Predicting
Success or Failure
in
Marriage

PRENTICE-HALL SOCIOLOGY SERIES

—edited by Herbert Blumer

RECENT TRENDS IN RURAL PLANNING, *by* William
E. Cole *and* Hugh Price Crowe

A HISTORY OF SOCIAL PHILOSOPHY, *by* Charles A.
Ellwood

SCIENTIFIC SOCIAL SURVEYS AND RESEARCH, *by*
Pauline V. Young

SOCIAL RESEARCH, *by* Manuel Conrad Elmer

SOCIETY IN TRANSITION, *by* Harry Elmer Barnes

INTRODUCTORY SOCIOLOGY, *by* Edward W. Gregory,
Jr., *and* Lee Bidgood.

PREDICTING SUCCESS OR FAILURE IN MARRIAGE, *by*
Ernest W. Burgess *and* Leonard S. Cottrell, Jr.

Predicting
Success or Failure
in
Marriage

by

Ernest W. Burgess
University of Chicago

and

Leonard S. Cottrell, Jr.
Cornell University

New York: 1939

Prentice-Hall, Inc.

PRINTED IN THE UNITED STATES OF AMERICA

TO THE

FIVE HUNDRED TWENTY-SIX COUPLES

Preface

IN modern society, knowledge is becoming indispensable in every phase of human living. The increasing knowledge of physical nature made possible the great inventions which are changing our institutions and our mode of living. Medical knowledge has removed or reduced the scourges of communicable and other diseases. Increase in our information about human nature and social relations is likewise essential for dealing with the many problems of human adjustment.

In few fields of human relations is the need for knowledge more evident, the demand for it more insistent, and the amount of verifiable information so scanty and fragmentary, as in the field of marriage adjustment. Marriage in the past was regulated by custom and tradition; the young married couple followed the parental pattern. Today the situation is entirely different. Young people begin married life on their own and often without guidance. Marriage no longer has its permanence guaranteed by custom and public opinion; today it is less and less influenced by the community, and more and more a matter of a personal relationship between husband and wife. It has entered upon a precarious existence, with its future dependent more than ever before in human history upon the affection, the temperamental compatibility, and the common objectives of husband and wife. Love and companionship are the personal ties that are replacing the communal and customary bonds which formerly held husband and wife together.

Each couple, accordingly, is on its own in marriage. The roles of husband and wife are no longer clearly defined, and each couple must work out its own patterns of relationship. The husband and wife of this generation are less disposed than in previous generations to ask or to take advice from their parents. On the other hand, they are interested in knowing what scientific knowledge is available which they may use in planning their joint career. There can be no doubt regarding the wide demand for this knowledge on the part of young people. Nearly every newspaper gives its advice to young people, sometimes through "the love-lorn column." Consultation centers that give premarital and marital advice have rapidly increased in the United States and, in 1937, numbered at least 42.[1] Demands are being made on all sides for education for marriage in churches, schools, and adult-education groups. Students in colleges and universities are bringing pressure upon the faculties to introduce courses in preparation for marriage.

Unfortunately little verified knowledge of factors making for marital happiness is available. There is abundance of theory and of speculation, but only a minimum of established factual data. Seven years ago one student in this field wrote:

We have very little scientific knowledge as yet concerning the less obvious aspects of married life. Few people who fully realize the complexity of personal interaction can advise others with confidence, and many well-informed people find difficulty in managing their own affairs.[2]

An examination of recent college texts on preparation for marriage shows how few of the statements have been substantiated by factual evidence.

A small but increasing body of information derived from research is now available regarding the factors associated with success or failure in marriage. This book [3] is a contribution to

---

[1] Robert G. Foster, "Servicing the Family through Counselling Agencies," *American Sociological Review*, 2, 1937, pp. 764–770.

[2] See Clifford Kirkpatrick, "Techniques of Marital Adjustment," *Annals of the American Academy of Political and Social Science*, 160, March 1932, p. 179.

[3] A preliminary statement of the methods and the findings of this study was reported at the 1935 meeting of the American Sociological Society and published under the title "The Prediction of Adjustment in Marriage" in *American Sociological Review*, 1, 1936, pp. 737–751.

the growing literature which seeks to discover by statistical and by case-study methods the factors associated with marital adjustment. It has also attempted the more difficult task of grappling with certain of the basic problems in prediction upon the solution of which further advance in our knowledge of human behavior depends.

The project reported in this book is an outgrowth of an earlier prediction study; namely, the attempt to predict before a man was released from prison whether or not he would succeed or fail on parole. The findings of the latter research,[4] published in 1928, showed the feasibility of classifying prisoners into different risk groups with reference to the probability of their observing or violating their parole regulations. The findings also indicated the desirability of applying the same or similar methods to other fields of human conduct. Accordingly, in 1931 the present study of predicting success or failure in marriage was begun. The writers realized from the beginning that predicting marriage adjustment was more difficult and complex than parole prediction because it involved not the behavior of one person but the conduct of two people in interaction with each other.

This study has been made possible by the interest and financial support of the Social Science Research Committee of the University of Chicago. Valuable suggestions utilized in the study have been made by W. F. Ogburn, L. L. Thurstone, Ruth Shonle Cavan, S. A. Stouffer, and Louis Wirth, the last two named having read parts of the manuscript.

It would have been impossible to carry on this study without the help of research assistants, to whom we express deep appreciation for their devoted and efficient services: to Richard O. Lang, now with the United States Census Bureau, who assisted in making the first tabulations of the data and whose

[4] A. A. Bruce, A. J. Harno, E. W. Burgess, and John Landesco, *The Workings of the Indeterminate-Sentence Law and the Parole System in Illinois,* Springfield, Illinois, Division of Pardons and Paroles, 1928. Part IV, "Factors Determining Success or Failure on Parole," pp. 205–249.

master's thesis *The Rating of Happiness in Marriage* contributed valuable findings, several of which have been utilized in this study; to Mary K. White, until recently connected with the research division of the Council of Social Agencies of Chicago; to Wilson M. Meeks, junior research sociologist, Division of the Criminologist, Illinois Department of Public Welfare; and to Paul Wallin, Marshall Field Fellow of the University of Chicago, who has read the manuscript and made valuable suggestions. The assistance of Roberta Burgess has been of great value, particularly in the difficult tasks of the checking of data and of the preparation of the index.

We are also grateful to the Works Progress Administration for assistance given during the past year by the project *Predicting Adjustment in Engagement and Marriage,* which was particularly valuable in providing the statistical calculations necessary for the preparation of Chapter XVI and for the final form of the statistical tables in Appendix A.

This study was fortunate in having the participation of teachers in colleges and universities in Illinois who encouraged their students to give their services in the placement of schedules with their friends and acquaintances.

Last but not least, we appreciate and have been stimulated by the fine response of the 526 couples without whose co-operation this study could not have been made.

Ernest W. Burgess
Leonard S. Cottrell, Jr.

Contents

	PAGE
PREFACE	vii
TABLES	xvi
CHARTS	xxi

CHAPTER

I. ADJUSTMENT IN MARRIAGE   1
   Marital Adjustment as a Social Problem   1
   Marriage in the Orient and the Occident   2
   Social Trends and the Family   4
   Changes in the Mores   7
   Marital Adjustment Defined   10
   Personality Interaction and Marital Adjustment .   11

II. SOCIAL CHARACTERISTICS OF THE COUPLES STUDIED   16
   Methods of Collecting Data   16
   Construction of the Questionnaire   17
   Distribution of the Questionnaire   18
   Social Characteristics of the Sample   20

III. HAPPINESS AS A CRITERION OF SUCCESSFUL MARRIAGE   30
   Marital-Happiness Ratings   32
   Objections to Happiness as a Criterion   37
   Reliability and Validity of Happiness Ratings . .   38
   Limitations of Happiness Ratings   44

IV. MEASURING ADJUSTMENT IN MARRIAGE   47
   Five Indications of Marital Adjustment   47
   Agreements and Disagreements   48
   Common Interests and Activities   52
   Demonstration of Affection and Confiding . . .   53
   Dissatisfaction with Marriage   54
   Feelings of Personal Isolation and Unhappiness. .   55

CHAPTER   PAGE

V. CONSTRUCTING AN INDEX OF MARITAL ADJUSTMENT   58
        Construction of a Numerical Adjustment Score . .   59
        Key for Scoring Adjustment Questions   63
        Marital-Adjustment Scores of the 526 Couples . .   68
        Reliability and Validity of the Adjustment Score .   70

VI. THE IMPRESS OF CULTURAL BACKGROUNDS . . .   75
        The Family as an Agency for Transmitting Culture   75
        Family Background   77
        Differences in Family Backgrounds   82
        Rural and Urban Rearing   85
        Other Cultural Differences   86

VII. PSYCHOGENETIC CHARACTERISTICS   90
        Family Relationships   92
        Happiness of Parents' Marriage   98
        Parents' Status   102
        Sibling Relationships   104

VIII. THE SOCIAL TYPE   114
        Age at Marriage   115
        State of Health at Marriage   118
        Weight Deviation   119
        Educational Status   121
        Religious Identification and Participation   122
        Membership in Organizations   126
        Friendship   128
        Previous Marital Status   132
        The Character of the Neighborhood   132

IX. THE ECONOMIC ROLE   136
        Occupation and the Person   136
        The Wife's Occupation   146
        Mobility and Stability   148
        Work Record and Occupational Stability   150
        Income and Economic Status   152
        Economic Security   154

CHAPTER   PAGE

X. RESPONSE PATTERNS: ROMANCE AND COMPANION-
SHIP 159
   Difference in Ages of the Married Couple 161
   Acquaintance, Courtship, and Engagement . . . 164
   Attitude of Parents Toward Marriages 168

XI. PERSONALITY FACTORS IN MARRIAGE ADJUSTMENT 172
   Assumptions and Procedures 174
   Case I.—An Adjusted Couple: James and Mary O. 178
   Case II.—An Unadjusted Couple: William and
      Laura A. 192
   Case III.—A Maladjusted Couple: Thomas and
      Frances G. 202
   Psychogenetic and Cultural Patterns in Marital Rela-
      tions 216

XII. THE SEXUAL FACTOR 218
   Problems of Sexual Adjustment Classified . . . 219
   Sexual-Adjustment Problems Due to Lack of Knowl-
      edge and Skill 221
   Sexual-Adjustment Problems Due to Organic Fac-
      tors 221
   Sexual-Adjustment Problems Due to Attitudinal
      Factors 225
   General Lack of Sexual Desire 228
   Specific Lack of Sexual Desire 235
   Alternating Periods of Desire and Aversion . . . 238
   Surface Evidence of Hypersexual Activity . . . 239

XIII. CONTINGENCY FACTORS: STABILITY AND SECURITY . 244
   Time and Marriage 246
   Stability and Mobility in Social Relations 248
   Stability and Kinship Relations 256
   Economic Security 261

XIV. THE PREDICTION OF MARITAL ADJUSTMENT . . . 269
   Reliability of Background Score 284
   Validity of Background Score 286

CHAPTER PAGE

XV. FIVE CASE STUDIES OF MARITAL ADJUSTMENT . . 290
Case I.—An Unadjusted Couple with Low Predic-
tion and Poor Adjustment Scores: William and
Laura A. 290
Case II.—A Well-Adjusted Couple with High Pre-
diction and Good Adjustment Scores: James and
Mary O. 293
Case III.—A Couple Changing from Poorly to Well
Adjusted with Low Prediction and Poor Adjust-
ment Scores: Charles and Virginia C. 295
Case IV.—A Fairly Well Adjusted Couple with Low
Prediction and Good Adjustment Scores: Robert
and Helen D. 300
Case V.—A Couple with Doubtful Adjustment with
High Prediction and Poor Adjustment Scores:
Howard and Eleanor E. 304
The Adjustment Score as a Fair Index of Marital
Adjustment 310
The Need for Supplementing the Prediction Score
by Case Studies 311

XVI. BASIC PROBLEMS IN PREDICTION 313
Adjustment and Prediction Scores 314
The Search for Basic Factors 317
Relative Significance of Husbands' and Wives' Pre-
marital Prediction Items 325
Multiple Correlation 327
Limitations of Statistical Methods 329
The Distinctive Value of the Case Study 332
Problems of the Case-Study Method 335

XVII. MAJOR FINDINGS AND THEIR INTERPRETATION . . 341

XVIII. THE FUTURE OF RESEARCH IN MARRIAGE
ADJUSTMENT 350
Review of Studies of Prediction of Marital Adjust-
ment 350
Comparing the Findings of the Different Studies . 355
Premarital Items Found to Be Significant by Two or
More Studies 359

CHAPTER   PAGE

XVIII. THE FUTURE OF RESEARCH IN MARRIAGE
ADJUSTMENT—(*Continued*)

A Plan for Further Research 361
An Institute for Research in Marriage Adjustment . 371
Prediction in the Psychological and in the Social
Sciences 373

APPENDIX A—TABLES NOT INCLUDED IN THE TEXT 375

APPENDIX B—SCHEDULE FORM USED IN THIS
STUDY 420

APPENDIX C—CASE-STUDY OUTLINE USED IN THIS
STUDY 430

BIBLIOGRAPHY 437

INDEX 465

Tables

TABLE   PAGE

1. The Age at Marriage of 526 Husbands and Wives . . .   20
2. Distribution of the Couples According to Length of Time Married 21
3. Distribution of the Couples According to Country of Birth of Fathers 22
4. Distribution of the Couples According to Religious Affiliations 22
5. Distribution of the Couples According to Where Childhood and Adolescent Years Were Spent 23
6. Distribution of the Couples According to Educational Status 24
7. Distribution of the Couples According to Income of Husbands at Time of Marriage 24
8. Distribution of the Couples According to Income of Wives at Time of Marriage 25
9. Distribution of the Couples According to Occupational Classification of Husbands at Time of Marriage . . 26
10. Distribution of the Couples According to Occupational Classification of Wives at Time of Marriage 26
11. Distribution of the Persons According to Neurotic Scores 28
12. Ratings of Marital Happiness as Given by Either Husband or Wife 32
13. Happiness Ratings of This Study Compared with Those of Lang's Study 34
14. Percentage Distribution of Happiness Ratings Found by Terman and His Associates in a Group Studied and in a Random Sample 36
15. Appraisals of Their Marriages by Husbands and by Wives 39
16. Appraisal of Husband's Parents' Marriage by Husband and by Wife 40
17. Appraisal of Wife's Parents' Marriage by Husband and by Wife 41

TABLE   PAGE

18. Appraisal of the Couple's Marriage by a Member of the Couple and by an Outsider 42

19. Appraisals of the Marriage by a Member of the Couple and by Judge Number 1 43

20. Appraisals of the Marriage of a Member of the Couple and by Judge Number 2 43

21. First and Second Appraisals of the Person's Own Marriage 44

22. The Correlation Between Ratings of Marital Happiness and Extent of Agreements and Disagreements . . . 50

23. Relation of Items of Agreement and Disagreement to Ratings of Marital Happiness 51

24. The Correlation Between Ratings of Marital Happiness and Mutuality of Interests and Activities 53

25. The Correlation Between Ratings of Marital Happiness and Demonstration of Affection and Mutual Confiding 53

26. The Correlation Between Ratings of Marital Happiness and Expressions of Dissatisfaction with Marriage . . 54

27. The Correlation Between Ratings of Marital Happiness and Feelings of Isolation and Unhappiness 56

28. The Correlation Between Ratings of Marital Happiness and Each Question Used in Computing the Adjustment Score 60

29. Extent to Which Couple Engaged in Outside Activities Together Compared with Their Ratings of Marital Happiness 62

30. Extent of Agreement of Couple in Handling Family Finances Compared with Their Ratings of Marital Happiness 62

31. Extent of Agreement of Couple on Religious Matters Compared with Their Ratings of Marital Happiness . 63

32. Scoring Key for Adjustment-Score Questions 64

33. Frequency of Regretting Marriage Compared with Ratings of Marital Happiness 66

34. Distribution of Answers to Questions on Frequency of Regretting Marriage Given by Persons Who Rated Their Marriages as Very Happy or Happy 66

35. Frequency Distribution of Marriage-Adjustment Scores for 526 Marriages 69

36. Correlation Table of Marriage-Adjustment Scores Calculated from Separate Schedules Filled Out by Husbands and Wives 70

TABLE   PAGE

37. Frequency Distribution of Marriage-Adjustment Scores
by Happiness-Rating Categories   72
38. Distribution of Marriage-Adjustment Scores by Groupings into Those Who Are Divorced, Separated, Have
Contemplated Divorce or Separation, and Have Not
Contemplated Divorce or Separation   73
39. Relative Weights in Marriage-Prediction Score of Items
Indicative of Cultural Background of the Husband
and the Wife   78
40. Index of Similarity in Family Backgrounds and Adjustment   84
41. Different Groups of Salesmen and Marital Adjustment . 145
42. Percentage Distribution of Marriage-Adjustment Scores
at Different Educational Levels 271
43. Relation Between Membership in Social Organizations
at Time of Marriage and Marriage-Adjustment Score 272
44. Relation Between Number of Persons of Opposite Sex
Husbands and Wives Went with Steadily Before Marriage and Marriage-Adjustment Score 273
45. Weighting Key for Prediction Score 275
46. The Relation Between the Prediction Scores and Marriage-Adjustment Scores 284
47. Correlation of Prediction Scores Computed from Schedules Filled Out Separately by Husbands and Wives . 285
48. Correlation Between Prediction or Background Scores
Computed from First and Second Schedules Filled Out
by Same Persons at Different Times (Time Interval:
Eight Months to Two Years) 287
49. Percentage Distribution of Prediction Scores for Those
Who Are Divorced, Are Separated, Have Contemplated
Divorce or Separation, and Have Not Contemplated
Divorce or Separation 288
50. Adjustment and Prediction Scores with Percentile Ranking and Actual Adjustment for Five Selected Couples 311
51. Intercorrelations of the Five Basic Factors 323
52. Zero-Order and Partial Correlations of the Five Factors
with Adjustment Score 324
53. Zero-Order and Partial Correlations of Husbands',
Wives', and Common Scores with the Adjustment
Scores 326

TABLE   PAGE

54. Zero-Order Correlations Between the Adjustment Scores (or Marital-Happiness Scale) and Husbands' and Wives' Scores 327

55. Percentage Distribution of Happiness Ratings for Different Marital Combinations of Strong and Weak Personalities 333

56. Cultural Backgrounds of Husband and Wife and Adjustment 375

57. Rural or Urban Residence in Childhood and Adolescence and Adjustment 376

58. Husband's Attachment to Parents and Adjustment . . 377

59. Husband's Conflict with Parents and Adjustment . . . 378

60. Wife's Attachment to Parents and Adjustment 379

61. Wife's Conflict with Parents and Adjustment 380

62. Appraisal of the Happiness of Parents' Marriage (Separate Ratings) and Adjustment 381

63. Appraisal of the Happiness of Parents' Marriage (Combined Ratings) and Adjustment 382

64. Parental Status and Adjustment 383

65. Size of Family and Adjustment 384

66. Place in Family and Adjustment 385

67. Place in Family of Husband and Wife and of Their Parents and Marital-Happiness Ratings 386

68. Sibling Attachment and Adjustment 387

69. Age at Marriage of Husband and Wife and Adjustment 388

70. Health Previous to Marriage and Adjustment 389

71. Weight Deviation and Adjustment 390

72. Educational Status and Adjustment 391

73. Age at Which Stopped Attending Sunday School and Adjustment 392

74. Church Attendance and Adjustment 393

75. Place in Which Married and Adjustment 394

76. Membership in Organizations and Adjustment . . . 394

77. Number of Husband's Friends and Adjustment . . . 395

78. Number of Wife's Friends and Adjustment 396

79. Number of Intimate Associations with Other Sex Before Marriage and Adjustment 397

80. Occupation of Husband at Marriage and Adjustment . 398

81. Occupations of 17,533 Husbands and Happiness Ratings by Friends or Acquaintances 399

TABLE   PAGE

82. Occupation of Wife at Marriage and Adjustment   . . .   401
83. Length of Time Held Position and Adjustment   . . .   402
84. Work Record Before Marriage and Adjustment   . . .   403
85. Income at Marriage and Adjustment   404
86. Savings of Husband and Adjustment   404
87. Savings of Wife at Marriage and Adjustment   405
88. Husband's Financial Index at Marriage and Adjustment   405
89. Difference in Age of Husband and Wife and Adjustment   406
90. Duration of Acquaintance Before Marriage and Adjust-
    ment   406
91. Duration of Keeping Company and Adjustment   . . .   407
92. Duration of Engagement and Adjustment   407
93. Attitude of Parents Toward the Marriage and Adjustment   408
94. Length of Time Married and Adjustment   409
95. Number of Years Married and Ratings of Marital Happi-
    ness by Close Acquaintances   409
96. Size of Community and Adjustment   410
97. Distance from Chicago and Adjustment   410
98. Character of Neighborhood and Adjustment   . . .   411
99. Type of Residence and Adjustment   411
100. Average Months per Residence and Adjustment   . . .   412
101. Home Ownership and Adjustment   412
102. Residence with Relatives and Adjustment   413
103. Frequency of Seeing Parents-in-Law and Adjustment . .   413
104. Number of Children and Adjustment   413
105. Desire for Children and Adjustment   414
106. Number of Rooms in Residence and Adjustment   . . .   414
107. Monthly Rent per Room and Adjustment   415
108. Employment of Husband and Adjustment   415
109. Average Number of Months Position Held by Husband
    and by Wife, and Adjustment   416
110. Financial Index and Adjustment   416
111. By Whom Married and Adjustment   417
112. Residence at Time of Marriage and Adjustment   . . .   418
113. Wife's Vocational Ambition Compared with Occupation
    Before Marriage and Adjustment   419
114. Wife's Intention Before Marriage Regarding Work Com-
    pared with Working After Marriage and Adjustment   419

Charts

CHART   PAGE

1. Comparison of Assumed Normal Distribution with Actual Distribution of Happiness Ratings 33
2. Actual and Assumed Normal Distribution of Happiness Ratings Based on Lang's 8,263 Couples Married from 1 to 16 Years 35
3. Family-Background Index and Marital Adjustment . . 79
4. Rural or Urban Residence in Childhood and Adolescence and Marital Adjustment 85
5. Husband's Attachment to Parents and Marital Adjustment 92
6. Husband's Conflict with Parents and Marital Adjustment 93
7. Wife's Attachment to Parents and Marital Adjustment . 95
8. Wife's Conflict with Parents and Marital Adjustment . . 97
9. Appraisal of the Happiness of the Parents' Marriage (Separate Ratings) and Marital Adjustment 99
10. Appraisal of the Happiness of the Parents' Marriage (Combined Ratings) and Marital Adjustment . . . 101
11. Parental Status and Marital Adjustment 103
12. Size of Family and Marital Adjustment 105
13. Place in Family and Marital Adjustment 107
14. Place in Family of Husband and Wife and of Their Parents and Marital-Happiness Ratings 109
15. Sibling Attachment and Marital Adjustment 111
16. Age at Marriage of Husband and Wife and Marital Adjustment 117
17. Health Previous to Marriage and Marital Adjustment . 118
18. Weight Deviation from Normal and Marital Adjustment 120
19. Educational Status and Marital Adjustment 121
20. Age at Which Stopped Attending Sunday School and Marital Adjustment 123
21. Church Attendance and Marital Adjustment 124
22. Place in Which Married and Marital Adjustment . . . 126
23. Membership in Organizations and Marital Adjustment . 127

CHART   PAGE

24. Number of Husband's Friends and Marital Adjustment . 128
25. Number of Wife's Friends and Marital Adjustment . . 130
26. Number of Intimate Associations with Other Sex Before
    Marriage and Marital Adjustment 131
27. Occupation of Husband at Marriage and Marital Adjust-
    ment 138
28. Occupations of 17,533 Husbands and Happiness Ratings
    by Friends and Acquaintances 140
29. Occupation of Wife at Marriage and Marital Adjustment 147
30. Length of Time Positions Held and Marital Adjustment 149
31. Work Record Before Marriage and Marital Adjustment . 151
32. Income at Marriage and Marital Adjustment 153
33. Savings of Husband at Marriage and Marital Adjustment 155
34. Savings of Wife at Marriage and Marital Adjustment . 155
35. Husband's Financial Index at Marriage and Marital Ad-
    justment 157
36. Difference in Ages of Husband and Wife and Marital
    Adjustment 162
37. Duration of Acquaintance Before Marriage and Marital
    Adjustment 165
38. Duration of Keeping Company and Marital Adjustment 166
39. Duration of Engagement and Marital Adjustment . . 168
40. Attitude of Parents Toward the Marriage and Marital
    Adjustment 169
41. Length of Time Married and Marital Adjustment . . . 247
42. Number of Years Married and Ratings of Marital Happi-
    ness by Close Acquaintances 248
43. Size of Community and Marital Adjustment 250
44. Distance from Chicago and Marital Adjustment . . . 251
45. Character of Neighborhood and Marital Adjustment . . 252
46. Type of Residence and Marital Adjustment 252
47. Average Months per Residence and Marital Adjustment . 253
48. Home Ownership and Marital Adjustment 254
49. Residence with Relatives and Marital Adjustment . . . 257
50. Frequency of Seeing Parents-in-Law and Marital Adjust-
    ment 258
51. Number of Children and Marital Adjustment 259
52. Desire for Children and Marital Adjustment 260
53. Number of Rooms in Residence and Marital Adjustment 262
54. Monthly Rent per Room and Marital Adjustment . . . 263

CHART   PAGE

55. Employment of Husband and Marital Adjustment . . 263

56. Average Number of Months Position Held by Husband
    and by Wife, and Marital Adjustment 265

57. Financial Index and Marital Adjustment 267

58. Graphic Representation of Clusters of Selected Items in
    Husband's Premarital Background as Indicated by In-
    tercorrelations of These Items by the Multiple-Factor
    Method 319

CHAPTER I

Adjustment in Marriage

As ANCIENT as human nature is the problem of the adjustment of man and woman in marriage. But in the past domestic discord was regarded almost entirely as a private question confined to the two interested persons. The recognition of marital incompatibility not only as a ground for the dissolution of a marriage, but as a social problem and therefore a subject of public concern, is only recent.

Marital Adjustment as a Social Problem

Historically, the emergence in Western society of marital adjustment as a social problem is to be traced to the individualistic movement ushered in by the Renaissance and the Reformation.[1] The transition from the conception of marriage as a sacrament to that of marriage as a contract was essentially a change from subordinating the person to the institution of marriage to making his interests paramount. If marriage be a contract rather than a sacrament, then divorce, as John Milton, the poet of Puritanism, argued, is the remedy for an unsatisfactory union.[2]

In the United States it was, in fact, the increasing divorce rate that called public attention to the problem of adjustment in marriage. The number of married people who sought the secular release of divorce from the holy bonds of matrimony multiplied in something like a geometric ratio. While the

---

[1] Ernest R. Mowrer, *The Family,* Chicago, University of Chicago Press, 1932, pp. 11–19.

[2] *The Doctrine and Discipline of Divorce, Restored to the good of both sexes from the bondage of Canon Law and other Mistakes,* London, 1643.

I

population increased only 215.7 per cent from 1870 to 1930, the number of divorces increased 1,647.8 per cent. The divorce rate grew from 28 per 100,000 population in 1870 to an estimated 193 per 100,000 population in 1937.[3] So rapidly has divorce gained upon marriage that in 1932 there was one divorce for every six marriages.

There is no conclusive evidence that the growing divorce rate actually indicates an increase in marital maladjustment. In fact, by terminating unhappy unions divorce may represent a decrease in marital discord. But divorce does constitute a social problem in that it has aroused public concern as to the causes of domestic discord and the possibility of its treatment and prevention.

If the increasing divorce rate does not represent increasing marital unhappiness, it does indicate a profound change in mores as to the inviolability of marriage. Fifty years ago the sanction of American mores was still enforced against divorce as inimical to social welfare. Today our mores condone, if they do not approve, divorce as one solution of the problem of marital unhappiness.

To be understood, marriage adjustment, like any other problem, must be examined in the context of culture and of social change. A perspective, then, of marital adjustment in American society is to be gained through comparison of its status in our culture with its status in other cultures, through an examination of trends in family life, and through a survey of the changes now in progress in sex and marriage mores.

Marriage in the Orient and the Occident

"Falling in love" is, in the United States, the right and proper basis for marriage. In China, and elsewhere in the Orient, love

---

[3] Divorce rate for 1937 estimated by S. A. Stouffer and Lyle M. Spencer in article "Recent Increases in Marriage and Divorce," *American Journal of Sociology*, 44, January 1939, p. 552.

comes after rather than before marriage, if it comes at all. Even in marriage respect has priority over love.

In American mores, marriages are arranged by the young people themselves, and parental interference is not sanctioned. During courtship and engagement the youth and the maiden are expected to find out whether they are really in love and well suited to one another. Chinese marriages are arranged by the parents or through a matchmaker, and the young people have little or nothing to say in the matter. Before marriage the bride and groom meet each other only formally.

Our mores encourage the newly married couple to set up a separate domestic establishment, and disapprove of their living after marriage with the parents of either the bride or the groom. In their own home they therefore have freedom to institute desired innovations. In India and Japan, as well as in China, the traditional course is for the young married couple to live after marriage with the bridegroom's parents. The bride becomes the assistant of her mother-in-law in the performance of the household tasks. Ceremonial forms regulate and control the relations of the young couple to each other and to the larger family group. It is difficult if not impossible for them to make innovations, since the whole situation is organized to perpetuate the customary and sanctioned ways of family life.

In the Orient the roles of husband and wife, parent and child, and the relation of a member of the small family to the large family group are clearly defined and regulated by custom. In the United States recent social changes have caused an increasing ambiguity in the definition of these roles, which ambiguity leaves the person without social orientation and therefore makes more important the individual patterns of behavior in adjustment in marriage.

In short, the entire course of selection of mates, marriage, and marital adjustment is regulated by Oriental mores with a minimum of personal freedom and initiative and a maximum of familial and social control. In American society the mores ensure a maximum of personal freedom in courtship, engagement, and marriage, but in a time of rapid social change provide little or no guidance for adjustment in married life.

Social Trends and the Family

The rapidity of social change in American society has outrun attempts to make the necessary institutional adjustments. The problems of marital adjustment need to be considered in their relation to past and present trends in family life.

In *Recent Social Trends* William F. Ogburn has described in detail the changes now taking place in the family and its functions. He thus states the two outstanding conclusions indicated by his data: [4]

One is the decline of the institutional functions of the family, as for example its economic functions. Thus the family now produces less food and clothing than it did formerly. The teaching functions of the family also have been largely shifted to another institution, the school. Industry and the state have both grown at the family's expense. The significance of this diminution in the activities of the family as a group is far-reaching.

The other outstanding conclusion is the resulting predominant importance of the personality functions of the family—that is, those which provide for the mutual adjustments among husbands, wives, parents and children and for the adaptation of each member of the family to the outside world. The family has always been responsible to a large degree for the formation of character. It has furnished social contacts and group life. With the decline of its institutional functions these personality functions have come to be its most important contribution to society. The chief concern over the family nowadays is not how strong it may be as an economic organization but how well it performs services for the personalities of its members.

Certain specific instances of shifts in functions of the family and the behavior of its members may be briefly summarized

---

[4] From *Recent Social Trends in the United States, Report of the President's Research Committee on Social Trends,* by permission of the publishers, McGraw-Hill Book Company, Inc.

from *Recent Social Trends* (pp. 664–700) to substantiate the above conclusions:

1. Many household economic activities, such as baking, canning, laundering, cleaning, dyeing, and sewing, have already been largely transferred from the home to outside industries.

2. Between 1920 and 1930 the number of married women working outside the home increased 60 per cent, while their total number in the population rose only 23 per cent.

3. An increasing number of labor-saving devices and conveniences have been introduced into the home.

4. Multi-family dwelling is on the increase. In recent years about one-half of the newly constructed homes in cities were apartment buildings, and only about one-third were one-family dwellings.

5. Protective functions such as health conservation, security against old age, unemployment insurance, and control of child labor are now largely in the hands of the state.

6. Family attendance at church and family prayers, as reported by one study, are twice as frequent in rural as in urban areas. This fact is perhaps indicative of the decline of religious influence upon the city family.

7. Recreational activities outside the home have greatly increased in recent decades, although the radio may be cited as one instance of a reversal of this general trend.

8. The status of the family is apparently declining in importance as the individualization of its members takes place. Increasing although not complete recognition has been given by law to the individualization of the married woman.

9. Since 1890, contrary to widespread opinion, the percentage of population in the United States that is married has increased with each decade and is larger in the rural than in the urban areas.

10. The study of a sample of families from different communities indicates that the average size of the family household

has declined from 4.30 persons in 1900 to 4.01 in 1930. The per cent decreases for different types of areas from 1900 to 1930 are: farms, 0.6 per cent; small towns, 3.5 per cent; cities, 4.5 per cent; and the metropolis, 21.2 per cent.

11.   The average size of the unbroken family (husbands and wives and children living at home) has only slightly decreased, the decrease being from 3.67 in 1900 to 3.57 in 1930.

12.   The number of unbroken families without children increased from 28 per cent in 1900 to 31 per cent in 1930.

13.   Homes broken by death decreased from 7.6 per cent in 1900 to 4.9 per cent in 1930, but those broken by divorce, annulment, or separation increased from 6.7 per cent in 1900 to 9.8 per cent in 1930.

14.   In 1930 there were 36 divorces for 10,000 married persons, as compared with 20 in 1900.   In 1930, 37 per cent of the divorces occurred within five years after marriage; in the period 1887–1906 only 28 per cent occurred within that time.

These changes in the functions and structure of the family have been accompanied by the emancipation of woman.   The wife and mother has been freed from the slavery of the kitchen and relieved of the greater part of household drudgery.   She is winning her right to an independent career outside the home either in an occupation or in some social, civic, or welfare activity.

The continuing loss of functions by the family may, in fact, make all the more important those remaining; namely, affection, companionship, and the rearing and informal education of children.   This may mean that the family today, more than ever before in human history, is specializing in its intrinsic functions of providing persons with the satisfactions of intimate personal relationships.

A knowledge of the trends now taking place in family life is an aid in giving the background necessary for an analysis of the factors underlying marital maladjustment in our society. Many of the problems of the family are incidental to the transition from a rural to an urban civilization.   The concepts of "cultural lag" and "cultural conflict" serve to identify and, in part, to explain the maladjustments which are concomitant with a period of social change.[5]

The family at present is in a process of adjustment to changes in our society in which the functioning of institutions and the attitudes and behavior of persons are being gradually accommodated to the technological conditions of modern existence, changes which may perhaps best be summed up by the use of the term "urbanization." Nowhere has the influence of urbanization been more profound than in the fields of child care, marital adjustment, and attitudes toward sex. In these fields vast changes have taken place in the folkways and the mores.

Changes in the Mores

In the field of child rearing the commandments of the mores have been definitely displaced by the authority of science. The young mother no longer asks her own mother how to bring up her child but appeals to the pediatrician and to the latest book on child psychology. Rapid has been the development of child study groups and associations, child research institutes, and journals for child welfare.[6]

In the area of husband-and-wife relations, the authority of tradition has been broken, but no substitute in science has yet been provided. Marriage consultation centers have been advocated and many have been instituted, but they are still in the experimental stage.[7]

The problem of the adjustment of modern youth in social

---

[5] F. Stuart Chapin, *Cultural Change*, New York, Century, 1928, Chapter 10, "The Cultural Lag in the Family."

[6] See L. K. Frank in *Recent Social Trends*, New York, McGraw-Hill Book Co., Inc., Chapter 15, "Childhood and Youth," pp. 751–800; and Florence L. Goodenough and John E. Anderson, *Experimental Child Study*, New York, 1931, D. Appleton-Century Co., Chapter 1, "Historical Beginnings."

[7] Best known of these are the Family Counsel, Philadelphia, Mrs. Mudd, director, and the Institute of Family Relations, Los Angeles, Paul Popenoe, director. A list of 32 family consultation centers is given in the *Journal of Social Hygiene*, No. 22, 1936, pp. 34–36. See also Ralph P. Bridgman, "Guidance for Marriage and Family Life," *Annals of the American Academy of Political and Social Science*, No. 160, March 1932, pp. 144–164; and Mary S. Fisher, "The Development of Marriage and Family Counselling in the United States," *Parent Education*, 3, April 1 and May 15, 1933, pp. 3–9.

relations, in courtship, in engagement, and in marriage needs
to be placed in the perspective of the great changes in sex mores
which have accompanied the lifting of the Puritan taboo upon
sex.

A main objective of the movement to end the policy of silence
surrounding sex was to give children information upon the
"facts of life."   The new freedom of sex discussion was quickly
capitalized upon by newspapers, popular magazines, "best-
seller" books, and the stage, and was exploited by the "yellow"
press and by melodramatic, risqué, sensational, and semiporno-
graphic publications.   The motion picture, the new means of
mass entertainment, quickly discovered in themes of love, sex,
and the eternal triangle a sure way of increasing attendance
and box-office receipts.   Competition soon forced producers
to vie with each other in "giving the public what it wanted."
The study *Movies and Conduct* by Herbert Blumer [8] portrayed
and analyzed the impelling influence of the motion picture on
the fantasies, lovemaking, and general patterns of behavior of
adolescents and youths.

Illustrations *ad infinitum* might be marshaled to indicate
the profound effects of this revolution in sex mores.   The
Methodist Episcopal Church lifted its ban on dancing.   Liberal
denominations sponsored dances.   The Y. W. C. A. conducted
"charm" classes.   Agitation for the introduction of sex instruction in the public schools has been continuous.   Cigarette smok-
ing is now permissible for youths of both sexes.   In the isolated
Southern mountain community where William Jennings Bryan
and Clarence Darrow debated the pros and cons of evolution,
newspaper reporters noted that lipstick and the vanity case had
already arrived.   The public is markedly responsive to adver-
tising with "sex appeal."   The bathing-beach costumes of last
summer if worn 20 or even 10 years ago would have been sufficient cause for arrest on the charge of indecent exposure or
disorderly conduct.   And, to cite an extreme case of social
change, witness the growth of the cult of nudism.

Most dramatic of all the changes in sex mores was the hard-

[8] New York, The Macmillan Co., 1933.

fought struggle regarding the limitation of the size of the family by means of contraception. Birth control, which had been a folkway of the educated classes for over a generation, has now entered the mores with the sanction both of the Federal Council of Churches and, in 1937, after many years of resistance, of the American Medical Association.

Syphilis, a long-neglected health problem of vital importance to the family, is now being attacked with unanimous public approval by the available scientific technique in the public health field.

No discussion of changes in the sex mores would be adequate or complete without recognition of the influence of psychiatry and particularly of psychoanalysis. The popularization of the discoveries of Dr. Sigmund Freud had much to do in directing the attention of the public to sexual maladjustment as the chief cause of marital unhappiness. This marked emphasis upon the sexual aspect of life by the followers of Freud may be regarded as a reaction to the earlier extreme of minimizing its influence upon human behavior. Through the growing number of psychiatrists, through the mental hygiene movement, through child guidance clinics, and through the psychiatric social worker, psychiatric study and treatment are now being given to many types of personality maladjustment, both within and outside of family relationships.

The impact of these changes upon the sex mores has naturally been strongest among youth. Undoubtedly sex is much more in the consciousness and in the conduct of young people of the present than it was in past generations.[9] Symptoms of this are the emergence of "necking" and "petting" and the interest in the "art of lovemaking." There is widespread evidence of increasing frequency of premarital sexual relations.[10] Little or no reliable information, however, is available about the

---

[9] Willard Waller, *The Family, a Dynamic Interpretation*, New York, Cordon, 1938, Part II, "Courtship and Interaction," pp. 171–302.

[10] See Ira S. Wile, Editor, *The Sexual Life of the Unmarried Adult*, Vanguard Press, New York, 1934; Dorothy Dunbar Bromley, *Youth and Sex*, New York, Harper and Brothers, 1938.

repercussions of these changes in attitude and behavior upon adjustments in married life.

Marital Adjustment Defined

Modern marriage in America differs widely not only from marriage in the Orient but from marriage in the United States of yesteryear. Marriage is becoming more and more an intimate and informal personal affair with less and less traditional control. It is regarded by young people as the fitting culmination of a romance rather than as a socially sanctioned institution. Marriage tends now to be considered as a continuation of a companionship instituted and tested in the period of courtship and engagement.

Marital adjustment must, then, be defined in the context of the modern conception of marriage. Adjustment is not insured here, as it is in the Orient, by customs and ceremonies minutely regulating the conduct of the young married people. If marriage has become a personal rather than a social relation, adjustment is to be defined in terms of personalities, their conflicts and accommodations, and the degree of assimilation taking place.

In certain of its phases, marital adjustment may be measured by accommodation, the mode of living that minimizes conflict and promotes harmony. Many, perhaps the majority of, marriages remain on the level of accommodation.

From the standpoint of assimilation, adjustment is to be defined as the integration of the couple in a union in which the two personalities are not merely merged, or submerged, but interact to complement each other for mutual satisfaction and the achievement of common objectives. The emphasis is upon intercommunication, interstimulation, and participation in common activities.

A well-adjusted marriage from the point of view of this study may then be defined as a marriage in which the attitudes and acts of each of the partners produce an environment which is favorable to the functioning of the personality of each, particularly in the sphere of primary relationships.

Four corollaries follow from this definition:

1. The degree to which the above conditions are met would be the degree of adjustment realized.

2. Since personality differs from individual to individual, a particular combination of traits highly favorable to adjustment for one personality may be entirely unsuited to another.

3. Since a personality is a composite of role patterns, a marriage which is favorable to the functioning of one part of the personality may not be favorable to that of another part.

4. Since personalities are not static but are in the process of development, a combination favorable to the functioning of the personality at one time may not be so for a later period in that personality's development; and hence a period, or recurring periods, of unadjustment may provide conditions of "growth" until a relatively mature and stable level of personality organization is achieved.

Personality Interaction and Marital Adjustment

The personality relations in marriage are so complex and so little understood that it is as yet impossible to deal with them adequately. For purposes of this research it was found necessary to deal separately with five groups of factors that seemed to affect marriage relationships. These five groups may be named as follows:

1. Cultural-background factors.
2. Psychogenetic characteristics.
3. Characteristics associated with the social type.
4. Economic factors.
5. Response attitudes and patterns.

It must be remembered that these groups of factors do not operate separately but interact with one another to affect the marriage adjustment.

Impress of cultural background. Every person bears the impress of his cultural background. His socially inherited cultural patterns are those attitudes and traits which he possesses in common with the other members of his primary social groups.

The early cultural patterns particularly significant for marital adjustment appear to be those transmitted in the family, the play group, and the neighborhood; namely, those of nationality, of a particular section or region of the country, of economic and social class, and of religion. These are constituted by the body of memories, sentiments, and attitudes acquired in childhood that make an adult feel "more at home" with persons similarly reared and "more a stranger" with those of different cultural backgrounds. Some indices of the impress of cultural background upon the person are certain fundamental attitudes and values, pronunciation and idioms in language, manners and mannerisms, and food preferences.

In general, even in American society, marriage takes place within cultural groupings. There seems to be generally, on the part of the person and almost always on the part of his social group, more or less resistance to marriage with the outsider. But intermarriage does take place, particularly when a man and a woman are in a situation of isolation from others of their own race, nationality, religion, and social class. In these cases of intermarriage between persons of widely different cultural backgrounds, one or both of the spouses may be more or less irritated by behavior and attitudes which reflect differences in their early rearing.

It might therefore be assumed, *a priori,* that similarity of cultural background is favorable and that dissimilarity, if sufficiently great, is unfavorable to adjustment in marriage.

The psychogenetic personality. Edward Sapir has defined the psychiatric (psychogenetic) personality as an "essentially invariable reactive system." [11] By this he means not only the temperament of the individual but, in addition, certain psychically conditioned responses organized into a configuration which may be conceived as "a comparatively stable system of reactivity." This is the precultural personality formed on the

---

[11] "Personality," *Encyclopaedia of the Social Sciences,* New York, The Macmillan Co., 1930–35, Vol. 12, p. 86.

basis of constitutional traits by prenatal and postnatal conditions in infancy and earliest childhood.

These reactive patterns are fixed neither by heredity nor by imitation but in the interaction of the infant and young child with mother and father, brother and sister. Some reactive patterns which may be significant for marital adjustment may include the following: extroversion, introversion, egocentricity, sociocentricity, emotional stability, emotional instability. Certain psychogenetic traits are aggressiveness and passivity, impulsiveness and deliberation, dominance and submission, control and feeble inhibition of temper, security and insecurity, sense of adequacy and inadequacy, and flexibility and rigidity.

With the passing of the well-defined traditional roles of husband and wife which, to some extent, controlled their relationship in the old American rural community, the adjustment of the psychogenetic personalities of the couple is becoming increasingly significant. In this study, therefore, an effort is made to determine whether or not and, if possible, to what extent marital adjustment is affected by the psychogenetic personalities of the husband and wife.

The social type. The social type of a person is the product of his roles as a member of different social groups. All these roles are derived from society, but they differ from the impress of cultural backgrounds in that the person appropriates them and makes them his own.

The roles to be considered in this study are the specific roles and patterns of behavior of given persons as they adjust to each other in courtship, engagement, and marriage.

Roles and expectations significant in marriage for the young man are, for example, his conception of himself as a husband and father, his ideal of a wife, his expectations of his career, his attitude toward a career for married women. These are related to his status as affected by his education, his religious identification and activity, and his participation in social life.

Economic status. By the "economic status" of a person we

mean the different factors such as occupation, occupational prestige, income, and prospects of success that determine the conception which he and others have of his economic career.

According to American mores, marriage should be for love and not for money. In the great majority of marriages in the United States, direct economic considerations are probably subordinate to personal and affectional influences. But the economic status of the young people and of their families plays a part in courtship, engagement, and marriage. A man's occupation is often the chief organizing factor in his social personality and plays the leading part in orienting and controlling his behavior. He is rated as a "marital risk" largely upon calculations of his chances for occupational advancement. After marriage the economic factor would seem to become increasingly important. The status of the family is closely linked with the husband's occupation and with his rise in it. Upon his income, chiefly, the family's necessities and luxuries of life depend. The question of whether the wife is to work may be influenced to a large extent by the economic competence of the husband.

In the economic aspect of personality adjustment, the significant question to be investigated is to what extent marital happiness is a function of size or stability of family income.

Response patterns. Two conceptions, not necessarily incompatible, dominate the attitudes of modern youth toward love and marriage. The first is that of romantic love with its notions of the ideal loved one, of love at first sight, of love transcending all else, and of supreme happiness in marriage. The second is that of affection developing out of companionship, mutual interests, and common activities. Besides these two major conceptions of love there are several specific reactions which affect adjustment in marriage. These include intensity of desire for demonstration of affection, gestural and verbal; the strength of the specifically sexual desires; the fixation in childhood of a particular response pattern; and aberrations of affectional and sexual responses.

In regard to response patterns the general question engaging our attention is: Which affords the more adequate basis for success in marriage—romantic love or affection developing out of companionship? The specific question will be: How are varying proportions of romance and companionship in the love relationship associated with adjustment in marriage?

Adjustment in marriage, it is now clear, involves a relation among several different aspects or characteristics of the two interacting personalities. Any study of marital accommodation and integration must accordingly take into account how the two persons interact with each other, both as persons with specific characteristics and as unified personalities.

The study reported in this volume is a pioneer and exploratory inquiry. It seeks, first, to define the problem of marriage adjustment; second, to find what factors present at the time of marriage are associated with marital success or failure; and third, to determine whether or not it is possible to devise a method of predicting before marriage its outcome in marital happiness or unhappiness.

Is it feasible to bring love and marriage within the purview of science, of prediction and control? Is it possible to increase our insight into and understanding of this realm of human life in which man's behavior seems governed least by his reason and most by his emotions and impulses? This study will attempt to give a preliminary answer to these questions.

CHAPTER II

Social Characteristics of the Couples Studied

THE VALIDITY of the findings of any research in the social sciences is largely dependent on the methods used in obtaining the data, a knowledge of the nature of the sample selected for the study, and the method of analyzing the data. We give, therefore, some explanation of the procedure employed in collecting the data offered in this study, certain important characteristics of the group of 526 couples studied, and the methods of analysis used, before we proceed to present and interpret the results.[1]

Methods of Collecting Data

Several methods of gathering data are open to the student of marriage adjustment:

1. Observation of the behavior of married persons with respect to selected variables to be correlated. This may be done with or without coöperation of the subjects of study.

2. Intensive case studies in which the subject is more or less aware of the purpose of the study and gives active coöperation by writing or reporting verbally on his behavior and experiences. This material may then be abstracted for statistical treatment, or each case can be analyzed into its dynamic factors.

3. Questionnaire studies in which the subject replies in writ-

---

[1] The methods of analysis of the data will be described at appropriate points in subsequent chapters.

ing to specific questions, the answers to which are then analyzed statistically.

4. Experimental studies in which the subjects are observed in a more or less controlled situation, or in which the observer can control some of the factors assumed to be related to the behavior of the subjects.

The present study relies chiefly on the questionnaire method supplemented by some intensive case studies.

Construction of the Questionnaire

A list of items which seemed to have some relevance to adjustment in marriage was drawn up. These items came from published results of research,[2] from preliminary investigations by the authors of the present study, and from suggestions by technical observers as well as lay married people. The list was divided into items that referred to more or less impersonal matters on which it was assumed information would be given readily, and items of a more intimate nature, such as those dealing with family interrelationships and sex. The first group of items was used to construct the questionnaire; the second group was worked into an outline to serve as a guide in interviewing and as a guide for persons writing autobiographical accounts of their marriages.[3] This division was made in order to minimize the resistance of persons filling out the questionnaire and also because it was felt that more reliable data on the intimately personal items could be obtained in case studies.

The items to be included in the questionnaire were arranged into the following sections: [4]

---

[2] E. R. Mowrer, *Family Disorganization*, Chicago, University of Chicago Press, 1927; G. V. Hamilton, *A Research in Marriage*, New York, 1929; Katherine B. Davis, *Factors in the Sex Life of 2,200 Women*, New York, Harper and Brothers, 1929; J. C. Flügel, *The Psychoanalytic Study of the Family*, London, International Psychoanalytic Press, 1921.

[3] See Appendix C for case-study outline.

[4] See Appendix B for questionnaire form.

1. Items on the husband's premarital background.

2. Items on the wife's premarital background.

3. Items on the postmarital attitudes and experiences of the couple.

4. An abbreviated personality inventory which might give some indication of the presence or absence of neurotic tendencies in the person filling out the questionnaire.

The questionnaire form was so constructed that one member of a couple could readily fill out all the items without the assistance of the other.[5]   Of the 526 questionnaires used in this study, 153 were filled out by the husband alone, 317 by the wife alone, 30 by both together, and 15 by one or both spouses with the assistance of an interviewer.   Eleven schedules carried no statement as to who filled them out.

A preliminary form of the questionnaire was tried on 100 subjects.   These returns were examined to discover questions which were not clear and which elicited ambiguous replies. Appropriate modifications were made and the final form was printed.

Distribution of the Questionnaire

About 7,000 questionnaires were distributed.   It is not known how many of these were brought to the attention of married couples.   The channels of distribution were students, other persons interested in the study, and a few social agencies that had certain nonrelief clients.   In addition a mailing list made up from newspaper reports of 400 divorces was used.   The experiment was also tried of placing 250 forms in mailboxes in apartment houses inhabited by young married people.

The questionnaire was prefaced by a statement explaining the purpose of the study, assuring anonymity, and soliciting co-

---

[5] Important methodological problems raised by this procedure are dealt with by L. S. Cottrell, *The Reliability and Validity of a Marriage Study Schedule*, Ph.D. thesis, University of Chicago Libraries, 1933.

operation. The total return was about 1,300 questionnaires, or 19 per cent. The returns were best from subjects who received the blank form from a friend or acquaintance. The personal contact facilitated a detailed explanation of the study, made it possible to secure a promise to coöperate, and permitted a follow-up contact to stimulate coöperation. Questionnaires distributed in the latter manner produced a 30 to 60 per cent return. Of the forms mailed to persons whose names appeared in the newspaper divorce reports, 4.5 per cent were returned, and only half of these were filled out sufficiently to be used. The apartment-house distribution yielded a 5 per cent return. It can be seen that returns were small, except where schedules were placed through personal contact.

The procedure in the collection of the data allowed for little or no control of sampling. This fact made it necessary to choose from the 1,300 returns those constituting a fairly homogeneous group of marriages. The criteria for the selection of the questionnaires to be used in the study were as follows:

1. The couple had to be residents of the State of Illinois at the time the questionnaire was filled out. This limitation was imposed in order to make the sample homogeneous as to the divorce laws under which the subjects lived.

2. The date of the marriage of the couple had to be not less than one nor more than six years previous to the time of filling out the blank.[6] This restriction was made in order to ensure a reasonable homogeneity as to length of time married. It was also assumed that the effect of premarital-background factors on adjustment would be more marked in the early married years than later; and it was with the effect of such factors that the study was primarily concerned.

Of the 1,300 returns, about 550 conformed to the above criteria. Some of these were inadequately filled out and were

---

[6] In the case of divorced couples, the date might be more than six years previous to the time of filling out the schedule, provided the divorce took place before the marriage was six years old.

discarded. The remaining 526 questionnaires were used as the basis for the present study.

Approximately three-fourths of the 526 schedules were obtained during 1931 and 1932, and the remainder in 1933.

As mentioned above, the procedure for securing returns allowed for little control of the sample collected. The questionnaire, however, contained a number of items on social and economic characteristics which permit a rather accurate statement of the nature and degree of homogeneity of the sample and serve to place the sample quite accurately in the general socio-economic order.

Social Characteristics of the Sample

Age. Table 1 shows the distribution of husbands and wives in the sample according to their ages at the time of marriage.

TABLE 1

THE AGE AT MARRIAGE OF 526 HUSBANDS AND WIVES

Age	Husbands	Wives
Under 20	11	56
20 to 24	176	255
25 to 29	178	112
30 to 34	53	23
35 to 39	24	11
40 and over	11	5
No reply	73	64
Total	526	526

Seventy-three husbands and 64 wives did not furnish information regarding age. Of the 453 husbands who replied, the great majority (89.9 per cent) were between 20 and 35 years of age when they married. The median age at marriage for the husbands is 26.1 years. Of the 462 wives who furnished information about age, almost eight-tenths (79.4 per cent) were between 20 and 30 years of age at marriage. Their median age at marriage is 23.4 years. The median ages of the husbands and wives of the group run about one year above the median age for marriage of men and women in the general population.

Length of time married. Table 2 shows the distribution of

TABLE 2

DISTRIBUTION OF COUPLES ACCORDING TO LENGTH OF TIME MARRIED

Months Married	Number
6 to 17	61
18 to 29	159
30 to 41	106
42 to 53	108
54 to 65	60
66 to 77	32
Total	526

the sample with respect to length of time married.[7] The majority of the couples in the sample (71.0 per cent) had been married two to four years, inclusive. The average length of marriage was three years and one month.

Nationality background. Table 3 shows the distribution of the sample according to place of birth of the fathers of husbands and wives. Information about 35 of the husbands' fathers and 27 of the wives' fathers is lacking. Of the 491 husbands' fathers for whom the information is given, about half (54.4 per cent) were native-born white Americans. Slightly more (61.0 per cent) of the 499 wives' fathers belonged to this category. If those born in Canada, England, and Ireland are grouped with the white Americans, 62.0 per cent of the husbands' fathers and 69.3 per cent of the wives' fathers can be classified as white, English-speaking persons. Scandinavian and German parentage accounts for an additional 15.5 per cent

---

[7] A few of the divorced couples had been married more than six years prior to the filling out of the questionnaire. No divorced couple was included, however, unless the interval between the marriage date and the divorce date was six years or less.

TABLE 3

DISTRIBUTION OF THE COUPLES ACCORDING TO COUNTRY OF
BIRTH OF FATHERS

Country of Birth	Husbands' Fathers	Wives' Fathers
United States (Negro)	11	12
United States (White)	267	304
Canada	10	9
England	15	19
Ireland	17	14
Norway or Sweden	32	26
Germany	44	33
Russia	50	52
Poland	13	9
Other Slavic	20	14
Other	12	7
No reply	35	27
Total	526	526

of the husbands' and 11.8 per cent of the wives' fathers. These figures would indicate a fair degree of homogeneity. It can be said that about eight-tenths of the sample come from north European cultures.

Religious affiliation. Table 4 indicates the distribution of the sample with respect to the religious affiliation of husbands and

TABLE 4

DISTRIBUTION OF THE COUPLES ACCORDING TO RELIGIOUS AFFILIATIONS

Religious Affiliation	Husband	Wife
None	89	48
Protestant	261	307
Catholic	54	57
Jewish	52	48
Other	3	4
No reply	67	62
Total	526	526

wives at the time of marriage. Of the 459 husbands whose religious affiliations are given, over half (54.7 per cent) are Protestant. Of the 464 wives who replied on this item, 61.2 per cent are Protestant. Of those who gave "none" as an answer to the question or who left the item blank, the majority (approximately 75 per cent) had Protestant parents. The sample is thus predominantly Protestant in religious background.

Rural-urban background. Most of the couples in this sample were living in Chicago and its suburbs when they filled out the questionnaire (69.1 per cent lived in the city of Chicago and 12.9 per cent in Chicago suburbs). Only 4.5 per cent lived in places of 1,000 or less population. All the couples lived in Illinois. Within the city, only 9.9 per cent of the sample lived in rooming-house, immigrant, hotel, or working-men's home areas. Forty-three per cent resided in apartment-house areas, and 43.2 per cent lived in better-class neighborhoods with single-family dwellings and in suburban sections.

From Table 5 it will be seen that the majority of husbands and wives were reared in a city. Of the 508 husbands for

TABLE 5

DISTRIBUTION OF COUPLES ACCORDING TO WHERE CHILDHOOD
AND ADOLESCENT YEARS WERE SPENT

Childhood and Adolescence Spent Chiefly in:	Husband	Wife
City	286	322
Small town	174	145
Country	48	40
No reply	18	19
Total	526	526

whom information is available, 56.4 per cent were reared in a city. Of the 507 wives, 64.5 per cent were city-bred. Only 9.5 per cent of the husbands and 7.9 per cent of the wives had spent their childhood and adolescence in the country. Most of this sample not only lived in an urban environment as married people but had been reared in cities and towns.

Educational status. The educational status of the sample is shown in Table 6. Of the 513 husbands whose educational

TABLE 6

DISTRIBUTION OF THE COUPLES ACCORDING TO EDUCATIONAL STATUS

Educational Status* (one or more years of:)	Husband	Wife
Grade school	51	27
High school	152	202
College	205	227
Graduate work	105	62
No reply	13	8
Total	526	526

* The person is assigned to the educational status of his last year of schooling.

status was given, 60.5 per cent had had some undergraduate or graduate work in college. Only 9.9 per cent had stopped at the grade-school level. Of the 518 wives, 55.7 per cent had attained the college or graduate level when they married. Only 5.2 per cent had stopped in the grades. Thus over half of the sample were college persons, and over nine-tenths had had at least some high-school training.

Income. Table 7 indicates the distribution of the sample

TABLE 7

DISTRIBUTION OF THE COUPLES ACCORDING TO INCOME OF HUSBANDS AT TIME OF MARRIAGE

Annual Income	Number	Per Cent
None	25	4.8
Under $1,800	129	24.5
$1,800 to $2,999	197	37.4
$3,000 to $4,199	49	9.3
$4,200 and over	55	10.5
Not given	71	13.5
Total	526	100.0

according to the annual income of the husbands at the time of marriage. A considerable proportion of those who either stated that they had had no income or failed to answer the question were students or were dependent on parents at the time of marriage. If half of those not replying to the question be regarded as having no earned income, then about three-fourths of the husbands of the sample were earning less than $3,000 a year at the time of marriage, and only one-fifth were earning $3,000 or more. Over half of the husbands were earning $1,800 or more.

Most of the wives of the sample were gainfully employed at the time of marriage, as Table 8 shows. Slightly over a fourth

TABLE 8

DISTRIBUTION OF COUPLES ACCORDING TO INCOME OF
WIVES AT TIME OF MARRIAGE

Annual Income	Number	Per Cent
None	67	12.7
Under $1,200	112	21.3
$1,200 to $1,799	143	27.2
$1,800 to $2,399	84	16.0
$2,400 and over	44	8.4
Not stated	76	14.4
Total	526	100.0

of the wives either left the question on income blank or specifically stated that they were earning no income when they married. A fifth were earning less than $1,200 per year, and the remaining 51.6 per cent were earning $1,200 and over, with only 8.4 per cent earning $2,400 or more.

Occupation. The occupational classification of the husbands at the time of marriage (Table 9) indicates that the sample is predominantly white-collar and professional. Only 11.6 per cent of the husbands were in unskilled, semiskilled, or low-paid clerical positions. Almost a fourth were in the skilled trades or operated small shops and businesses, and 52.5 per cent

TABLE 9

DISTRIBUTION OF COUPLES ACCORDING TO OCCUPATIONAL
CLASSIFICATION OF HUSBANDS AT TIME OF MARRIAGE

Occupational Classification	Number	Per Cent
None	8	1.5
Unskilled industrial	12	2.3
Clerical and semiskilled	49	9.3
Skilled and small-trades	122	23.2
Sales and semiprofessional	119	22.6
Professional	127	24.2
Larger business; managerial	30	5.7
Farmer	13	2.5
Unclassified; student	22	4.2
Not stated	24	4.6
Total	526	100.1

were in the semiprofessional, white-collar, professional, or upper business positions. About one-tenth had no occupation or
were not classifiable, or gave no information on the question.

The occupational table for the wives (Table 10) indicates
that the wives were of about the same occupational status as

TABLE 10

DISTRIBUTION OF COUPLES ACCORDING TO OCCUPATIONAL
CLASSIFICATION OF WIVES AT TIME OF MARRIAGE

Occupational Classification	Number	Per Cent
None	76	14.4
Domestic	15	2.9
Unskilled industrial	3	0.6
Clerical and semiskilled opera- tors, salesgirls, etc.	62	11.8
Skilled secretarial work	127	24.1
Nursing	15	2.9
Teaching and social work	140	26.6
Other professions	6	1.2
Highly paid business positions	9	1.7
Unclassified; students	32	6.1
Not stated	41	7.8
Total	526	100.1

the husbands.   Only 15.3 per cent of the wives belonged to the low-status occupational groups such as those including domestic servants, unskilled industrial workers, semiskilled industrial workers, lower-paid clerical workers, and so on.   Over half of the group, or 56.5 per cent, belonged to the more skilled secretarial, professional, and managerial business groups.   More than one-fourth of the sample either failed to state an occupation or had none, or could not be classified.   Most of these actually had no occupation.

Employment.   The problem of unemployment had not been serious for this group during the years since marriage up to the time the questionnaire was filled out (1931–1933).   Slightly over a tenth (10.5 per cent) did not answer the question on unemployment since marriage.   Of the 471 replying to the question, 71.8 per cent stated that the husband had been continuously employed or had not been out of employment as much as one month since the time of marriage.   Fifty-six of the husbands (11.9 per cent) had been out of work from one to less than six months, and 77 (16.4 per cent) had been unemployed a total of six months or more during the marriage period.

The general conclusion to be drawn from the income and occupational data is that at the time of marriage most of the husbands and wives were gainfully employed in white-collar and professional occupations and were earning incomes which place them in the lower half of the middle-income group of the population.   The employment data indicate that the sample was fairly homogeneous with respect to steadiness of employment.   It is evident that the study does not include the upper middle class, the laboring class, or the farm population.

Number of children.   Although the average length of marriage in this sample is three years and one month, 56.3 per cent of the couples had no children.[8]   About a third (33.1 per cent)

---

[8] Counting every birth, whether the child lived or not.

had one child; the remainder (10.5 per cent) had two or more children. This reproductive rate is apparently consistent with the other social characteristics noted above.

Personality characteristics. It has sometimes been stated that the subjects who respond to questionnaires on personal matters have certain personality characteristics that weight the results. Thus it is argued that only people with personality problems will respond to requests that they fill out such forms. So-called normal people, it is said, ignore such requests. If this be true, there is an uncontrolled bias in this and all other similar studies. Adequate evidence is lacking to prove or disprove that a psychological bias is present in this study. This study, however, includes the responses to a neurotic inventory [9] made by one member of each couple studied. Table 11 shows the distribution, by neurotic scores, of the persons who filled out the schedules.

TABLE 11

DISTRIBUTION OF THE PERSONS ACCORDING TO NEUROTIC SCORES

Neurotic Score	Number
0 to 5	78
6 to 11	145
12 to 17	122
18 to 23	80
24 to 29	42
30 and over	24
No reply	35
Total	526

In the inventory there were 42 questions, with neurotic and non-neurotic answers possible for each one. If a subject checked all the neurotic answers, his neurotic score would be 42 and he would be classified as extremely neurotic. If he

[9] The inventory used is an abbreviated form made up of the 42 most discriminating items in L. L. Thurstone's *Personality Inventory,* Chicago, University of Chicago Press.

checked none or only a few of the neurotic answers, his score would be low and he would be classified as non-neurotic. If it be assumed that a person checking as many as 18 or more of the neurotic answers is neurotically inclined, then we find that of the 491 persons filling out the inventory, 70.3 per cent are non-neurotic and only 29.7 per cent are neurotically inclined. If the figures are broken down according to the sex of the persons filling out the inventory, it is found that 21.8 per cent of the men and 33.9 per cent of the women would be classified as neurotically inclined persons.

Some of the subjects may have falsified their replies, and there may be more neurotically inclined persons in the sample than the test scores indicate. But so far as the test can show, there is no loading of the sample with neurotic subjects.

A review of the characteristics of the sample used in this study points to the general conclusion that it is a roughly homogeneous, young, preponderantly non-neurotic, middle-class, native-white American, urban group. Whatever degree of validity the findings of this study may have, therefore, they are applicable only to the social strata from which the sample has been drawn. Any application of the findings to other groups should be made with great caution and in an exploratory manner.

CHAPTER III

Happiness as a Criterion of Successful Marriage

DEEPLY rooted in the common-sense philosophy of the American people is the notion that happiness is the principal criterion of the success of any marriage. The expectation of supreme happiness in marriage is a corollary to the prevalent faith in romantic love as the right and proper basis for marriage. Over and above all other conditions implied in the marriage contract is the right to be happy and the obligation of husband and wife to make each other happy: a right and an obligation which emphasize the personal character of marriage in our individualistic society.

This belief in happiness as indispensable to marriage is very modern.[1] Havelock Ellis went so far as to question the very existence of marital happiness in the past:

One may even doubt if the happiness today demanded in marriage —whether or not often found—had any existence in ancient days. Marriage then was a duty for the partners who were bound together in wedlock, and a convenience, socially or financially, for the families who usually had the chief part in so binding them. Many love letters have come down to us from the days of old—beautiful and romantic many of them—but they were written by unmarried lovers. I know that I might search long to find among the old letters of married women what I see in a letter I chanced to receive this morning from an American woman, married and a mother: "We are happy, our love is beautiful; our lives, our interests grow ever closer and dearer."

---

[1] See sections 2 and 3 in Bernhard J. Stern, *The Family, Past and Present*, New York, D. Appleton-Century Co., 1938.

The established permanence of marriage in old days offered no practical alternative to acceptance. If the germs of discontent were generated, they may have led to a slow spiritual death below the surface, but to no open conflict between the forces of happiness and unhappiness. If marriages often appear less happy today it is because we are less willing to submit to unhappiness or to the make-believes of convention.[2]

Since happiness is by common consent the criterion for judging the success or failure of modern marriage, it is taken as the point of departure for the evaluation of the success of the 526 marital unions of our study. Each couple was asked to fill out the item: "Appraisal of marriage: very unhappy........; unhappy ....; average........; happy........; very happy........." No attempt was made in the schedule to define the term "happiness." The question was left for each person to answer in the light of his own understanding of its meaning. It was assumed that husbands and wives would be competent to report whether or not they were happy in their married life. It is highly probable that in checking this question they understood the term "happiness" in accordance with its popular usage as reported in *Webster's New International Dictionary:*

a state of well-being characterized by relative permanence, by dominantly agreeable emotion ranging in value from mere contentment to positive felicity, and by a natural desire for its continuation.

This definition of happiness in terms of a relatively permanent state of feeling ranging from contentment to felicity emphasizes its subjective nature. The admitted lack of objectivity in the concept of happiness should perhaps have prejudiced the writers against any attempt to use it in this research. On the other hand, it seemed of some interest to know how people rate their own marriages and to find empirically, rather than by relying entirely upon speculation, the values and limitations of happiness ratings.

---

[2] In *Esquire,* November 1936, p. 58. Copyright, 1936, by Esquire-Coronet, Inc., 919 N. Michigan Ave., Chicago, Ill.

Marital-Happiness Ratings

All but five of the 526 couples included in the study gave a rating of the happiness of their marriages. This disposed at once of two objections: first, that a large number of persons are unable to state whether or not they are happily married; and second, that they would have great difficulty in stating the degree of happiness of their marriages.

The ratings of marital happiness as given by either husband or wife are given in Table 12. Examining these figures, one

TABLE 12

RATINGS OF MARITAL HAPPINESS AS GIVEN BY EITHER HUSBAND OR WIFE

Happiness Rating	Number	Per Cent
Very happy	224	42.6
Happy	108	20.5
Average	76	14.4
Unhappy	71	13.5
Very unhappy	42	8.0
No reply	5	1.0
Total	526	100.0

is struck by the fact that nearly one-half (42.6 per cent) of the marriages are reported as very happy and one-fifth (20.5 per cent) as happy, as against one-seventh (14.4 per cent) as average, one-eighth (13.5 per cent) as unhappy, and only one-twelfth (8.0 per cent) as very unhappy. In short, the very happy and happy predominate over the average, unhappy, and very unhappy couples. These percentages do not present the normal curve of distribution which might have been expected by the form in which the question was asked. On the contrary, if plotted, the data show a marked skew (see Chart 1).

A comparison of the actual with the expected distribution of cases at once raises pertinent questions: Are the findings regarding this group of 526 couples representative of marital happiness in general? Does not this study include too large a proportion of happily married couples?

These questions cannot be given satisfactory answers, since a rigorously controlled sampling of the population for marital-happiness ratings has never been made. There are, however, available the findings of a study by Dr. R. O. Lang [3] on the ratings of the happiness of the marriages of their close acquaint-

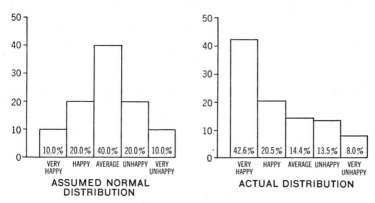

CHART I.—COMPARISON OF ASSUMED NORMAL DISTRIBUTION WITH ACTUAL DISTRIBUTION OF HAPPINESS RATINGS

ances [4] by a widely distributed group of students in colleges and universities. The ratings obtained in this study are presented in comparison with those of our 526 couples in Table 13.

The group of couples in Lang's study married from one to six years is more comparable with the 526 couples in this study who have been married not less than one nor more than six years. But whichever group in Lang's investigation is taken, it has a smaller proportion of "unhappy" and "very unhappy" ratings than has the present study.

Two factors explain the discrepancy. First, 69.2 per cent

[3] *The Rating of Happiness in Marriage*, unpublished M. A. thesis, Chicago, University of Chicago, 1932.
[4] *Ibid.*, p. 35.

TABLE 13

HAPPINESS RATINGS OF THIS STUDY COMPARED WITH THOSE OF
LANG'S STUDY

Happiness Rating	This Study (married 1–6 yrs.)	Lang's Study*	
		(married 1–6 yrs.)	(married 1–16 yrs.)
Very happy	42.6	44.4	39.5
Happy	20.5	24.1	25.4
Average	14.4	16.5	19.2
Unhappy	13.5	9.3	10.0
Very unhappy .	8.0	5.7	5.8
No reply	1.0		0.1
Totals..............	100.0	100.0	100.0
No. of cases	526	4,750	8,263

* Figures are adapted from Lang's tables by including the divorced and separated couples which he tabulated separately.

of our cases were from a city with over 3,000,000 population. Lang's study showed that a higher proportion of "unhappy" and "very unhappy" ratings came from large cities of 200,000 or over than from smaller cities. Secondly, a definite effort was made to seek out cases of separated and divorced couples for inclusion in our study. If the ratings of outsiders can be taken as indicating the state of happiness of a married couple,[5] then we must conclude that the 526 cases in our study have, if anything, a disproportionate number of unhappy rather than of happy marriages.[6]

Until more adequate data are available the findings of Lang upon the distribution of happiness may be taken as representative of the state of marriage adjustment in the United States. In Chart 2 are presented the findings of Lang's study in terms of a normal distribution curve of happiness ratings.

In the actual distribution of Lang's cases the proportion of

---

[5] This question is discussed on pp. 40–42.
[6] In Lang's study the proportion of divorced and separated couples in the period one to six years after marriage is 11.5 per cent; in this study, 24.0 per cent.

"very happy" couples, 39.5 per cent, is approximately the same as the total of "average," "unhappy," and "very unhappy" couples (35.0 per cent). The group of "happy" couples, 25.4 per cent, is in an intermediate position.

If it be assumed that happiness is the modal state of marriage, then in an assumed normal distribution the group of "very happy" should be distributed in the same proportion as the

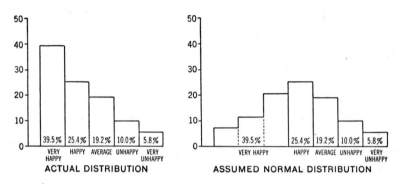

CHART 2.—ACTUAL AND ASSUMED NORMAL DISTRIBUTION OF HAPPINESS RATINGS BASED ON LANG'S 8,263 COUPLES MARRIED FROM 1 TO 16 YEARS.

"average," "unhappy," and "very unhappy" couples in the actual distribution shown in the figure on the right.

How do Lang's findings compare with those of other studies of happiness in marriage? G. V. Hamilton, a psychiatrist, interviewed 200 married individuals [7] under controlled experimental conditions and found that 45 per cent of them were seriously maladjusted, some being actually on the brink of separation. This high proportion of unhappy marriages can be accounted for either by the selection in his study of a disproportionate number of maladjusted cases or by the larger percentage of marital maladjustment discovered by his more intimate and intensive method of study.

[7] The 200 married individuals were equally divided between husbands and wives. Married couples numbered 55, leaving cases including 45 men and 45 women in which only one spouse was interviewed. See *Research in Marriage*, New York, A. and C. Boni, 1929.

Katherine B. Davis,[8] in her study of the sex life of 2,200 women, stated the happiness of 988 marriages on the basis of returns from a questionnaire. Using only two categories, she found 88.4 per cent "happy" and 11.6 per cent "unhappy." The proportion of marriages reported as "unhappy" by Dr. Davis is smaller than the combined group of the "unhappy" and "very unhappy" in Dr. Lang's study, probably because Dr. Davis did not include divorced and separated couples.

Terman and his associates [9] found the following percentage distribution of self-ratings by 792 couples included in his study, and by 902 husbands and 644 wives in a random sample of married persons in attendance at meetings, representing a wide range of gatherings. Again we find the typical lumping of

TABLE 14

PERCENTAGE DISTRIBUTION OF HAPPINESS RATINGS FOUND BY TERMAN AND HIS ASSOCIATES IN A GROUP STUDIED AND IN A RANDOM SAMPLE

Happiness Rating	Group Studied		Random Sample	
	Husbands	Wives	Men	Women
Extraordinarily happy	29.5	34.6	25.5	27.2
Decidedly more happy than average	36.8	35.9	29.4	28.0
Somewhat more happy than average	16.3	14.7	13.1	10.1
About average	12.9	9.2	18.2	16.3
Somewhat less happy than average	2.9	3.0	6.6	7.3
Decidedly less happy than average	1.6	1.8	3.2	4.0
Extremely unhappy	0.1	0.8	4.0	7.1

cases at the "happy" end of the scale. The unusually low proportion in the "less happy" categories in the study of 792 couples is partially explained by the fact that Terman's procedure both

---

[8] *Factors in the Sex Life of Twenty-Two Hundred Women,* New York, Harper and Brothers, 1929.

[9] L. M. Terman, *et al., Psychological Factors in Marital Happiness,* McGraw-Hill Book Co., New York, 1938, p. 78.

selected the happier couples in attendance at meetings and ruled out all separated and divorced couples.

Certain reasons for this characteristic skewness of the happiness rating may be suggested. One is that there is a cultural expectation of happiness which might cause an unconscious "generosity" in the rating. Another is that marriage is a personal relation established after considerable selection has taken place: the crudely maladjusted couples would be eliminated in courtship. Again, with a relatively high separation and divorce rate, the very unhappy relations tend to dissolve. Although we made special efforts to obtain such cases as the latter, they were much more difficult to obtain than the undissolved-marriage cases.

Objections to Happiness as a Criterion

Certain objections to the use of happiness as a standard in judging the success or failure of marriage must already have occurred to the reader as they occurred to the research workers in the planning of this study. Among the possible objections to placing confidence in the happiness ratings are these:

1. Happiness is something that cannot be objectively defined. How, therefore, can it be measured and reliably rated upon a continuum?

2. Conceptions of happiness vary too much from person to person for various estimates to be compared.

3. An individual's conception of his own happiness varies too much from day to day to be consistently rated.

4. A marriage may be quite happy for one spouse and quite unhappy for the other. Hence the ratings of two partners would not agree.

5. Persons will not or cannot be entirely honest in recording their judgments as to how happy their marriages are, even though they consciously strive to be honest.

6. There is no way of checking up on a person's rating of

his marriage, because it is impossible for an outsider to give accurate ratings. Ratings by outsiders will diverge a great deal from the self-ratings which married persons give.

The only possible answer to these objections is to determine as far as possible the extent to which they are supported or refuted by empirical data. The tables that follow represent attempts to evaluate the degree of reliability and validity with which happiness in marriage is rated.

Reliability and Validity of Happiness Ratings

Independent ratings of the happiness of their marriages by husbands and wives among 251 couples were secured. Table 15 shows the result of a comparison of these ratings.[10]

It will be noted that there are some divergences in these ratings, but only nine of the 251, or 3.6 per cent, show disagreement between husband and wife by as much as two scale steps.[11] The remaining 242 either show identical ratings or agree within one step.[12] These figures would indicate that husbands

---

[10] Owing to the manner in which we collected the ratings tabulated in Tables 15, 16, and 17, we could not rigorously control the amount of collaboration between husband and wife. The instructions were explicit and emphatic that there should be no consultation between husband and wife on these ratings either before or after filling out the schedules. Moreover, the schedules were to be mailed to us in separate envelopes. On the basis of a partial check, we have reason to believe that most of the subjects followed the instructions. However, many of them probably did not. The agreement in ratings probably would not be quite so close had we been able to secure all ratings by husbands and wives under controlled conditions.

[11] The coefficient of contingency for Table 15 is .805. The upper limit for a coefficient of contingency on a 5×5 table is .894. Hence, the actually computed coefficient of contingency is .900 of its upper limit. Persons not familiar with the coefficient of contingency as an index of association may refer to G. U. Yule, *Introduction to the Theory of Statistics*, London, Griffin, 1937.

[12] If this 5×5 table be turned into a 2×2 table by drawing the lines of division between the steps "happy" and "average," a tetrachoric correlation coefficient may be computed. The correlation coefficient thus computed is .89, which is a fairly high index of reliability.

For a demonstration of the mathematical basis for the computation of the tetrachoric coefficient of correlation—that is, a coefficient of correlation computed from data distributed in a fourfold table—see Karl Pearson's article "Mathematical Contribution to the Theory of Evolution," Section 7, on the correlation of characters not quantitatively measurable, *Philosophical Transactions*, No. 195, Series A, pp. 1–47.

and wives agree fairly closely in their estimates of the degree of happiness of their marriages.

In Table 16 are shown the results of a comparison of independent ratings by husband and wife of the husband's parents' marriage. In this instance, therefore, two people are giving independent estimates of the degree of happiness in the marriage of couples with whom they are reasonably well acquainted.

TABLE 15

APPRAISALS OF THEIR MARRIAGES BY HUSBANDS AND BY WIVES

Appraisal of Marriage Wife's rating:	Husband's Rating					Total	Percentage Distribution
	Very Un- happy	Un- happy	Aver- age	Happy	Very Happy		
Very happy			3	24	112	139	55.4
Happy			12	38	12	62	24.7
Average		3	14	7	6	30	11.9
Unhappy	1	11	2			14	5.6
Very unhappy	5	1				6	2.4
Total	6	15	31	69	130	251	100.0
Percentage Distribution	2.4	6.0	12.3	27.5	51.8	100.0	

	Number	Percentage
Ratings that agree...	180	71.7
Ratings that agree within one category..................	62	24.7
Ratings that disagree by two or more categories......	9	3.6

Here again, in spite of some divergence in the ratings, is found rather close approximation between the independent estimates.

See also P. F. Everitt, "Tables of the Tetrachoric Functions for Fourfold Correlation Tables," *Biometrica*, No. 7, pp. 437–451; and his "Supplementary Tables for Finding the Correlation Coefficient from Tetrachoric Groupings," *Biometrica*, No. 8, pp. 385–395; and Karl Pearson's "On the Probable Error of a Correlation Coefficient as Found from a Fourfold Table," *Biometrica*, No. 9, pp. 22–27.

Persons not interested in the lengthy mathematical proofs in the above references who wish to find out how to compute a tetrachoric coefficient are referred to Leone Chesire, Milton Saffir, and L. L. Thurstone, *Computing Diagrams for the Tetrachoric Correlation Coefficient,* which may be obtained from the University of Chicago Bookstore, Chicago, Ill.

Of the 198 independent ratings only six, or 3 per cent, disagreed by two or more scale steps.[13]

In Table 17 is presented a similar comparison of independent ratings by husbands and wives, but in this instance the marriage of the wife's parents is being rated.   Here again the agreement

TABLE 16

APPRAISAL OF HUSBAND'S PARENTS' MARRIAGE BY HUSBAND AND BY WIFE

Appraisal of Marriage / Wife's rating:	Husband's Rating					Total	Percentage Distribution
	Very Un-happy	Un-happy	Aver-age	Happy	Very Happy		
Very happy...	1*			9	47	57	28.8
Happy			10	36	14	60	30.3
Average	1	5	35	10	2	53	26.8
Unhappy	1	17	6	1	1	26	13.1
Very unhappy	2					2	1.0
Total	5	22	51	56	64	198	
Percentage Distribution	2.5	11.1	25.8	28.3	32.3	100.0	100.0

	Number	Percentage Distribution
Ratings that agree.....................................	137	69.2
Ratings that agree within one category..................	55	27.8
Ratings that disagree by two or more categories......	6	3.0

* Probably an error in checking the wrong end of the scale.

between the ratings is quite close.   Of the 189 pairs of ratings, only seven show a disagreement by two or more scale steps.[14]

In Table 18 are given 272 paired ratings of happiness in marriage.   In each pair one rating is by a member of the couple whose marriage is being rated.   The other rating is by an outsider who is more or less acquainted with the marriage.

[13] The tetrachoric correlation coefficient for Table 16 is .91.   The coefficient of contingency is .778.   Since the upper limit of a contingency coefficient on a 5×5 table is .894, the obtained coefficient is .870 of its upper limit.

[14] The tetrachoric coefficient for this table is .90.   The coefficient of contingency is .803, which equals .898 of its upper limit.

While we were not altogether able to control the amount of collaboration between husbands and wives in the happiness ratings tabulated in Tables 15, 16, and 17, we were able to control the ratings tabulated in Table 18. We secured these ratings under conditions which made it impossible for any pair of raters to collaborate. Moreover, neither the outsider

TABLE 17

APPRAISALS OF WIFE'S PARENTS' MARRIAGE BY HUSBAND AND WIFE

Appraisal of Marriage / Wife's rating:	Husband's Rating					Total	Percentage Distribution
	Very Un-happy	Un-happy	Aver-age	Happy	Very Happy		
Very happy...			4	15	41	60	31.7
Happy			16	38	7	61	32.3
Average		2	37	5	2	46	24.3
Unhappy	2	8	5	1		16	8.5
Very unhappy	6					6	3.2
Total	8	10	62	59	50	189	100.0
Percentage Distribution	4.2	5.3	32.8	31.2	26.5	100.0	

	Number	Percentage Distribution
Ratings that agree	130	68.8
Ratings that agree within one category	52	27.5
Ratings that disagree by two or more categories	7	3.7

who rated a marriage, nor the member of the couple who gave a self-rating, knew that the two ratings would be compared. It will be seen from this table that the ratings are fairly close in agreement. Of the 272 pairs of ratings only 24, or 8.8 per cent, show a disagreement by two or more scale steps.[15]

Another attempt to test the consistency of happiness ratings was made as follows: Detailed case studies were made of 34 marriages. Two judges were asked to read the case histories

[15] The tetrachoric coefficient of correlation for this table is .91. The coefficient of contingency is .680, which is .761 of its upper limit.

TABLE 18

APPRAISALS OF THE COUPLE'S MARRIAGE BY A MEMBER OF THE COUPLE AND BY AN OUTSIDER

Appraisal of Marriage Outsider's rating:	Rating by a Member of the Couple					Total	Percentage Distribution
	Very Un-happy	Un-happy	Aver-age	Happy	Very Happy		
Very happy....			4	16	57	77	28.3
Happy		2	4	31	35	72	26.5
Average	1	4	6	16	8	35	12.9
Unhappy	10	27	20	3		60	22.0
Very unhappy	11	11	5	1		28	10.3
Total	22	44	39	67	100	272	100.0
Percentage Distribution	8.1	16.2	14.3	24.6	36.8	100.0	

	Number	Percentage Distribution
Ratings that agree	132	48.5
Ratings that agree within one category...................	116	42.7
Ratings that disagree by two or more categories....	24	8.8

and make a happiness rating of each marriage.[16] The judges' ratings were then compared with the rating given by a member of the couple whose marriage had been studied. Tables 19 and 20 show the result of these comparisons. Here again the ratings of happiness are in fairly close agreement.[17]

Table 21 shows the result of an attempt to estimate the consistency with which the same people on two different occasions rate the degree of happiness of their own marriages. For a small number of cases (38) a second rating was obtained after a lapse of time ranging from eight months to two years. Of course, one may not conclude too much from such a small sample, but this table does indicate relatively little variance in

---

[16] The cases were disguised so that the persons involved could not be identified.
[17] The tetrachoric coefficient of correlation for Table 19 and for Table 20 is .96.

TABLE 19

APPRAISALS OF THE MARRIAGE BY A MEMBER OF THE COUPLE AND BY JUDGE NUMBER 1

Appraisal of Marriage By Judge No. 1:	Rating by a Member of the Couple					Total
	Very Un-happy	Un-happy	Aver-age	Happy	Very Happy	
Very happy..					1	1
Happy				7	5	12
Average			3	1		4
Unhappy	5	7		2	1	15
Very unhappy	2					2
Total	7	7	3	10	7	34

TABLE 20

APPRAISALS OF THE MARRIAGE BY A MEMBER OF THE COUPLE AND BY JUDGE NUMBER 2

Appraisal of Marriage By Judge No. 2:	Rating by a Member of the Couple					Total
	Very Un-happy	Un-happy	Aver-age	Happy	Very Happy	
Very happy ...				1	3	4
Happy				7	3	10
Average			3	2		5
Unhappy	1	2		3	1	7
Very unhappy	5	2				7
Total	6	4	3	13	7	33

the way people on two different occasions estimate the happiness of their marriages.[18]

In summary, happiness ratings on a five-point scale appear to be reliable and stable when comparisons are made (1) between independent ratings by husbands and wives of their own marriages and of their parents' marriages; (2) between

---

[18] The tetrachoric coefficient of correlation for this table is .86.

TABLE 21

FIRST AND SECOND APPRAISALS OF THE PERSON'S OWN MARRIAGE

Appraisal of Marriage First rating:	Second Rating					Total
	Very Un-happy	Un-happy	Aver-age	Happy	Very Happy	
Very happy			2	3	17	22
Happy			1	7	2	10
Average			2			2
Unhappy		1				1
Very unhappy	1	2				3
Total	1	3	5	10	19	38

independent ratings made by a member of the couple and by an outsider; (3) between independent ratings made by a member of the couple and by a judge who has read the case history of the marriage; and (4) between two ratings of his own marriage made by the same person after an interval of 8 to 24 months. It must be admitted, however, that the evidence presented in the above tables on comparative ratings does not enable us to say how much of the apparent agreement in the estimation of happiness in marriage is due to a generalized unconscious tendency to rate marriages as they are supposed to be rather than as they are.

Limitations of Happiness Ratings

Most of the objections to the use of happiness as a criterion of success in marriage are at least in part refuted by these findings. Happiness, although it is a subjective concept interpreted by each person in accordance with his own feelings and reactions, turned out to be a rather reliable and stable instrument for measuring differences in the satisfaction or dissatisfaction of married couples with their union. There are, however, two major limitations in the acceptance of ratings of happiness as anything more than a preliminary instrument for measuring marital success and failure.

First, since the state of feeling described as happiness is so subjective, it is highly probable that attempts to get at finer estimates than those on a five- or possibly a seven-point scale [19] would yield results of little value. Hence, while the ratings are shown to be relatively satisfactory for crude groupings into five scale steps, if a more precise and discriminating index of adjustment is desired some other means will have to be devised.

In the second place, this question can be raised: Is a happiness rating the most significant criterion of adjustment in marriage? Happiness ratings, although reliable as a report of the state of feeling of the person toward his marriage, only partially indicate the nature of the adjustment achieved in the marriage relationship.

What is wanted, then, is a concept which will express the nature and the state of the interaction of the two persons with each other and in the activities and objectives of married life. A concept useful for this purpose is that of marital adjustment of the two personalities to each other and then as a married couple to their common environment. Indications of the adjustment of husband and wife may be found in their agreements and disagreements, in the convergence or divergence of their interests and activities, in the expression or withholding of affection and confidences, in satisfaction or dissatisfaction with their marriage, and in feelings of optimism or pessimism, of companionship or lonesomeness, of well-being or *anomie*.

Happiness ratings may be very helpful as a guide in the construction of an instrument for the measurement of marital adjustment. They are so used in this study. They will always have a value in giving a rough but apparently reliable index of the degree of satisfaction which husband and wife find in the marriage relationship.

---

[19] See discussion of marital-adjustment scale, pp. 58, 68–69.

The points presented in this chapter may be briefly summarized as follows:

1. Happiness in the minds of present-day Americans is the major criterion of successful marriage.

2. In spite of difficulties of definition and in spite of the varying conditions under which different marriages are happy, most persons can give an estimate of what they consider to be their degree of happiness in marriage.

3. Husbands and wives usually agree in estimates of their marital happiness.

4. An outsider who is fairly well acquainted with a married couple will generally agree with a member of the couple in his happiness rating of the marriage.

5. Two outsiders reasonably familiar with a given marriage will usually agree in their appraisals of the marriage.

6. People's estimates of the happiness of their marriages do not fluctuate markedly over short periods of time.

7. Happiness ratings, although reliable and stable on a five-point scale, are satisfactory for crude classification, but not for precise and discriminating measurement of adjustment in marriage.

8. Happiness ratings report the state of feeling of the married couple but give no indication of the conditions making for the success or failure of the marriage.

9. Happiness ratings, however, may be found of value as a guide in the construction of an index of marriage adjustment.

CHAPTER IV

Measuring Adjustment in Marriage

A WELL-ADJUSTED marriage may be defined as one in which the patterns of behavior of the two persons are mutually satisfying. It is evidently impossible to measure *directly* the degree to which any given marriage approximates this definition. But if adjustment cannot be satisfactorily defined or measured directly, it is nevertheless true that one is more or less vaguely aware of the extent to which people are well adjusted. Common-sense estimates of how well or poorly people are adjusted are made on the basis of certain symptoms or indications of their feelings and attitudes toward their mates and their marriages. This fact is the clue to the way an index of the degree of adjustment in marriage might be constructed. Such an index, to be sure, will not be as exact as might be desired: but it may be precise enough for the purposes of the present research.

If affection and intimate companionship be the essential condition of successful marriage in American society, the indices of marital maladjustment will be found in those items of behavior and attitude which reflect a weakening, or a disturbance, or a disintegration of this relationship.

Five Indications of Marital Adjustment

In our attempt to measure marital adjustment the following assumptions were therefore made:

1. It was assumed that one important indication of adjustment in marriage is essential agreement between husband and

wife upon matters that might be made critical issues in the relationship. Couples who testify to agreement in such things as handling finances, dealing with in-laws, friends, demonstration of affection, and so on, are much more likely, in general, to be well adjusted in their marriages than couples who decidedly disagree on one or more of such items.

2. It was assumed that a substantial number of common interests and joint activities was a favorable indication of adjustment, and that where such common interests and activities were lacking or where there was wide divergence, the likelihood of good adjustment was much less.

3. It was assumed that the more frequent the overt demonstrations of affection and mutual confidences, the greater would be the probability of a well-adjusted marriage.

4. It was assumed that couples whose marriages were poorly adjusted would register a larger number of complaints about their marriages than would those who were well adjusted.

5. It was further assumed that husbands and wives who were poorly adjusted would report, more often than well-adjusted couples, feelings of being lonely, miserable, irritable, and would be troubled by some particular useless thought and lacking in self-confidence.

The above five assumptions were employed as a basis for selecting questions indicative of the degree of marital adjustment. These questions will be listed under each of these assumptions in the form in which they appeared in the Marriage Study Schedule.

Agreements and Disagreements

Eleven important matters in family life were selected to measure the extent of agreement and disagreement between husband and wife. These were: (1) handling family finances, (2) recreation, (3) religion, (4) demonstration of affection, (5) friends, (6) intimate relations, (7) caring for the baby, (8) table manners, (9) conventionality, (10) philosophy of life, and (11) ways of dealing with in-laws.

The married person filling out the schedule was asked to check the extent of agreement or disagreement in terms of "always agree," "almost always agree," "occasionally disagree," "frequently disagree," "almost always disagree," "always disagree," as shown in the following question taken from the schedule:

21. State approximate extent of agreement or disagreement on following items:

(Please place a check opposite every item.)

Check One Column for Each Item Below	Always Agree	Almost Always Agree	Occasionally Disagree	Frequently Disagree	Almost Always Disagree	Always Disagree
Handling family finances						
Matters of recreation						
Religious matters						
Demonstrations of affection						
Friends						
Intimate relations						
Caring for the baby						
Table manners						
Matters of conventionality						
Philosophy if life						
Ways of dealing with in-laws						

To bring out any important disagreements not included in this table and to ascertain how disagreements were settled, two further questions were asked:

Specify other matters of disagreement: ....

When disagreements arise, they usually result in: husband giving in ......; wife giving in ......; agreement by mutual give and take ......

The question can quite fairly be raised whether or not agreements and disagreements constitute a satisfactory criterion of marital adjustment. It may be pointed out that differences are "the spice of life" and that complete agreement would make married life monotonous.

In order to check this objection, the extent of disagreements and the manner of settling them were correlated with ratings of happiness in marriage as shown in Table 22.

TABLE 22

THE CORRELATION BETWEEN RATINGS OF MARITAL HAPPINESS AND EXTENT OF AGREEMENTS AND DISAGREEMENTS

Items of Agreement and Disagreement	Correlations of Ratings of Marital Happiness with Extent of Agreement	
	Coefficient of Contingency (C)	Tetrachoric Coefficient of Correlation (r)
Handling finances	.504	.69
Recreation	.477	.65
Religious matters	.281	.38
Demonstrating affection	.451	.65
Friends	.469	.60
Intimate relations	.503	.61
Caring for baby	.409	.40
Table manners	.215	.33
Matters of conventionality	.433	.51
Philosophy of life	.478	.62
Dealing with in-laws	.456	.66
Manner of settling disagreements	.452	.70 —

All the 11 individual items of extent of agreement correlate positively with the ratings which the couple gave of their marriage as very happy, happy, average, unhappy, or very unhappy. The correlation is not complete, probably indicating both that other factors than extent of agreement and disagreement enter into marriage adjustment and that, in the case of certain couples at least, a report of happiness in marriage does not depend upon unanimity of attitude and opinion upon the major issues of married life.

As can be seen from Table 22, there is considerable variation in the degree of correlation between happiness ratings and the extent of agreement on the various items. Table 23 classifies the items according to the degree of correlation between them and the rating of happiness.

Apparently, according to the testimony of our group of

TABLE 23

RELATION OF ITEMS OF AGREEMENT AND DISAGREEMENT TO RATINGS
OF MARITAL HAPPINESS

Items of Agreement and Disagreement		
Marked Correlation	Moderate Correlation	Low Correlation
Handling finances	Caring for baby	Religious matters
Recreation	Matters of	Table manners
Demonstration of	conventionality	
affection		
Friends		
Intimate relations		
Philosophy of life		
Dealing with in-laws		

married persons, and popular opinion to the contrary notwithstanding, disagreements over religion and over table manners play only a relatively small part in marital unhappiness. There is reason to believe that in the cases of religious differences before marriage a selective factor operates in preventing many unions where disagreement would have resulted in great unhappiness.[1] Case studies seem to indicate that irritation caused by table manners, generally the table manners of husbands, is discounted to some extent as a cause of marital discord because of a rational recognition of its very triviality. Disagreements over caring for the baby and matters of conventionality, although relatively frequent, have only a moderate relationship with marital unhappiness.

The seven items of agreement and disagreement having a rather marked correlation with domestic unhappiness are: handling finances, recreation, demonstration of affection, intimate relations, friends, ways of dealing with in-laws, and philosophy of life. These are all questions upon which serious

---

[1] Examination of individual cases seems to indicate that religious differences are likely to come to a head with reference to the religious rearing of the children. This situation has little influence in a series of cases which are limited to the period of one to six years after marriage.

differences of opinions are likely to arise and which may imperil the relationship.

It might be assumed that certain items of agreement and disagreement would behave as independent variables. On the contrary, each was correlated quite highly with all the others. This fact of general intercorrelation suggests, perhaps, that particular items of disagreement may be symptomatic of an underlying maladjustment of the two personalities.

This hypothesis, then, may be stated: that the basic factor in adjustment in marriage is an intimate and affectionate companionship. Where this exists the couple is well adjusted; disagreements do not arise, and if there are occasional differences of opinion they do not disturb the equilibrium of adjustment. This hypothesis is suggested but not conclusively established by the findings of this study.

Common Interests and Activities

Two questions were asked in order to find out the extent of the sharing of interests and activities by husband and wife:

Do husband and wife engage in outside interests together? (*check*) all of them ......; some of them ......; very few of them ......; none of them ....

In leisure time husband prefers: (*check*) to be "on the go" ......; to stay at home .... Wife prefers: to be "on the go" ......; to stay at home ....

The responses to both of these questions correlate moderately with marital happiness as indicated in Table 24. This positive relationship between common interests and leisure-time preferences on the part of husband and wife may be taken as further evidence in support of the hypothesis of affectionate and intimate companionship as basic to marital adjustment.

TABLE 24

Interests and Activities	Correlations Between Marital Happiness and Interests and Activities	
	Coefficient of Contingency (C)	Tetrachoric Coefficient of Correlation (r)
Engage in outside interests together	.477	.76
Agreement on leisure-time preferences	.444	.70

Demonstration of Affection and Confiding

The marriage relationship in American culture centers around affection and intimacy. It was, therefore, to be expected that the following two questions on demonstration of affection and confiding in each other as indices of marital adjustment should show some relationship to marital happiness:

Do you kiss your husband (wife)? every day ......; occasionally ......; almost never ....

Do you confide in your husband (wife)? almost never ......; rarely ......; in most things ......; in everything ....

The relation between the answers to these questions and marital unhappiness is shown in Table 25.

TABLE 25

Affection and Confiding	Correlations Between Marital Happiness and Affection and Confiding	
	Coefficient of Contingency (C)	Tetrachoric Correlation (r)
Frequency of kissing spouse	.447	.69
Do you confide in your spouse?	.471	.53

The correlations of demonstration of affection and of mutual confiding show a moderate relation to marital adjustment.

Dissatisfaction with Marriage

Expressions of dissatisfaction with marriage are no doubt the best indication of marital maladjustment. Four items were inserted in the schedule in order to probe into present attitudes toward marriage and toward one's spouse:

Do you ever wish you had not married?   frequently ......; occasionally ......; rarely ......; never ......

If you had your life to live over, do you think you would: marry the same person ......; marry a different person ......; not marry at all ......?

What things annoy and dissatisfy you most about your marriage?......
....

What things does your husband (wife) do that you don't like?............
....

The relation between the replies to these questions and marital unhappiness is given in Table 26.

TABLE 26

THE CORRELATION BETWEEN RATINGS OF MARITAL HAPPINESS AND
EXPRESSIONS OF DISSATISFACTION WITH MARRIAGE

Dissatisfaction with Marriage	Correlation of Marital Happiness and Marital Dissatisfactions	
	Coefficient of Contingency (C)	Tetrachoric Coefficient of Correlation (r)
Frequency of regretting marriage.........	.634	—.86
Would marry different person or would not marry.................	.583	—.87
Number of complaints about marriage	.408	—.55
Number of complaints about spouse ...	.354	—.53

Significantly high are the correlations between unhappiness in marriage and the frequency of regretting marriage, and the desire, if life were to be lived over, not to marry at all or to marry another person. These correlations are much higher than the moderate positive relationship shown between marital unhappiness and the number of complaints about marriage and about one's spouse.

It is interesting to note that the statement of a generalized attitude toward the marriage, such as the frequency of regretting its occurrence, should be a better index of marital unhappiness than specific complaints about one's marriage and about one's mate. This finding suggests again that the generalized attitude toward the marriage is of more basic significance than specific concrete disagreements or complaints.

Feelings of Personal Isolation and Unhappiness

Included in the schedule were the following seven questions calling for replies indicative of feelings of being lonely, miserable, ill-tempered, and without self-confidence:

Do you often feel lonesome, even when you are with other people? Yes........ No........ ?........

Are you usually even-tempered and happy in your outlook on life? Yes........ No........ ?........

Do you often feel just miserable? Yes........ No........ ?........

Does some particular useless thought keep coming into your mind to bother you? Yes........ No........ ?........

Are you usually in good spirits? Yes........ No........ ?........

Do you often experience periods of loneliness? Yes........ No........ ?........

Are you in general self-confident about your abilities? Yes........ No........ ?........

These feelings of personal isolation and unhappiness were all found to have a low but rather consistent relation to marital unhappiness, as indicated in Table 27.

TABLE 27

CORRELATION BETWEEN RATINGS OF MARITAL HAPPINESS AND FEELINGS OF ISOLATION AND UNHAPPINESS

Feelings of Isolation and Unhappiness	Tetrachoric Coefficient of Correlation (r) with Feelings of Isolation and Unhappiness
Do you often feel lonesome even when with others?	—.31
Are you usually even-tempered?	+.30
Do you often feel miserable?	—.31
Does some particular useless thought bother you?	—.30
Are you usually in good spirits?	+.35
Do you experience periods of loneliness?	—.47
Are you self-confident about your abilities?	+.27

It is quite likely that these feelings of *anomie,*[2] to use the French term, arise from, or at least are accentuated by, marital maladjustment. If the intrinsic value of marriage inheres in relationships of response and intimacy, frustration may be expected to result in the reactions of being lonely, miserable, irritable, and in losing self-confidence in one's ability.

On the other hand, it may be pointed out that these feelings might have had a part to play in producing marital unhappiness. So far as the findings of the present study go, no decisive answer can be given to these two explanations. In fact, the valid explanation may turn out to be another case of circular reaction; namely, that these neurotic feelings are factors in marital unhappiness and are intensified by domestic discord.[3]

In the attempt to measure marital adjustment, attention has been given to 27 individual items classified under the five head-

---

[2] Compare the use of this term by Émile Durkheim in his study of *Suicide.*

[3] In a study of engaged couples now in progress, an attempt will be made to determine the answer to this question by securing returns on these seven questions before and after marriage.

MEASURING ADJUSTMENT IN MARRIAGE 57

ings "agreements and disagreements," "common interests and activities," "demonstration of affection and mutual confiding," "dissatisfaction with marriage," and "feelings of isolation and unhappiness." Each of these individual items shows a measurable relationship to the ratings given by couples of the degree of the happiness or unhappiness of their marriage. The next step is to devise a means of combining all the individual items into a single score which will indicate the degree of adjustment in marriage.

CHAPTER V

Constructing an Index of Marital Adjustment

HAPPINESS in marriage, as reported by married persons, was found to be a satisfactory criterion of marital adjustment, particularly in regard to reliability and validity. It was feasible, as indicated in Chapter IV, to identify 27 items which have correlations with ratings for marital happiness and which might serve as fairly reliable indicators of the degree of adjustment in a given marriage. As criteria of marital adjustment they may be combined into an index of marital adjustment more serviceable for statistical purposes than marital-happiness ratings. Since the score lends itself to more precise discrimination of degrees of adjustment, it is more adaptable to statistical manipulation than the five-step rating scale. It is also more stable, even with slight instabilities in the answers to the 27 questions; whereas with the rating scale, a fluctuation of one step reclassifies the case. Furthermore, most of the 27 items refer to rather concrete and objective behavior and therefore are not so open to the criticism of subjectivity as is the rating of happiness.

In order to construct an index of marital adjustment it is necessary to assume (1) that the answers to the questions covered by the 27 items upon marital adjustment could be given appropriate numerical values, and (2) that when the answers of a given couple to a set of such questions are assigned these numerical values, the sum of these numerical values can be regarded as a fairly satisfactory index of the relative degree of adjustment of such a couple's marriage.

Construction of a Numerical Adjustment Score

The first problem was to determine what numerical values to assign to the different possible answers to the various items. For example, item 13 asks, "Do husband and wife engage in outside interests together?" What numerical value or how many points were to be given for the answer "All of them"? What value was to be given to "Some of them" or "Very few of them" or "None of them"?

The procedure followed was to relate the answers for each of the selected items to the ratings of the happiness of the marriage, as checked by the married person on the following scale:

Very unhappy ......; unhappy ......; average ......; happy ......; very happy ....

It was possible in this way to measure the association between the happiness ratings of the marriage and the way the different questions were answered.

Table 28 shows the correlation between the happiness ratings and each of the selected adjustment items. These correlations are expressed in two ways: as the coefficient of contingency and as the tetrachoric coefficient of correlation.

By examining the two indices of the degree of association, one can see that some questions are more closely correlated with the happiness ratings than others. For example, the relation between agreement on finances or on dealing with in-laws and the happiness rating is closer than the relation between agreement on religion or on table manners and the happiness rating. In other words, the items of agreement on finances and in-laws appear to be more valuable for discriminating between ratings of happy and unhappy marriages than are the items of agreement on religion or table manners. Hence, when numerical values are given to the different degrees of agreement, this difference must be taken into account. That is to say, if a

TABLE 28

THE CORRELATION BETWEEN RATINGS OF MARITAL HAPPINESS AND EACH
QUESTION USED IN COMPUTING THE ADJUSTMENT SCORE

The degree of correlation is shown both by the coefficient of contingency *(C)* and the tetrachoric coefficient of correlation *(r)*.

Marital-Adjustment Items	Coefficient of Contingency (C)	Tetrachoric Coefficient of Correlation (r)
I. Extent of Agreement on		
1. Handling finances.........	.504	.69
2. Recreation	.477	.65
3. Religious matters	.281	.38
4. Demonstrating affection	.451	.65
5. Friends	.469	.60
6. Intimate relations	.503	.61
7. Caring for the baby........	.409	.40
8. Table manners	.215	.33
9. Matters of convention- ality	.433	.51
10. Philosophy of life.........	.478	.62
11. Dealing with in-laws ...	.456	.66
12. Manner of settling dis- agreements	.452	.70
II. Common Interests and Activities:		
13. Do couple engage in outside interests to- gether?	.477	.76
14. Leisure-time preferences	.444	.70
III. Demonstration of Affection and Confiding:		
15. Frequency of kissing spouse	.447	.69
16. Do you confide in your spouse?	.471	.53
IV. Dissatisfaction with Marriage:		
17. Frequency of regretting marriage	.634	.86
18. If you had your life to live over, would you marry the same person?	.583	.87
19. Number of complaints about marriage	.408	.55

TABLE 28 (*Continued*)

THE CORRELATION BETWEEN RATINGS OF MARITAL HAPPINESS AND EACH
QUESTION USED IN COMPUTING THE ADJUSTMENT SCORE

The degree of correlation is shown both by the coefficient of contingency *(C)* and the tetrachoric coefficient of correlation *(r)*.

20. Number of complaints about spouse	.354	.53
V. Feelings of Anomie:		
21. Do you often feel lonesome when with others?	(*)	.31
22. Are you usually even-tempered?	(*)	.30
23. Do you often feel miserable?	(*)	.31
24. Does some particular useless thought bother you?	(*)	.30
25. Are you usually in good spirits?	(*)	.35
26. Do you experience periods of loneliness?......	(*)	.47
27. Are you self-confident about your abilities?..	(*)	.27

* Coefficient of contingency not computed.

person checks "Always agree" on finances, he should receive more points on the adjustment score than he receives for checking "Always agree" on religion.

This difference in discriminative value is brought out even more clearly when the tables are studied than when sole reliance is placed upon the coefficients. Compare the distribution in the "Very Happy" column in Tables 29, 30, and 31.

The range of variation is quite wide both for the item "extent to which couples engaged in outside activities together" (4.5 per cent to 67.3 per cent) and for the item "extent of agreement of couple in handling family finances" (0.0 per cent to 61.3 per cent), but considerably narrower for the item "extent of agreement of couple on religious matters" (4.2 per cent to 47.5 per cent).

TABLE 29

EXTENT TO WHICH COUPLE ENGAGED IN OUTSIDE ACTIVITIES TOGETHER
COMPARED WITH THEIR RATINGS OF MARITAL HAPPINESS

(Percentage distribution)

No. of Activities Engaged in Together	Happiness Ratings					No. of Cases
	Very Unhappy	Un-happy	Aver-age	Happy	Very Happy	
All of them...............	3.9	2.6	6.5	19.6	67.3	153
Some of them	5.3	12.8	20.4	24.3	37.2	226
Few of them	27.6	34.5	22.4	10.3	5.2	58
None of them	36.4	31.8	13.6	13.6	4.5	22
Total	9.1	12.9	16.0	20.5	41.5	459

* The total is less than 526 because some persons did not reply to the questions.

TABLE 30

EXTENT OF AGREEMENT OF COUPLE IN HANDLING FAMILY FINANCES
COMPARED WITH THEIR RATINGS OF MARITAL HAPPINESS

(Percentage distribution)

Extent of Agreement	Happiness Ratings					No. of Cases
	Very Unhappy	Un-happy	Aver-age	Happy	Very Happy	
Always agree	3.1	5.2	10.0	20.4	61.3	191
Almost always agree....	4.1	8.9	17.1	29.2	40.7	123
Occasionally disagree .	12.7	13.9	30.4	17.7	25.3	79
Frequently disagree....	18.7	46.9	18.7	6.3	9.4	32
Almost always disagree	36.8	42.1	15.8	5.3	0.0	19
Always disagree	50.0	35.8	7.1	7.1	0.0	14
Total	9.0	13.1	16.2	20.3	41.5	458*

* The total is less than 526 because some persons did not reply to the questions.

TABLE 31

EXTENT OF AGREEMENT OF COUPLE ON RELIGIOUS MATTERS
COMPARED WITH THEIR RATINGS OF MARITAL HAPPINESS

(Percentage distribution)

| Extent of Agreement | Happiness Ratings | | | | | No. of Cases |
	Very Unhappy	Un-happy	Aver-age	Happy	Very Happy	
Always agree	7.3	10.2	12.6	22.4	47.5	246
Almost always agree	6.6	11.0	18.7	17.6	46.1	91
Occasionally disagree	6.0	22.0	18.0	20.0	34.0	50
Frequently disagree	4.8	23.8	28.6	23.8	19.0	21
Almost always disagree	57.1	14.3	0.0	0.0	28.6	7
Always disagree	29.2	29.2	20.8	16.7	4.2	24
Total	8.9	13.5	15.5	20.5	41.7	439*

* The total is less than 526 because some persons did not reply to the questions.

The study of the percentages in the "Very Happy" columns indicates that the question on agreement in religious matters evokes replies that are much less discriminating than the replies to the questions on agreement on finances and on the extent to which the couple engage in outside activities together.

Key for Scoring Adjustment Questions

All of the items were studied in this fashion and, with the percentage distributions of replies and the sizes of the coefficients of association as guides, numerical values were assigned to all the possible answers to each of the selected questions. To be sure, the assignment of values was somewhat arbitrary and not precise, but the values were crudely proportional to what appeared to be the relation existing between the answers and the happiness ratings.[1] The numerical values or weights assigned to each of the items are shown in Table 32.

[1] The reader has no doubt already raised the question as to the justification of using happiness ratings as a guide in assigning the numerical values. This point will be dealt with later (pp. 67–68).

TABLE 32

Scoring Key for Adjustment-Score Questions

State approximate extent of agreement or disagreement on following items:

Check Each Column	Always Agree	Amost Always Agree	Occa- sionally Disagree	Fre- quently Disagree	Almost Always Disagree	Always Disagree
1. Handling family finances........	10	8	6	4	2	0
2. Matters of recreation	10	8	6	4	2	0
3. Religious matters	5	4	3	2	1	0
4. Demonstration of affection........	10	8	6	4	2	0
5. Friends	10	8	6	4	2	0
6. Intimate relations	10	8	6	4	2	0
7. Caring for the baby*						
8. Table manners	5	4	3	2	1	0
9. Matters of conventionality	10	8	6	4.	2	0
10. Philosophy of life	10	8	6	4	2	0
11. Ways of dealing with in-laws	10	8	6	4	2	0

12. When disagreements arise, they usually result in: husband giving in............(1); wife giving in............(1); agreement by mutual give and take............(10).

13. Do husband and wife engage in outside interests together? all of them............(10); some of them............(10); very few of them ....(1); none of them............(0).

14. In leisure time husband prefers: to be "on the go"............; to stay at home............; wife prefers: to be "on the go"............; to stay at home............. (If both husband and wife had checked "stay at home," 10 points were given; if both checked "on the go," 3 points. If they checked differently, 4 points.)

15. Do you kiss your husband (wife) every day?............(10); occasionally?............(1); almost never?............(0).

---

* This item was not used in the adjustment score, since such a high proportion of our sample had no children.

TABLE 32 (*Continued*)

SCORING KEY FOR ADJUSTMENT-SCORE QUESTIONS

State approximate extent of agreement or disagreement on following items:

16. Do you confide in your husband (wife)? almost never............(0); rarely............(0); in most things............(10); in everything ....(10).

17. Do you ever wish you had not married? frequently............(0); occasionally............(2); rarely............(4); never............(15).

18. If you had your life to live over, do you think you would: marry the same person?............(15); marry a different person?............(1); not marry at all?............(0).

19. What things annoy and dissatisfy you most about your marriage? nothing listed............(10); one listed............(7); two listed............ (1); three or more listed............(0).

20. What things does your husband (wife) do that you don't like? nothing listed............(7); one listed............(5); two listed............(1); three or more listed...........(0).

21. Do you often feel lonesome, even when you are with other people? *Yes* (0); *No* (1); ? (0).

22. Are you usually even-tempered and happy in your outlook on life? *Yes* (1); *No* (0); ? (0).

23. Do you often feel just miserable? *Yes* (0); *No* (1); ? (0).

24. Does some particular useless thought keep coming into your mind to bother you? *Yes* (0); *No* (1); ? (0).

25. Are you usually in good spirits? *Yes* (1); *No* (0); ? (0).

26. Do you often experience periods of loneliness? *Yes* (0); *No* (1); ? (0).

27. Are you in general self-confident about your abilities? *Yes* (1); *No* (0); ? (0).

The maximum values for each question were assigned roughly in accordance with the relative size of the coefficients of correlation.[2] This maximum value was allotted to the answer which was given most frequently by those couples who rated their marriages as "very happy." The other answers were assigned score points in accordance with the way the combined "very

---

[2] With the exception of items 21 to 27. For these questions the favorable response was arbitrarily assigned a value of 1, and the unfavorable response a value of 0.

happy" and "happy" ratings were distributed in these answers.

To illustrate, item 17 ("Do you ever wish you had not married") may be taken. Table 33 is a distribution of answers to this question compared with the ratings of happiness.

TABLE 33

FREQUENCY OF REGRETTING MARRIAGE COMPARED WITH RATINGS
OF MARITAL HAPPINESS

Happiness Ratings	Frequency of Regretting Marriage				No. of Cases
	Never	Rarely	Occasionally	Frequently	
Very happy	162	26	3	0	191
Happy	42	26	20	7	95
Average	8	18	39	9	74
Unhappy	4	5	20	31	60
Very unhappy	3	2	8	29	42
Total	219	77	90	76	462

If all those who rated their marriages as very happy or happy are combined, we have the result shown in Table 34.

TABLE 34

DISTRIBUTION OF ANSWERS TO QUESTION ON FREQUENCY OF REGRETTING
MARRIAGE GIVEN BY PERSONS WHO RATED THEIR MARRIAGES AS
VERY HAPPY OR HAPPY

Happiness Rating	Frequency of Regretting Marriage				No. of Cases
	Never	Rarely	Occasionally	Frequently	
Ratings of very happy or happy	204	52	23	7	286
Percentage	71.3	18.2	8.0	2.5	100.0
Score points assigned	15	4	2	0	

In Table 34, of the 286 persons who rated their marriages as very happy or happy, 204, or 71.3 per cent, said they never wished they had not married; 52, or 18.2 per cent, said they rarely had such a wish; 23, or 8.0 per cent, said "occasionally";

and only 7, or 2.5 per cent, said they frequently had such a wish.

As already shown in the scoring key, a maximum score of 15 points was assigned to the answer "never," which was most frequently given by people who rated their marriages as very happy. Less score points were assigned to the other answers in accordance with the way the "happy" and "very happy" ratings are distributed in these answers. Thus 18.2 per cent is roughly one-fourth of 71.3 per cent, and therefore the answer "rarely" was given roughly one-fourth of the maximum value; namely, 4 points. Eight per cent is roughly one-half of 18.2 per cent, and so the answer "occasionally" was alloted a score of 2 points. Two and one-half per cent is so much less than one-half of 8.0 per cent that the answer "frequently" was assigned a score of 0.

Other methods of scoring will no doubt occur to the reader. The procedure selected is admittedly crude but is reasonably conservative. Moreover, as will be seen later, an index of adjustment based on this procedure is fairly discriminating and valid. In this connection it is interesting to note that Professor Terman used, with slight modifications and one addition, the items on our schedule to compute his marriage-adjustment index on the sample he studied. He determined the weights to assign replies to the items by a more rigorous statistical procedure.[3] His method of weighting, however, does not appear to add anything to the reliability or validity of the index. We used his method of weighting on our own sample and correlated the new adjustment scores thus obtained with our original scores. The correlation coefficient was $+ .90 \pm .008$. This might indicate that there is a point of diminishing returns in the application of more elaborate statistical procedures to data as crude as those on our schedule.

One question that can be raised is: Why go to all the trouble of assigning these values on the basis of marital-happiness

---

[3] L. M. Terman, *Psychological Factors in Marital Happiness*, New York, McGraw-Hill Book Co., 1938, pp. 56–57.

ratings when one would assign about the same score values arbitrarily? As a matter of fact, an experiment was made of scoring by assigning arbitrary values to the various items. The arbitrary weighting of the items yielded scores that correlated closely with scores arrived at after using the marital-happiness rating as a guide in assigning score values.[4] The answer to the above question is that a somewhat sounder footing is obtained when guesses are checked by an empirical method than when the guessing procedure alone is followed.

Marital-Adjustment Scores of the 526 Couples

A method of scoring the answers to each of the test items having been established, any schedule may be taken on which a person has recorded his replies to the questions, his replies may be scored, and the scores may be added to give a marriage-adjustment score. This was done for our group of 526 cases.[5] Table 35 gives the frequency distribution of the marriage-adjustment scores thus obtained.

While the adjustment scores thus obtained leave much to be desired in the way of precision in description of the degree of adjustment in marriage, they offer, for the purposes of this study, some improvement over the use of such rough qualitative categories as good, fair, and poor adjustment; or very happy, happy, average, unhappy, and very unhappy marriage.

It might be asked why the qualitative ratings of happiness would not be sufficiently precise for the purpose of this study. There are two advantages in the adjustment score as compared with the happiness ratings. One is that the adjustment score does make finer discriminations possible and permits a more precise statement of the relative degree of adjustment repre-

---

[4] The correlation between the adjustment scores, with arbitrary weighting and empirical weighting, was +.96.

[5] This is the group used throughout the study described in this volume. They are people who were living in Illinois at the time they filled out the schedule. Their marriages were more than one year and less than seven years old at the time the schedules were returned.

TABLE 35

FREQUENCY DISTRIBUTION OF MARRIAGE-ADJUSTMENT SCORES FOR 526 MARRIAGES

Adjustment Scores	Number	Percentage	Cumulative Percentage
190 to 199	19	3.6	100.1
180 to 189	51	9.7	96.5
170 to 179	82	15.6	86.8
160 to 169	74	14.1	71.2
150 to 159	50	9.5	57.1
140 to 149	32	6.1	47.6
130 to 139	41	7.8	41.5
120 to 129	33	6.3	33.7
110 to 119	25	4.7	27.4
100 to 109	20	3.8	22.7
90 to 99	23	4.4	18.9
80 to 89	19	3.6	14.5
70 to 79	16	3.0	10.9
60 to 69	21	4.0	7.9
50 to 59	12	2.3	3.9
40 to 49	5	1.0	1.6
30 to 39	2	0.4	0.6
20 to 29	1	0.2	0.2
Total	526	100.0	

sented by a given couple than the happiness rating permits. If a couple makes a score of 150, we can say that such a couple is higher in our scale than 48 per cent of the sample. This is more precise than merely giving the rating of happiness. A second advantage is that the marital-adjustment score is based on 26 [6] separate responses rather than on a single rating, and is thus subject to fewer major fluctuations than a single rating might be.

---

[6] The item on caring for baby was omitted; see p. 64n.

Reliability and Validity of the Adjustment Score

The question may now be raised as to how consistently the adjustment score behaves and how indicative it is of actual social adjustment in marriage.[7]   Table 36 shows the fairly close

TABLE 36

CORRELATION TABLE OF MARITAL-ADJUSTMENT SCORES CALCULATED FROM SEPARATE SCHEDULES FILLED OUT BY HUSBANDS AND WIVES

Scores from Husbands' Schedules	Scores from Wives' Schedules																No. of Cases
	40–49	50–59	60–69	70–79	80–89	90–99	100–109	110–119	120–129	130–139	140–149	150–159	160–169	170–179	180–189	190–199	
190 to 199												1			1	2	4
180 to 189									1					1	5	1	8
170 to 179													3	2	1	3	9
160 to 169								1	1	2	1		2	2	1		10
150 to 159								1	1				1				3
140 to 149							1			2	2	2	1				8
130 to 139										2			1	1			4
120 to 129						1				1	1						3
110 to 119				1						1							2
100 to 109		1						1									2
90 to 99				1	1	1											3
80 to 89			1		1	1	2	1	1								7
70 to 79					1												1
60 to 69			1														1
50 to 59	1																1
40 to 49																	0
No. of Cases	1	0	3	2	3	3	2	3	5	7	5	4	8	6	8	6	66

correspondence between the adjustment score computed from 66 pairs of schedules filled out independently by husbands and wives. The Pearsonian coefficient of correlation is $+.884$, with a standard error of .027.

While this coefficient of reliability is not so high as one might

---

[7] See Leonard S. Cottrell, Jr., *The Reliability and Validity of a Marriage Study Schedule*, unpublished Ph.D. thesis, University of Chicago, 1933, for a more detailed study of this instrument.

desire, it is sufficiently high to support a reasonable amount of confidence in the consistency with which the score discriminates among marriages. The number of cases is, of course, too small to furnish conclusive evidence on the reliability of the score, but the results are in conformity with the findings of the study of the happiness ratings. Hence more confidence can be placed in them than would be the case in the absence of such supporting evidence.

If it is tentatively accepted that the adjustment score measures whatever it measures with a reasonable consistency or reliability, then the question may be asked: Does the score measure marital adjustment? One way to answer this question is to see whether the score corresponds very closely to, or is very different from, the way subjects rate their happiness in marriage.

Since the happiness ratings were used as a guide in assigning numerical scores to the selected questions, it was to be expected that the adjustment scores would correlate fairly closely with the happiness ratings.[8] It is reassuring to find that such a correlation exists. Table 37 gives the frequency distribution of the scores in each rating category. The tetrachoric coefficient of correlation between the ratings and the scores is +.92.[9]

The relation between the subjects' estimates of the happiness of their marriages and the adjustment scores would be more convincing if the two variables could be correlated on a new sample of cases. It was possible to do this on 68 new cases. The distribution is similar to the one in Table 37 and the tetrachoric coefficient of correlation is +.95.

Another indication of the validity of the score is the way it distinguishes, on the one hand, between the subjects who are either divorced or separated or have contemplated such a step, and on the other hand between those who are not separated or

---

[8] For a discussion of the reliability and validity of happiness ratings, see Chapter III, pp. 38–44.

[9] To compute this coefficient, the distribution of ratings was split into two groups so as to include the ratings of "happy" and "very happy" in one group and all other ratings in another. The adjustment scores were split into two groups at the median of the distribution.

TABLE 37

FREQUENCY DISTRIBUTION OF MARRIAGE-ADJUSTMENT SCORES
BY HAPPINESS-RATING CATEGORIES

Adjustment Score	Happiness Rating						Total	Percentage Distribution
	Very Unhappy	Unhappy	Average	Happy	Very Happy	No Rating		
180 to 199				34	65		72	13.7
160 to 179			5	7	118	1	155	29.4
140 to 159			12	31	32	1	79	15.0
120 to 139	2	9	27	24	6	2	70	13.3
100 to 119	3	13	23	8			47	8.9
80 to 99	13	19	5	3		1	41	7.8
60 to 79	15	17	3		3		38	7.2
40 to 59	7	8		1			16	3.2
20 to 39	2	5	1				8	1.5
Total	42	71	76	108	224	5	526	
Percentage distrib.	8.0	13.5	14.4	20.5	42.6	1.0		100.0

Mean Score = 140.8.
$\sigma =$ 38.8.

divorced or claim not to have considered such a step. Table
38 gives this distribution. The tetrachoric coefficient of correlation for this table is $+.89$.[10]

In summary, the procedure for constructing an index of marital adjustment was as follows:

1.   Each adjustment item in the schedule could be answered
in two or more ways.

2.   Accordingly, the different answers to each item were correlated with the rating for marital happiness.

3.   The various answers to each of the 26 adjustment items

[10] To compute this coefficient, the distribution was split so as to put those who
had not contemplated divorce or separation in one group and all others in a second
group. The adjustment-score groupings were split so as to place those cases with
a score of 140 or more in one group and all remaining cases in the other.

TABLE 38

DISTRIBUTION OF MARRIAGE-ADJUSTMENT SCORES BY GROUPINGS INTO
THOSE WHO ARE DIVORCED, SEPARATED, HAVE CONTEMPLATED
DIVORCE OR SEPARATION, AND HAVE NOT CONTEMPLATED
DIVORCE OR SEPARATION

Adjustment Score	Marital Status				No Reply	Total
	Divorced	Separated and Not Divorced	Have Contemplated Divorce or Separation	Have Not Contemplated Divorce or Separation		
180 to 199				64	8	72
160 to 179	3		4	141	7	155
140 to 159	1	6	8	54	10	79
120 to 139	9	6	19	29	7	70
100 to 119	10	13	13	11		47
80 to 99	15	12	9	4	1	41
60 to 79	12	18	4	3	1	38
40 to 59	6	8	2			16
20 to 39	5	2	1			8
Total	61	65	60	306	34	526

were then assigned their appropriate weights, as indicated by the above procedure.

4. An adjustment score for each couple was computed by taking the sum total of the weights of the answers given to the 26 items by the husband or the wife.

5. The reliability of the adjustment score was estimated by comparing the scores computed from 66 schedules filled out independently by husbands and wives (Pearsonian correlation, +.88).

6. The validity of the adjustment score was determined by comparing it with the marital-happiness rating (tetrachoric correlation, +.92), with an adjustment score derived from arbitrary weights assigned by common sense (tetrachoric correlation, +.95), and with the question whether the couple were divorced or separated, or contemplated divorce or separa-

tion, or had not contemplated that step (tetrachoric correlation, $+.89$).

The foregoing summary restates the available statistical evidence which could be assembled to answer the question of how reliably and validly the adjustment score indicates adjustment in marriage. The general conclusion is that the score is reasonably dependable though necessarily crude.

In further support of this conclusion an examination was made of our case-study series of about 50 marriages upon which detailed interview material was assembled. Summaries of several of these cases are given in Chapter XV. The reader is invited to examine these cases in order to obtain a general impression of the marital-adjustment level and to compare his own estimate with the adjustment score and its percentile rank. This series of 50 cases, used to test the validity both of the happiness rating and of the adjustment score, adds further support to the confidence placed in the marital-adjustment score.

Having established the reliability and validity of the adjustment score, it was then possible to find out what degree of association, if any, there would be between this score and the different answers given by the 526 couples to each of the questions concerning premarital items. In the following chapters the premarital items found to be correlated with adjustment in marriage will be discussed under the general headings (1) the impress of cultural backgrounds, (2) psychogenetic characteristics, (3) the social type, (4) economic role, and (5) response patterns.

CHAPTER VI

The Impress of Cultural Backgrounds

T HE ROLE of the family in the personality development
of the child is twofold. On the one hand the family is
a social institution through which the culture of one generation is transmitted to the next; on the other, the family as a
unit of interacting personalities is a major determinant in the
personality formation of the child. These two processes, one
of cultural and the other of psychogenetic conditioning, cannot,
perhaps, be absolutely differentiated from each other. Their
effects upon personality development are, however, quite different, and for purposes of the present study they will therefore
be considered separately: the cultural process in the present
chapter and the psychogenetic process in the chapter following.[1]

The Family as an Agency for Transmitting Culture

Quite naturally and inevitably, and by a mechanism as arbitrary in its workings as the conditioned reflex, the child tends
to exhibit in his behavior the cultural patterns of his family
and of the society in which he is cradled.

The life history of the individual is first and foremost an accommodation to the patterns and standards traditionally handed down
in his community. From the moment of his birth the customs into
which he is born shape his experience and behavior. By the time he
can talk he is the little creature of his culture, and by the time he is

---

[1] In Chapter XI, "Personality Factors," both cultural and psychogenetic aspects in
personality development will be considered.

grown and able to take part in its activities, its habits are his habits, its beliefs his beliefs, its impossibilities his impossibilities.[2]

This impress of cultural patterns upon the individual is what is emphasized when personality is defined as "the subjective aspect of culture." [3]

A distinction should be made between the cultural patterns which are impressed upon the person in infancy and childhood and those which he accepts more or less by choice in his adolescence and youth. By "impress of cultural background" we mean those basic values and attitudes, sentiments and memories, habits of speech and manner, which the person acquires unconsciously and unwittingly from his family and his playmates in the early years of his life. He is rarely aware of his possession of them until he first meets those who have been culturally conditioned otherwise. So deeply entrenched in the person are these basic attitudes and reactions that he finds it difficult, if not impossible, to change them. Examples of the impress of cultural background upon the person are the Southern drawl, food preferences, deeply ingrained tendencies to saving or to spending money, and nationality, religious, and racial prejudices.

In our heterogeneous American society is found, to be sure, a common culture, but it is one with great variations with regard to sections of the country, rural and urban population, racial and national origins, economic and social class, and religious affiliation. The cultural backgrounds of any man or woman will vary more or less according to the particular permutation of his family in the above groupings.

In his social relations the person is then first identified through these groupings. He is a Southerner, of pre-Colonial old English stock, of an impoverished aristocratic family, residing in a small town, and he is a Methodist. Or he is an

---

[2] Ruth Benedict, *Patterns of Culture*, Boston, Houghton Mifflin Co., 1934, pp. 2–3.
[3] Ellsworth Faris, *The Nature of Human Nature*, New York, McGraw-Hill Book Co., 1937, Chapter 3, "The Subjective Aspect of Culture," pp. 21–35.

Easterner, of Irish ancestry, of an unskilled worker's family, living in the large city, and he is a Catholic.

Social life is organized largely within cultural groupings. Friendships are formed typically by persons of similar cultural backgrounds. Marriages normally take place within the same socio-economic classes, and each cultural group is somewhat resistant to marriages to "outsiders." The public in general believes that marriages between persons of different race, nationality, religion, and class are generally foredoomed to failure.

The hypothesis to be tested in this chapter is that similarity in impress of cultural backgrounds of husbands and wives makes for, and dissimilarity works against, domestic harmony. The items in the schedule bearing upon the impress of cultural backgrounds will be presented in four sections: (1) family background of husband and wife, considered separately, (2) differences in their family backgrounds, (3) rural or urban rearing of husband and wife, and (4) other cultural differences between husband and wife.

Family Background

Included in this study were several items indicative of the impress of cultural backgrounds on the husband and on the wife. The majority of these had to do with the cultural status or social affiliations of the parents of both the husband and the wife. These items were

1. Occupations of their fathers.
2. The education of parents, as measured by formal educational attainment.
3. Their religious preference.
4. Their activity in church (members, held office, regular attendants, sometimes attended, never attended).
5. Their economic status (very wealthy, wealthy, well-to-do, comfortable, meager, poor).

6. Their social status in the community (leading family, upper class, reputable, inferior, very inferior, uncertain).

7. The number of their brothers and sisters.[4]

8. Their place in order of birth among brothers and sisters (only child, oldest, youngest, middle).[4]

9. The happiness of their marriage.[4]

These are only a few of the possible items indicative of cultural background. They are, perhaps, sufficient to test this question: Do cultural backgrounds as indexed by the economic, occupational, religious, and social status of the parents influence the adjustment of husband and wife in marriage?

The relative weight of these items of cultural background for marital success is shown in Table 39. The chief point of interest in this table is the much higher weight to be assigned

TABLE 39

RELATIVE WEIGHTS* IN MARRIAGE-PREDICTION SCORE OF ITEMS INDICATIVE OF CULTURAL BACKGROUND OF THE HUSBAND AND THE WIFE

Cultural Background Items: Parents of Husband and Wife	Weight in Relation to Marital-Adjustment Score	
	Husband's Family	Wife's Family
1. Occupation of father	10	5
2. Education	20	9
3. Religious preference	15	9
4. Religious activity	15	15
5. Economic status	5	5
6. Social status	5	5
7. Number of brothers and sisters	20	10
8. Order of birth	20	10
9. Happiness of the marriage	10	5
Total	120	73

* Weights were assigned to each of these items according to its association with the marital-adjustment score. For detailed explanation of this procedure see Chapter XV. Only maximum weights are given in this table.

[4] These items may be classified according to certain aspects as either cultural or psychogenetic. The happiness of the parents' marriage is probably indicative of psychogenetic influence and is taken up later (see pp. 98-102).

to the cultural background of the husband. Theoretically it is possible for the husband to have a total score 64.4 per cent greater than is possible for the wife. A study of the table will also show that for both husband and wife the economic and social status of the parents seem less important factors in marital success than the other items studied.

Instead of employing these items separately in the prediction of marriage adjustment, it was decided to combine them into an index of family background. Each of the subcategories of the above items was given a numerical value, and a total score was derived for the cultural background of the husband and of the wife.

The relation between the familial backgrounds of husbands and wives and their adjustment in marriage is shown in Chart 3. The tables in Appendix A from which the charts are derived (in this case Table 56) should be consulted particularly for the number of husbands or wives in each group represented by a bar on the charts.

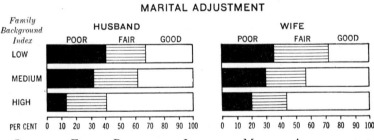

CHART 3.—FAMILY-BACKGROUND INDEX AND MARITAL ADJUSTMENT.

In this chart the marriage-adjustment scores are shown grouped into three divisions. Scores ranging from 20 to 119 points, inclusive, have been grouped into what we have called our "poor" adjustment group. Those marriages receiving 120 to 159 points on the adjustment scale have been designated our "fair" adjustment group. Finally those marriages with scores of 160 to 199 points are designated as our "good" adjustment group. Of the 526 couples 28.5 per cent were in the "poor,"

28.3 per cent in the "fair," and 43.2 per cent in the "good" adjustment group.

An examination of this chart shows both for husbands and wives a decided decline in the proportions of "poorly" adjusted marriages corresponding to a rise in the family- (or cultural-) background index. Of those marriages in which the husbands have less than 70 points on the family-background index, 40.6 per cent are poorly adjusted; of those in which the husband received 90–119 points, only 13.7 per cent fall in the "poor" adjustment group. In the "good" adjustment group the percentages change in the opposite direction. Of those marriages in which the husband received less than 70 points on the family-background index, only 32.5 per cent are in the well-adjusted class, as against 59.0 per cent for marriages in which the husband received 90 to 119 points.

These differences are fairly large and seem to indicate that there is a significant relation between what we have called cultural background and adjustment in marriage. However, when statistical comparisons are made with small numbers involved, observed differences in proportions may be due to chance fluctuations rather than to any significant relations between the variables compared. When large numbers are used in such comparisons, greater reliance may be placed on observed differences. In this study we are forced to use small numbers, since our total sample is only 526 couples. Thus it is necessary to test each variation in percentages to see whether the observed differences are too great to be accounted for by chance fluctuations. For comparing percentage differences this test is made by computing the standard error of the difference between two given proportions and finding the ratio between the observed difference and the standard error of the difference. This ratio is usually called the critical ratio (CR). If the ratio is as much as 3.0 (that is, if the observed difference is three times the standard error of that difference), then it is practically certain that the observed difference is not due to chance fluctuations. The probability that a difference with a critical ratio of 3.0 is due to chance is about 1 in 369. Thus critical ratios of approximately 3.0 or above indicate practical certainty that observed differences with such critical ratios are significant—significant in the sense that the differences are due to other than mere chance factors.

The use of the critical ratio in this manner may be seen by examining the differences noted above in the husbands' background scores. In the case of the poorly adjusted group, there were 40.6 per cent of the marriages in which the husband's cultural-background score was under 70. There were only 13.7 per cent of the marriages in the 90–119 score group. The observed difference is 26.9 per cent. The standard error of this difference is 5.2 per cent.[5] This means that the observed difference is 5.2 times the error of the difference; or, in other words, the critical ratio (CR) is 5.2. The observed difference is therefore not due to chance.

If we turn to the column of "good" adjustment and compare the percentages, we find that of those marriages in which the husband has a low cultural-background score, 32.5 per cent are well adjusted. Of those marriages with the highest background scores for the husbands, 59.0 per cent are well adjusted. The observed difference is 26.5 per cent, which is 4.6 times its standard error. Again the difference is found to be significant in that it could not have been due to chance.

The cultural-background score groupings of the wives can

---

[5] The probabilities of "good" and of "poor" adjustment in relation to the sub-categories for the different items (such as cultural background) will be expressed in terms of the critical ratio (CR); that is, the ratio between the observed difference of two percentages and the standard error of the difference. In the example in the text the difference between .406 and .137 is .269; the standard error of this difference is .0519; and the critical ratio (CR) is 5.2.

$$\sigma_{diff.} = \sqrt{\frac{p_1 (1 - p_1)}{n_1} + \frac{p_2 (1 - p_2)}{n_2}} \text{ or } \sqrt{\frac{.406 \times .594}{123} + \frac{.137 \times .863}{161}}$$

where $\sigma_{diff.}$ represents the standard error of the difference between the proportions compared, p_1 and p_2 the proportions compared, and n_1 and n_2 the numbers on which the proportions are based. See Appendix A, Table 56, for the figures on which Chart 3 was constructed (CR $= d/\sigma$, or .269/.0519 $= 5.2$).

Most recent standard texts in statistics include a demonstration of the method of computing the error of the difference. *An Introduction to the Theory of Statistics* (1937 edition), by G. Udny Yule and M. G. Kendall (London, Griffin, 1937, Chapter 19, especially pp. 359–362) contains a good discussion of the use of this measure.

be tested in the same way. Of those marriages in which the wife's cultural-background score was under 55, there were 35.0 per cent in the poorly adjusted group. Of those in which the wife's cultural-background score was 65 and over,[6] 19.9 per cent were in the poorly adjusted group. The critical ratio of this difference is 2.7. This is not quite high enough for certainty that the difference is significant, but the probability that this much difference is due to chance is about 1 in 195. Turning to the column of well-adjusted marriages, we find that of those marriages in which the wife made a background score under 54, 28.2 per cent were in our "good" adjustment group. Of those marriages in which the wife made 65 or over on the cultural-background scale, 55.9 per cent were in the "good" adjustment group. The critical ratio of this difference is 4.7, which means that it is a statistically significant difference.

In regard to both husband and wife, these differences are statistically significant; there is practical certainty that they are real differences. There seems little doubt, then, that cultural background works for or against marital harmony.

Interestingly, the range of scores on the family-backgrounds index was found to be wider for the husband than for the wife. The husband's scores varied from 30 to 119 points, while those of the wife ranged from 30 to 79 points. The husband's family background, as represented by the items in our schedule, appears to be more significant for success in marriage than the family background of the wife.

Differences in Family Backgrounds

In our society, preparation for marriage is still largely confined to the experiences of the person in his own family. Case studies show that the cultural pattern of one's family influences in a positive or sometimes negative way the conceptions of

6 It will be noted that the wives' background scores are lower than those of the husbands and that the range is not so great. This is due to the fact that we used different weight values for the different items in the backgrounds of the two groups. For a more complete statement regarding this difference, see footnote 3 for Table 56 in Appendix A.

marital and familial relationships held by husband and wife. Other influences are friends, reading, the motion picture, and the theater.

These and other considerations suggest the hypothesis that the greater the similarity in the cultural backgrounds of husband and wife, the smaller is the likelihood of conflict in their concepts of marital and familial relationships and, accordingly, the greater is the probability of marital success.

Certain items in our schedule made it possible to construct an index of similarity in family background by means of which this hypothesis could be tested. A glance at these items shows that they take into account only a few of the many factors entering into cultural likenesses and differences between the families of bride and groom. They may perhaps be indicative of more subtle factors that are difficult to reduce to numerical terms. They are

1. Religious preferences of parents of husband and wife.
2. Their degree of active participation in church.
3. Their formal educational attainment.
4. Occupation of father.
5. The social and economic status of parents.
6. Their social status in the community.

The families of certain couples may manifest marked similarity in all or nearly all these cultural items; others may be markedly dissimilar; while in some cases there may be similarities in certain items but differences in other cultural factors.

In regard to each of these items the association of different degrees of similarity and difference for the four parents with the marital adjustment of the couple was determined, and the appropriate numerical weight was assigned. The total score of each couple for the above six items was then taken [7] as the index of similarity.

---

[7] For a detailed explanation of this procedure, see pp. 269–275.

When this index of similarity in family background of husband and wife is correlated with the adjustment score (Table 40), it becomes apparent that the greater the similarity in family backgrounds, the larger is the proportion of couples in the very high adjustment class.

TABLE 40

INDEX OF SIMILARITY IN FAMILY BACKGROUNDS AND ADJUSTMENT
(Percentage distribution)

Index of Similarity in Family Backgrounds *	Adjustment			No. of Cases
	Poor	Fair	Good	
19 to 21 points	41.1	27.7	31.2	141
22 to 24 points	31.4	31.4	37.2	86
25 to 27 points	21.1	32.8	46.1	180
28 to 30 points	22.7	20.2	57.1	119
All cases	28.5	28.3	43.1	526

* Higher scores indicate greater similarity.

It will be noted that in the column for those with "poor" adjustment there is a decline from 41.1 per cent of the lowest group (19 to 21 points) to 22.7 per cent [8] of the highest group (28 to 30 points). Similarly there is a marked rise in the proportion of those with "good" adjustment from 31.2 per cent of those with least similarity in cultural background to 57.1 per cent [9] of those with the greatest similarity.

Some readers will doubtless be surprised that there is not an even more marked association between similarity in family backgrounds and marital adjustment. It must be remembered, however, that this is only one of a number of factors entering into the situation. Another explanation is that in certain instances, as revealed by case studies, marital integration is achieved either because of or in spite of diversity in family background. Another point is that our index of similarity of family back-

[8] CR 3.2.
[9] CR 4.3.

grounds includes the more external and tangible rather than the more subtle and imponderable manifestations.

Rural and Urban Rearing

The cultural conditioning of a person depends to a considerable degree upon whether he is reared in the country, the town, or the city. One question in the schedule bears upon the differential influence of rural and urban environment. Each person was asked whether his childhood and adolescence had been spent mainly in the country, in a small town, or in the city. The point to be tested was whether or not the early impressions of childhood and adolescence as represented by the difference in rural and urban viewpoints, standards, and mores exert an effect upon marital adjustment.

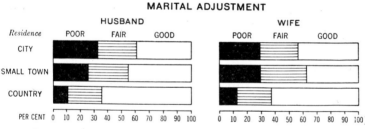

CHART 4.—RURAL OR URBAN RESIDENCE IN CHILDHOOD AND ADOLESCENCE AND MARITAL ADJUSTMENT.

Our data show that fewer husbands (286) than wives (322) were reared in the city, and correspondingly more husbands (222) than wives (185) in the small town and country.

The outstanding relation shown in Chart 4 between place of residence in childhood and youth and marital success is the high degree of association between rural rearing and marital happiness both for husbands and wives, as indicated by the large proportions with "good" adjustment (64.6 and 62.5 per cent, respectively). The corresponding percentages of those in the groups "poorly" adjusted are only 10.4 per cent and 12.5

per cent. For the husband, to be reared in the small town appears to be slightly more advantageous for "good" adjustment (44.8 per cent) than being reared in the city (39.2 per cent). The opposite holds for the wife, for whom a childhood and adolescence spent in the city (43.5 per cent) have a little margin over the small town (37.2 per cent). These small differences are not statistically significant. A larger number of cases would be necessary to enable one to draw decisive conclusions about the relation of city or small-town rearing to marital happiness.

It should be pointed out that those with rural rearing in this study are a selected group. Only 7 of the 48 husbands and 3 of the 40 wives brought up in the country were living there at the time of marriage. The figures available on married life in rural communities tell a different story. In a study of over 7,000 marriages,[10] a sample of 376 couples living on the farm represented the lowest percentage reported as "very happy" among 11 groups of communities classified according to size of population.

A rural background, however, for a person who migrates to the city, seems to be more favorable than a childhood spent in either the town or the city.

Other Cultural Differences

This study contains data bearing upon certain differences between husband and wife that are popularly considered adverse to marital adjustment, such as differences in the formal education of the bride and groom or differences in religious affiliations.

These items, it is true, are more indirect than direct indexes of differences in the impress of cultural backgrounds. Differences in educational level of the couple will reflect in large

[10] Richard O. Lang, *The Rating of Happiness in Marriage,* unpublished M. A. thesis, Chicago, University of Chicago, 1932, p. 25.

part their parents' educational interests, and the religious affiliation of the young people is in the great majority of cases the same as that of their parents.

The educational status of husband and wife was indicated as "grades only," "high school," "college," and "graduate or professional." The marriages were then grouped as (1) at the same level, (2) husband one level higher than the wife, (3) husband two levels higher than the wife, (4) wife one level higher than the husband, and (5) wife two levels higher than the husband. Here again only small differences appeared, none of them being of statistical significance.

Data upon religious membership and preference were obtained for both husband and wife. It was therefore possible to compare the probabilities of success in marriage where husband and wife were of the same or different religious faiths according to the broad groupings "Protestant," "Catholic," and "Jewish." Again, interestingly enough and contrary to popular opinion, no differences of statistical importance appear when a comparison is made between marriages of persons of the same and of different religious beliefs.

Further research will be required for any conclusive explanations as to why these two rather significant cultural differences appear to have little or no effect upon marital adjustment. It may of course be true that young people hesitate to wed if there are marked differences in educational level and religious faith. The assumption, then, would be that the few marriages of this type turn out to be of average success. In many instances the individuals concerned are emancipated from religious controls, and therefore conflict over religious differences may not arise.

Another point worth attention is the short time after marriage covered by this study. It may be that if the love and affection of husband and wife have been strong enough to overcome all the resistance of cultural differences, it continues to be of sufficient strength to mediate the adjustments of the early years of marriage. The real test would come then, according to this reasoning, after the sixth year of marriage. This is probably particularly true of marriages of persons of different religions in whose case conflict typically arises about the question of the religious rearing of the child. Then, too, the point might be made that the important religious differences today are not between Catholic, Protestant, and Jew, but between modernism and fundamentalism, between belief and disbelief in God and immortality, and between devotion to and neglect of religious duty.

Evidence for this last point is provided by a tabulation of the rates of church attendance after marriage for husbands and wives. Of 456 couples, 329 report the same rate of attendance, 60 a slight difference, and 67 a great difference. The proportion of the very happy is 46.2 [11] per cent where both husband and wife report the same degree of church attendance; 38.4 [12] per cent where there is a slight difference in frequency of attendance; and only 20.9 per cent in the case of great difference. These findings seem to indicate that likenesses and differences in the religious practices of the couple rather than in religious affiliation "inherited" from their parents is associated with happiness in matrimony.

This study of the relation between the cultural background and marital adjustment of 526 couples resulted in findings that were both expected and unexpected. Among the expected findings are (1) that certain indexes of the cultural background of both husband and wife are associated with marital success; (2) that likeness in the impress of cultural backgrounds of the couple is associated with happiness, and marked difference with unhappiness, in marriage.

The unexpected findings of this study are (1) that the cul-

---

[11] CR, .462 and .209, 4.4. (This footnote is to be read "The critical ratio of 4.4 in this instance means that the difference between .462 and .209 is 4.4 times the standard error of the difference." See pp. 80–82 for fuller explanation.

[12] CR, .384 and .209, 2.2.

tural level of the husband's parents is more important than that of the wife's for success in marriage; (2) that certain cultural differences between husband and wife popularly assumed to be inimical to successful marriage, such as differences in educational status and wide differences in religious affiliations, show no relation to marital adjustment, at least in the first six years of married life; and (3) that residence in the country during childhood and adolescence is favorable, and residence in the city during those periods unfavorable, to marital adjustment.

CHAPTER VII

Psychogenetic Characteristics

THE INITIAL adjustment of any two persons to each other is almost always in terms of some cultural characteristic. The other person is characterized as a Frenchman or a lawyer, or a Westerner or an urbanite. The next adjustments are likely to be on the basis of some temperamental or other personality trait indicative of what Edward Sapir has termed the psychiatric (or perhaps more properly the psychogenetic) personality. This aspect of personality, which is not entirely predetermined by heredity and which apparently is influenced little or not at all by culture, is defined thus by Sapir: [1]

The psychiatrist's concept of personality is to all intents and purposes the reactive system exhibited by the precultural child, a total configuration of reactive tendencies determined by heredity, and by prenatal and postnatal conditioning up to the point where cultural patterns are constantly modifying the child's behavior. The personality may be conceived of as a latent system of reaction patterns and tendencies to reaction patterns finished shortly after birth or well into the second or third year of the life of the individual. With all the uncertainty that now prevails with regard to the relative permanence or modifiability of life patterns in the individual and in the race it is unwise, however, to force the notion of the fixation of personality in time.

The genesis of personality is in all probability determined largely

---

[1] From article "Personality," *Encyclopaedia of the Social Sciences,* New York, the Macmillan Co., 1930–35, Vol. 12, p. 86.

by the anatomical and physiological makeup of the individual but cannot be entirely so explained. Conditioning factors which may roughly be lumped together as the social psychological determinants of childhood must be considered as at least as important in the development of personality as innate biological factors.

The psychogenetic personality may, for purposes of analysis, be quite sharply distinguished from what might be termed the cultural person discussed in the last chapter. Specific habit formation is the chief mechanism of the process of cultural conditioning. In the psychogenetic process the mechanism is rather the fixation of "a total configuration of reactive tendencies." Attempts to classify personality types as extrovert and introvert, as aggressive and passive, as egocentric and sociocentric, as balanced and unbalanced, as dominating and submissive, are symptomatic of this interest in isolating and defining systems of reaction patterns.

No effort was made in this study to work out a systematic classification of psychogenetic personality types.[2] Neither our statistical nor our case-history data were adequate for such an attempt. Our data did, however, indicate that many couples with the same cultural backgrounds might be highly incompatible apparently because of clashes of temperament and because of other psychogenetic reactions. The careful study of the life histories of some of our couples suggested that the ease or difficulty of a person's adjustment to another personality in marriage had some association with his own relations as a child to his parents and to his brothers and sisters.

On the assumption, then, that the psychogenetic personality is formed chiefly in familial interaction, it may be studied indirectly through an analysis of the different kinds of parent-child and sibling relationships.

---

[2] See Chapter IX, "Personality Factors in Marriage Adjustment," in which the psychogenetic personality is studied through interview materials.

Family Relationships

What association, if any, between family relationships and marital happiness can be established by an examination of the crude statistical data available in this study? Does marital adjustment seem to be influenced much, little, or not at all by the particular sort of parent-child relationships and of brother and sister relationships in the backgrounds of husband and wife?

The items on parent-child relationships obtained in this study are: the degree of attachment or conflict between husbands or wives and their fathers and mothers; happiness of the parents' marriage as reported by their children; and marital status of parents at the time of the marriage of husband and wife.

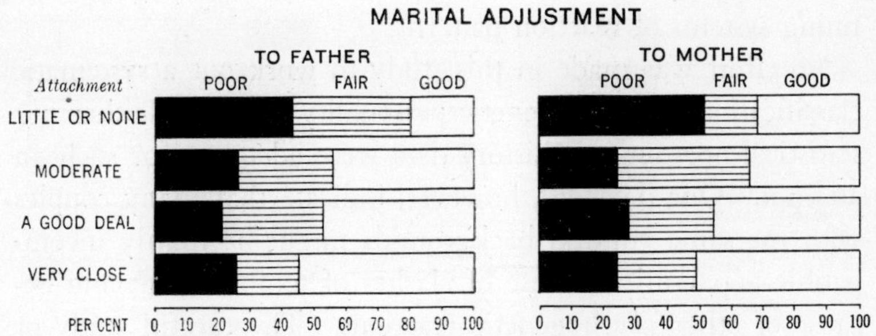

CHART 5.—HUSBAND'S ATTACHMENT TO PARENTS AND MARITAL ADJUSTMENT.

Relations of husband and wife to parents. Two questions in the Marriage Study Schedule furnish information on the emotional relation of the husband to his father and mother and of the wife to her father and mother; namely, the amount of attachment and of conflict between them.

Relation of husband to father and mother. What relation if any is shown between a report of the degree of harmony and disharmony between parents and their son and his success in marital adjustment?

It is interesting to note first that the son has a good deal of attachment, or is very close, to his father in five-tenths, and to his mother in seven-tenths, of the cases reporting.   Chart 5 shows that the degree of attachment to the father seems to present a wider range of the probabilities of "good" adjustment (from 20.0 per cent where "very little" or "no" attachment is reported to 54.1 per cent [3] where they were "very close" to each other), as compared with the smaller spread in the relation of his attachment to the mother (from 31.1 per cent, where there is "little or none," to 50.5 per cent,[4] where there is a "good deal"). The high percentage of cases of "poor" adjustment falls where attachment both to the father and to the mother is "little or

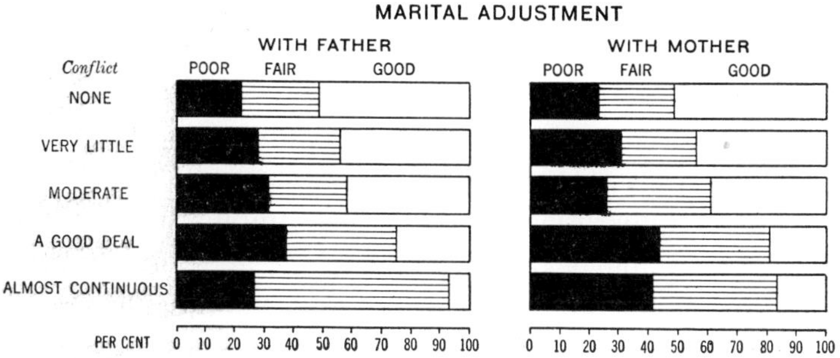

CHART 6.—HUSBAND'S CONFLICT WITH PARENTS AND
MARITAL ADJUSTMENT.

none" (42.7 [3] and 51.7,[5] respectively), as compared with the much lower percentages in the other categories.

Quite as significant as relations of attachment are those of conflict (Chart 6 and Table 59, Appendix A).   Sons report fewer cases of "moderate," "a good deal," and "almost continuous"

---

[3] CR, .200 (very little or no attachment) with .541 (very close attachment), 5.01; with .439 (moderate attachment), 3.93; and with .477 (a good deal of attachment), 4.32.   The differences between .439, .477, and .541 are not statistically significant.

[4] CR, .311 with .505, 2.08.   CR, .339 (moderate attachment) with .450 (a good deal of attachment), 1.82; and with .505 (very close attachment), 2.85.

[5] CR, .427 with .262 (moderate attachment), 2.46; with .203 (a good deal of attachment), 3.3; and with .257 (very close attachment), 2.4.

conflict with the mother (79) than with the father (127) although the difference is not so great (16.7 per cent as against 26.4 per cent) as might be expected according to the theory of the Oedipus complex. The absence of conflict with both the father and the mother shows the highest relationship to "good" adjustment—51.4 per cent [6] and 49.0 per cent.[7] The smallest percentages of the couples with "poor" adjustment are found where there is no conflict: with the father, 22.0 [8] per cent, and with the mother, 24.2 per cent.[9]

The variation of these figures on attachment and conflict are in the direction suggested by the theory of the Oedipus complex, which assumes a natural tendency for close attachment between mother and son and for conflict between father and son. The differences, however, are much smaller than the powerful influence attributed by psychoanalysts to the Oedipus complex would lead one to expect. The psychoanalysts can doubtless point out that the replies to these questions are self-conscious statements dictated by conventional attitudes, rather than indications of unconscious impulses. In psychoanalytic terminology the responses to the above questions indicate in part the dominance of the superego over the ego and the id, making for the repression of conscious avowal of deep-seated parent-child conflict.

Relationship of wife to father and mother. The relationship of attachment and conflict of the son to his parents seems to bear a small but definite relationship to marital adjustment. Is there a similar association between happiness in marriage and the affection or antagonism of the daughter to her father and mother? The answer to this question is presented in

---

[6] CR, .514 and .211 (combining cases of "a good deal" and "almost continuous" conflict), 4.75.

[7] CR, .490 and .167 (combining cases of "a good deal" and "almost continuous" conflict), 4.6.

[8] CR, .220 and .351 (combining cases of "a good deal" and "almost continuous" conflict), 1.9.

[9] CR, .241 and .444 (combining cases of "a good deal" and "almost continuous" conflict), 2.3.

Charts 7 and 8. Study of Table 60, Appendix A, indicates that a larger proportion of wives express a very close attachment for their mothers than for their fathers (45.7 per cent and 32.8 per cent, respectively, of those reporting). The difference between the corresponding percentages for the husband is in the same direction but smaller (39.3 per cent and 23.2 per cent).

The degree of attachment of the daughter to her father shows almost no relationship to marital adjustment except where "little or no" attachment is reported (64 cases, with only 35.9 per cent [10] in the "good" adjustment class). The same

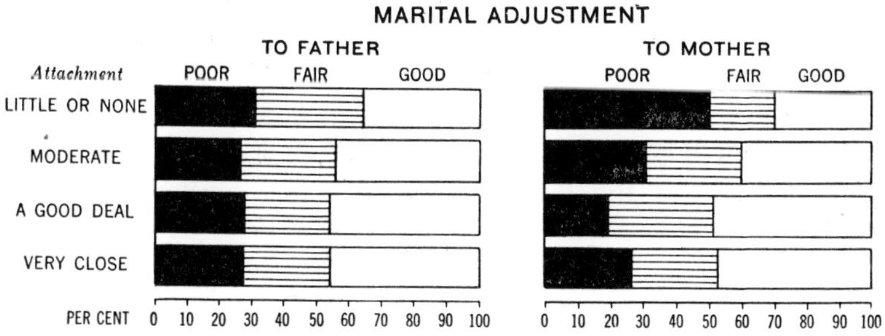

MARITAL ADJUSTMENT

CHART 7.—WIFE'S ATTACHMENT TO PARENTS AND MARITAL ADJUSTMENT.

may be said for the amount of attachment between daughter and mother, with the reservation that where there is "little or no" attachment the proportion with "good" adjustment is small (29.4 per cent versus 46.6 per cent [11] where there is a "very close" relationship). The percentages with "poor" adjustment vary correspondingly (50.0 per cent when there is "little or no" attachment, as against 26.9 per cent where attachment is "very close").[11]

The degree of conflict between son and parents appeared to indicate a small negative relation to adjustment in marriage. Is this true of antagonism between mother and daughter? Be-

---

[10] CR, .359 and .462 ("very close" attachment), 1.43. In our larger group of 1,064 cases, CR of the corresponding percentages is 2.7.
[11] CR, .294 and .466, 2.02. CR, .500 and .269, 2.58.

fore we answer this question, it is interesting to ask whether
or not husbands and wives included in this study differ as to
the proportion who have not been in conflict with their fathers
and mothers.

Table 61 [12] indicates that wives who report no conflict with
their fathers number 258 and with their mothers 211. It shows
a disproportion in the opposite direction from the figures for
the husbands, in which cases those with no conflict with their
fathers total only 218, but with their mothers, 257. Similarly
the daughters who have had "a good deal" or "almost continuous" conflict with their fathers are 46 and with their mothers
60; the corresponding figures for the sons are 57 and 36. In
other words, while the great majority of both husbands and
wives report very little or no conflict with either parent, there
is a slight tendency for the son to have less conflict with the
mother and for the daughter to have less conflict with the
father.

Psychoanalysts will tend to explain this statistical difference
in terms of natural preference of the son for the mother and of
the daughter for the father. It should also be pointed out that
the conflict may arise out of resentment against control which
is, on the whole, more likely to result in conflicts between
father and son and mother and daughter than between father
and daughter and mother and son. In the matter of attachments, as we have seen, both sons and daughters more frequently indicated "very close" attachment for mother than for
father and "little" or "no" attachment for father than for
mother.[13]

But what is the relationship of the presence or absence of
conflict between parents and daughter to the latter's adjustment
in marriage? The figures given in Chart 8 appear to show no
consistent pattern of variation such as was found in the association between the husband and his parents.[14] The only gen-

---

[12] See Table 61 in Appendix A.
[13] See Charts 5 and 6, pp. 92–93.
[14] The largest differences are between the proportions of those reporting "no

eralization, perhaps, that can be made from an examination of this chart is that where there is no conflict between father and daughter the percentage with "good" adjustment is somewhat higher than the average (47.7 per cent compared with 43.2 per cent). Where there is conflict of whatever degree, the percentage is lower than the average.

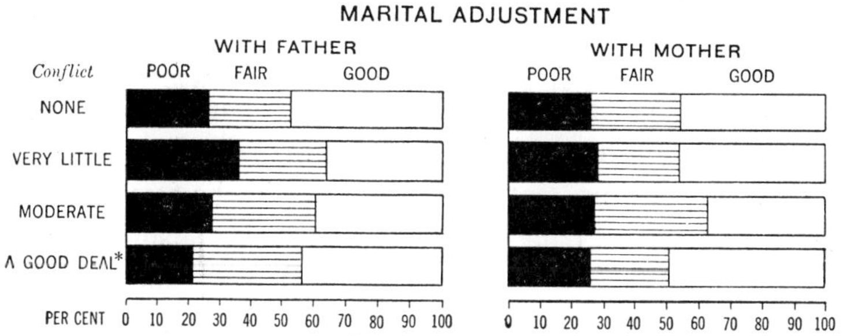

MARITAL ADJUSTMENT

* Includes 12 cases of "almost continuous" conflict with father and 8 cases of "almost continuous" conflict with mother.

CHART 8.—WIFE'S CONFLICT WITH PARENTS AND MARITAL ADJUSTMENT.

The point may well be made that the number of cases reporting the presence of conflict is much smaller than might be expected. This is partly due, no doubt, to a tendency to minimize the degree of conflict, or to ignore it altogether when filling out a schedule. Then, too, a person may forget conflict experiences of the past. Again, the schedule called for the answer to this question "as if at the time of marriage" rather than in childhood or youth, and this probably lessened the number who admitted conflict relations.

The chief results of this examination of the effect of parent-child relationships upon adjustment in marriage may be summarized as follows:

1. Wives report a greater degree of attachment to both parents than do husbands.

conflict" and those reporting "very little conflict." Those with "poor" adjustment: CR, .263 ("none") and .352 ("very little"), 1.77; and with "good " adjustment: CR, .477 ("none") and .367 ("very little"), 2.1.

2. Both husbands and wives assert that they are more attached to the mother than to the father, although the margin of difference between these attachments is greater in the case of the husband than of the wife.

3. The absence of conflict with the parents is practically the same for sons as for daughters, but wives report relatively less conflict with fathers than with mothers, and husbands admit proportionately less conflict with mothers than with fathers.

4. Closeness of attachment and absence of conflict in the association of parents and son show a consistent although small positive relation to marital adjustment.

5. No such consistent pattern appears in the association between parents and daughter, although "no" attachment to the father and "little" or "no" attachment to the mother appear to work against a high marital-adjustment score.

6. If attachment to and conflict with parents may be taken as indicative of early child-parent relations which give rise to psychogenetic characteristics, then the above data suggest a slight but definite relation between such characteristics and marital adjustment. The association between these two factors (conflict and attachment) and marital adjustment is slight, however, and might be explained by other factors.

Happiness of Parents' Marriage

What effect, if any, does the happiness of parents in their own married life have upon the adjustment in marriage of their children? Clinical studies indicate the effect of domestic discord upon the personality development of the child, and psychiatrists report that many behavior problems of children are frequently due to parental conflicts. The further assumption might be made that the child unadjusted or maladjusted because of the unhappy marriage of his parents reproduces in his married life a similar state of disharmony. This is at least one formulation of the hypothesis of the relation of the psychogenesis of personality to marital adjustment. A comparison of the happiness of the parents' marriage with the marital adjustment of their children should have some bearing on this theory.

The husband or wife who filled out the schedule was asked to appraise the marriage of the parents as "very happy," "happy," "average," "unhappy," or "very unhappy." As already indicated, the criterion of reports of happiness, subjective as this term seems to be, was shown to be statistically highly reliable when ratings by different persons were compared.[15]

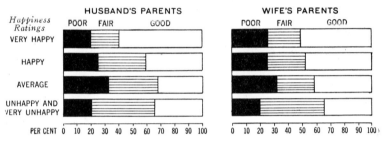

CHART 9.—APPRAISAL OF THE HAPPINESS OF THE PARENTS' MARRIAGE (SEPARATE RATINGS) AND MARITAL ADJUSTMENT.

In Chart 9 are presented the happiness ratings of the marriages of parents as related to the marital adjustments of their sons and daughters.

The correlation of the happiness ratings of the parents' marriages with the marital adjustments of the couples in this study appears to be more pronounced in the case of the husband than of the wife. For instance, 60.3 per cent [16] of the husbands whose parents' marriages were rated "very happy" fall in the group with "good," and only 19.9 per cent [17] in the group with "poor,"

---

[15] See Chapter III, "Happiness as a Criterion of Successful Marriage," particularly pp. 38–44.

[16] CR, .603 ("very happy"), with .419 ("happy"), 3.27; with .319 ("average"), 6.68; and with .354 ("unhappy and very unhappy"), 3.22.

[17] CR, .199 and .397 ("average"), 3.7. CR, .250 ("happy") and .397 ("average"), 2.8.

adjustment. The corresponding figures for the wives of "very
happily" married parents are 49.3 per cent [18] for wives with
"good" and 26.4 per cent with "poor" adjustment. Where the
husband's parents' marriage is rated only "average," the proportion with "good" adjustment falls to 31.9 per cent,[19] and
the proportion of the "poorly" adjusted [20] rises to 39.7 per cent.
Corresponding figures for the wives were 40.1 per cent with
"good" and 32.8 per cent with "poor" adjustment.

Chart 9 treats independently the effect of the marital happiness of the parents of the husband and that of the wife's
parents upon the adjustment of the young couple. Actually,
however, every permutation of the combined ratings of the
happiness of the husbands' and wives' parents is represented
in marital unions. There is no doubt that a tabulation giving
the possible 15 combinations of happiness ratings of the husbands' and of the wives' parents would afford a more accurate
picture of the relation of the harmony or disharmony of the
parents' marriages to the marital adjustments of the couples.

The number of cases in this study was too small for such a
detailed classification. In Chart 10, however, are presented
five combinations of the happiness appraisal of the parents'
marriage in relation to the marital adjustment of their children.
A comparison of the findings of Chart 10 with those of Chart
9 quite convinces one of the value of combining for each couple
the happiness appraisals of the parents' marriage rather than
of treating them separately for husband and wife.

Chart 10 presents a consistent pattern with very marked
differences between the extremes in the happiness ratings. In
the case of a couple where the marriage of both sets of parents
was rated "very happy" 72.9 [21] per cent had "good" adjustment
and only 11.9 per cent [22] were "poorly" adjusted. On the other

---

[18] CR, .493 and .333 ("unhappy" and "very unhappy"), 2.31.
[19] See footnote 16.
[20] See footnote 17.
[21] CR, .729 and .279, 6.3.
[22] CR, .119 and .378, 4.0.

hand, where the parents of both bride and groom were rated as "average," "unhappy," or "very unhappy" only 27.9 [21] per cent of the couples had "good" adjustment and 37.8 per cent [22] were "poorly" adjusted.

The conclusion reached, then, is that the domestic happiness of the parents does appear to be definitely correlated with the marital adjustment of the children. The nature of the association remains, however, undetermined. Three hypotheses may

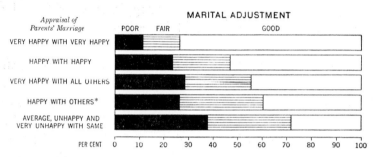

* Except with "very happy."

CHART 10.—APPRAISAL OF THE HAPPINESS OF PARENTS' MARRIAGE (COMBINED RATINGS) AND MARITAL ADJUSTMENT.

be offered which independently or in conjunction may explain this association:

1. It is conceivable that domestic accord of the parents is favorable to the development of a stable type of personality in children, and a stable personality in turn makes for good adjustment as adults in marriage. Conversely, the parental conflict may lead to the formation of an unstable personality in the child who, in later life, is maladjusted in marriage.

2. It may be argued that the domestic accord or discord of the parents is an expression of biologically inherited instability which is transmitted to their children by biological inheritance rather than through social interaction.

[21] See footnote on preceding page.
[22] See footnote on preceding page.

3. It may be contended that reliance need not be placed upon either of the foregoing explanations, since the happiness or unhappiness of the parents in marriage may be the resultant of a cultural or social pattern of behavior which is carried over by their children in their marriage.

The data in the present study cannot be used to prove or disprove any of the above theories. It must be left to future studies to determine whether or not "family atmosphere," as represented by parental happiness or unhappiness, conditions the personality of the growing child for or against adjustment in marriage.

In conclusion it should be pointed out (and this is true of all items taken individually) that in any case the happiness of the parental marriage is not in itself *all*-important. Even where both sets of parents were "very happily" married, some couples report marital disagreements and dissatisfactions. And where parents of both husband and wife have been "unhappy" or "very unhappy" in their marriage, a considerable proportion of couples live in agreement and contentment.

Parents' Status

If family relations are significant in personality formation, it is to be expected that the status of the parents of the young couple should show a relationship to the adjustment of the husband and wife in marriage. Chart 11 provides some data on this relationship derived from Table 64 in Appendix A.

The largest group (those with both parents living), when compared with all other categories of parental conditions, does not differ significantly in the proportion of couples with "good" adjustment.[23] Nor is there any significant difference between the proportion in the very high score group of those couples

---

[23] CR, .458 (where wives' parents are both living together) and .392 (proportion of all other groups in known marital status), 1.41.

whose parents are married and both living and those couples whose parents are both dead.[24]

In the case of both husband and wife, however, there is to be noted a considerably lower percentage with "good" adjustment (31.2[25] and 34.4[26] per cent, respectively) where the parents are separated or divorced at the time of the couple's marriage, as compared with the corresponding figures (40.4 per cent and 45.8 per cent) where the parents were alive and living together. With the small numbers sampled, these differences are not statistically significant. They will probably prove to be real

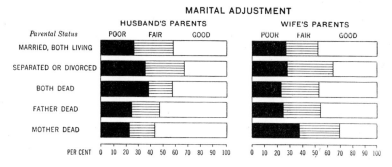

CHART 11.—PARENTAL STATUS AND MARITAL ADJUSTMENT.

differences when larger numbers of cases are available for comparison.

Two possible explanations may be offered for the smaller proportion of those with "good" adjustment where the parents are divorced or separated. First, the tension between the parents leading to separation and divorce may have been a result of temperamental traits that were inherited by their children and became one factor making for maladjustment. Second, the disharmony between the parents may have been emotionally or otherwise disturbing to their children in a way that dimin-

[24] CR, .492, (where one or both parents of the husband are dead) and .404 (where both are alive and living together), 1.9.

[25] CR, .312 and .404 (both parents living together), 0.7.

[26] CR, .344 and .458 (both parents living together), 1.2.

ished their chances for marital happiness. At any rate, this finding is consistent with the finding which indicated that children of unhappily married parents have fewer chances for marital adjustment than children of happily married parents.

Interesting in its relation to domestic happiness is the question of the effect upon marital adjustment of the death of one parent. In the case of the husband, the probabilities of successful marital harmony seem higher than the average when his father is dead (50.6 per cent [27]) and still higher when his mother is not living (55.8 per cent [28]). The Freudian explanation would doubtless be that the death of his father removes a rival for the affection of his mother, and the passing of his mother leaves his wife without a competitor.

The death of the father of the wife has no apparent effect on marriage adjustment. But our data indicate a lower proportion in the class with "good" marriage adjustment (only 29.4 per cent [29]) when the wife's mother is dead. This may represent a situation in which the wife is experiencing conflict in her affection for her husband and for her father.

These findings, if corroborated by other studies, suggest that in a certain proportion of cases the severance by death of certain filial affectional relationships reacts upon the adjustment of husband and wife in marriage. More intensive case study and statistical research is required, however, to determine the actual operation of factors of personality, of emotional response, and of feelings of duty in the complex interplay of filial and marital relations.

Sibling Relationships

The first adjustments of a person are made within the family circle to brothers and sisters as well as to parents. The psy-

---

[27] CR, .506 and .404 (both parents living together), 1.7.
[28] CR, .558 and .404, 2.1.
[29] CR, .294 and .458 (both parents living together), 2.0.

chiatric theories regarding the influence of family interaction upon personality development hold that relationships between siblings exert a formative influence almost if not quite as strong as relationships between the child and the parents.[30]   Therefore the size of the family, the order of birth among children, and attachments to brothers and sisters may be investigated on the assumption that if they condition a person's early social responses, they may also influence his later adjustments, including his adjustments in marriage.

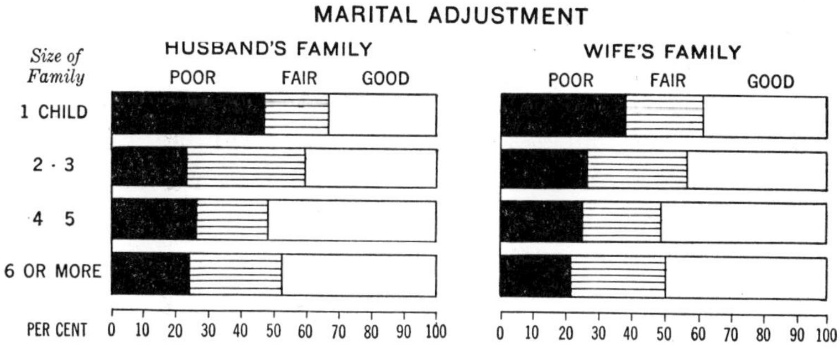

MARITAL ADJUSTMENT

CHART 12.—SIZE OF FAMILY AND MARITAL ADJUSTMENT.

Size of the family.   One of the outstanding differences between families is in the number of children.   The coming of each child changes the constellation of familial interaction.   It was, therefore, of interest to find out whether the size of the family of the husband and of the wife had any association with their marital adjustment and, if so, how much.

The number of cases in which the husband or the wife is the only child is small (55 and 63, respectively).   The largest number of our cases (164 and 206) come from families with two to three children; the next largest number (139 and 125) come from families with four to five children; and the third largest

---

[30] See William A. White, *Mechanisms of Character Formation,* New York, The Macmillan Co., 1916.

group (129 and 97) come from families with six children and more.[31]

The relation of size of family to marriage adjustment is clearly seen in the case of the husband. The percentage with "good" marital adjustment is only 30.9 when the husband was the only child, 40.8 when there were two or three children, and 51.1 when there were four to five children.[32] The percentages of "poorly" adjusted couples are practically identical for husbands from families with two to three children (23.2 per cent), four to five children (26.6 per cent), and six or more children (24.0 per cent); but each of these figures is significantly different from the figure (49.1 per cent) for families with one child.[33]

The same pattern of association with "good" adjustment is to be seen with size of the wife's family but to a lesser degree: 38.1 per cent where there was one child, 42.7 per cent for two or three children, 48.8 for four or five children, and 47.4 per cent for six or more children.[34]

Falling in the group of "poorly" adjusted couples are 38.1 per cent of the wives from one-child families but only 26.7 per cent from families with two and three children; 25.6 per cent from families of four and five children; and 22.7 per cent from families of six or more children. These differences are probably significant.[35]

In summary, it is evident that the size of the family is a more important factor in marital adjustment for the husband than for the wife. In his case the probabilities of "good" adjustment

[31] In our sample there appears to be a larger proportion of husbands than of wives from families with four or more children; and, conversely, a larger percentage of wives than husbands from families of three or less children. This may be due to a tendency of men to marry women from socio-economic classes slightly higher than their own. Since there is a negative correlation between socio-economic status and size of family. this would mean that men from larger families would more frequently marry women from slightly smaller families.

[32] CR, .309 and .408, 1.3; .309 and .511, 2.68; .408 and .511, 1.78; and .309 and .465, 2.05.

[33] CR, .491, with .232, 3.4; with .266, 2.9; and with .240, 3.3.

[34] None of these differences, however, is significant.

[35] CR, .381, with .267, 1.66; with .256, 1.69; and with .227, 2.07.

are greater if he be one of two or three children than if he is an only child, and still higher if he had three or more brothers and sisters. Where the wives and the husbands are only children, a very large proportion are in the "poorly" adjusted group.

Place in family. More significant perhaps than the mere size of the family is the place of the person within it. There is a growing literature upon order of birth as a factor in personality formation.[36] The different positions of the eldest, middle, and youngest children in the family constellation might very well produce or influence certain personality traits which would affect social adjustments, including those of the marriage relationship. Our data upon this subject are presented in Chart 13.

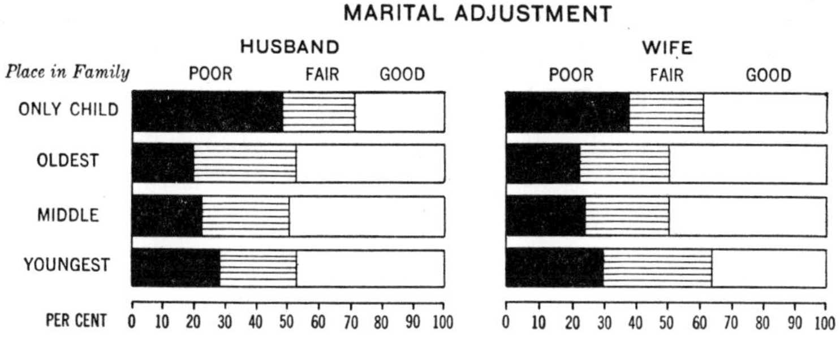

CHART 13.—PLACE IN FAMILY AND MARITAL ADJUSTMENT.

Actually the findings presented in this chart show little if any relationship between birth order and marital adjustment except in the case of the only child. In the case of both husbands and wives, the only child has a lower-than-average expectation of falling in the class with "good" adjustment (30.9 per cent [37] and 38.1 per cent [38]), and there is a higher probability that he will

---

[36] For a review of the literature and a recent study, see W. Paul Carter, *The Only Child and Other Birth Orders,* doctoral dissertation, Chicago, University of Chicago Libraries, 1937.

[37] CR, .309 (only child) with .470 (oldest), 2.05; with .489 (middle), 2.37; and with .461 (youngest), 1.87.

[38] CR, .381, with other percentages for "good" adjustment is not statistically significant.

fall in the group of "poorly" adjusted couples (49.1 per cent [39] and 38.1 per cent [40]).

When the husband and wife are either the eldest or middle children, there appears to be a somewhat higher-than-average probability that a larger proportion will be found among those with good marital adjustment (47.0 and 48.9 per cent for the husbands, 49.2 and 49.0 per cent for the wives). The percentage of youngest children in this class shows practically the same proportion in the case of husbands (46.1 per cent), but drops sharply (to 35.8 per cent [41]) in the case of wives.

The tentative conclusion may be drawn that only children have lower chances for very high marital-adjustment scores than other children. This seems more certain for only-child husbands than for only-child wives. Both husbands and wives who are only children are found in the "poorly" adjusted group in larger proportion than husbands and wives of any other birth-order position. It seems probable also that wives who are youngest children are poorer marital risks than oldest and middle children.

Rather than simply relating order of birth to marriage adjustment for husbands and wives independently, we really should correlate marriage adjustment with the different combinations of birth order, such as an oldest child mated with an only child, an oldest with an oldest, an oldest with a middle, an oldest with a youngest, a middle with an only, a middle with a middle, and so on. The number of cases in the group of 526 marriages was too small for the 10 combinations required.

Accordingly all the data in our study bearing upon the relation of birth order to marital happiness were utilized. These include not only the main group of 526 couples in Illinois, but the couples outside that state and their parents, wherever their

---

[39] CR, .491 (only child) with .197 (oldest), 3.87; with .227 (middle), 3.54; and with .284 (youngest), 2.56.

[40] CR, .381 (only child) with .227 (oldest), 2.15; with .249 (middle), 1.88; and with .301 (youngest), not statistically significant.

[41] CR, .358, with .492 (eldest), 2.16; and with .490 (middle), 2.24.

place in the family was indicated. In Chart 14 are presented
the findings regarding place in the family in relation to ratings
of marital happiness for 3,566 couples. Happiness ratings are
employed in this tabulation because detailed data upon marital
adjustment were not available for the parents of the couples.[42]

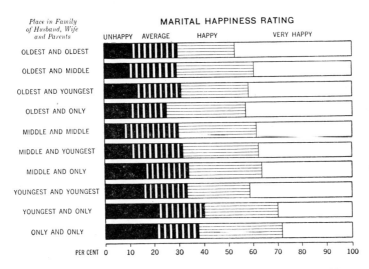

CHART 14.—PLACE IN FAMILY OF HUSBAND AND WIFE AND OF THEIR
PARENTS AND MARITAL-HAPPINESS RATINGS.

A careful study of this chart indicates the value of combining
the husband's and wife's place in the family instead of considering them separately as in Chart 13. It is now possible to
make certain rather definite statements about the relation of
place in the family to happiness in marriage:

1. Where both husband and wife are eldest children, the
proportions of "very happy" marriages are the highest among
the 10 combinations.[43]

---

[42] As will be recalled, there is a high correlation between happiness ratings and
marital-adjustment scores. See Chapter III, "Happiness as a Criterion of Marriage
Success."

[43] CR, .471 (oldest and oldest) with .383 (oldest and middle), 2.58; with .398
(oldest and youngest), 1.89; with .417 (oldest and only), not significant; with .375
(middle and middle), 2.83; with .370 (middle and youngest), 2.90; with .402 (mid-

2. Where both husband and wife are only children [44] or are both youngest children,[45] or where one is an only child and the other a youngest child,[46] the percentages of "very happy" marriages are the lowest, and of "unhappy" and "very unhappy" marriages the highest, among these groupings.

3. The lowest proportion of "unhappy" and "very unhappy" marriages is found in the unions of middle children. This appears to be a significant difference from the other combinations,[47] except in regard to marriages of eldest and eldest, eldest and middle, and eldest and youngest children.

4. The other groupings of the oldest children with middle, with youngest, and with only children, and of middle children with youngest and with only children,[48] have an intermediate proportion of "very happy" marriages in comparison with the group mentioned above.

These differences, while probably statistically significant, are not great. They are not important except perhaps in the case of the marriages of youngest and only children. Even here a

---

dle and only), not significant; with .357 (youngest and youngest), 2.47; with .288 (youngest and only), 3.55; and with .260 (only and only), 2.98.

[44] CR, .260 ("very happy") with .471 (oldest and oldest), 2.98; with .383 (oldest and middle), 1.83; with .398 (oldest and youngest), 1.99; with .417 (oldest and only), 1.96; with .375 (middle and middle), 1.72; with .370 (middle and youngest), not significant; with .402 (middle and only), 1.92. CR, .218 ("unhappy and very unhappy") is significant with only two other groupings; with .106 (oldest and middle), 1.81; and with .085 (middle and middle), 2.16.

[45] CR, .357 ("very happy") is significant only with .471 (oldest and oldest), 2.47. CR, .173 ("unhappy and very unhappy") appears significant with .113 (oldest and oldest), 1.77; with .106 (oldest and middle), 2.20; with .085 (middle and middle), 2.96; with .114 (middle and youngest), 1.91.

[46] CR, .288 ("very happy") with .471 (oldest and oldest), 3.52; with .383 (oldest and middle), 2.05; with .398 (oldest and youngest), 2.22; with .417 (oldest and only), 2.02; with .375 (middle and middle), 1.89; with .370 (middle and youngest), 1.75; with .402 (middle and only), 2.05. CR, .225 ("unhappy and very unhappy") with .113 (oldest and oldest), 2.56; with .106 (oldest and middle), 2.89; with .137 (oldest and youngest), 2.03; with .111 (oldest and only), 2.29; with .085 (middle and middle), 3.43; with .114 (middle and youngest), 2.67.

[47] CR, .085 ("unhappy and very unhappy") with .137 (oldest and youngest), 2.61; with .114 (middle and youngest), 1.85; with .164 (middle and only), 2.76; with .173 (youngest and youngest), 2.96; with .225 (youngest and only), 3.43; and with .218 (only and only), 2.16.

[48] CR, .164 ("unhappy and very unhappy") for marriages of middle and only children are probably significant with similar percentages for two other groupings: with .106 (oldest and middle), 1.99; and with .085 (middle and middle), 2.76.

much larger number of cases is required to determine the weight that should be placed upon birth order in relation to marital happiness.

Attachment to brother or sister. If familial interaction is significant in personality formation, the attachment of the husband and the wife to a particular brother or sister might be correlated with adjustment in marriage. Accordingly, the question was asked to which brother or sister the husband and the wife was most attached. The findings are presented in Chart 15 and, in full, in Table 68 in Appendix A.

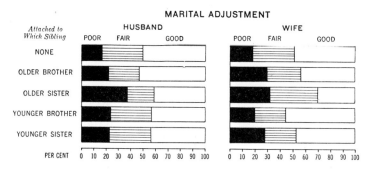

CHART 15.—SIBLING ATTACHMENT AND ADJUSTMENT.

A larger number of husbands (148) than of wives (100) stated that they had no attachments to any of their brothers and sisters. Husbands are more likely to be attached to a younger brother (62) or younger sister (66) than to an older brother (43) or to an older sister (48). Wives show a similar but smaller preference for younger siblings, but this fact is outweighed by their attachment to an older sister (68) and a younger sister (76) as compared with an older brother (43) and a younger brother (54).

In this sample of married couples, the attachment of a husband to his older brother and of a wife to her younger brother show the highest association with "good" marital adjustment

(51.2 per cent and 53.7 per cent).[49] The attachment of the husband to an older sister is associated with a higher proportion (37.5 per cent [50]) of "poorly" adjusted couples. The attachment of the wife to an older sister indicates a lower proportion than the average in the class with "good" adjustment (29.4 per cent [51]) and a higher proportion than the average in the "poor" adjustment group (32.4 per cent [52]). The only statistically significant conclusion to be drawn from these data is that the attachment of either husband or wife to an older sister appears to have a negative association with domestic harmony.

Further research upon a larger sample of cases will be required to determine whether or not any other than the above stated association of sibling relationship to marital happiness may be considered stable and valid.

In this chapter the bearing of the psychogenetic personality upon marital adjustment has been dealt with not directly but indirectly, in accordance with the assumption that certain emotional attachments formed during childhood in the family would affect the marriage relationship. The important findings may be summarized as follows:

1. The most significant association of any childhood familial factor with marital accord or discord established in this study is that of the reported happiness of the marriages of the parents of the husband and of the wife.

2. Next in significance appear to be the closeness of attachment of the husband and the wife to their parents and, in the case of the husband, the absence of conflict with his father and mother.

3. Less important in view of the small number of cases, but

---

[49] The differences between these percentages and other percentages in the table are not statistically significant.

[50] CR, .375 and .169 ("no attachment" for any sibling), 2.68.

[51] CR, .294 and .490 ("no attachment" for any sibling), 2.63.

[52] CR, .324 and .190 ("no attachment" for any sibling), 1.94.

of great interest for further research, appears to be the marital status of the parents.

4. Being a member of a family of four or more children appears to be, especially for the husband, a favorable factor for matrimonial life.

5. The only child and the youngest child, in the present findings, seem to be poor marital risks unless mated with an oldest or middle child. Marriages of eldest with eldest children appear to offer the best chance of happiness.

6. The only finding of probable statistical significance in this study of sibling preferences was the apparently unfavorable relation to marital adjustment of attachment of either husband or wife to an older sister.

Generalizing upon the basis of these findings, we may say with some certainty that the family constellation of relationships of attachment or of conflict exert an influence upon the person which may fit or unfit him for marriage. The further unraveling of the tangled skein of these conscious and unconscious influences will require much careful, detailed, and discriminating research—research that will necessitate case study as well as statistical procedure.[53]

---

[53] See Chapter XI, "Personality Factors in Marriage Adjustment."

CHAPTER VIII

The Social Type

THE REACTION of a person to others with respect to either his cultural background or his psychogenetic personality is determined for him in early childhood by his family: by the social world of which it is a microcosm and by its given constellation of interpersonal relations. These reactions of the person are therefore largely preconditioned, unconscious, and difficult if not impossible to change.

Related to these two aspects of the personality, but to be distinguished from them, is the social type which the person is or aspires to be. For purposes of this study the social type may be defined as the sum and coördination of the social roles of the person. A social role is a differentiated activity assumed by or assigned to a member of a group. A person has, accordingly, as many social roles as the number of groups to which he belongs.

Both the person and the group are highly conscious of his social roles. The youth, in particular, conceives and rehearses his roles in his imagination and practices them in conversation and action among his fellows. The group continually rates and re-rates its members in terms of their proficiency in their various roles.

In the present study the available data do not permit so detailed and so delicate an analysis as would be desired of the social type and social roles of the person in relation to marriage adjustment. Considerable information was, however, gathered upon his status and participation in social groups. This may be examined in the light of the above discussion of social types and social roles.   The data cover

1. Age and physical status.
2. Educational status.
3. Religious identification and participation.
4. Participation in social life.
5. Previous marital status.
6. Residential status.

The above data will be analyzed not merely in terms of these concrete items but in the perspective of their bearing upon the person's social type in its relation to married life.   What type of a man or woman readily adjusts to marriage?   What type finds adjustment difficult?

Age at Marriage

Age may be taken as an index of two related but somewhat different aspects of human development.   Increasing age is correlated, in general, with increasing maturity but with decreasing flexibility in social adaptation.   From the standpoint of adjustment in marriage it may be assumed that both maturity and flexibility are desirable qualities.   The questions for research to answer are, then,

1. Do early marriages turn out better than the average, because of the greater flexibility of the two personalities to each other, or do they turn out worse because of the immaturity of the young couple?

2. Is there, hypothetically, an optimum age for marriage when the most favorable balance would be struck between the two factors of flexibility and maturity?

Hornell Hart and Wilmer Shields [1] in a pioneer study gave to both of these questions an answer based upon a comparison

---

[1] "Happiness in Relation to Age at Marriage," *Social Hygiene,* 12, 1926, pp. 403–410.

of the ages at marriage of couples appearing in the Domestic
Relations Court of Philadelphia and the ages given by couples
applying in the same city for licenses to marry. They summarize their findings as follows: [2]

. . . that the ideal age for marriage is about 29 for the groom and
24 for the bride; that deviations of four years on either side of the
ideal age for the groom, or of two years on either side of the ideal
age of the bride, make no appreciable difference; that marriages in
which the bride is under 21 years of age, or the groom under 24, become rapidly more dangerous as younger ages are considered; that
marriages in which either party is 19 or younger are from 10 to 100
times as risky as are marriages at the ideal age; and that marriages
of persons over 38 years of age are from two to five times as likely to
result in domestic difficulties as are marriages at the ideal age: such
are outstanding conclusions with regard to Philadelphia marriages as
indicated by age data collected from the Domestic Relations Court
and the Marriage License Bureau of that city.

These findings by Hart and Shields were severely criticized
by Paul Popenoe, especially on the ground that cases from the
Domestic Relations Court are highly selected and therefore can
only with extreme caution and many reservations be compared
with marriages in the general population. [3] It is therefore of
more than usual interest to determine what is the relation of
age to adjustment in marriage as derived from the data of the
present study. These are shown in Chart 16. An examination
of this chart indicates the very high proportion of "poorly"
adjusted, and the very low proportion of "well"-adjusted,
couples where the wife was under 19 years and the husband
under 22 years of age at the time of marriage. In the great
majority of cases there seems to be no doubt regarding the
unfortunate effects of very early marriages. Many of these
marriages are hasty unions, often after short acquaintance, generally entered into despite the opposition of parents, with the

---

[2] *Ibid.*, p. 403.   Reprinted by permission of the American Social Hygiene Association.
[3] Paul Popenoe, "Early Marriage and Happiness," *Social Hygiene*, 12, 1926, pp.
544–549.

wife unprepared for the duties of managing a household and with the husband unable to support a wife.

Our data give no clear answer to the question of the optimum age for marriage. There is some indication that the age group 28 to 30 years (practically identical with Hart's age of 29) is the most favorable period for men to marry, but the number of

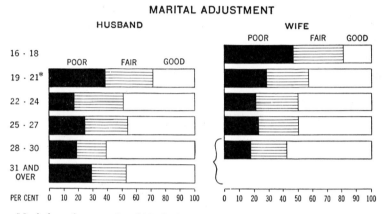

MARITAL ADJUSTMENT

*Includes a few cases in which the husband was 17 or 18.

CHART 16.—AGE AT MARRIAGE OF HUSBAND AND WIFE AND ADJUSTMENT.

cases is too small to be conclusive. Cases in larger numbers will also be necessary to determine whether or not marriage during the age period 19 to 21 is to be regarded as unfavorable to adjustment.

The chart shows a marked increase of the "poorly" adjusted and a decided decrease of those with "good" adjustment among the men who marry at 31 years or later, while for women in the age group of 28 and over the reverse is indicated. It will be interesting to observe whether further research, with a sufficient number of cases to give reliable findings, will corroborate these indications of relationship.

State of Health at Marriage

Health like age is a biological factor but is likewise significant in personal relations and in the role of the individual in the group. For this reason both husband and wife were asked to make a statement on the state of their health at the time of marriage. The report made must, however, be understood as that of a layman. The findings regarding health in relation to marital life are presented in Chart 17.

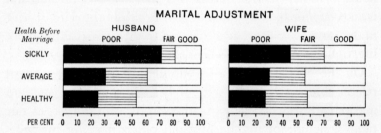

CHART 17.—HEALTH PREVIOUS TO MARRIAGE AND MARITAL ADJUSTMENT.

The number of persons who reported themselves as "sickly" previous to marriage is small (husbands 11; wives 20). Both these groups show a much lower proportion than the average in the "very high" marital-adjustment class, but because of the small number of cases the difference with regard to the other group is not statistically significant.

For the husband there is quite likely a significant difference in proportion in the class of "good" adjustment between those who report themselves as "healthy" and those who report themselves as "sickly" combined with those in "average" health (46.1 per cent [4] and 36.4 per cent [5]). The difference between the corresponding percentages for those "poorly" adjusted (25.8 per cent and 34.9 per cent) is also probably significant.[6]

---

[4] CR, .461 (healthy) and .381 (average), 1.56.
[5] CR, .461 and .364, 1.95.
[6] CR, .258 and .349, 1.92.

For the wives the figures apparently indicate that "sickness" is adverse and "health" is favorable to marital happiness (30 per cent as against 44.1 per cent among those with "good" adjustment, and 45.0 per cent compared with 25.9 per cent for the "poorly" adjusted), but because of the small number of cases in the "sickly" group these differences are not significant.

If it is assumed that the state of health before marriage is somewhat indicative of health after marriage, we are faced with the question of why the husband's health seems to have some significance for marriage adjustment and the wife's little or none. The explanation may be that poor health of the husband is an economic handicap, while poor health of the wife, at least in the early years of wedded life and in many cases throughout life, tightens rather than loosens the bonds of affection.

On the whole, the data in our sample show only a small relationship between the state of health before marriage and marital adjustment. This relationship is, on the basis of our figures, significant for the husband rather than for the wife. In all probability our findings give an underestimate of the relation between state of health before marriage and marital happiness.

Weight Deviation

Height and weight are indexes not only of physical but also of social status, and as such might be expected to show some association with domestic felicity. But when height and weight were considered separately from each other, they disclosed little or no relation to marital adaptation. Because of this, and because today in the United States persons are becoming self-conscious regarding weight in relation to height, the weight deviation of husband and of wife from the standard norms according to height by age and sex was figured.

The distribution by weight deviation at time of marriage shows a slight tendency in our sample of cases toward overweight in husbands and a marked tendency toward under-weight in wives. For the husbands the figures suggest an association between the state of being 15 pounds or more under-weight and marital adjustment, but none of the differences in percentages can be relied upon because of the small number of cases in each weight-deviation group.

With the wives the strong contrast is at the extremes in weight deviation. The small group who are 15 pounds or more overweight contribute the highest proportion to the "poorly" adjusted class and represent the smallest percentage with high

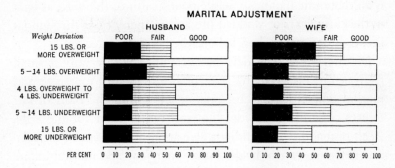

CHART 18.—WEIGHT DEVIATION FROM NORMAL AND MARITAL ADJUSTMENT.

chances of "good" adjustment (50 per cent [7] and 27.3 per cent,[8] respectively). The large group who are 15 pounds or more underweight provide the lowest percentage of the "poorly adjusted" and the largest proportion of those with "good" adjustment (20 per cent [7] and 52.6 per cent,[8] respectively).

Another interesting and probably significant difference is that between wives who are 5 to 14 pounds underweight and those who are 15 or more pounds overweight. The wives in the former group provide 32.7 per cent [9] of those with "poor"

---

[7] CR, .500 and .200, 2.70.
[8] CR, .273 and .526, 2.47.
[9] CR, .327 and .200, 2.63.

adjustment and only 37.2 per cent [10] of the group with "good" adjustment.

The present vogue for the slender female figure and the fashion of dieting are sufficient explanation for the particular association with marital adaptation found in the two extreme groups of wives. It is more difficult to explain why the large group of those 5 to 14 pounds underweight should include a low proportion of wives with "good" adjustment. A possible reason is that these wives included a number who were com-

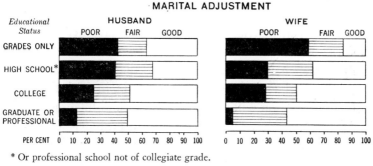

* Or professional school not of collegiate grade.

CHART 19.—EDUCATIONAL STATUS AND MARITAL ADJUSTMENT.

pelled to continue dieting to maintain a condition of underweight, and were therefore nervous and irritable. There is, however, no evidence in our data to support this interpretation.

Educational Status

In American society the level attained in formal education enters into a person's conception of himself and into his status in the eyes of other people. It is generally assumed that educational achievement is associated with increased personal efficiency and stability. So far as marriage is concerned this assumption may be tested by the data presented in Chart 19 and in Table 72 in Appendix A.

[10] CR, .372 and .526, 2.85.

The large proportion of husbands and wives with college, graduate, or professional education is a reminder that our sample is overweighted with persons of higher education. At the same time there is in our group a sufficient proportion of persons with a high-school education to make feasible a comparison between educational levels with regard to marital success. The percentages give a quite consistent picture of the increased chances of success in marriage that go with a rising level of educational achievement of both husband [11] and wife.

But education is bound up with economic status, type of neighborhood, and other social indexes positively correlated with success in marriage. We may then have here the effect of ·these other factors as well as the single one of education. On the other hand, it may be asserted that educational opportunities should, and to a growing extent do, increase the probability that a person will be more objective and intelligent in his social relationships, more tolerant in attitude, and better equipped with reliable information about the sexual and other adjustments of married life. It also seems true that the higher the educational level, the longer marriage is postponed. Our figures point to increased chances of success in marriage with increasing age at time of marriage.[12] So there is perhaps an association between age and educational progress in the latter's relation to marital success.[13]

Religious Identification and Participation

As much, or more, than educational achievement, religious identification and activity may be taken as an index of social and personal attitudes. The denominational preference of a

---

[11] The only exception in the table is the lower per cent (33.6) of husbands of high-school level as compared with the per cent (37.2) of those of grade-school level. This difference, however, is reversed in our larger group of 1,064 cases. In both samples, however, differences are not statistically significant.

[12] See pp. 115–117.

[13] For the relation of difference in educational status of husband and wife to marriage adjustment, see p. 87.

person, it is true, is generally the same as that of the parents, but the degree of participation in church activities represents in all probability the person's own religious interest.

The great majority of persons in our study reported a religious affiliation at the time of marriage. Only 89 husbands and 48 wives reported no affiliation, and 70 husbands and 62 wives gave no reply. In the case of both bride and groom, those reporting no church connections ranked lower than the average in "good" adjustment, constituting only 33.7 per cent and 39.6 per cent, respectively, of the well adjusted.

More significant than church affiliation as indicative of religious interest and participation is attendance at church and Sunday school. Chart 20 presents the extent of Sunday-school

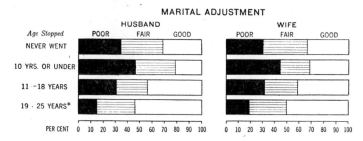

* Includes those still attending at time of marriage.

CHART 20.—AGE AT WHICH STOPPED ATTENDING SUNDAY SCHOOL AND MARITAL ADJUSTMENT.

attendance of bridegroom and bride as correlated with marital success. If the first two groups (those who never went and those who stopped attending at 10 years of age or less) are combined, a regular and consistent pattern of the relation between Sunday-school attendance and marital happiness is obtained. Both husbands and wives who never went to Sunday school or who stopped going after 10 years of age show a markedly lower proportion of highly successful [14] and a

---

[14] For the husbands with "good" adjustment, CR, .528 (19 to 25 years) with .206 (10 years and under), 3.96; and with .309 (never went), 2.90. CR, .455 (11 to 18

higher proportion of unsuccessful [15] marriages as measured by
the adjustment score.   On the other hand, those who continued
going to Sunday school until they were 19 to 25 years old, or
even older, have a distinctly higher chance than other groups
for marital success [14] and a lower chance for failure.[15]

In addition to Sunday-school attendance, Chart 21 presents
church attendance before marriage as an index of religious
interest and participation.   This chart shows that wives before

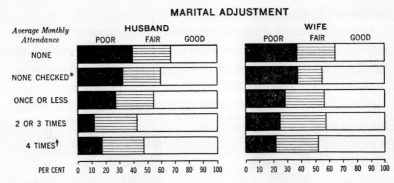

* But a church member.
† Includes those which indicate other church activity if attendance is not checked.

CHART 21.—CHURCH ATTENDANCE AND MARITAL ADJUSTMENT.

marriage were on the average more frequent in church attendance than husbands. For both husband and wife, but distinctly more markedly for the husband, religious activity as
indicated by church attendance is positively correlated with
probabilities of marital success.

For the husband both Sunday-school and church attendance
seem to have practically the same relationship to marital

years) with .206 (10 years and under), 3.26; and with .309 (never went), 2.09.
For the wives with "good" adjustment, CR, .523 (19 to 25 years) with .412 (11 to 18
years), is 2.25; with .310 (10 years and under), 2.27; and with .325 (never went),
2.38.
[14] See footnote on preceding page.
[15] For "poorly" adjusted husbands, CR, .155 (19 to 25 years) with .291 (11 to
18 years), 3.23; with .470 (10 years and under), 3.47; and with .346 (never attended), 2.71. For "poorly" adjusted wives, CR, .184 (19 to 25 years) with .314
(11 to 18 years), 3.11; with .448 (10 years and under), 2.72; and with .300 (never
went), 1.48.

success; for the wife Sunday-school attendance affords a better criterion.

The husbands who never attend church are the "poorest" matrimonial risks, those who attend once or less a month "average," and those who attend two, three or four times a month the "best." [16] The 175 wives who attend church four times a month include a smaller proportion (22.3 per cent) of those "poorly" adjusted than those who never attend (37.1 per cent or who did not check attendance although they are church members (37.5 per cent).[17]

A final indication of the relation of religious interest to marital adjustment may be derived from our data regarding the place where the marriage took place and the person who performed the wedding ceremony. The questions are, which marriages turn out to be the more successful: (1) those taking place in church, or at home, or elsewhere; and (2) those in which the ceremony is performed by ministers or by civil officials?

In our group of 526 couples all but 9 reported the place of marriage. In these cases 253, or nearly one-half, had been married at church or in the parsonage, 157 at home, and 107 elsewhere.

As shown by Chart 22, those married at church or in the parsonage contribute a larger proportion (49.4 per cent) of couples with "good" adjustment than those whose wedding ceremonies took place at home (39.5 per cent) or elsewhere (35.5 per cent).[18] Correspondingly, church and parsonage weddings are associated with a lower percentage of couples falling in the "poorly" adjusted group (22.5 per cent) than weddings at home (34.3 per cent) or elsewhere (34.6 per cent).[19]

---

[16] For "poorly" adjusted husbands, CR, .397 (none) with .271 (once or less), 2.27; with .119 (two or three times), 4.19; and with .176 (four times), 4.00. For husbands with "good adjustment" CR, .325 (none) with .452 (once or less), 2.23; with .571 (two or three times), 2.83; and with .520 (four times), 3.19.
[17] For "poorly" adjusted wives CR, .223 with .371, 2.15; and with .375, 2.11. For the wives no other differences in percentages for Chart 21 are statistically significant.
[18] CR, .494 with .395, 1.99; and with .355, 2.50.
[19] CR, .225 with .343, 2.56; and with .346, 2.28.

Adjustment in marriage is probably not bettered by the sheer external fact of a church wedding. The point is that the religious and certain other sentiments and attitudes of the couple and of their families which demand a church ceremony seem to be associated with marital adjustment.

The overwhelming proportion of our group of couples, 467, were married by minister, priest, or rabbi, as against 51 who

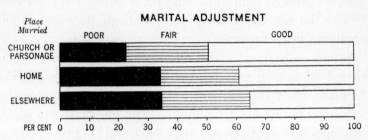

CHART 22.—PLACE IN WHICH MARRIED AND MARITAL ADJUSTMENT.

were joined in wedlock by civil officials (8, no reply). Of those married by civil officials only 19.6 per cent [20] fall in the class with "good" adjustment, while 54.9 per cent [21] are in the class with "poor" adjustment. In cases in which the wedding was solemnized by a religious ceremony, 46.0 per cent [20] are in the category of "good," and 25.7 per cent [21] in the classes with "poor," adjustment.

Whatever data were examined to test the relation to marital adjustment of religious sentiments, interests, and activities— Sunday-school or church attendance, place of marriage, or official performing the ceremony—all agree in showing a positive association.

Membership in Organization

Both husband and wife were asked to check the type of organizations of which they were members and were regularly

[20] CR, .549 and .257, 4.02.
[21] CR, .196 and .460, 4.39. Also see Table III in Appendix A.

attending at the time of marriage. The extent of membership in organizations such as clubs, luncheon groups, fraternal orders, and labor or farmers' organizations may perhaps be taken as one indication of participation in social life outside the home and church. Accordingly the number of organizations of which the husband and wife were members or regular attendants was correlated with marital adjustment.

In our sample of 526 couples, fewer husbands (75) than wives (88) are not members or regular attendants of social organizations. On the other hand, more wives (208) than husbands (185) are affiliated with two or more organizations. Identification with one formal social group is most frequent both with husbands (210) and with wives (161).

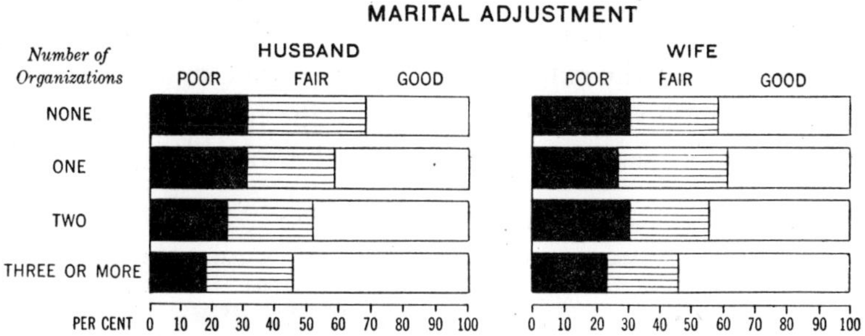

CHART 23.—MEMBERSHIP IN ORGANIZATIONS AND MARITAL ADJUSTMENT.

Chart 23 indicates that there is in the group studied a positive relation between the number of organizations to which one belongs and the chances for success in marriage. For the husbands the percentage with "good" adjustment appears to increase regularly from no membership (32.0 per cent) to membership in three or more organizations (54.3 per cent),[22] and correspondingly to decrease in the proportion of those "poorly" adjusted (from 30.7 per cent to 18.5 per cent[23]). In

[22] For husbands CR, .543 (three or more) and .320 (none), 2.89; and with .429 (one), 1.75. CR, .320 with .429 (one), 1.71; and with .471 (two), 2.08.
[23] For husbands CR, .185 (three or more) with .307 (none), 1.78; and with .300 (one), 2.15.

the case of the wives, there is slight difference in the percentage of those with "good" adjustment for no or one membership (42.0 per cent and 38.5 per cent) but a difference of probable statistical significance for membership in three or more organizations (54.7 per cent [24]).

This analysis indicates that membership in organizations is almost if not quite as satisfactory an indication of marital success as educational level and church and Sunday-school attendance.

Friendship

Educational attainment, church activity, and membership in organizations are formal expressions of social participation. In order to secure data on the more intimate and informal aspects of sociability, husband and wife were asked to answer questions about the extent of friendship before marriage with persons of both sexes as well as to state the number of persons of the opposite sex with whom they had associated steadily.

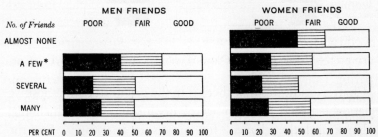

*Includes eight cases reporting "almost none." 242 husbands report "many" men friends and only 156 "many" women friends. See Table 77 in Appendix A.

CHART 24.—NUMBER OF HUSBAND'S FRIENDS AND MARITAL ADJUSTMENT.

In Chart 24 are presented the findings regarding the relation between men and women friends of the husband and success in marriage. These findings are in agreement with the com-

[24] For wives CR, .547 (three or more) with .420 (none), 1.73; and with .385 (one), 2.54.

mon-sense observation that husbands tend to have more men than women friends. The number of men friends shows an interesting relation to marital adjustment. A "few" friends seem to be unfavorable, but "several" and "many" close acquaintances favorable, to marital success.[25]

Likewise the number of women friends of the husband before marriage shows an interesting but not so clear-cut an association with marriage happiness. Judging from the figures, "almost no women friends" at the time of marriage is not associated with domestic felicity, for almost one-half (48.2 per cent) of the men with "almost no" women friends fall into the "poor" adjustment group, as compared with about one-fourth (28.4, 22.0, and 26.9 per cent) for each of the other friendship categories.[26] For the "good" adjustment class, "several women friends" appears to be the relation most favorable for marital adjustment, although this percentage is probably the only statistically significant difference from that for "almost no" friends.[27] It will be important to note whether or not a larger number of cases will definitely place "many women friends before marriage" as an unfavorable indicator.

Similar data for the wife regarding the number of men and women friends before marriage in relation to marital success are presented in Chart 25 and Table 78 in Appendix A. Comparing Tables 77 and 78, it will be noted that women tend more than men to report "many" friends with one's own and with the opposite sex, and correspondingly tend less to report "few" friends of both sexes.

If the wives are divided into two groups, those with "many" women friends before marriage and those with "almost none," a "few," and "several" combined, it is evident that the chances

---

[25] With men friends in the "poorly" adjusted groups CR, .400 (few) and .212 (several), 3.37; and with .269 (many), 2.47. Under the heading of "good" adjustment, CR, .308 (few) with .470 (several), 2.77; and with .483 (many), 3.32.

[26] CR, .482 (almost none) with .284 (a few), 2.57; with .220 (several), 3.43; and with .269 (many), 2.78.

[27] CR, .518 (several) with .333 (almost none), 2.41; with .419 (a few), 1.71; and with .423 (many), 1.64.

of the first group for matrimonial happiness would be better than the chances of the second group.

The husband with "several" women friends had the best, and with "almost none" the poorest, chances for a successful marriage. Does Chart 25 give similar figures for the wife in her

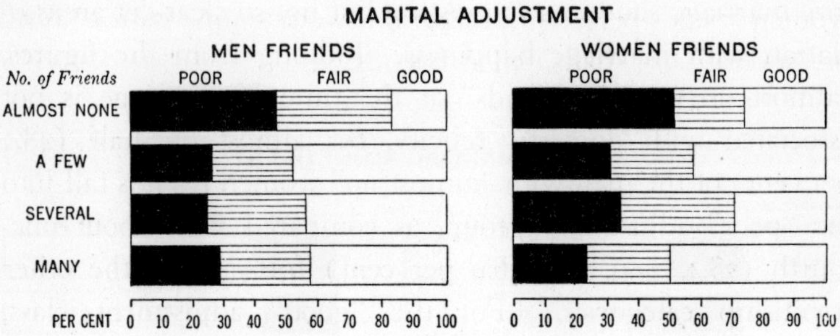

CHART 25.—NUMBER OF WIFE'S FRIENDS AND MARITAL ADJUSTMENT.

relation with men friends? The first clear conclusion is that the wife with "almost no" male friends before marriage is the poorest matrimonial risk.[28] But the other groupings with a "few," "several," and "many" are all equally favorable for marital adjustment.

The number of women friends of the wife before marriage does not show the same definite relation to marriage adjustment as was found for the number of men friends of the husband. "Almost no" friends of one's own sex appears to be unfavorable, but the number of cases to judge from is small. A "few" women friends shows the average expectancy for marital adjustment. Consequently the only comparison remaining is between the bride with "several" or "many" women friends,[29] and here there is a statistically significant difference

---

[28] With men friends under the head of "poor" adjustment CR, .450 (almost none) with .260 (few), 2.18; with .248 (several), 2.36; and with .282 (many), 1.95; under "good" adjustment, CR, .175 (almost none) with .481 (few), 4.14; with .456 (several), 3.94; and with .437 (many), 3.68.

[29] Under "poor" adjustment CR, .347 (several) and .237 (many), 2.24; under "good" adjustment CR, .290 (several) and .498 (many), 4.20.

indicating that "many" women friends before marriage is favorable and "several" unfavorable to the wife's marital adjustment.

In summary, we have the picture of the man or woman more likely to succeed in marriage as one who possesses "many" friends among one's own sex; if a man, one with "several" women friends before marriage; if a woman, one with a "few" or "several" or "many" men friends.

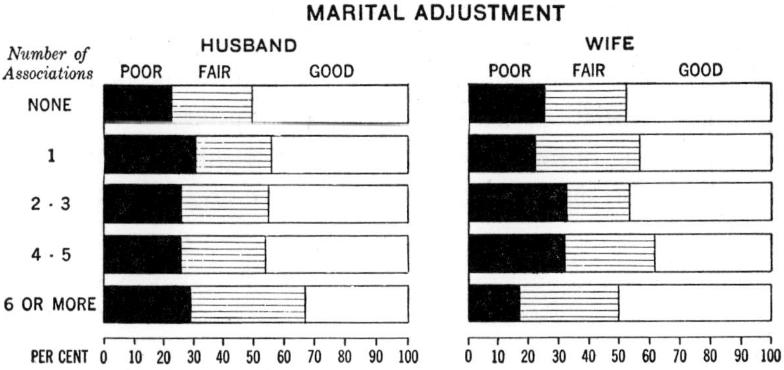

MARITAL ADJUSTMENT

CHART 26.—NUMBER OF INTIMATE ASSOCIATIONS WITH OTHER SEX BEFORE MARRIAGE AND MARITAL ADJUSTMENT.

Close companionship before marriage with a person of the opposite sex is to be differentiated from friendship. "Keeping company" implies a relation of intimacy and close association, generally over a period of months and years. What, then, is the most favorable experience for marital adjustment: that the person shall have kept company with (1) only his spouse; or, if not, with (2) what other number of persons? The data in Table 79 in Appendix A answer a question regarding the number of persons besides each other with whom the bridegroom and the bride had "gone steadily."

The husbands and wives in our study apparently fall in about the same proportion into each subgroup of "no," one, two or three, four or five, six or more persons, with whom they "had gone steadily" before marriage. The largest subgroup is that of 139 husbands and 149 wives who had two or three close friendships with the opposite sex before the one resulting in marriage. The second largest subgroup is that of 128 husbands and 112 wives who had had no love affair previous to the one which ended in marriage. The subgroups of either "one" or "four or five" persons for steady company have almost the same numbers: 80 and 80 for husbands, and 84 and 85 for wives. Finally there is the subgroup of six or more cases of intimate association with the other sex.

A careful examinaton of Chart 26 reveals no consistent pattern in the relation to marital adjustment of the number of intimate associations with the opposite sex prior to the association resulting in marriage. The differences in percentages are small, and in only one case are they perhaps statistically significant.[30]

Previous Marital Status

The overwhelming majority (484 and 481, respectively, out of 526) of the husbands and wives definitely stated that they had not previously been married. Only 19 men and 15 women were reported as divorced, and 8 men and 10 women as having lost their spouse. These latter numbers are too low to warrant credence in the stability of our figures, which indicate that a lower-than-average proportion of divorced and widowed fall into the class with "good" adjustment scores for marriage adjustment.

The Character of the Neighborhood

Neighborhoods within the city become more and more differentiated from each other in the process of urban growth. The greater the degree of differentiation, the greater is the homo-

---

[30] This is in "poor" adjustment for wives where CR .322 (two or three) and .175 (six or more), 2.06.

geneity of the neighborhood and of the economic and cultural characteristics of its inhabitants. Accordingly, the kind of neighborhood in which people live may be taken as at least a crude index of their social type.

The classification of neighborhoods made for the purpose of this study is admittedly crude. It was based upon readily observable characteristics of their residential structure and upon evidence of occupation by immigrants or by native-born persons. It proved satisfactory enough, however, to indicate something of the relation of the character of the neighborhood in which the husband and wife lived at the time of marriage to their later marital adjustment.

At the time of their marriage the husbands and the wives of this study resided in many different kinds of neighborhoods within and outside of Chicago. For example, the 474 husbands who gave pertinent information upon place of residence were distributed by type of neighborhood as follows: 58 in single-home residential districts, 16 in areas of first immigrant settlement, 56 in areas of second immigrant settlement, 114 in apartment-house districts, 22 in rooming-house regions, 50 in Chicago suburbs, 99 in cities other than Chicago, 52 in small towns outside of the Chicago metropolitan district, and 7 in rural neighborhoods. The 480 wives answering this question gave their residence at time of marriage as follows: 49 in single-home neighborhoods, 16 in areas of first immigrant settlement, 50 in areas of second immigrant settlement, 104 in apartment-house districts, 22 in rooming-house regions, 52 in Chicago suburbs, 121 in cities other than Chicago, 63 in small towns outside of the Chicago metropolitan district and 3 in rural neighborhoods.

The number of cases is too small in the majority of these nine different types of residential neighborhoods to warrant too great reliance upon the differences apparent by an inspection of Table 94 in Appendix A.[31] It is clear, however, that the hus-

---

[31] "Small towns" and "cities" outside the Chicago metropolitan region, although not properly "neighborhoods," are so classed for purposes of comparison.

band's residence at the time of marriage is more important than
that of the wife for adjustment in marriage.   For example, the
proportions of husbands with "poor" adjustment have a range of
10.0 per cent (living in a Chicago suburb) to 40.9 per cent (residence in rooming-house region), while the percentages of
"poorly" adjusted wives vary from 21.1 per cent (living in a
Chicago suburb) to 36.4 per cent (residence in a rooming-house
district).   In the cases of those with "good" adjustment, much
the same differences are found: for husbands a range of from
58.0 per cent (living in Chicago suburb) to 31.8 per cent (residing in a rooming-house district); and for wives a variation of
from 55.6 per cent (living in a small town outside the metropolitan region) to 35.6 per cent (residing in an apartment-house
district).

The comparison of these different types of neighborhoods indicates, with greater statistical significance for husbands than
for wives, that residence before marriage in a Chicago suburb
is favorable to marital success as compared with living in an
apartment-house or rooming-house area.[32]   Residing in a small
town outside the metropolitan area also appears to be associated
with "good" adjustment in marriage.[33]

When we summarize the findings of this chapter, it appears
that the social type which readily adjusts in marriage is the
socialized person.   Indexes of socialization evident in the data
of the study are maturity, educational opportunity and achievement, participation in religious activities (such as attending

---

[32] For husbands with "good" adjustment, CR, .580 (living in Chicago suburb)
with .318 (residing in rooming-house region), 2.2; and with .368 (residence in
apartment-house district), 2.6.   For "poorly" adjusted husbands, CR, .100 (living
in Chicago suburb) with .409 (residing in rooming-house region), 2.7; and with .378
(residence in apartment-house district), 4.4.

For wives with "good" adjustment, CR, .481 (living in Chicago suburb) and .356
(residing in apartment-house district), 1.5.   For "poorly" adjusted wives, CR, .211
(living in Chicago suburb) and .356 (residing in apartment-house district), 2.0.

[33] For husbands with "good" adjustment, CR, .500 (living in small town outside
metropolitan region) and .368 (residing in apartment-house district), 1.6.   For
"poorly" adjusted husbands, CR, .173 (living in small town) with .378 (residing in
apartment-house district), 3.0.   For wives with "good" adjustment, CR, .556 (living in small town) with .356 (residing in apartment-house district), 2.5.

Sunday school and church), participation in social life as manifested by number of friends, membership in organizations, and residence in neighborhoods of the single-family dwelling type. This socialized person is, perhaps, characterized by traits of stability, conventionality, and conformity. He has been molded by and has participated in our social institutions. He is, therefore, well fitted by training and experience to make the adjustments required in marriage.

CHAPTER IX

The Economic Role

THE ECONOMIC role, one of the many played by a person in the human drama, is so obvious and necessary in his life that it is often treated apart from his other roles as if these others were unimportant or subsidiary functions of the personality. It is in the study of the interaction of these different roles that an understanding of personality is to be achieved. The economic behavior of the individual needs always to be viewed in its social setting. The fallacy of the "economic man" of the classical economists lay in the narrowness of the abstraction and in its divorce from the other aspects of the personality.

The two economic factors considered in this study, occupation and income, are significant for marriage adjustment in their relation to the person's conception of his career, his standard of living, and the mobility inherent in his occupation.

Occupation and the Person

Occupation is both an expression of personality and an influence which enters into its making. Common-sense observation as well as systematic studies [1] show not only that physique, temperament, interest, and aptitude are involved in occupational selection, but that, once selected, the trade or the profession regulates conduct. Division of labor rests upon and promotes economic, personal, and cultural differentiation.

---

[1] W. V. D. Bingham, *Aptitudes and Aptitude Testing,* New York, Harper and Brothers, 1937; Douglas Fryer, *The Measurement of Interests in Relation to Human Adjustment,* New York, Henry Holt and Co., 1931; E. K. Strong, *Change of Interest with Age,* Stanford University, Stanford University Press, 1931.

The favorable or unfavorable influence of an occupation on
marital adjustment seems to depend on the occupation's status
as regards social control and on its mobility.

The two hypotheses to be tested by our data upon occupation
are

1. The greater the control exercised by society over the
conduct of the person in a given occupation, the higher is the
association of that occupation with good adjustment in marriage.

2. The greater the personal mobility required by the occupation, the lower is the association of that occupation with good
adjustment in marriage.

In the modern world, occupational differentiation has become too complex for 500 cases to offer an adequate representation of the multitude of different kinds of employment.   The
United States Census in 1930 used a classification of 534 occupations.   It is not surprising, then, that our attempt to group
cases by trades, businesses, and professions was none too satisfactory, as is indicated by the following classification of the
occupations at marriage of husbands in our sample of 526 cases:

No occupation	8
Unskilled industrial	12
Clerical or semiskilled	49
Farming	13
Small trades and skilled	122
Sales and semiprofessional	119
Teaching	46
Ministry	10
Medicine, law, and other professional	71
Large business, manager, entrepreneur	30
Other	22
No reply	24
Total	526

Only three specific occupations are listed here: farming,
teaching, and the ministry.   And only for the teacher does the

size of the group approach a number which warrants a special classification. In Chart 27 are presented only those occupations and occupational groups represented by 30 or more cases.

The pattern of distribution of the cases seems to indicate an increasing proportion of husbands with "good" adjustment as we move from those engaged in clerical, small trades, and skilled work to those in the professions and large business. Conversely, the percentages with "poor" adjustment are smaller

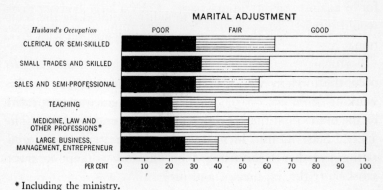

* Including the ministry.

CHART 27.—OCCUPATION OF HUSBAND AT MARRIAGE AND
MARITAL ADJUSTMENT.

in the latter groups and larger in the former. The teaching profession shows the highest proportion of husbands in the class with "good" adjustment (60.9 per cent compared with the average of 43.2 per cent) and the lowest proportion in the class with "poor" adjustment (21.8 per cent in contrast with the average of 28.5 per cent for all occupations).

The number of cases in all but two of the occupational groups is too low for indicating significant differences. The differences, however, between husbands in teaching and in small trades and skilled work is 22.4 per cent, which is 2.64 times its standard error. Since this difference could only occur once out of 240 times by chance alone, it may be regarded as highly significant.

The data in this chart indicate the probability of a high relationship between occupation and adjustment in marriage. But many times this number of cases and much greater specificity in the enumeration of occupations are necessary for an adequate analysis of the effect of the occupation of the husband upon the success of his marriage. For example, the group of salesmen comprises several distinct occupations—those of traveling salesmen, retail-store salesmen, automobile salesmen, life-insurance salesmen—each of which has its characteristic traits that make for or against stability in marriage. Only a large body of cases would provide data adequate for a discriminating differentiation.

Fortunately data on the relation of happiness in marriage to occupation are available in Lang's study[2] for 17,533 couples working in 60 occupations.[3] These marriages were not rated by the married partners themselves but by friends and acquaintances. Such ratings, however, have a correlation of .9 with ratings by either the husband or the wife and are therefore quite satisfactory for our present purpose.

Of the 17,533 cases in which the husband was in one of the 60 occupational groups, 10,798 (61.6 per cent) were rated as "very happy" and "happy"; 3,322 (18.9 per cent) as "average"; and 3,413 (19.5 per cent) as "unhappy" and "very unhappy," or separated or divorced. The distribution by occupation of these cases into the above categories of marital happiness is given in Chart 28.

The first impression gained from an examination of this chart is that of wide divergence in happiness ratings between certain occupations. For example, only 34.9 per cent of laborers fall into the group of married couples rated as happy and very happy, as compared with 82.7 per cent of chemical

---

[2] *The Rating of Happiness in Marriage,* unpublished M. A. thesis, University of Chicago, 1932, pp. 53–59.

[3] An additional number of couples, 4,653, were not used because they were too widely scattered in various other occupational groups with very small numbers in each group.

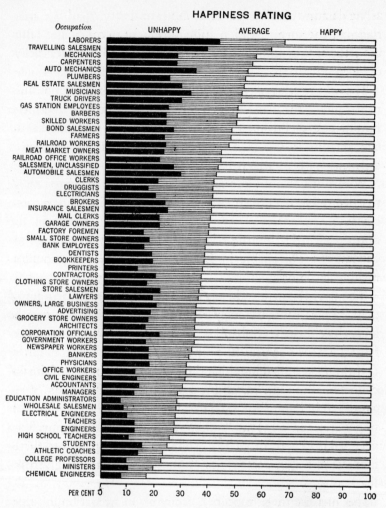

CHART 28.—OCCUPATIONS OF 17,533 HUSBANDS AND HAPPINESS
RATINGS BY FRIENDS AND ACQUAINTANCES.

engineers. Then, too, 40.5 per cent of the former, but only
7.5 per cent of the latter, have marriages either characterized as
unhappy or very unhappy or broken by separation or divorce.
Another striking comparison is that between ministers and
traveling salesmen: 79.5 per cent of the clergy but only 39.9
per cent of the gentlemen of the road have marriages classified

as very happy and happy, and only 11.2 per cent of the marriages of the former and as high as 35.9 per cent of the latter are rated as very unhappy and unhappy or end in separation or divorce.

The occupations at the extreme ends of the table are certainly in striking contrast with each other. On the other hand, the middle half of the classes fall in the range of 56.9 per cent to 67.8 per cent in the group of very happy and happy unions, a difference of only 10.9 per cent.[4]

Within the two middle sections the occupations do not show marked differences from each other. It will therefore be more significant to make a comparison of the occupations in the upper and lower quartiles in order to test our hypotheses regarding the relation of social control and mobility to adjustment in marriage.

The occupations in the upper quartile arranged in order of their ratings as "very happy" and "happy," from highest to lowest per cent, are: chemical engineer, minister, college professor, athletic coach, student, high-school teacher, engineer (type not specified), teacher (type not specified), electrical engineer, wholesale salesman, educational administrator, manager, accountant, civil engineer, and office worker. In this upper quartile are found, in fact, the six occupations with a very high degree of public control over personal conduct— namely, minister, college professor, athletic coach, high-school teacher, and educational administrator. Moreover, in the upper quartile there appears no occupation with a high degree of mobility. These facts are in correspondence with the theory of the direct relation of social control and the inverse relation of mobility of occupation to marital happiness.

In the lower quartile are found the following occupations, listed in order of lowest to highest percentages in the ratings for "very happy" and "happy" marriages: laborer, traveling

---

[4] The three quartile points in this distribution are: upper quartile, 67.83 per cent; median, 62.46 per cent; lower quartile, 56.92 per cent.

salesman, mechanic, carpenter, automobile mechanic, plumber, real-estate salesman, musician, truck driver, gas-station employee, barber, skilled worker, bond salesman, farmer, railroad worker, meat-market owner, and railroad-office worker. The two occupations lowest in the rating for happiness—unskilled laborer and traveling salesman—have, perhaps, the maximum degree both of mobility and of the absence of control by the community over the private conduct of its members. In none of the occupations in the lowest quartile does the public exert any special control over the conduct of its members, and many such members are exceptionally free from community surveillance. Nearly every one of these occupations has associated with it, in one form or another, a high degree of mobility. The outstanding exceptions, and both are near the upper ratings for happiness in this quartile, are the occupations of farmer and meat-market owner. Representatives of the latter occupation are relatively few in number; hence their presence in the lower quartile may be due to chance. The happiness ratings for farmers, however, are based on a relatively large group of farmers—1,230.

Why should a presumably stable group such as farmers rate so low in the scale for marital happiness? Possibly the answer is that no distinction was made in the classification of occupations between farm owners with a low degree of mobility and tenants with a high degree of mobility of residence.

The theory, then, that social control exerts a favorable, and mobility an unfavorable, effect upon marital happiness seems borne out by these findings. A closer study of the table, however, indicates that factors other than these two must be taken into account in comparisons of marital adjustments according to occupation.

To what extent are ratings of marital happiness correlated with economic and educational status? How is the happiness rating of certain particular occupations to be explained: for instance, all groups of engineers in the upper quartile; musicians, the only profession in the lowest quartile; the presence of different groups of salesmen in all four quartiles—variations that seem to defy explanation in terms of mobility, social control, and economic and educational status?

These questions are easier to raise than to answer. Certain comments, however, are in order.

Economic status and security. The low-income occupations are definitely concentrated in the lowest quartile of the marital-happiness ratings. The highest-income occupations, however, such as owner of large business, corporation official, and banker are not in the highest quartile but in the upper middle quartile. The more remunerative professions such as medicine, law, and dentistry are also in the upper middle quartile while the less remunerative professions, such as engineering, teaching, and the ministry, are in the highest quartile. The tentative conclusion, then, is that while there appears to be a relation between economic status and marital happiness, it is probably not so direct and so decisive as a low degree of mobility and a high degree of community control over the occupation. In fact, there is some evidence in the distribution to indicate that it is not the amount of income but its degree of certainty which is related to marital happiness. In the lower middle quartile, for example, are found brokers and garage owners with relatively high incomes. Most of the occupations in the highest quartile for marital happiness are the small-salary incomes which give more security than the larger incomes derived from ownership of a business or from fees for services—incomes from occupations that fall in the two middle quartiles.

Educational status. As with economic status, there appears to be a rough correspondence between the degree of formal education and ratings of marital happiness. But there are striking exceptions. Physicians and lawyers have probably received on the average as much education as engineers, teachers, and ministers, but they rate a quartile below them in marital happiness. The relation of educational status to marital happiness appears to be less direct and decisive than that of the degree of community control and of the absence of mobility.

Personality types and occupational selection. The low rating of the musician and the high standing of the engineer on the marital-happiness scale call for explanations other than those in terms of social control, absence of mobility, economic status, economic security, or education. Another hypothesis could be formulated in terms of occupational selection as related to personality types. According to this theory the musician would be representative of the "temperamental," artistic type, a type that has difficulty in marital adjustment, whereas the engineer would be representative of the objective, practical, stable type of personality, one more certain of marital happiness.

That the engineer, whether because of his personality or of his occupation or both, is a preferred matrimonial risk there seems little or no doubt. The difference in percentages in "very happy" and "happy" ratings of all engineers and all physicians [5] is quite significant, and when lawyers [6] are substituted for physicians, the difference is even more pronounced in favor of the engineer.

Significant for further study are the selection of occupation according to personality traits and interests, and the relation of the control of the person by his occupation to social and marital adjustment.

Detailed occupational analysis. One of the most interesting disclosures of the table of ratings of marital happiness by occupations is the divergence of the different groups of salesmen. For convenience in reference these data are given in Table 41. The differences in "very happy and happy" ratings range from 39.9 per cent for traveling salesmen to 71.4 per cent for wholesale salesmen. This range is almost as great as the range for all occupations: 34.9 per cent for unskilled laborers to 82.7 per cent for chemical engineers. Within these two extremes are

---

[5] CR, .742 (engineers) and .672 (physicians), 2.8.
[6] CR, .742 (engineers) and .641 (lawyers), 4.1.

TABLE 41

DIFFERENT GROUPS OF SALESMEN AND MARITAL ADJUSTMENT

Subgroup of Salesmen	Marital-Happiness Rating			No. of Cases
	Unhappy and Very Un-happy, Sep-arated or Divorced (per cent)	Average (per cent)	Very Happy and Happy (per cent)	
Wholesale	8.1	20.5	71.4	161
Retail store	21.3	15.3	63.4	483
Insurance	23.4	16.0	60.6	655
Automobile	29.0	13.0	58.0	200
Unclassified*	26.6	16.3	57.1	857
Bond	27.3	19.4	53.3	139
Real estate	27.7	22.7	49.6	141
Traveling	35.8	24.3	39.9	198
All cases	24.8	17.1	58.1	2,834

* The unclassified group of salesmen is made up of those who were reported, without specific designation, as "salesmen." When the classified groupings of salesmen are combined into one group, the ratings are "very happy and happy," 58.5 per cent; "average," 17.4 per cent; and "unhappy, very unhappy, divorced, and separated," 24.1 per cent.

store salesmen, with 63.4 per cent; insurance salesmen, 60.6 per cent; automobile salesmen, 58.0 per cent; bond salesmen, 53.3 per cent; and real-estate salesmen, 49.6 per cent.

The differences between the percentages of "very happy" and "happy" for the successive subgroups of salesmen are not significant, except probably for those between wholesale and store salesmen [7] and between real-estate and traveling salesmen.[8]   On the other hand, each of the three upper groupings of wholesale, store, and insurance salesmen is significantly different in percentage from each of the two lower groupings of real-estate and traveling salesmen.   This fact gives us a continuum of significant variations in the high ratings of marital happiness

[7] CR, .714 and .634, 1.91.
[8] CR, .496 and .399, 1.78.

from wholesale salesmen through retail-store and real-estate salesmen to the traveling type.

Salesmanship is the common characteristic involved in all these groupings. The chief oustanding difference affecting marital adjustment appears to be that of the greater mobility of the real-estate than of the wholesale or the store salesman, and the much greater mobility of the traveling salesman. In the case of the traveling salesman, his going "on the road" may be, in some cases, the result as well as a cause of marital unhappiness.

There can be little or no doubt that the occupation of the husband is correlated with marital adjustment. The explanation of this relationship is, however, wide open for further study. Present evidence points to the influence of mobility of occupation as an adverse factor and to the control of the community over the conduct of its members as a favorable factor for happiness in marriage.

It is apparent, however, that other factors must be carefully analyzed; for example, the income level and the education required by the occupation. Finally there are the tantalizing but intriguing questions of personality traits and occupational selection, and the effect of occupation upon the personality in relation to marital adjustment. The cutting of the Gordian knot of circular causation offers the best promise for an understanding of the interaction of personal and economic factors.

The Wife's Occupation

In regard to the relation of the occupation of the wife to marital adjustment we are limited to the findings upon our 526 cases, presented in Chart 29. Several important facts will be noted from this chart and Table 82 in Appendix A.

First, a high proportion of wives in this group had been gainfully employed before marriage. Of the 526 wives, only 76 stated that they had not been gainfully employed before mar-

riage; and 41 gave no reply to the question.   Second, teachers
have a better prospect of marital success and a lower chance
of failure[9] than other women who were gainfully employed
before marriage.   Third, it seems that women who were employed in skilled office positions had a higher probability of
attaining success in marriage than those doing clerical or semiskilled work.   Fourth, women who had not worked before

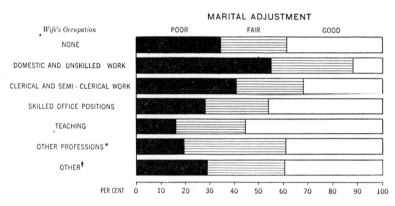

MARITAL ADJUSTMENT

*Including medicine, law, social work, and higher-paid positions in business and
nursing.
†Includes students.

CHART 29.—OCCUPATION OF WIFE AT MARRIAGE AND
MARITAL ADJUSTMENT.

marriage seem less likely to succeed in marriage than teachers
and (the cases being too small in number for certainty) perhaps
than women in skilled office positions.

The wife was asked to state her vocational ambition before
marriage.   This made it possible to learn whether or not the
last position she held before marriage was in harmony with her

---

[9] With "good" adjustment, the difference between the per cent of teachers (55.0)
and the per cent of other occupations is: *(a)* no occupation (38.2), 16.8 per cent
(CR, 2.36); *(b)* clerical and semiclerical work (30.6), 24.4 per cent (CR, 3.6); *(c)*
skilled office positions (45.7), 9.3 per cent (CR, 1.5).
   With "poor" adjustment, the difference between the per cent of teachers (16.3)
and the per cent of other occupations is: *(a)* no occupation (34.2), 17.9 per cent
(CR, 2.8); *(b)* clerical and semiclerical work (41.9), 25.6 per cent (CR, 3.6); and
(c) skilled office positions (28.3), 12.0 per cent (CR, 2.3).

stated vocational ambition. Where the harmony existed, the probabilities were higher for "good" adjustment in marriage. But if the wife had no vocational ambition, or if her occupation was greatly different from the one of her choice, then the chances for poor adjustment were increased.[10]

From the data it would seem that the occupation of the wife before marriage in the group included in this study [11] is indicative of personality traits which play as important a role in marital adjustment as do the factors associated with the occupation of the husband. It is therefore highly desirable that an adequate number of cases be secured for data on the employment of the wife previous to marriage. Those data might be analyzed to indicate which of the factors associated with employment, such as income, social status, personality traits, or social control, are significant for marital adjustment.

The status of a woman's occupation and the degree of social control exerted upon it by the public appear to be important for marital adjustment. The occupation of school teacher still retains its high status as the most appropriate and respected occupation for women. It is also the profession in which personal conduct is most strictly under social control. In the gainful employment of females mobility does not appear to be an important factor.[12]

Mobility and Stability

The length of time that the husband or wife had held his or her last position at the time of marriage may be an index

---

[10] See Table 113 in Appendix A.

[11] It should be emphasized that these findings are for a predominantly urban, white-collar, and professional middle-class group of native, white, American Protestant persons. Preliminary findings for 200 rural couples indicate that the premarital employed wife is not so well adjusted. See Edith Webb Williams, *Factors in Adjustment of Rural Marriage*, unpublished Ph.D. thesis, Cornell University, 1938.

[12] In the occupations listed in Chart 29, the one in which mobility enters most clearly, namely domestic and unskilled work, has too few cases to provide a satisfactory basis for comparison with the other occupations.

of one or two rather different personal characteristics. Long employment may be indicative of stability and reliability, and as such might be expected to show a positive relation to success in marriage. But it may also mean failure to advance because of lack of initiative, ambition, or ability which might, particularly in the case of the husband, reduce the probabilities of success in marriage.

The findings regarding the relation to marital success of the

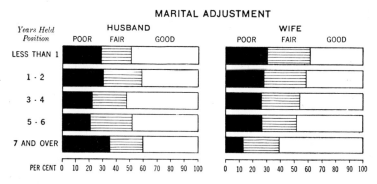

CHART 30.—LENGTH OF TIME POSITIONS HELD AND
MARITAL ADJUSTMENT.

length of time the husband and the wife had held his or her last position before marriage are presented in Chart 30. A study of this chart reveals certain points rather clearly.

First, the marital-adjustment score of the wife shows a regular pattern of progression, so that the number of years in the last occupation held varies inversely with "poor" adjustment [13] and also varies directly with "good" adjustment.[14] In other words, if the length of time a job has been held is indicative of the traits of stability and regularity, these traits seem to be associated with marriage adjustment.

Second, no such consistent pattern is to be seen in the case

---

[13] CR, .318 (less than one) and .135 (seven and over), 2.17.
[14] CR, .364 (less than one) and .596 (seven and over), 2.34.

of the husband. Less than one year [15] and three to four years
at the same job appear to be favorable to marriage adjustment,
while one to two years and especially seven years and over appear to be somewhat unfavorable.[16] Men who delay marriage
seven years and longer may be rather different personalities
from women who delay marriage. It may be that men who
wait until they are rather secure economically are either more
emotionally self-sufficient or more psychologically insecure than
women, whose delay may not be entirely from choice.

The explanation of this apparent lack of a regular relation
between period of employment and marital success may lie in
the antagonistic operation of two factors indicated by the number of years in the present job. These factors are stability
and progress, the former indicated by holding, the latter often
by changing, jobs. For changing jobs may signify either economic failure or success. In future research it will be desirable
to distinguish between change of employment due to incompetence or restlessness and that denoting advancement.

Work Record and Occupational Stability

More pertinent as an index of occupational and personal
stability than number of years in the last job should be the
regularity of employment before marriage. Was the husband
or wife regularly or irregularly employed? In our group 323
husbands were regularly employed, 82 were irregularly employed or continually changing positions, 87 had never worked
except during vacations, and 34 did not reply. Of the wives,
319 had been employed regularly, 76 had occasionally worked,
15 were housekeepers at home, and 19 had been engaged in
other nonremunerative activity; 75 had never worked, and 22

---

[15] Husbands who held a position less than one year before marriage are probably,
in the main, college or professional-school graduates with positions of sufficient income and stability to make early marriage feasible.

[16] CR, .509 (three to four) with .422 (one to two) is only 1.20; and with .406
(seven and over) only 1.47.

gave no reply.   The relation to marital success of these different kinds of work records previous to marriage is shown in Chart 31.

In the husband's work record the significant comparison in the percentages of "good" adjustment is in favor of those with regular rather than irregular employment: 47.4 per cent versus 31.7 per cent.   To the "poor" adjustment group 42.7 per cent are contributed by those with irregular, as against only 24.8 per cent [17] by those with regular, work records.   The significance

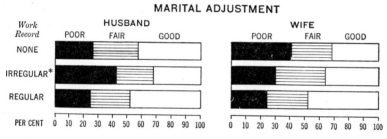

MARITAL ADJUSTMENT

* Includes cases of "continually changing" positions.

CHART 31.—WORK RECORD BEFORE MARRIAGE AND MARITAL ADJUSTMENT.

of both these differences is high (reaching practical certainty in the case of the second).

The significant difference in the work records of wives is between those who worked regularly as against those who did not work at all (47.3 per cent versus 30.7 [18] with "good" adjustment and, conversely, 24.4 per cent versus 41.3 per cent [19] with "poor" adjustment).   The differences between these percentages have a fairly high probability of being statistically significant.   Apparently regular work experience develops qualities making for success in marriage.   Or it may equally well be argued that the traits leading women into regular employment are the same traits making for marital adjustment.

[17] CR, 3.0.   CR, .474 and .317, 2.7.
[18] CR, 2.8.
[19] CR, 2.7.

In our group the women who have occasionally worked before marriage include a higher proportion with "good" adjustment and a lower percentage with "poor" adjustment than women without any work experience. On the other hand, those with occasional employment are found in smaller proportion than those with a regular work record in the class with "good" adjustment (36.8 per cent versus 47.3 per cent). It should be borne in mind, however, that the ratio of this difference to its standard error is 1.7, which would indicate chances of only 21.4 to 1 that a real difference exists.

Income and Economic Status

Almost all husbands and the great majority of wives in our study were gainfully employed at the time of marriage. A somewhat larger proportion of husbands was found in the higher-income groups. Of the 526 husbands, 129 reported that they were earning under $150 a month; 197, $150 to $249; 49, $250 to $349; and 55, $350 or more. No income was reported in 25 cases,[20] and 71 made no reply. The 526 wives indicated the following distribution of incomes: 112, under $100; 143, $100 to $149; 84, $150 to $199; 44, over $200; 67, no income; and 76, no reply.

The relation of income at time of marriage to subsequent adjustment is shown in Chart 32.

The husbands who at marriage had an income of between $150 and $249 a month constitute a smaller proportion of the "poorly" adjusted and a larger proportion of the class with "good" adjustment (21.3 per cent and 49.2 per cent[21]) than those with lesser incomes (monthly earnings under $150 a month, 34.1 per cent and 38.8 per cent) or those with greater incomes (monthly salary $250 or more, 36.5 per cent and 41.4

[20] Some of the no-income group are probably college students with allowances from parents.
[21] CR, .213 with .341, 2.5; and with .365, 2.7. CR, .492 and .388, 1.86.

per cent). There is a high probability that these differences are real differences. The small differences in percentages on the adjustment score between those with monthly incomes under $150 and over $250 are not significant.

With husbands, then, the tentative conclusion is that a moderate income at marriage is indicative of higher chances of marital success than either a low or a high income. Further research is needed to determine what is the character of the factor or factors actually in operation here. It is not the asso-

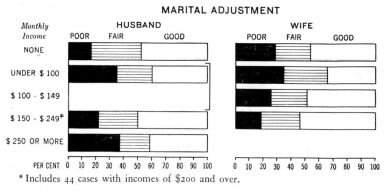

MARITAL ADJUSTMENT

* Includes 44 cases with incomes of $200 and over.

CHART 32.—INCOME AT MARRIAGE AND MARITAL ADJUSTMENT.

ciation of older age and higher income, for instance, because the proportion of successful marriages was found to increase with age at marriage.[22]

The data for the wives give a consistent picture of a positive relation between size of income at marriage and the probability of success in marriage. The group with the smallest income (under $100) has the higher percentage, and the group with the highest income ($150 and over) has the lowest percentage, in the class with "poor" adjustment (34.8 per cent versus 21.1 per cent).[23] Conversely, wives with meager wages have the smallest, and those with the higher salaries the greatest, proportion in the class with "good" adjustment (33.9 per cent

---

[22] Pp. 116–117.
[23] CR, 2.37

versus 50.8 per cent).[24]   It is highly probable that these differences are significant.   The group of wives with earnings at marriage of $100 to $149 [25] show percentages which are intermediate but closer to those with higher than with lower wages.

Apparently in the case of wives the traits which make for success in the business world as measured by monthly income are the traits that make for success in marriage.   The point, of course, may be made that income indirectly measures education, since the amount of educational training influences income. If this point should prove to be correct it would hold for the wife but not for the husband, where the highest income group has a lower-than-average expectation of marital success.

Economic Security

The correlation of moderate incomes with marriage adjustment suggests that security rather than the size of the income is perhaps the factor that is actually related to marital happiness. If this should be the case, savings at the time of marriage should represent both the value placed by the person upon security and its role in married life.

Savings. The capacity to save is different from earning ability. Furthermore, the savings of a single person, other things being equal, may represent serious preparation for marriage.

Of the 526 husbands, 136 stated that they had saved nothing before marriage; 140 reported savings of under $1,000; 63, $1,000 to $1,999; 28, $2,000 to $2,999; 51, $3,000 and over; and 108 gave no information.   To show the relation of savings to marital success, the last three groups are combined into one group with savings of $1,000 and over (see Chart 33).

In Chart 33 no significant difference in expectation of marital

---

[24] CR, 2.7.
[25] For those with "good" adjustment CR, .388 (with incomes under $100) and .492 (with incomes of $100 to $150), 1.9.

success appears between the groups with savings under $1,000 and with savings of $1,000 and more. The real differences appear to be between those with no savings and those with savings.[26] The data in this table indicate a high probability that savings are correlated with successful adjustment in marriage.

Of the 526 wives, 115 reported no savings before marriage; 107, savings of less than $500; 88, savings of $500 to $1,499; 17, $1,500 to $2,449; 18, $2,500 and over; and 181 gave no data. The number of wives reporting "no savings" is less than the

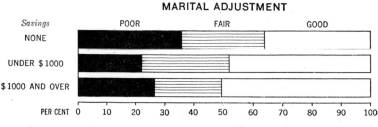

CHART 33.—SAVINGS OF HUSBAND AND MARITAL ADJUSTMENT.

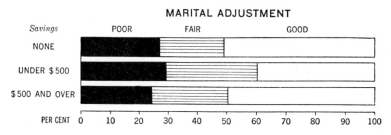

CHART 34.—SAVINGS OF WIFE AT MARRIAGE AND MARITAL ADJUSTMENT.

corresponding number of husbands; but this is far more than counterbalanced by the much larger number of wives than husbands who gave no reply.

The three groups with savings of $500 and over are combined into one group for purposes of tabulation to indicate the relation of savings to marital success (see Chart 34). For wives

---

[26] CR, .353 (no savings) and .229 (savings under $1,000), 2.3. CR, .360 (no savings) and .471 (savings under $1,000), 1.9.

there appears to be no clear association of savings with marital success. In fact the bride who reports no savings seems quite as likely to make a highly satisfactory marriage adjustment as the one who has saved $500 and over, and is likely to be better adjusted than the one who has managed to save less than $500. The favorable position of the wife who begins marriage with more rather than less than $500 to her account [27] may not be due to the amount saved but to the fact that greater savings may be due to employment in higher-paid occupations. With women the better-salaried positions seem, as we have noticed, to increase [28] probabilities of marital success.

The largest group of women represented in Chart 34 are those who did not make any answer to the question of savings before marriage. It is reasonably fair to assume that the great majority in this group had saved little or nothing and that the correct answer would have been "no savings." The lack of reply is probably quite significant [29] as contrasted with the reply "none." "No reply" may very well be an index of an attitude of unwillingness to report a fact which to the person is unpleasant.

Financial index. The sheer amount of savings is obviously not a satisfactory indication of economic security. The sense of security is relative to the given standard of living, which is largely dependent upon the income level. Evidently, then, an adequate measurement of security must take into account the relation of savings to income.

This point being kept in mind, a financial index was derived by taking the savings of the husband at marriage as the numerator and the product of his age at marriage times his salary per month at marriage as the denominator. The grouping of our couples on this scale is shown in Chart 35.

A study of this chart shows that the financial index of the

---

[27] CR, .392 and .488, 1.5.
[28] Pp. 153–154.
[29] For those with "good" adjustment CR, .376 (no reply) and .496 (none), 2.1.

husband at marriage in each of the three groupings above zero had a high positive correlation with a high marital-adjustment score. No valid discrimination, however, can be made on the basis of the present data between these three different groupings. If the findings regarding the financial index be compared with those regarding savings, there seems to be little or

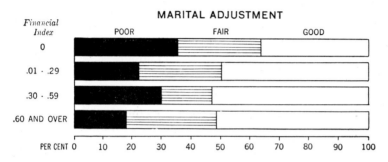

CHART 35.—HUSBAND'S FINANCIAL INDEX AT MARRIAGE AND
MARITAL ADJUSTMENT.

no additional value to be gained from the construction of the financial index.

It may very well be that, in the case of the unmarried man, economic security is not yet a value of sufficient importance so that the ratio of savings to income will be of any greater importance than the mere amount of savings. After marriage economic security does become a great value, and the financial index is highly discriminating.[30]

The findings regarding the relation of the economic role of the person to marital adjustment may be briefly summarized thus:

1. The occupation of the person rather than the amount of his income shows the highest degree of association with marital happiness.

2. An analysis of the differential association of various occupations with happiness in marriage seems to verify the hy-

---

[30] See Chapter XIII, "Contingency Factors," pp. 244–268.

pothesis that a high degree of mobility in an occupation is adverse, but that a high degree of community control over the private life of the members of an occupation is favorable, to marital happiness.[31]

3. Other factors associated with a given occupation which also appear to affect marital adjustment, but in lesser degree, are its income level, its educational status, and its relation both as cause and as effect to personality traits and types.

4. In regard to the gainful occupation of wives before marriage, mobility was not found to be an important factor. Work, however, as teacher and perhaps also in skilled office positions was found to be more highly associated with adjustment in marriage than the status of having no gainful occupation before marriage.

5. The occupational mobility of the person as measured by the number of positions held before marriage shows a consistent pattern adverse to marital adjustment in the case of the wife, but it shows no consistent pattern in the case of the husband. Future studies should differentiate between the change of jobs because of promotion and changes resulting from the incompetence or restlessness of the person.

6. As an index of stability, a regular work record of the husband correlates favorably with marital adjustment, as compared with irregular employment indicative of mobility. Regular work experience of the wife is related favorably, and no work experience is related unfavorably, to marriage adjustment.

7. The correlation of a moderate monthly income of the husband at marriage with marital happiness suggests that security and stability rather than the income level itself are important for successful marriages. This evidence seems to be borne out in the positive correlation found between adjustment in marriage and both savings and ratio of savings to earnings at time of marriage.

---

[31] Possibly the different occupations select different types of psychogenetic personalities which affect marital adjustment differentially.

CHAPTER X

Response Patterns: Romance and Companionship

"FALLING in love" in our society is both an intimate personal experience and the socially approved prelude to marriage. As a social pattern for youth, love tends to be defined in its romantic aspects. The attention of the public and of young people is focused upon romantic love as it is portrayed in literature, upon the stage, and by the moving picture.[1] The notions of romantic love, of one's affinity, of the ideal lover, and of passionate love overcoming all barriers of culture, class, and prudence, make a powerful appeal to the imagination of adolescents and youths and become the warp and woof of their daydreams and expectations.[2]

These glamorous conceptions of romantic love often remain dominant for years in the phantasy life and imagination of the person. There they live and grow, nourished by literature, drama, and art, but generally having little obvious part in the overt love life of the person. Sometimes, however, almost in the full measure of the romantic expectations, they find realization in courtship and marriage or, outside of marriage, in clandestine relations, in philandering, or perchance in a fruitless quest for "The Bluebird" of romance. Increasingly in America, and to some extent in other countries, the philosophy of romantic love is in itself a major factor in the dissolution of

---

[1] Herbert Blumer, *Movies and Conduct*, New York, the Macmillan Co., 1933.
[2] See Henry T. Finck, *Romantic Love and Personal Beauty*, New York, The Macmillan Co., 1887; and *Primitive Love and Love Stories*, New York, Scribner's 1899.

one marital relationship and the consummation of a new union.

Over against this romantic conception of love is the more prosaic notion of a love which gradually develops out of a companionship. "Friendship deepening into love" is the phrase of definition given by young people. Here the emphasis is not upon personal beauty, sex appeal, or other external characteristics, but upon congeniality, mutual interests, and comradeship.

This love "deeper than friendship" is not the same as conjugal affection which emerges after marriage from participation in the joint interests and enterprises of married life.[3] Love arising out of intimate companionship is peculiarly characteristic of America and results from the freedom accorded the sexes in social relations before marriage. This very freedom of social intercourse acts as a check upon romantic conceptions of love and marriage, and encourages instead mutual affection developing out of common interests and activities.

Few marriages, perhaps, can be classified as wholly romantic or as based entirely on companionship. The two aspects of the sentiment of love blend in every union of affection but in varying proportions. Romance and companionship are but two focal points for the organization of much the same emotions and sentiments. The sentiment of love has been analyzed into the components of sexual desire, personal beauty, rapport, admiration and respect, love of approbation, self-esteem, pleasure of possession, extended liberty of action, exaltation of the sympathies, and intellectual comradeship.[4] Of these, sexual desire, personal beauty, or self-esteem appear to be dominant in romantic love; while respect, exaltation of the sympathies, or intellectual comradeship are generally prominent in companionship relations.

In the perspective of this analysis of romantic love and of

---

[3] For a description of conjugal affection, see Henry T. Finck, *Primitive Love and Love Stories*, pp. 304–307.

[4] Herbert Spencer, *Principles of Psychology* (3rd edition), New York, D. Appleton-Century Co., 1892, pp. 487–488.

deep-seated affection, the following query can be put to the test of our data:

Is affection growing out of companionship a better guarantee of domestic happiness than romantic love?

The data that may be of assistance in answering this question are: difference between ages of bride and groom, duration of acquaintance, length of time of keeping company, period of engagement, and attitude of parents toward the marriage. These are all topics of interest in themselves; they may also have a bearing upon the relative adequacy of romantic love or companionship for marital success.

Difference Between Ages of the Married Couple

Age difference between husband and wife in its relation to happiness in marriage has always been a subject of popular discussion.   Where parents arrange marriages, either in the Orient or in Europe, the husband frequently, if not typically, is much older than the wife.   Parents in America often prefer for their daughter the older suitor as more stable and as a better provider than his younger rival.   Our marriage folkways, in line with the romantic concept, have favored marriages in which the bridegroom is older but not too much older than the bride. Our data on age, therefore, permit us to test the validity of the popular and romantic notion that the husband should be slightly older than the wife.

In 425 of our 526 cases, the ages of husband and wife are given.   The married pair are the same age in 46, or 10.8 per cent, of the 425 cases; the husband is older by one to three years in 168, or 39.5 per cent; four to seven years older in 110, or 25.9 per cent; eight years or more older in 45, or 10.6 per cent, of the marriages.   The wife is one or more years older than the husband in 56, or 13.2 per cent, of the cases.   In other words, the folkway of the husband's being older but not too much older than the wife is followed by 278, or 65.4 per cent, of our couples.

But what age difference between husband and wife tends to be associated with the more satisfactory marital adjustment? The findings upon this point, while not conclusive, may be of interest. The main conclusion to be drawn from Chart 36 is that age differences in the couples included in this study are not a major factor in marital adjustment, at least for the first six

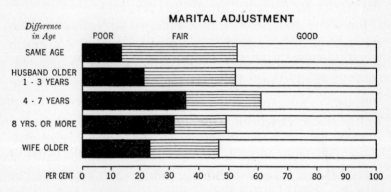

CHART 36.—DIFFERENCE IN AGES OF HUSBAND AND WIFE AND MARITAL ADJUSTMENT.

years of marriage. Other conclusions which may be tentatively stated after a study of this chart are as follows:

Contrary to the American folkway that the wife should be younger rather than older than her husband, the figures indicate that in a group of 56 marriages in which the wife is a year or more older than her mate, 53.6 per cent [5] have a "good" and only 23.2 per cent a "poor" adjustment.[6]

In contradiction to the prevalent opinion that the husband should not be many years older than the wife is the finding in a group of 45 cases, in which he is eight or more years older than his mate, that 51.1 per cent fall in the class with a "good"

---

[5] CR, .536 with .382 (where the husband is four to seven years older), 1.90. The differences between .536 and the percentages for the other age differences are not statistically significant.

[6] CR, .232 and .354 (where the husband is four to seven years older), 1.68. This and differences from the other percentages for age differences are not statistically significant.

adjustment. This difference, however, may be due to chance because of the small group of cases.

Where husband and wife are of the same age, or the husband is one to three years older than the wife, the percentage that falls into the group with "good" adjustments (47.8 per cent and 47.6 per cent, respectively) is not very much higher than the average for the entire group (43.2 per cent).

But where the husband is from four to seven years older than the wife, the percentage in the class with a "good" adjustment is only 38.2 per cent [7] and the proportion of "poorly adjusted" rises to 35.4 per cent. This latter percentage is statistically significant in comparison with similar percentages for two out of four of the other age-difference groups.[8]

These differences in adjustment for the various "age at marriage" combinations, while not very great, may be indicative of certain factors associated with age differences. It may well be that the *adjustment index* does represent fairly well the factor of congeniality and of common interests where both partners in marriage are of the same age or the husband is older than the wife by only one to three years.

In cases in which the wife is older than the husband, she may tend to take more of a maternal attitude toward her husband and he may be the more inclined to accept it. Where the husband is eight or more years older than the wife, he likewise may be more disposed to take the paternal role, and the wife may be disposed to accommodate herself to it. In short, these age differences may be associated with a tendency to superordination and subordination, whereas when husband and wife are of the same age or the husband is slightly older, the age similarity may be associated with a tendency to coördination of the partners in marriage.

But where the husband is four to seven years older, the ten-

---

[7] CR, .382 and .536 (where the wife is older than the husband), 1.90.

[8] CR, .354 with .131 (where couple are of the same age), 3.30; with .214 (husband one to three years older), 2.51; and with .232 (where wife is older), 1.68.

dencies to coördination on the one hand and to superordination on the other may be much more likely to be in conflict with each other. Possible evidence of this is the finding that, compared with the 35.4 per cent of the couples in this group, only 13.1 per cent of the couples of the same age and 21.4 per cent of those with husband from one to three years older fall into the class with "poor" adjustment.

When we summarize the findings regarding age differences, the popular romantic notion that, for marital happiness, the husband should be somewhat older than the wife, is not substantiated for the group studied.

Acquaintance, Courtship, and Engagement

The relations to marital compatibility of the length of the period of acquaintance, of keeping company, and of engagement are of interest to every engaged couple. Data upon love subjected to the test of time also permit certain inferences to be drawn with reference to the question of romance versus companionship as making for marital adjustment. The inferences are based on the assumption that marriages of romantic love in contrast to those of companionship take place upon short acquaintance, a whirlwind courtship, and a brief engagement period, and that accordingly, all other things being equal, the shorter time spans will be representative of marriages of romance and the longer time periods those of companionship.

The data on the relation of time of acquaintance before marriage to the marital-adjustment score are presented in Chart 37. Striking is the regular and consistent picture given by the figures. In "poor" adjustment the decline is regular according to time of acquaintance from the very high proportion (47.0 per cent) who had known each other under six months, to the low percentage who had been acquaintances for five years and more (14.7 per cent). In contrast is the steady rise in percentages of those with "good" adjustment from the low point of

the 22.4 per cent who knew each other less than six months
before marriage to the 53.3 per cent whose period of acquaintance was five years and more.

Not only does the table give this consistent picture of the
regularity of the direct positive relation of length of acquaintance with marital compatability, but further examination shows
the difference between the percentages to range with only two
exceptions from fair probability to certainty.[9]

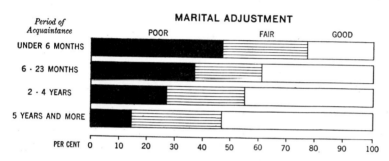

CHART 37.—DURATION OF ACQUAINTANCE BEFORE MARRIAGE AND
MARITAL ADJUSTMENT.

"Keeping company" implies closer association than acquaintance. It denotes a period of close association which may
or may not develop into engagement and marriage. "Keeping
company" is an old American custom which arose when it became usual for young people rather than their parents to arrange marriages. Courtship, in cases of nonromantic unions,
is the period during which it is determined whether or not
there exists sufficient mutuality of love, congeniality of inter-

---

[9] The two exceptions are: in the "poorly" adjusted group the difference between
.470 (under 6 months) and .377 (6 to 23 months) and in the group with "good"
adjustment the difference between .377 (6 to 23 months) and .438 (2 to 4 years).
For the "poorly" adjusted group CR, .470 (under 6 months) with .278 (2 to 4
years), 2.45; and with .147 (5 years and more), 4.20. CR, .377 (6 to 23 months)
with .278 (2 to 4 years), 1.82; and with .147 (5 years and more), 4.37; CR, .278 (2 to
4 years) with .147 (5 years and more), 3.04. In the group with "good" adjustment
CR, .224 (under 6 months) with .377 (6 to 23 months), 2.07; with .438 (2 to 4 years),
3.15; and with .533 (5 years and more), 4.01. CR, .377 (6 to 23 months) with .533
(5 years and more), 2.61; and with .438 (2 to 4 years) with .533 (5 years and more),
1.76.

ests, and companionship for the plighting of marriage vows.

Is a long or short period of intimate association related to successful marriage adjustment? The figures in Chart 38 indicate rather clearly that longer rather than shorter periods of keeping company are associated with successful adjustments in marriage. The figures plainly indicate: (1) that keeping company for less than one year is related to a high proportion of couples with "poor" adjustment and a lower-than-average

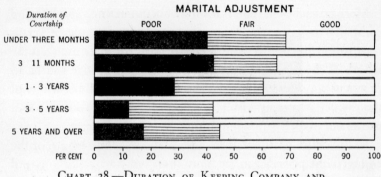

CHART 38.—DURATION OF KEEPING COMPANY AND
MARITAL ADJUSTMENT.

percentage with "good" adjustment; (2) that couples who have been going together from one to three years have average chances of matrimonial success; and (3) that the longer period of three years and over has the highest association with success in marriage. Couples who kept company less than 12 months show a significant statistical tendency toward the "poorly" adjusted class as compared with each of the three groups of those who had kept company longer.[10] The same is true of "going together" for a period of one to three years as compared with three years and more.[11]

In the proportion of those with "good" adjustment the sig-

---

[10] CR, .429 (three to eleven months) with .289 (one to three years), 2.42; with .126 (three to five years), 5.24; with .172 (5 years and over), 3.71.

[11] CR, .289 with .126 (three to five years), 4.48; and with .172 (five years and over), 1.99.

nificant difference is between keeping company under three years and keeping company three years and over. This may be seen in the percentages of 32.1, 33.3,[12] and 39.3 [13] for the first period and of 56.8 [12, 13] and 55.2 [12, 13] for the second period.

For the educated, lower middle-class group from which the cases in this study are drawn, it would seem that keeping company over a three-year period increases the chance of successful marriage. Perhaps the test of intimate association for three or more years weeds out many poor matrimonial risks.

More crucial even than duration of acquaintance and keeping company in its bearing upon the question of romance versus companionship as the more adequate basis for matrimony, is the length of the period of engagement. Romantic love spurns all practical considerations, even the test of time. But time is of the essence in a relationship of affection which is rooted in and grows out of association and intimacy.

In the entire group of 468 couples who gave the length of the engagement period, 249, or more than one-half, were engaged less than 9 months, and of this number 70 were engaged for less than 3 months. These two groups, engaged less than 3 months or from 3 to 8 months, are assumed to include more of the romantically inclined couples than those who delayed their marriages for 8 to 23 months and even for 24 months or more after engagement.

Most discriminating are the consistent and regular findings presented in Chart 39. As duration of engagement increases, the proportion of couples with "poor" adjustment steadily declines from 50.0 per cent [14] (under 3 months) to 33.0 per cent [15] (3 to 8 months) to 18 per cent [14, 15] (9 to 23 months), and to only 11.0 per cent [14, 15] (24 months and over). Corresponding to the lengthening of the engagement period, the percentage of

---

[12] CR, .333 (three to eleven months) with .568 (three to five years), 3.62; and with .552 (five years and over), 2.74.

[13] CR, .393 (one to three years) with .568 (three to five years) 3.00 and with .552 (five years and over), 2.15.

[14] CR, .500 with .330, 2.45; with .180, 4.65; and with .110, 5.71.

[15] CR, .330 with .500, 2.45; with .180, 3.07; and with .110, 4.57.

couples with "good" adjustment mounts from 25.7 per cent (under 3 months) to 40.2 per cent [16, 18] (3 to 8 months), to 46.1 per cent [16, 17, 18] (9 to 23 months), and finally to 62.6 per cent [17] (24 months and over).   It is apparent that duration of engagement is positively associated with probabilities of good adjustment in marriage.   There is probably a point at which increasing length of engagement may reduce the probabilities, but our data are not sufficient to discover this point.

To sum up the findings regarding length of acquaintance,

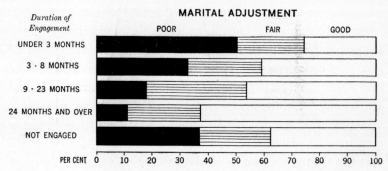

CHART 39.—DURATION OF ENGAGEMENT AND MARITAL ADJUSTMENT.

"keeping company," and engagement, it is evident that the longer the period of intimate association before marriage, the greater are the probabilities of harmonious marital adjustment. Companionship tested by time appears therefore to be a better basis for successful marriage than the emotional feeling of certainty inspired by short-lived romantic love.

Attitude of Parents Toward Marriages

American mores sanction the right of young people to control their own destiny in the selection of marriage partners. The request by the suitor addressed to the father for the hand

---

[16] CR, .257 with .402, 2.27; with .461, 2.99; and with .626, 5.07.
[17] CR, .626 with .257, 5.07; with .402, 3.58; and with .461, 2.45.
[18] CR, .402 with .461, not statistically significant.

of his daughter is now a formality, a vestigial survival of a custom which once placed absolute control of marriage in the hands of parents.

Although customs have changed, parental attitudes remain. The mothers and fathers of the engaged couple cannot but be interested in the marital future of their children, and they usually give expression to their approval or disapproval of the marriage. The young couple, in turn, are in most cases concerned with the reaction of their parents.

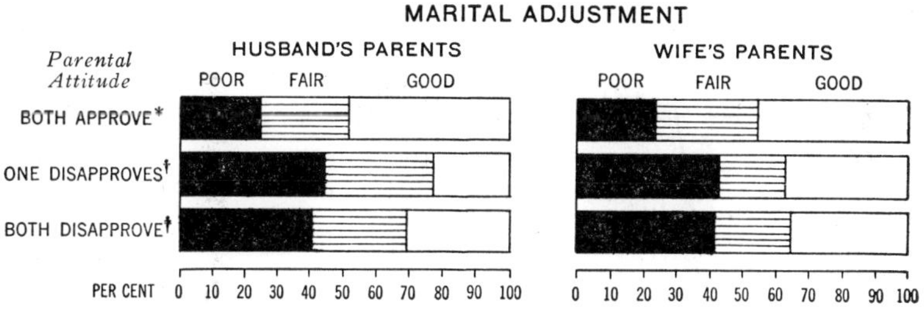

MARITAL ADJUSTMENT

CHART 40.—ATTITUDE OF PARENTS TOWARD THE MARRIAGE AND MARITAL ADJUSTMENT.

* Includes a few cases in which one parent approves and the other is dead or does not reply.
† Includes a few cases in which one parent may be dead.
‡ Includes a few cases in which there is no reply for one parent, although he or she is still living.

Parents in general, at present as in the past, are strongly inclined to place prudential considerations above those of romance. They are likely to emphasize qualities such as stability and earning capacity in the young man and domesticity and consideration for others in the girl. Accordingly, findings regarding parental approval or disapproval of a marriage have a bearing upon the question of whether romance or companionship is the more adequate basis for adjustment in marriage.

In 481 of the 526 marriages studied, a statement was made regarding the attitude of the parents toward the marriage of their children. It is interesting that the great majority of parents, four-fifths of the fathers and mothers of the prospective husbands and three-fourths of the fathers and mothers of the brides, are reported as having favored the marriage. It should be noted that disapproval by one or both parents is somewhat more frequent in the case of the bride's than of the groom's parents (one-fourth as compared with one-fifth). The chief question of interest, however, is the way in which parental approval or disapproval of the marriage is associated with marital success or failure.

Where both parents are reported to have been in favor of the marriage of their son or daughter, a percentage somewhat higher than the average for couples (48.7 per cent and 47.4 per cent, respectively) fall in the group with "good" adjustment. But where one or both parents are stated to be unfavorable to the marriage, a much lower proportion of couples is to be found in the "good" adjustment category and a much higher percentage in the group has "poor" adjustment. It is interesting and perhaps significant that when one or both of the husband's [19] parents disapprove, the probabilities for good adjustment in marriage are considerably lower than when one or both of the wife's [20] parents disapprove of the marriage. Should this finding stand the test of a larger number of cases, it may indicate that the husband's parents are more discerning as to the traits in the wife that will make for unhappiness in marriage than are the bride's parents of the corresponding characteristics of the husband, or that the success of the marriage is dependent to a greater extent on the goodwill of the husband's parents.

If, in general, parental approval tends to be bestowed on marriages because of prudential rather than romantic considerations,

---

[19] In the case of the husband's parents, for the "poorly" adjusted CR, .236 (where both approve) with .440 (one disapproves), 2.77; and with .408 (both disapprove), 2.34. For those with "good" adjustment CR, .487 (both approve) with .240 (one disapproves), 3.76; and with .306 (both disapprove), 2.56.

[20] In the case of the wife's parents, for the "poorly" adjusted CR, .231 (both approve) .435 (one disapproves), 3.06; and with .429 (both parents disapprove), 2.84. For those with "good" adjustment CR, .474 (both approve) with .355 (one disapproves), 1.80; and with .339 (both disapprove), 1.97.

the findings here again indicate that unions of romantic love have less chance than those of companionship for marital contentment.

All the available evidence—age difference between the bride and groom, duration of acquaintance, "keeping company," engagement, approval or disapproval of parents—is consistent in its indication that marriages based on companionship will, in general, result in more harmonious unions than those chiefly inspired by romantic attitudes.

Factors other than companionship affecting response relations in marriage, such as early affectional conditioning—particularly to parents—and experiences of a sexual nature in childhood and adolescence will be considered in the next two chapters.

CHAPTER XI

Personality Factors in Marriage Adjustment

THE PURPOSE of this chapter is to explore the way in
which personality factors affect marital adjustment.[1] The
items in our schedules measured the influence of personality
traits only indirectly. But case studies of 100 married couples
revealed the dynamic role of personality factors in marriage
adjustment. The hypothesis derived from an inductive study
of these cases is that marital compatibility is primarily influenced in each given case by the person's specific patterns of
affectional relations to parents and siblings, which are formed
in early childhood and tend to persist throughout life.

The results of studies of personality factors in marital adjustment which use standardized forms, inventories, and tests
of assumed personality "traits" are as yet quite inconclusive.

---

[1] The following are representative of a gradually increasing literature in which
personality factors in marriage are given specific research attention: Burgess, E. W.,
"The Family and the Person," *Publications of the American Sociological Society*, Vol.
22, December 1927, pp. 133–143; Cottrell, L. S., Jr., "Roles and Marital Adjustment," *Publications of the American Sociological Society*, Vol. 27, May 1933, pp.
107–115; Hamilton, G. V., *A Research in Marriage*, New York, Boni, 1929; Kelly,
E. L., unpublished materials on a research to cover seven years of observational contact with a sample of married couples; Krueger, E. T., "A Study of Marriage
Incompatibility," *The Family*, Vol. 9, 1928, pp. 53–60; Mowrer, E. R., *Family Disorganization*, Chicago, University of Chicago Press, 1927; Mowrer, Harriet R., *Personality Adjustment and Domestic Discord*, New York, American Book Co., 1935; Terman, L. M., and Buttenwieser, P., "Personality Factors in Marital Compatibility,"
Journal of Social Psychology, Vol. 6, May 1935, pp. 143–171, continued in August
1935, pp. 267–288; Terman, L. M., *Psychological Factors in Marital Happiness*, New
York, McGraw-Hill Book Co., 1938; Waller, Willard, *The Old Love and the New:
Divorce and Readjustment*, New York, Liveright, 1930; *The Family, a Dynamic Interpretation*, New York, 1938; Mudd, Emily H., "An Analysis of One Hundred Consecutive Cases in the Marriage Counsel of Philadelphia," *Mental Hygiene*, Vol. 21,
April 1937, pp. 198–217. Other important material is to be found in numerous
case materials from records of psychoanalytic and similar studies in which marriage
relations constitute a considerable part of the problem, and in reports from marriage-
counseling clinics.

These results tend to support the contention that personality factors studied apart from the dynamics of personality development will throw little light on the relation of personality to marital happiness. For example, Terman and his associates, using Strong's Interest blank and Bernreuter's Personality Inventory, find "a low or negligible correlation between the total scores and marital happiness" but "more than a quarter of the items taken singly appear to have an appreciable validity as indicators of marital compatibility." [2]

On the basis of their preliminary studies, Terman and his associates selected a total of 132 items from the Bernreuter Personality Inventory (67 items), the Strong Interest blank (50 items), and a set of opinions about marriage (15 items). These items were weighted according to the extent of their association with a marriage-adjustment index. The resulting personality scores (sum of the weights of the 132 items) for the husbands correlated .47 with their marriage-adjustment index. The corresponding correlation of wives' personality scores with their marriage-adjustment index was .46.[3]

An approximate description of the personality of the happily married person is given as a composite of the responses to the 132 selected items. In general, happy wives are found to be secure, outgoing, optimistic, coöperative, benevolent, and conservative. Unhappy wives are found to be insecure, hostile, individualistic, assertive, and radical. Happy husbands are found to be emotionally stable, coöperative, benevolent, outgoing, responsibility-assuming, and conservative. Unhappy husbands are described as neurotic, emotionally unstable, insecure, domineering, withdrawing, and radical.[4]

More research is needed to discover the extent to which the noted characteristics are antecedent to or follow upon good adjustment in marriage. One weakness in the Terman study

---

[2] Terman, L. M., and Buttenwieser, P., *op. cit.*, p. 288.
[3] L. M. Terman, *Psychological Factors in Marital Happiness;* see Chapters VI, VII, and XIII.
[4] See *ibid.*, Chapter VII, for a more complete description.

is that the results are based upon responses to the personality items by people who have been married from less than one year to over 27 years, with an average length of marriage of 11.4 years. It is necessary to get responses of this type before persons enter the marriage relation and to correlate the pre-marital responses with adjustment later achieved.[5]

Standardized devices for measuring personality traits have been worked out so recently that the value of the tests as a whole, and of their individual component items, for an under-standing of human behavior has not as yet been definitely deter-mined. Such basic questions as the extent to which different personality traits or patterns of behavior are organic, psycho-genetic, or culturally determined, fixed or relative to situations, stable or unstable, are problems for further study. At this stage of research development, probably the most important kind of investigation would therefore be intensive case studies of specific personality patterns and traits in specific marriage situations. In the present study an attempt has been made to secure and analyze from this standpoint a limited number of case histories of married couples.

In this chapter it is proposed to illustrate the nature of the case materials secured and how they were analyzed; and to in-dicate some of the general findings that the case studies yielded on personality factors in the marriage-adjustment process.

Assumptions and Procedures

The general procedure of collecting the case materials and the methods of analyzing them were based on the following assumptions: [6]

1. Married couples come to the marriage situation with

---

[5] Studies of this sort are being done by E. W. Burgess and Paul Wallin at Chicago and by E. Lowell Kelly at Storrs, Connecticut.

[6] These assumptions grew out of a considerable amount of analytical experience in dealing with family case materials and were then more systematically applied to the case studies of this research.

certain preëstablished reaction patterns and expectations regarding the marriage relationship and their own and their mates' roles in it. These reaction patterns and expectations are conceived to be complex integrations of wishes and attitudes appropriate to a given role in a given field of social interaction, such as the response relation.

2. These reaction patterns and expectations in the field of love and marriage are developed and made relatively permanent in the interaction of the child and adolescent with his early social environment, particularly his family milieu. For example, the activities, attitudes, and expectations which constitute the behavior complex which we call the son's pattern of relation to his mother may be assumed to have an important effect on the pattern of relation he will seek to establish with the woman he marries.

3. These patterns may be and frequently are partly or wholly unconscious in the person manifesting them. For example, a husband who complains that his wife is inconsiderate and selfish may mean that she does not act toward him in the indulgent, "mothering" way that he unconsciously desires. Or he may be sexually impotent, and explain it by saying that his wife is sexually repulsive to him, whereas he is unconsciously reacting to her as a symbol of a sexually tabooed mother.

4. The marriage reaction pattern may not correspond to the relationship in the family experience of the person, but may be antithetical. Thus a wife whose relation to her father has been bitter and resentful because the father preferred her sibling, may be supremely happy in a marriage with a man who is fatherly and indulgent. She has achieved a relation which she wanted but was denied in experience and which she built up in phantasy. Upon the arrival of a child that captures some of her husband's attention and affection, she may relapse into the resentful, hostile pattern of behavior that existed in the father-daughter relation.

5. Married couples do not have one pattern of relationship,

but usually manifest several that they have brought from their formative milieus. They have a repertoire of several roles which they may act out with one another in different situations or in composite forms in a single situation. It is well known to clinical workers, particularly those employing prolonged therapeutic interviewing, that a "transfer situation" develops between subject and interviewer which is not merely a relation in which the subject develops affectional and dependent attitudes toward the interviewer, but a relation in which the subject reënacts all his more important relational patterns. The interviewer will at various times be made the benevolent parent, the punishing parent, the hated rival sibling, and so on. The same kind of phenomena obtain in the marriage situation. There tend to be, however, one or two patterns of relationship which are most consistently maintained in the marriage. These may not appear to the observer as the most "pleasant" or "satisfactory" patterns, and yet they may be satisfying to certain components of one or both of the personalities involved.

6. More than one interpersonal pattern may be operating in a given concrete behavior sequence. For example, a husband who begins to drink excessively and gamble recklessly and show other irresponsible behavior, even though he is aware that it is endangering job, home, and social position, may be causing his wife and friends to show intense concern and to attempt all kinds of protective and punishing behavior. He may also be getting the satisfaction of revolting against and hurting the persons who attempt to be parental toward him. He is thus forcing his wife to play the role of the concerned parent and at the same time revolting against this parent.

7. The relational patterns of married persons may be classified as cultural and individual (or psychogenetic). Certain patterns of husband-wife behavior are defined in the folkways and mores of a given cultural group. In addition, the individual, owing to his own special family experience, brings certain more or less unique personal patterns to the marriage. Some-

times the cultural and the individual patterns are in harmony and are integrated in the role the person plays most consistently in his marriage. Sometimes they conflict, as in the case of the man who has an individual pattern of passive dependence on an aggressive female, but who is expected by his culture to play the role of the "head of the house," and this role he consciously attempts to play.

With these working assumptions, the procedure in the case studies was to get as full a picture as possible of the subject's important relational patterns in his family experience, and to see how far these patterns obtained in his marriage or had any relation to the patterns which did characterize his marriage. The analysis of the materials consisted chiefly in demonstrating the relation between the marriage roles and their interaction and the patterns which had developed in the earlier family life of the partners.

The case studies were made chiefly by interviews. Some of the persons were interviewed once; others as many as 20 to 30 times. All interviewing was done by the same interviewer. Some of the studies were made with both partners coöperating; others with only the husband or the wife. Some of the case materials are autobiographies, written by persons who used the interview and autobiographical outline as a guide.[7] Most of the subjects had some problem in their marriage, but several appeared to have no special problem and simply agreed to coöperate in being interviewed for scientific research purposes.[8]

Subjects were interviewed at the office of the interviewer or in their homes, and in both places. Husbands and wives were interviewed separately, although in some conferences they were seen together. The interview material was dictated from notes as soon as possible after each session with the person.

---

[7] See Appendix C.

[8] In nearly all the problem cases, some positive therapeutic results could be noted, although in some instances it was very slight. If the marriage was already broken, frequently the increased insight made for better personal adjustment, according to the statements of those who contributed any subsequent testimony.

With this introductory statement of assumptions and procedures, three case histories [9] are presented which illustrate concretely the hypothesis that the particular affectional relationships with parents and siblings affect adjustment in marriage.

The first case indicates how the relational patterns of both husband and wife as developed in their respective family associations predisposed both of them to be compatible with each other. The other two cases are significant examples of the continuance in marriage of the same personal-conflict patterns that had arisen in interaction with parents and siblings.

The material presented in these three cases indicates the correspondence [10] between the patterns of affectional relations of the person with parents and siblings and those with husband or wife. Upon this point they are typical of the 100 case studies made. If we generalize from this group of cases, it appears certain that personality factors as evidenced in and conditioned by relationships to father and mother, brother and sister, play a dynamic role in marital adjustment.

Case I.—An Adjusted Couple: James and Mary O.

Mr. and Mrs. O. (married four years) coöperated in this study by filling out a schedule, and they volunteered for a few periods of interviewing. They claimed to have no adjustment problems but were interested in knowing how their marriage adjustment compared with that of other couples studied. They rated their marriage as very happy and regarded it as permanent. They scored high on the adjustment questions, falling into the top quartile of the sample of 526 cases. The premarital score was also high. The family background and

---

[9] The cases which follow present only an abstracted picture which brings out the relational patterns and their operation in the marriage. It must be kept in mind, therefore, that there are other factors operative in these cases which are not brought out here. Moreover, anyone working with a different set of social-psychological assumptions would probably derive somewhat different results.

[10] This correspondence is generally positive; under certain conditions it may be negative, as pointed out earlier (see p. 175).

the economic, educational, social, and other items of this case
are given in Chapter XV, where the schedule items furnished
by this couple are discussed. It is sufficient here to note that
their backgrounds were very similar; the vocational and financial items were favorable; both were college graduates with
some additional training; both were participants in several
organized groups; they had several well-developed interests
in common; they have no children, though both claim to want
children and expect to have them. So, through the schedule,
most of the items showed favorable probabilities for their successful adjustment.

The primary aim here is to analyze the personality patterns
of Mr. and Mrs. O. to see how far these patterns make for
good and poor adjustment in their marriage.

In neither the interviews with the husband nor those with
the wife was there any hint of serious dissatisfaction or doubt
about the marriage. So far as the interviewer could discover,
there was no attempt to conceal possible negative factors. Elements of resentment and hostility were admitted, but the attitude seemed to be that no relation is free from occasional
transient irritations and frustrations. It so happened that
interview studies were made of two other couples who knew
the O.'s quite well. In both cases the couples gave unsolicited
comments about what they regarded as the exceptional harmony of the O. marriage. So far as can be judged from schedule, interview, and outside-observer evidence, this is a well-
adjusted marriage. The following material is an attempt to
state the nature of the personal relations and the important
personality patterns that seemed to make this relationship possible.

In the interviews with this couple, no systematic attempts
were made to increase their insights or to clarify for them what
appeared to the interviewer to be the significant personality
patterns in the relationship. Some increase in their grasp of
the psychological structure of their relationship occurred in-

cidentally during the interviewing. Their increased consciousness of the nature of their relationship did not appear to damage it, though in some types of relationship this is possible and
does occur.

From the interview material and the interviewer's observations, certain important characteristics of the marriage relationship of the O.'s emerge and may be briefly stated. The first
word that comes to mind in describing the relation is "companionship." There seems to be a strong element of *camara-
derie* and equalitarian give-and-take in the whole range of
their domestic life. Since both were working during their
four years of married life, they had little leisure time, but practically all of it was taken up with activities which both husband and wife seemed to enjoy thoroughly. Both maintained
that it was difficult for them to "have a good time" unless they
were engaged in joint activities. The companionship pattern
carried over into more serious aspects of life.

During the interviews two important problems came up.
One was the question of investing a small amount of money
they had accumulated. The other was a question of a position offered to the husband in another state. In both instances
there was no doubt about the reality of the "talking-it-over"
process. There were differences of opinion, occasional irritations and piques; but at no time was there any indication that
either entertained any idea of making an independent decision
and overriding the objection of the other. Both stated that
this was the usual pattern in matters calling for decision. However, the interviewer's impression was that certainly, in many
small ways, the husband maintained a certain dominance which
the wife seemed to accept unconsciously. Occasionally when
the husband seemed to assert this dominance too obviously, the
wife would stage a mild rebellion by reacting in a negativistic
manner. The husband reported this type of interaction and
stated that, when his wife showed slight "signs of being balky,"
he had learned to take it as an indication that he was being too

assertive and would deliberately assume a more passive role in the situation.

A second feature of this relationship seemed to be its affectionate character. Both reported a rather constant give-and-take of overt expressions of affection in the home. In the presence of outsiders this aspect of the relation is lacking to such an extent that they sometimes give the impression of being indifferent to each other. The interviews, however, brought out abundant evidence of strong affection and its free expression. The wife was considerably more demonstrative than the husband. She gave no evidence, however, that her husband's expressions were insufficient. Each gave the impression that he regarded the affectional output of the other as entirely appropriate and satisfactory.

The great sense of security husband and wife seem to feel about their relationship is a third characteristic of this marriage. Neither expressed any doubts or fears as to how the other felt about the marriage. According to their reports, there never has been any occasion during the marriage when either member felt insecure or jealous, notwithstanding the fact that in their work both persons have considerable dealings with eligible members of the opposite sex. Both husband and wife, in answer to interview questions regarding possible attractions to other persons, stated that they had met several persons "who might be interesting" and to whom they might be strongly attracted if they were "looking for that sort of thing." Each made statements to the effect that in such instances they did not find it difficult to control the amount of attention directed toward the outside attraction. Both of them seemed to feel that this was possible only because the marriage itself was satisfactory.

Another very evident and highly significant feature of the O. marriage is the manifold character of the relationship. In a good many of the marriages studied, particularly the problem cases, husband and wife seemed limited to one or two roles in their relationships to one another. If conditions called for a different pattern, the roles were shifted only with great difficulty and with great tension, or a shift was found impossible. For example, a husband may be very passive and dependent in his relations with his wife. He maintains the cultural role of head of the house, decision maker, and parent person on whom others can depend, only with great internal tension or through much *sub rosa* contrivance by his wife. He may be unable to assume the role at all. Likewise the domineering, dictatorial wife is sometimes confronted with the choice of losing her husband or playing a more passive, dependent role. If she attempts the latter, the effort may create great stress in her personality. The situation is frequently complicated by the fact that the resentful husband in the case is basically passive and dependent himself. A part of his personality resents the woman's dominance; another part desires it. Hence if the wife attempts the more passive role, stresses of insecurity may arise in the husband. In such cases, if any adjustment is reached, it is largely due to the skill of the wife in maintaining a neat balance between "playing the part of the woman" and seeing that in unobtrusive ways she supplies initiative, decisiveness, and reassurance where her husband lacks or needs it.

The foregoing digression is for the purpose of emphasizing the fact that the O. couple is especially marked by an ability to shift from one pattern of relation to another with what appears to be little conscious effort or stress in their personalities. This was revealed in their individual interviews and when they were being interviewed together. At the time of the interviews both husband and wife were able to play superior, equalitarian, and inferior parts, parental and dependent child roles, and a number of other roles in their marriage drama, with considerable facility. This varied role-taking was spontaneous, nondeliberate, and quite unconscious for the most part. While

these multiple possibilities were evident in the marriage, still
there were certain role relationships to which the couple tended
to gravitate. These will be better understood after the childhood and adolescent family relational patterns of each are
described. It is also evident that the wife's is the more mobile
personality; and the history of the marriage shows that it was
rather difficult for the husband to shift the relational patterns
at first. According to both his own and his wife's report, he has
shown increasing mobility of personality throughout the marriage.

It was interesting to see to what extent there were hostile elements in what appeared to be such a satisfying relationship.
The husband reported that he had had fairly pronounced resentments in the earlier part of the marriage. These hostile
attitudes were caused by ideas and wishes of the wife that ran
counter to his own in such matters as finances, friends, in-laws,
and recreation. He said, "Most of the time I knew she was
right on the question, but I couldn't stand having her tell me
what to do." This dislike of a woman's telling him what to
do is better understood when his early family relationships are
outlined.

At the time of the interview, there were no focal points of
conflict and hostility. Both husband and wife, however, reported what appeared to be spontaneous shifts from very positive and emotionally close relationships to mildly hostile or
emotionally distant relationships. There was no regularity
about these alternate moods, and contact with the case was not
long enough to establish the sequence of these shifts. With respect to all of their hostilities, however, this couple seemed able
to work through the important known conflict situations; and,
without any feelings of insecurity, to look upon the spontaneous
and transient periods of emotional distance as natural and inevitable changes in mood. Each has learned to sense the onset
of the negative phase and each then follows what they term a

"let-alone policy." Less secure persons seem to overreact to such moods and place undue strains on the relationship by so doing.

It was very difficult for this couple to describe any characteristic relational patterns in their day-to-day interaction when events move along more or less routinely. But it was quite evident that when problems arise action has to be taken and plans carried through, the husband assumes a decisive, directive position, sometimes to the point of arousing the wife's resistance to his "ordering her around." His general attitude toward her somewhat resembles an older, responsible sibling's bearing toward a younger, dependent one. This is perhaps the best single characterization of the relation that could be made. For the most part the wife seems to expect and automatically accept this form of the relationship. Both seem able to function smoothly and unconsciously in this manner much of the time. On the other hand, it is interesting to note that under some circumstances the husband becomes rather completely dependent upon the wife, expecting her to assume the initiative, make the decisions, and in general be a parental person. This she seems able to do without any evidence of marked tension or insecurity.

The above description is sufficient to give the reader some idea of the character of the relations that are maintained in this marriage. Attention can now be turned to summary statements of the familial relations of the two.

Mr. O. was the oldest of four children. He reacted with strong hostility against his displacement by the second child. He said:

I fought my brother until we were in our teens. At the same time we were inseparable companions. Everything we did was together. At home we were constant enemies and gave my parents much trouble. My mother gave me up as an incurably mean person. Strangely enough, when we were out of the home we were boon companions. We shared possessions, didn't want to go places without each other, and so on. I was very protective of him, and most of

my fights were with bullies who bothered him. I guess I bossed
him a lot, and if we went to some friend's home I corrected his manners—pretty much like a parent. Even now when he is with me he
expects me to say what is to be done.

The assumption of responsibility seemed to characterize
Mr. O. early.

My parents always left me in charge of things when they went
away. When the younger children came along, I had to take care
of them a lot. As all the children got older they seemed to look to
me to tell them what to do about as much as they looked to our
parents.

Mr. O.'s siblings have always, even to the present time, regarded him as possessing superior strength, skill, and wisdom.
A characteristic weapon in arguments with siblings or parents
was "You ask Jim if it isn't so"; or, "Jim said it was so." Even
after the children grew up and developed skills or strengths
superior to his, the tacit assumption seemed to be that James
could equal or better the performance if he cared to or if he
would "practice up a little." The parents also seemed to regard Mr. O. more as a third parent than as a child on an equal
basis with the others. Family problems and plans were discussed with him and not with the others.

He was known as a dominant and responsible person in his
treatment of his siblings. He always gave directions and
orders that could not be challenged. Occasionally the younger
children would rebel. The rebellion would never last long
because James was usually doing things that they desired to
participate in, and the simple threat of "Go ahead, then, but
you can't go fishing with me tomorrow," or some equivalent
intolerable deprivation, was sufficient to bring the rebels into
line.

Coupled with his tyranny was a strong affection for his
siblings. Much of his time was spent in making toys for
them. His threats of excluding them from specified activities
were rarely carried out, because he preferred to operate with

the obedient and admiring sibling audience rather than alone or with nonfamily friends. After some conflict had occurred and he had struck or otherwise hurt one of the siblings, he would feel very guilty and, without admitting having such an attitude, would contrive to "do something special" for the injured party.

As the children grew older and more capable of competing with James and beating him in fights or feats, he tended to withdraw from direct competition and to rest his reputation on his school standing, his social-group activities, and his *savoir faire*. The legend of his superiority has never been exploded, and the children still look to him as a person whose advice and good opinion are important. With his removal from areas of competing interest, the conflicts and hostile components in the relationship have disappeared and a rather close, friendly, somewhat sentimental relation remains. These attitudes are strengthened rather than weakened by distance and infrequency of contacts.

The husband-wife pattern presented by Mr. O.'s parents is interesting, since Mr. O. plays much the same role as his father. The parents were quite affectionate and demonstrative even in the presence of the children. Mr. O. states that his father took a "cherishing" attitude toward his (father's) wife. He was extremely chivalrous and attentive. He always called her "my little girl," and was very protective. The mother was devoted to the father; and the children always felt that her warmest feelings were for him rather than for any of the children. She made "quite a fuss over him" and "babied" him. He was very dependent on her. She was actually in many respects a stronger and more assertive personality than he was. Certainly she was the more feared authority and punisher of the two. The children were very affectionate toward their father, but their attitude was at the same time mildly derogatory and tolerant. They seemed to feel that he was never the adequate person the mother was. In spite of that attitude, which Mr. O. thinks at least amused the mother if, indeed, it was not secretly shared by her, the relations of father and children were close. Regardless of what the mother's conscious estimate of the father was, she successfully played the role of the pleased woman, flattered and made happy by the continuous courting of her romantic husband.

To some extent Mr. O. seemed to identify himself with his father. Not only did he resemble his father in appearance, but he was constantly picked out by friends and relatives as most like his father generally. The identification shows up at least in his chivalrous and cherishing attitude toward women. This has been his most characteristic attitude toward women and certainly shows up in his behavior toward his wife. This pattern is modified of course by the sibling relationship pattern, which also shows up very definitely in his relations with his wife.

A decided ambivalence has characterized Mr. O.'s relation with his mother. He still shows some resentment and hostility toward her; he also shows decided affection and deep admiration for her. His resentment is related in his mind to his belief that his mother has always preferred his younger brother to him. Discussion of this aspect of his family brought back to Mr. O.'s memory many feelings of inferiority with respect to his brother. He felt the brother was better looking than himself and that he was a more likable personality and attracted people more readily; that the relatives, particularly on the mother's side, liked the brother more than they liked him. This of course was a basis of hatred for the brother, but much of the hostility was directed toward the mother as well. His most intense memories of hatred for the mother center about her real or fancied rejection of him in favor of the brother.

It was during this part of the interview that he made the remark that Mrs. O.'s indulgent and devoted behavior made him feel like a favorite child. At another time he said that since his marriage he has been able to appreciate the satisfaction his father got out of being the center of so much feminine attention. In some respects his marriage is the realization of the affectional satisfaction of which he was deprived in the family. The interpretation might be offered that his marriage enabled him to take the role of his father in the affections of a woman who stood for his mother; it also enabled him to be "the favorite child" of this mother-person; and it may possibly have stood for his restoration as the only child, a role he occupied before his brother was born. A possible confirmation of this interpretation is the fact that the interviews brought out mildly ambivalent attitudes toward having children. It would be interesting to see what reactions occur on his part if a child is born to the couple, and if the wife deflects a considerable amount of attention and affection toward the child. It is probable, of course, that by that time he will have experienced a secure affection from the wife for a sufficient period so that he will not feel any dangerous threats from a child.

With all his hostile attitudes Mr. O. had strong affection for his mother and went to great lengths to give her gifts. A part of his drive for good grades and recognition in other ways seemed to have been an effort to win her approval.

Another interesting aspect of his relation with his mother was Mr. O.'s immediate resistance to any attempt on her part to "tell him what to do." It has been noted that the mother was apparently a stronger and more positive personality than the father. She apparently refrained from using obvious directive pressure on her husband; it appears probable that she was more assertive in her control over the children, even in their adolescence. The interviews did not proceed far enough to uncover the mechanism of what was apparently an over-reaction to assertive acts by a woman. Possibly Mr. O. was overreacting to a passive component that he had by virtue of his identification with his father. At any rate he quickly becomes annoyed by any effort of his wife to tell him what he ought to do.

The material given above is sufficient to give some idea of Mr. O.'s position in his family and the significant patterns of relationship in it which seem to have some relevance for an understanding of his marriage relationships. Since contact with him was limited to a few interviews, there are many gaps in our information and many unanswered questions. By using prolonged interview methods, a more adequate description of his marriage and his family relations could be gained and a more convincing connection between family pattern and marriage pattern probably could be established.

A description of Mrs. O.'s family relationships and her position in them follows:

Mrs. O. (Mary) was the next to the youngest child in a family of six children. The oldest was a boy, the next was a girl, then two boys. Mrs. O. was next, followed by another girl. Mary's relationships in her family were fairly clear-cut. She worshiped her oldest brother from afar. He was much older than she and did not have much to do with her, but to Mary he was a very romantic person. She fell desperately in love with his friends, who used to visit the home, and would be very embarrassed if these friends paid her any attention. She was attached to her older sister and rather dependent upon her for guidance in her adolescent activities. The brother just older than she was her closest companion in the family; they spent much of their childhood together. She still regards him as her closest friend in the family. The brother was very fond of her and demonstrated his deep attachment to her by marrying a girl very much like her in personal characteristics. In his absent-minded moments he calls his wife "Mary." For the most part Mary played the younger-sibling subordinate role in this relation, with only occasional rebellions against her brother's dominance.

Mrs. O.'s relations with her younger sister have always been strained and attended by a strong hostility and sense of guilt. This youngest sister was the father's favorite child. Mrs. O. has always been deeply devoted to her father, and most of her childhood memories of him are connected with unsatisfied longings that he would notice her and show the affection for her that he showed for her sister. He never paid her much attention, and when he did, it was likely to be somewhat unfavorable. This favoritism caused strong resentments. There are no conscious memories of antagonism or hatred for the father, but many memories were presented of spiteful behavior toward her sister, thinly disguised wishes for her death, and feelings of guilt about this hatred. At the same time she took a very parental and protective attitude toward this sister in extrafamily relations. She still feels animosity for this sister, but also feels personally responsible for her though the sister seems able enough to take care of herself.

Mrs. O.'s parents were very close and affectionate but much less demonstrative than Mr. O.'s parents. Her mother was more demonstrative than her father. He was a rather reserved and somewhat stern patriarch. His relations with his children were more formal and distant than was true of Mr. O.'s father. The family, particularly the mother and daughters, were strongly attached to him. They vied with each other in "looking after father."

Mrs. O. identified herself very closely with her mother, and was probably the mother's favorite daughter. She feels that she is closer to her mother and understands her better than any of the other children. It has already been pointed out that she had a strong attachment for her father but had never felt that her father had much affection for her.

In the first interview Mrs. O. volunteered the statement that the longer she knew her husband, the more similarities she discovered between him and her father. In a later interview she made the remark that marrying her husband seemed like marrying her brother (the one next older than herself). Throughout the interview material there is further evidence that Mrs. O. partially identifies her husband with her father and her brother. In her relations with her husband she is probably realizing a role she desired to play with respect to her father. She is now the favorite daughter. She is also able to play—and it is quite evident that she does play—a loved and mildly bullied younger-sibling role.

Both husband and wife made the point several times that, almost from the moment they met, they felt at home and relaxed in one another's company. Apparently they had not felt the same degree of familiarity in any other similar relationship. A part of this is no doubt due to their very similar family backgrounds. However, a good part is probably due to the fact that their individual personality patterns geared rather closely together.

It is evident that the role patterns the husband and wife brought to the marriage do not explain all the marriage adjustment. But it does not seem too much to claim that they furnish a considerable basis for the relationship that has developed.

Contact with this case was not thorough enough to reveal in detail the sexual patterns in the marriage. At the time of the interviews both felt that sexual adjustment was highly satisfactory. The only complaint was that their work was sometimes too fatiguing to allow for enough sexual activity. They reported that sexual adjustment was not immediately achieved at marriage, and they attributed the delay to ignorance and lack of skill in handling contraceptive devices. But judging from what information was obtained, it is probable that there were some deeper factors that partly inhibited them. Whatever the difficulties were, they seem to have been successfully overcome.

Case II.—An Unadjusted Couple: William and Laura A.

Mr. and Mrs. A., who had been married about a year and a half, were referred to us by a physician who stated that he had treated both of them for minor ailments and had advised Mrs. A. on a matter of nutritional difficulty. The husband had come to him stating that the marriage was very unsatisfactory to him and asking advice as to a divorce. The doctor had found that sexual relations were unsuccessful and unsatisfactory. The husband was clumsy, lacking in knowledge and technique, and somewhat diffident. The wife did not have strongly negative attitudes towards sexual activity, but did not experience much satisfaction in the act. The physician had counseled them and had referred them to appropriate reading. The sexual relations improved only slightly, and the doctor therefore felt that there were other important personality factors in the situation.

The A.'s had some differences in background. Their parents were foreign-born. Mr. A.'s parents were born in Russia; Mrs. A.'s in Austria. Both families are Jewish, but Mrs. A.'s parents rarely attended synagogue. Mr. A.'s family was more religious. Mr. A.'s father had had little education and had worked in a wholesale house as a shipping clerk with no promotions throughout his working years. Mrs. A.'s father had had two years of college and was an independent business man. But, owing to the irregular and unstable work habits of Mrs. A.'s father, the actual economic status of the two families was not very different.

Mr. A. (age 24) is the youngest of a family of seven. When asked to tell about his childhood, he launched into a rather enthusiastic account of his happy and satisfactory family life. From his story one gathers that his mother was a powerful and aggressive personality, the chief center, drive, and control factor in the family. She ran the father's affairs, planned the children's vocational and social activities, maneuvered the daughters into marriage, and tried to maneuver the sons into marriage. Mr. A. boasts of her iron will. He is proud of her determined look, and tells how her spirit never sagged. He tells how she faced death with the same unshaken will and determination never to admit defeat.

The father is described as a pleasant, reliable and steady, quiet and meek person who seemed to figure merely as an unimportant though kindly fixture in the household. He worked steadily, turned his earnings over to his wife, never seriously opposed her, and after her death agreeably allowed his daughters to place him in an old people's home.

The three sisters, particularly the two older ones, are described as being very much like the mother. The two sisters have husbands with whom they play quite the same role which their mother played with her husband. The youngest sister, Martha, is two years older than Mr. A. Although not quite so Amazonian as her sisters, she is fairly aggressive, active, and adequate in meeting situations. She has played a decidedly mothering role with Mr. A., especially since the death of their mother when Mr. A. was about 15 years old. He says of Martha,

We have always been very close together. She has comforted me and consoled me in my troubles. I have confided in her and she has shielded me. She used to advise me and tell me what to do.

He used to sleep with his sister, and he tells of his surprise on discovering recently that people thought such an arrangement strange. He says, "Even after I was 16 or 17, if I was blue or worried about my future she would take me to bed with her and comfort me." This occurred more frequently after the mother's death. Soon after his marriage he felt he *had* to leave his wife, to get away and think things out. He went home for a visit. The first few days he was very worried and upset; he couldn't sleep at night, and one night he fell to weeping. Martha took him to bed with her and consoled him. He says, "I felt a motherly warmth and felt released from my troubles and went to sleep. After that I slept in her room every night and felt much better." Mr. A. denies ever having had sexual impulses or ideas regarding Martha at any time, although they have discussed sex quite freely.

In speaking of all the sisters he says: "I was always proud to go places with my sisters. They were lively and popular and I was proud of them. I could walk around and enjoy myself, and they could take care of themselves." (This was said in a comparison of his sisters with his wife, who depends too much on him, he says, for pleasant times at social gatherings.)

Mr. A. does not feel that there was much conflict in his home. Things seemed to be secure and to run smoothly under the orderly supervision of the mother. He feels that the home life was happy. He reflects:

There was always something going on at my home. My mother and sisters were always doing interesting things, having people over and having jolly times that I like to remember. They didn't sit around as she does [alluding to his wife] and wait for something to happen. My father is quiet and never participated much in what was going on, but he enjoyed watching and listening to other people. I am like my father. I liked to watch and listen, and, if I felt like it, put in a word or do something. I hate to feel I *have* to talk or take the initiative. [This remark also was made with reference to his wife's irritating dependence upon him.]

Mr. A.'s two brothers are interesting. The older brother, who is also the oldest child, is called the "black sheep." His relations with the mother and with the sister next to him in age were particularly hostile. He rebelled and left home early. The next brother is the middle child, the mother's favorite. He was and still is a dependable, quiet, kindly, nonaggressive person. The children say he is the mainstay of the family. Mr. A. describes him as a kind of parent to the younger children.

Mr. A. says that his parents and siblings were always kind to him.

They always took care of me, and my brother told me he would send me to school. My sisters like to have me come to their homes, and they enjoy giving me the comforts of a home. They say, "You need the comforts of a home"; and I believe they are right, because I often wish I could feel that I had a father and mother and a home I could go back to.

He was punished very little. A typical instance of his treatment is revealing. His mother and brother scolded him and threatened to punish him for not practicing his music. They told him he should be willing to practice for them if they paid for his lessons. Mr. A.'s comment is interesting: "I remember I was very angry that they should expect anything from me just because they paid for the lessons. I hated to feel obligated." (This represents an attitude characteristic of Mr. A.—that of expecting the environment to minister to him with no obligation or responsibilities on his part.)

One gets the impression from Mr. A.'s conversation that he was an extremely dependent, much indulged and coddled child; that he resented any responsibility or expectation or demand from him on the part of the environment; and that he felt insecure in situations in which he was thrown on his own initiative. He tended to assume a passive role, expecting the environment to furnish aggressive support, backing, and leadership. On several occasions he made what he describes as attempts to win his independence by leaving home. He usually went under the tutelage of a decisive and aggressive boy friend who told him he ought to learn to stand on his own feet. On each occasion when he faced a shortage of jobs or money he felt forced to retreat home. After a few attempts he was ashamed to go home and would retreat to the family of the girl he finally married. He said, "I just can't bear feeling all alone in a strange place with no money and no home I can go to."

Mr. A. met his wife shortly before his mother's death. He says, "I was timid and bashful, but she was pleasant and talked to me and I felt comfortable with her." Soon after Mr. A.'s mother died, the girl's family moved to another city. Mr. A. wept the night before her departure, and said to her, "First I lose my mother; then I lose you." (The girl had the same first name as Mr. A.'s mother.) He told her he loved her at that time, but felt that he had said more than he meant; and the next day he contrived to arrive at the railroad station too late to see her off. Largely through the girl's efforts, a correspondence was kept up between the two. Later, after some of his unsuccessful forays into the world of affairs, he would travel to the city where her parents lived to seek the shelter of the girl's home. She would be very sympathetic about his trials and tribulations, and she readily accepted his alibis for failure and excused him to himself. When she consoled him in his retreats from unsuccessful attempts to make good in the world (which he expected to do in short order), he would tell her that she was just like his sister. As he was forced to repeat his returns to the girl's family, he became more and more uncomfortable; he felt himself more and more obligated to assume responsibilities with respect to the girl. He seemed unable to do without a good deal of sympathetic reassurance; but he became increasingly panicky as it grew more evident that marriage was expected of him.

Before discussing further the relations between Mr. A. and his wife, it is necessary to describe briefly Mrs. A.'s family. The families of both Mr. and Mrs. A. represent the same cultural and economic levels. If there is any difference, it is slight and in favor of Mr. A.'s family.

Mrs. A. (aged 23) describes her father as a successful merchant until a few years ago, when he developed an interest in gambling and taking extended vacations. He had never saved money, but his business had kept the family in good circumstances. For some time now, however, he has been very improvident and irresponsible. He has obtained good positions, but has given them up for very trivial reasons. Mrs. A. says she used to admire and respect her father, but since he has allowed the family to come upon evil days she has lost respect for him and feels very resentful toward him. The father accuses the mother of being responsible for the condition of the family. He says, "You should have taken the money from me and not allowed me to gamble"; and "You should have made me attend to our business." Mrs. A. feels that her father has acted as something of a spoiled child toward his wife.

The mother is described as patient, long-suffering, submissive. Mrs. A. feels that she is close to her mother because, as she says, "I am very much like my mother and can understand her." She has always taken sides with her mother in family arguments, which seem to align the father and older brother against the mother and Mrs. A. These arguments are in the form of tongue-lashings from the father and older brother, with the mother and daughter passively resisting.

The oldest brother is very harsh toward the mother, and she submits to his dominating and overbearing treatment. She appears to resent it somewhat, but she excuses him. When he flies into rages and leaves home to avoid paying room and board, the mother will feel sorry for him and will cook up cakes and other dainties, which she carries to his abode and lays at his feet. She treats the father in much the same way, patiently accepting his occasional beratings. When some of the children complain of their father's incompetence, the mother will make excuses for him. She will say, "Your father has worked hard all his life, and now just look at him. It isn't fair."

There are three children in the family: an oldest son, Mrs. A., and her younger brother. Mrs. A. speaks bitterly of her intense hatred for her older brother, who appears from her description to be a very domineering, overbearing, egocentric person. But she follows her statements of hostility toward him with the admission that she secretly admires his aggressiveness and capabilities and envies his assertiveness. She has wished all her life that he would love her. When on rare occasions he would be kind to her or give her a birthday gift, she would feel much encouraged and hope for better relations. She would experience great disappointment when he resumed his usual tactics.

The son's hostility toward his mother and sister seems to date from early childhood. Mrs. A. has fought back somewhat, but she usually cries, feels "blue," suffers inwardly. She still dreams of having bitter fights with him, but in these dreams her role is one of defending herself against his attacks. Occasionally she will dream of a more aggressive role in which she vehemently commands her brother to get out of the house. She says that one reason she liked Mr. A. was that he seemed to be the opposite of her brother in every way.

Mrs. A. is fond of her younger brother and feels that they were quite close as children, though their relationship is not so close now.

Mrs. A.'s conversation gives one the impression of a person with some hostile drives, who, nevertheless, tends to assume a passive role in all situations. She tends to wait for something to happen, for others to make suggestions and to take the initiative. Her lack of decisive self-assertion is a characteristic which drives her husband, so he says, to distraction.

With this account of the backgrounds of our subjects, let us turn again to their relationship with one another.

Mr. A. became more and more frightened and restless as it became clearer to him that the natural and expected result of his relationship to Mrs. A. was marriage. He made some attempts to extricate himself by protesting to her that they were in no position to marry, and by leaving her home. In an interview he said, "I wanted to be away, to be free to work out my prob-

lems alone, but I felt myself dragged deeper and deeper."
Early attempts to leave and get a job resulted in failure and an
inevitable return to the girl, who was always ready with her
sympathy and mothering solicitude. Her family was hos-
pitable; but what worried Mr. A. was that they assumed his
frequent returns for prolonged visits to mean that he was
intent on marriage. The father finally became more urgent
and tried to encourage the diffident young man by letting him
know that what he needed to settle him down was marriage.

These urgings and expectations on the part of the family
plus the pleas of the girl, plus his own inability to do without
some sympathetic reassurances, proved too much for him.
Finally, he says, he shut his eyes and jumped. For two days
he suffered mental anguish as he walked the streets trying to
make up his mind. "Then," he says, "with superhuman effort
I forced myself to go to the courthouse and say, 'I want a marriage license!'"

After the marriage Mr. A. began to have many fears and
forebodings. He was afraid Mrs. A.'s mother or father would
die and he would have to help take care of Mrs. A.'s younger
brother. He feared that he had wrecked his chances to realize
his best self, and that he should get out of the marriage. He began to find Mrs. A. ugly; and this, he said, outraged his aes-
thetic sensibilities. But the main theme throughout his interviews is:

My wife is a drag on me. She depends too much on me. Instead
of feeling myself being pulled forward, I feel like she is pulling me
backward. Why can't she be like my sisters? She is weak and casts
a gloom over my spirit that I can't shake off. I must go away so I
can feel free again and be on my own.

He did break away once to go to his sister for comfort and
solace. He said:

While I was there I was happy again unless I thought of my plight.
My sister said, "All you need is the comfort of your home," and she
was right. While I was with her I felt all right.

The wife complained that she didn't feel secure with her husband. She wished that he could be like other men who seem to know what they want to do and how to go about it, who seem to take charge of things and forge ahead and not appear so helpless. She resented the fact that although her husband was out of work and she was supporting him, he seemed to take that for granted as his due. Moreover, he showed great irritation toward her if she came home tired and, as he puts it, "Sad and weak-looking." He says, "I simply can't stand that sad, wilted look."

Their sexual adjustment is interesting when seen on this background. Their first attempts at intercourse were clumsy and unsuccessful; neither knew how to proceed. The husband's history shows considerable curiosity during childhood, and avoidance and fear in adolescent encounters. Even after receiving coaching from a physician and becoming somewhat adept in sexual technique, he is still described by his wife as clumsy and diffident in his approaches. He himself reveals a certain resentment against and resistance to assuming the role of aggressor in relation with his wife. In the sexual situation he has to assume a role that runs contrary to his desires.

In both husband and wife there are evidences of strong repressions of sexual drives. These specifically sexual attitudes are undoubtedly a part of the situation, but they may also be thought of as parts of the basic role patterns, particularly in the case of the husband.

This represents an outline of some of the outstanding points in the case, but presentation of all the material would hardly do more than amplify the picture which must be evident from even such a scant description.

The central problem in this case is a problem of basic roles, which are apparently the result of the early family relationships. The husband is looking for a solicitous, protecting, aggressive, decisive, parent environment which the wife, who expects something of the same sort, cannot supply. She was able to furnish sympathy and to that extent supplied the role of mother and sister in the husband's family. But she is not equipped to assume the more positive and aggressive roles that these people played in Mr. A.'s personality development.

Neither of the couple is quite fully aware of what the root of their trouble is. The husband thinks his marriage is a mistake, that he is not cut out for marriage, that his temperament needs complete freedom to realize itself. The wife thinks the husband is sulky, inconsiderate, selfish, and jealous of her interest in her family.

From the psychoanalytic point of view, Mr. A. would probably be classified as a homosexual type, and the difficulties would be interpreted on that basis. If it be recognized that for the male the category "homosexual" applies to general psychosexual traits of passivity rather than merely to certain specific sexual attitudes, then the classification is probably valid. But it should be pointed out that such a classification is not fully descriptive of the role-pattern Mr. A. represents. He is not only passive, but he has an infantile dependent attitude or role which is not necessarily characteristic of the homosexual.

The case might also be interpreted as a result of guilt feelings which arise when Mr. A. engages in sexual activity with a person who stands as a substitute for his sister Martha. Sexual impulses with reference to his sister must have been strongly repressed, and when they are allowed expression on a love object that stands for her, they give rise to strong guilt feelings from which Mr. A. seeks to escape by terminating the marriage. Even here, however, we find ourselves using the concept of roles. But it is apparent that this specifically sexual explanation leaves out of account too much of Mr. A.'s general pattern of response to all types of situations.

Case III.—A Maladjusted Couple: Thomas and Frances G.

Mrs. G. (age 26) appealed to her physician for help in meeting what she regarded as a crisis in her marriage. She stated that Mr. G. was drinking heavily and with increasing frequency. His gambling was becoming almost incessant and was increasingly reckless to a point where it was threatening the economic security of the family. In his relation with her he alternated between periods of great self-condemnation, pleas for forgiveness, and promises to "straighten out," and harsh words, swearing at her, and telling her she could get out and go if she didn't like the way he acted—he would be "damned glad to get rid of her." Bills were piling up, and the drinking and gambling were not leaving enough to live on. Mrs. G. was afraid, too, that Mr. G. would lose his position and ruin his health.

According to her history of the husband's behavior, this was the second critical episode since their marriage six years ago. Excerpts from her story reveal the general picture of the relationship, particularly as it is high-lighted by the crisis situation. Mrs. G.'s statement follows:

I knew he was a little wild when I married him. He lived in the same little town I did and ran around with a wild bunch of fellows who drank and gambled quite a bit. Several times his father had to pull him out of a hole by paying off some of his gambling debts and setting him straight. His mother would cry and beg him not to disgrace her and send her to her grave. It would nearly kill her. He was always sorry, but would get going again. I learned more about him from his mother after I married him. His parents thought I would be good for him and steady him. My father couldn't "see" him at all, and my brother couldn't stand the idea of my marrying him. Neither my father nor my brother would speak to us for quite a while after we were married.

After we married we moved to R. [a large city] about 200 miles from our home town. Both of us worked hard. He was grand for a while, then seemed to get going with the wrong crowd again and got worse and worse. I have often wondered if my making more money than he did at that time had anything to do with it. Anyway, I would beg and plead and cry. He would get mad and say, "Good God, you're worse than my mother!" Then he would be sorry and ask me to forgive him, and he would be better. We both decided that it would be best for him to get away from that town and get a job, and for me to stay home and keep house. We were planning to move when he got influenza and then pneumonia, and nearly died. We went to his parents' home, and I stayed right with him and nursed him through it all. He just couldn't seem to stand it if I was out of his sight five minutes while he was sick; he said he loved me more than anybody in the world. He was sick most of eight months. We were in debt and had no jobs. I had a friend in B. [a small city about 50 miles from Mr. G's home town], and she helped me get a pretty fair job [office secretarial work in a wholesale house]. I left him at his parents' home and came to B. I looked around and finally heard of a job that I thought he could do. A friend of his helped me; we got him lined up for the job, and he came here and they gave it to him. It was new work for him, and he was terribly afraid of the job. He was scared he wouldn't make good—worked like a dog and became one of the two best men in the area. [The job was that of a sales representative of a district office of a large concern.]

He was making fairly good money, and we pulled out of debt with a little help from his father. Tom was earning $200 to $250 a month by the time we had been here a year, and he hadn't had nearly the experience of some of the other fellows in the office. Well, we decided that now was the time for me to quit work and have a baby. He seemed to want one more than I did, though I always planned to have one. He said it would make him feel more responsible. He had started drinking and gambling a little, but not enough to worry about, though I used to worry quite a bit and, I guess, I showed it. He would get "sore" if I said anything and let him know I was afraid he was going to get worse.

I became pregnant and stopped work, and something happened to start him off with a bang. He began drinking more heavily and lost more money than he should have at gambling. I started crying and begging him to stop, but that didn't do any good. Then I got good and mean to him; I bawled him out and threatened to leave him. Sometimes he would cry and beg me not to leave him—he would say if I did leave him it would be the end of him. At other times when he was good and drunk he would say, "Go, God damn you, go! I'll be glad to be free from you!" Then I went to the minister and had a talk, and made Tom go for a talk with him. He did and said he was sorry, and promised me to be good, but that lasted about a week.

We were good friends with the sales manager of the area and his wife. He is a fine man and took a real interest in the younger men like Tom who worked under him. I went to him with my troubles. He and I worked out a scheme so that he and I controlled Tom's pay check and knew when and where the money went. Tom was humiliated to death and was meaner to me than ever. He threatened to quit the job and said he wasn't going to have people taking care of his money as if he were a two-year-old. The next day he took the money I gave him to pay the bills and went on a big drunk. After that he got around me on the expense money: he borrowed from the fellows at the office, and I would have to pay them back.

I wrote to his father and mother. They sided with me. His father wanted to come right up and clean house with him. They came for a visit about the time the baby was born and stayed about two months. His father bawled him out and paid up some of his back gambling debts. His mother cried and told him he was driving her to her grave. I guess he felt pretty bad; and I don't know if it was the thing to do or not, but it was some comfort to me to have a little help. It was better for a little while, but by the time his parents left I could see that he was going to be just as bad as ever. His boss and I had let him handle his own checks again, but we were trying to work out some way of my letting the boss know how much he was spending. He took a flyer and lost a lot of money gambling one week and then got so drunk that his mind went completely blank for a couple of days. I was scared, because he always seemed to know what was going on no matter how drunk he was. His boss called him in and we thought he was going to get fired, but he got the worst bawling out I ever heard. I was there. I thought Tom would certainly throw the job at the boss's head, but he took it and admitted he was a damn fool. I would never take a trimming like that from anybody. But it looked to me like Tom was losing his grip and was confused and didn't know what to do about it. He looked to me as if he knew he was getting in a worse mess all the time, but just didn't know where to turn or what to do.

I thought he might have something really the matter with him, and so I went to the doctor, and he said we should see you. I talked Tom into coming here, although I don't think he was at all keen on doing it. I think now, though, he feels maybe there might be something wrong that you could help us in, so I brought him up here to talk to you.

Mrs. G. had taken the initiative and had called for an appointment for her husband. When it was suggested that he could come alone for the first interview, she said he was timid in such matters and would probably not come unless she brought him.

I don't know—sometimes I wonder if all of my working on him hasn't just made him worse instead of better. Maybe he is just bound and determined not to let a woman tell him what to do. He has told me several times that his mother has just run over his dad all the time they were married and that he would be damned if he ever let a woman run over him like that. He is really fond of his father and is like him in a good many ways. But I think he hates his mother like poison. She kisses him but he never kisses her; he turns away so that she just kisses him on the cheek. He can't stand being around her very long at a time, either. His mother and father get along, but I think myself it is because the father has just given in to whatever the mother wants. She is a fine housekeeper but rather tyrannical. If she doesn't get her way in the family, she gets quite sick. I am at the end of my rope. I get the jitters when I think of divorce. I know I'll still care for Tom and worry about what's happening to him. I know he'll go to the dogs. I would have to go back to work, and then what would happen to my baby? He needs me now. Tom seems to care for me one time and hate me another. He is wild about the baby and says he will take him away from me if I leave him. He is still good at his work, but how he can stand the strain of it all, I don't know. I don't believe he can stand it much longer. Something's got to break.

Mrs. G. was questioned regarding the sexual relations. Her attitude shifted from one of frankness to that of partly evading and partly dismissing the question as "of no particular importance in our case." But the following material was elicited: She was strictly reared, knew very little about the "facts of life," had no remembered childhood or adolescent sex experiences either in autoerotic activities or with other children. She picked up her sexual information from other children but had no special conscious curiosity or feelings of guilt. She thought her husband was satisfied with their sex relations, though they had never discussed this area of their marriage very much. She stated she was satisfied with the relations, though for the four years before they had the child she had not experienced orgasm. Since the birth of the child she has occasionally had an orgasm. There is little foreplay. She claims to feel no sense of deprivation or desire to improve the sexual relations with her husband.

About two or three months after her pregnancy, her husband stopped intercourse with her. "He seemed to take on a purity complex." Since the birth of the child, intercourse has been resumed but is less frequent than before (it was twice a week and is now less than once a week). The husband generally shows less zest in sexual activity than formerly. She has wondered whether he is interested in another woman and has suggested it to him at various times when he has been intoxicated. She feels there is probably no other woman because he has been so positive and scornful in his denials of such an interest.

She feels she must be uncompromising in her stand against his drinking and gambling, and now refuses to allow him to drink at home. "One drink and he is gone. He starts and simply cannot stop. He's the same way about gambling." She has tried drinking with him to "shame him." "I can drink, and have drunk, him under the table. I think that humiliated him, but it didn't do any good."

Mrs. G. is of medium height, attractive in appearance, well-dressed, and showing a tendency toward "smart" clothes. She shows considerable tension and strain, but manages to keep it pretty well concealed. She weeps slightly during the interview when she reaches points in her story where she has to admit

failure of her plans and uncertainty as to what she thinks should
be done next.

Mr. G.'s statement follows:

Mr. G. (age 28), a tall, slender, asthenic, rather pale man,
showed a great deal of nervousness and tension at the beginning of the first interview. He was extremely diffident and
not nearly so articulate as his wife. His tension subsided
noticeably as the interview progressed. With occasional exceptions the tension has not been so marked in subsequent
interviews. The lowering of the tension level was particularly noticeable after he had given expression to feelings which
he had suppressed and about which there was considerable
sense of guilt.

When asked to state the situation as he saw it, he rehearsed
his history of alcoholic indulgence which periodically reached
excessive peaks. His story confirmed that of the wife. He did
not mention gambling. He attributed his first excessive drinking episode, which had led to their moving from R., to the
fact that he "got in with the wrong crowd." The recent excesses, he said, were due to the intolerable strain of his work.

When I took this job I had just come out of a year of illness. It
was different from any work I had ever done before. [He had been
a worker in a machine shop before.] I walked the floor at night
and was afraid I couldn't do the job. When I thought I had not
done enough business, I couldn't bear to face the boss with the
week's report. A drink or two would help me forget. But I
would be in a saloon and couldn't keep from drinking more and
more. It wasn't a crowd that kept me drinking, as I drink alone
most of the time now. I think if my wife didn't have such a fear
of my drinking and would let me drink at home and go to bed, I
wouldn't be so bad about it. My wife is overanxious about drinking because her father and brother are such heavy drinkers. Her
brother is just a bum on account of it now. She used to try to
control them as she does me now, but it didn't help them any and
I don't suppose it will help me either.

He said he was still afraid that his work would be unsatisfactory, but added that his record is "far from the lowest." He admitted on questioning that he was among the two or three best men on the field staff, and also that his superior liked his work and was interested in him. He did not mention the financial arrangements his wife and superior had worked out to control his drinking and gambling.

It was suggested that people sometimes attributed their fears and worries to such things as job situations when, in reality, they were due to other problems which they were unable to solve or unwilling to face. He hesitated considerably and then replied,

Well, I guess the main problem is my wife and me, but that's all my fault and I'll have to work it out somehow; but I don't see how as yet. It isn't as it ought to be with us, but I guess it's me.

He then resumed his discussion of his job situation and seemed inclined to evade further elaboration on the marriage situation. It was suggested that he probably needed to confront the problems in the marriage. He answered that he did not know how to state or discuss the problems.

We have never discussed our problems, and I don't think it will do any good now. I'm to blame, I know. She has stuck by me and done all she could, but I get more irritable and mean to her all the time, and now she isn't attractive to me any more. When we were first married, we were in love and very romantic. I suppose all young people are like that. But now—I don't know, now it is different.

Mr. G. continued to talk in general terms until specific questions brought out that he never felt satisfied with his sexual relations with his wife.

We didn't want children right away, and we used methods to prevent it. [They first used *coitus interruptus* and then, later, rubber condoms.] We both had a feeling that there was probably something not quite right about using these methods, but we went ahead and used them anyway.

Neither method was particularly satisfactory to him, and he felt that his wife did not get much satisfaction out of any of their sexual relations. She refused to use a pessary or contraceptive jellies, explaining that she did not believe that they were safe.

I had been around before I was married, and I knew how it could be. I had one girl that used to enjoy it as much as I did. My wife never got the satisfaction this girl did. I knew she wasn't putting all she had into it and wasn't getting much out of it, but I didn't know what to do about it. I suppose it was due to our trying not to have a baby. I have thought that I would be better off if I had married the other girl, but I thought she was too loose for a man to marry. I think differently about such things now.

About the time my wife got pregnant, I met a girl and had an affair with her for about a year. She was as highly sexed as I am and enjoyed it. It was very satisfactory to me, except that I felt pretty bad about it. We finally decided that the thing couldn't go on, so we both decided to quit. It could start up again quite easily. I suppose one of my worries was that I felt like a cheater and a dog about the way I was treating my wife. Now I feel like I want to renew the affair, and yet I don't want to because I know it isn't the way to treat my wife.

My wife gets more satisfaction from sex relations now than she did before the baby was born. But I know she must suspect that I don't care for relations with her as I used to. It is more of a duty with me now than anything else, and I get no particular satisfaction.

He reports that he has felt rather intense resentment at not getting complete response from his wife. He has also wondered about his own adequacy, fearing that the deficiency is in himself and that he is not able to call out the full sexual response from his wife.

Further discussion reveals that his feeling of revulsion from his wife is not all due to the deficiencies in the sexual relation. Some of his most intense resentments have centered around his wife's efforts to control and direct him.

I don't know why, but the more she works on me and tries to keep me straight, the more I hate her and the more I'm bound to go in the opposite direction. Yet I know that she is doing everything she can for me and to make me happy. When I think of that, I feel rotten.

Asked if he had other complaints regarding his wife, Mr. G. said that his wife was not efficient in her housekeeping. "My mother had to have everything clean and in place and on time and all that sort of thing. I suppose it's the way I was brought up that makes me notice my wife on this." He reports that his wife is inclined to let things pile up, that the house is not tidy, and that meals are not always on time. He adds that part of the irregularity is due to the fact that he does the shopping now, and his irregular work hours affect the home schedule. He feels he is inclined to blame more of the laxity and irregularity on his wife than is just, but he recalls wishing for the rather strict regularity and order of his mother's home.

When asked if he has any solution for his problems or plans for dealing with the situation in the future, he answers that he has none. "Something is eating on me, I don't know what. I just decide to let things drift along as long as they can. Then I guess we will have some kind of crack-up."

These materials, taken from preliminary interviews with husband and wife separately, are sufficient to give a rough picture of important relational patterns in this marriage. The specialist, experienced in analyzing marriage problems from the point of view herein represented, will already have seen the important dynamic patterns at work. Even the nontechnical reader will doubtless have some sense of the situation.

A brief summary of the backgrounds and family-relationship patterns of husband and wife will help make the patterns more explicit.

Mr. G. is the younger of two boys. The older brother died in his earlier twenties. His father and mother are native, white

Americans of German extraction. The family is Lutheran in religious affiliation and moderately regular in attendance at religious services. His father is a highly skilled worker and has supported the family in moderately comfortable circumstances. They have lived in a small industrial city all of Mr. G.'s life. The family was considered one of the leading families in the local community.

Mrs. G. is the middle of three children. She has an older sister and a younger brother. Her parents are native, white Americans of German extraction. They are Lutheran and are moderately regular in attendance at church. Her father is a skilled worker by trade but has built up a small independent shop of his own (a garage). He has supported his family in moderate comfort, and the family is regarded as one of the leading families of the community. The two families lived in the same small city, but in different neighborhoods of about the same status.

As can be seen from the above information, the social-economic backgrounds are essentially similar. The husband and wife had approximately the same amount of education. She had taken two years of high school and a year of business-school training. Mr. G. had three and a half years of high school. He dropped out after he was suspended, as he said, "Because I was a damn fool and wouldn't obey some of the rules." At the time of marriage he was working regularly and earning about $1,500 dollars a year. Mrs. G. had just finished her business-school training. They had each saved about $300 or $400. Mr. G. had a history of more social participation in organized groups than had his wife.

With these background facts, we may turn to the family relationships of husband and wife.

Mr. G.'s family relationships are very interesting in the light of his marriage difficulties. He starts his discussion of his parents by saying, "I have very fine parents, and I owe it to them to do something about myself. I am the only one they have left now." (His older brother died about eight years ago.) As he discusses the family picture, it becomes clear that he identifies himself quite closely with his father and has a rather definite ambivalent attitude of intense hatred for and dependence upon his mother.

I am a lot like my father in many ways. The family always said I was his boy and that we look and act alike. I think, though, that he favored my brother more than he did me, probably because I was always getting into trouble. My brother was one of those model fellows. He never gave them any trouble and was good in his school work. My mother thought he was just about perfect, I guess. She was broken up completely when he died and hasn't really got over it yet. She is a good mother and gave us a good home. She kept the cleanest home I ever saw. It was a kind of obsession with her, and it used to gripe me a lot, but I notice it makes me sore when my wife is sloppy in housekeeping. I guess it was drummed into me pretty deep. I don't think my mother ever cared a lot for me, at least not as she cared for my brother. I think she had a natural mother love for me. At least she used to get plenty worried when I would get drunk and stay out all night with the gang. She would cry and go on, or get sick, or get mad. I felt sorry for hurting her so, but it didn't last long—I was soon doing the same thing again. I was called the black sheep of the family. Maybe I am what they call a problem child. [Laughs.]

My father was always very, very considerate of my mother. I guess he is the only man in the world who could have lived with her. He would give in to her and humor her in whatever she wanted to do. He had practically no say in the way the money was spent. He just handed it over to her. She would give him hell, and he would take it and say it was because she was sick. She was what you would call neurotic, I guess. If she didn't get people to do what she wanted, she would get sick and say we were all driving her to an early grave. I would never take from any woman what my father took from my mother. She dominated him, imposed on him, and couldn't stand to take any opposition from him. I suppose he just resigned himself to it. At least he never left her and never declared his independence in any way I know of.

I have always liked my father much better than I have my mother.

When I am home, I enjoy being around with him, but I can stand my mother so long and then I have to get out.

When I was a kid I used to admire my brother quite a bit. He was four years older than I was and was my mother's favorite. Half the time I hated him because she was always pointing out how much better he was and how he caused her no trouble. When she would do that, I would feel like being as different from him as I could. If he did a thing a certain way, I wanted to do it a different way so as not to be like him. It's funny to me now because I did also feel a kind of pride about him and admired him.

It was my pig-headedness that got me canned at high school. I just decided they couldn't make me obey one or two of their rules. I got canned twice and then got a job. It looks very silly to me now when I look back on it, but then I felt I could tell them all where to go.

Both my parents had strict morals. Anything suggesting sex was a mortal sin to my mother. As I look back at it now, I don't believe my parents ever had sex relations except to have children. If they did I doubt that my mother ever had any satisfaction. She probably thought it was something that men wanted but women didn't and weren't supposed to get any satisfaction out of it.

This is enough material to give a picture of Mr. G.'s family relational pattern and his role or position in it. Further material merely elaborates the basic pattern of a neurotically dominating mother; a passive and somewhat dependent father who doubtless gets certain satisfaction out of his role; an older son who has accepted without conscious protest the pattern of behavior his mother imposes on him and thereby gains her approval; a younger son who is hated by the mother and who is identified in part with the father, but who revenges himself on the mother by being a rebel and a black sheep. In spite of his rebellion, however, he still unconsciously wishes for the mother's direction and domination. His pattern of behavior calls for the mother on whom he can depend and against whom he can fight. His "wayward" behavior is therefore functionally related to his mother-son pattern of interaction.

This is sufficient to give some conception of the general pattern of relations in Mr. G.'s family. We can now turn to Mrs. G.'s family pattern.

Mrs. G. is the middle child of three. The oldest child, a girl, has been sickly and practically an invalid since she was ten or twelve years of age. The youngest child, a boy, was three years younger than Mrs. G. and was the person she felt most attached to in her family after her mother died. Her mother was very ill for two years when Mrs. G. was eleven to thirteen years of age, and died during Mrs. G.'s thirteenth year. Mrs. G. remembers her mother with the warmest affection and says her mother had the reputation of being one of the kindest persons in the community. She feels she is very much like her mother in appearance and in personal characteristics. All her relatives pointed to her as the child most like her mother. The mother depended on her a great deal even before she was ill, and when the mother became ill, most of the responsibilities for running the household rested on Mrs. G.'s shoulders. Her mother gave Mrs. G. her own wedding ring shortly before she died, and the family more or less made Mrs. G. the mother of the household.

She thinks her mother and father were quite happy in their marriage. From her description, the relation was much more equalitarian than was the case in Mr. G.'s family. The chief point of disagreement was the occasional celebrations of the father, in which he would get drunk and become quite noisy and jolly. This humiliated the mother, but she never remained angry very long and tended to make excuses for her husband.

My father drank in a crowd, and his drinking was always a kind of celebration. When he was drunk, he was noisy but never cruel or nasty to us. My mother excused him by saying it was a weakness of his character and he couldn't help it. It didn't happen very often, only about once every month or two. My husband's drinking is more unsociable, and he gets bitter and hateful when he is drunk. It used to embarrass me terribly if the neighbors would find out that my father was drunk—he was so foolish and silly. After my mother died, he drank more frequently, and

I used to pray that he would stop. My brother got to drinking with him, and I used to try to keep back his money so he couldn't drink so much.

Both my father and my brother were against my marrying Tom. I think they would have been against anyone I married, though. My brother was especially opposed. My sister and I figured he must have a sister complex on me and can't stand anybody having his sister. I suppose it is because I have been something like a mother to him. He has always been my special job, even before mother was sick. If he had any trouble in school, I was the one who had to straighten him out. Since I married he has got to drinking more and more. He is in business with my father [auto garage and repair shop], and I suppose they just get to drinking together. He says I am the only person who can keep him straight, but my marriage doesn't show I can even keep a husband straight.

This is sufficient material to give an outline picture of the relational pattern of Mrs. G.'s family, and particularly Mrs. G.'s own role in the situation. Obviously her role is that of a responsibility-assuming parent in relation to rather dependent persons. Particularly is this true in her relation to her brother. This brother has certain "wayward" patterns which, in gross overt form, are similar to the patterns of her husband.

It is probably no accident that Mrs. G. selected a personality to marry who seemed to fit into the wayward, younger brother-son role. Nor is it probable that Mr. G.'s choice of a woman who had the behavior and attitude patterns appropriate to a mothering role—a role for which he has both strong dependent and hostile rebellious attitudes—was accidental. Of course these were not the conscious bases of choice, but the reaction systems built up in the formative years tended to guide such choices quite unconsciously.

The marriage situation seems to be, in part at least, a drama in which these reaction systems are acting themselves out. Mr. G.'s "wayward" behavior, of course, is not a simple pattern of satisfying one drive-action complex. There is a multiple satisfaction in his behavior. It seems clear that this mode of action stimulates his wife and his friends [11] as well to intensive protective, supervising, and other parental behavior.   It also seems clear that his behavior is a means of aggression against his wife and of hurting her.   He needs to attack and revenge himself on a mother-person.[12]   His alcoholism is also without doubt an attempt to escape in a regressive manner from the tension-laden relations in home, business, and other departments of life.

Mrs. G. certainly suffers in the situation, but one seems to detect a certain satisfaction of deeply imbedded action patterns in her martyrlike, mothering role.

Space limitations preclude the use of other cases.   But the foregoing cases illustrate the general analytical approach employed in the marriages studied.

Psychogenetic and Cultural Patterns in Marital Relations

In some cases the situation turns primarily on attitude-behavior patterns which are cultural in the sense that they are held by the group to be the expected patterns of husband-wife relations.   Thus, if a Southern rural boy whose cultural patterns call for a chivalrous, indulgent, but dominant husband and a dependent, "feminine" wife marries an urban girl brought up in a social milieu which expects the woman to be aggressive, self-sufficient, and career-minded, a clash of cultural patterns may cause maladjustment.   In all cases there is usually some integration of individual and cultural patterns. Thus a part of Mr. G.'s behavior toward his wife is related to his particular mother-son structure; but there is also the general cultural pattern of male dominance and female subordination

---

[11] Note that the other persons Mrs. G. "mobilizes" stand in a parent relation to Mr. G.; viz., his boss, the minister, the family doctor.

[12] The mother-person withheld love and full response in Mr. G.'s childhood family, and the wife-mother withholds complete response in the sexual relations in marriage.   In both situations the mother-person is rebelled against.

which adds force to his attitudes of revolt. ("I would never let a woman run over me like my mother has done to my father.") And a part of Mrs. A.'s disappointment in her husband is his poor rendition of the cultural role of the adequate-provider husband.

In many instances the cultural patterns are in direct opposition to the individual patterns. Thus the male who is passive and dependent and who marries an adequate and aggressive female is in chronic conflict because the cultural expectations demand that he be the leader, initiator, provider, and sexual aggressor, while his basic personal patterns run counter to this expected role.

The number of cases studied in the manner described in this chapter is too small to furnish a basis for a classification scheme of psychogenetic and cultural patterns in relation to adjustment in marriage. Further research must produce a more adequate base of data before such an attempt can be made. The study of these cases, however, does indicate that specific interpersonal patterns of behavior arise in the intimate interaction of the person with his parents and siblings, and that these patterns are dynamic in determining compatibility or incompatibility in the intimate relations of married life.[13]

---

[13] For a statement of the way in which case-study data may be used in forecasting adjustment in marriage, see pp. 337–339.

CHAPTER XII

The Sexual Factor

THE SCHEDULE filled out by the 526 couples of the present study contained no premarital items regarding the sexual factor in marriage adjustment. This omission was intentional. In organizing the study it was decided to concentrate upon the economic and social aspects of marriage, aspects that had been more or less omitted or neglected in previous research.

The omission from the schedule of data on the sexual life of the person before marriage does not imply any disposition to minimize the importance of the sex factor. On the contrary, in the interviews careful attention was given to problems of sexual adjustment before and after marriage. Effort was especially directed to finding out (1) the nature of sexual adjustment in marriage, (2) the way in which sexual factors were interrelated with other factors in making for or against satisfactory adjustment in marriage, and (3) whether or not the probability of sexual compatibility could be predicted before marriage.

The following discussion of sexual factors in marriage is based upon a limited number of cases in which material was collected through the interviews or through written autobiographical documents. Of 100 cases thus studied, only 49 furnished sufficient material on sexual adjustment for an interpretation of the problems existing in the sexual aspect of the marriage. With so small a number of cases no attempt can be made at a systematic discussion of all factors affecting sexual adjustment.

In the analysis of the material on sexual behavior obtained from these couples it was soon apparent, first, that no absolute standard of "normal" or nonproblem sexual behavior can be set up; and, second, that sexual behavior in nearly all cases must be studied in relation to the attitudes and social experience of the person.

There is, actually, no normal sexual act in the sense of a mechanically standardized routine of actions or experiences. There is wide variation in the sexual act from couple to couple and from time to time in the activity of the same couple. There is variation in the intensity of desire, the kinds of acts which stimulate sexual desire, the nature and extent of preliminary sexual . interstimulation before coitus, the postures taken in coitus, the height of feeling in the orgasm, the time taken in the sexual activity, and the intervals between coitus. The variations do not constitute problems unless they operate to produce chronic frustrations of sexual satisfaction, or chronic negative attitudes toward sexual activity. It is, therefore, necessary to conceive of the normal sex act in relative terms if one is to evaluate properly sexual adjustment in marriage.[1]

A study of the cases included in this research clearly indicates what every experienced clinical worker knows; namely, that it is impossible to deal analytically or therapeutically with most sexual behavior apart from other aspects of the personality. Sexual attitudes and patterns are inextricably bound up with the total personality organization and can be dealt with only as a part of the total personality.[2]

Problems of Sexual Adjustment Classified

In analyzing marital adjustment, particularly for purposes of prediction, it is necessary and convenient to abstract various fac-

---

[1] See Th. H. van de Velde, *Ideal Marriage,* translated by Stella Browne, New York, Covici-Friede, 1930, Chapters 8–12.

[2] In the case of Mr. and Mrs. A. (see Chapter XI) the physician had made rather prolonged attempts to deal with the problems of adjustment by centering attention on the sexual techniques and attitudes of the couple. This treatment did not improve the situation and, if anything, intensified the problems. It was only after attention was focused on the more generalized, basic personality patterns that any insight was gained and any therapeutic progress made, even in the sexual relationship.

tors and deal with them more or less apart from the others. Thus, cultural factors, personality factors, and sexual factors are discussed in separate chapters in this study. But the reader needs to bear in mind that this separation is for purposes of analysis and does not appear in the dynamic clinical picture of a given case.

With this point in mind the problems of sexual adjustment found among the couples interviewed may be discussed under the following headings:

1. Problems due primarily to lack of knowledge and skill in sexual activity.

2. Problems due primarily to organic factors.

3. Problems due primarily to conscious or unconscious attitudes toward sexual activity.

In this, as in any classification, a certain violence is done to the concrete phenomena. A case of poor sexual adjustment may have some organic factor present; but it may be that the chief difficulty is in attitude toward sexual activity. The physical factor may serve as a rationalizing explanation. A problem in which there is conflict over the merits of contraceptive devices may be basically one of attitudes towards sex in general. For example, a wife may have the attitude, possibly not entirely conscious, that sex is sinful and thus any contraceptive device which allows more sexual activity is undesirable to her. On the other hand, she may also be fearful of conception when so-called "natural" methods of contraception are used and hence not respond even in the sexual acts she does engage in.

Anything that seriously blocks or impairs the sex act in any of its phases will create a problem of sexual adjustment. It is important to know, if possible, what experiences or conditions prior to marriage affect sexual behavior after marriage. Is it feasible to predict sexual compatibility or incompatibility in a given marriage on the basis of (1) lack of sufficient knowledge and skill in sexual matters at the time of marriage, (2) organic difficulties in sexual adjustment, and (3) conscious or unconscious attitudes toward sexual activity?

Sexual-Adjustment Problems Due to Lack of Knowledge and Skill

A large group of sexual-adjustment cases represent no particular organic or attitudinal difficulties. The problems of this group are for the most part those of recently married persons whose knowledge of the anatomy, physiology, and psychology of sex or contraceptive procedures is so limited that they feel insecure or awkward in their sexual relations. Ten of the 49 couples studied intensively with respect to sexual adjustment stated that their early sexual relations were handicapped by varying degrees of ignorance. All felt that more adequate information would have made adjustment easier.

Several of the 51 couples who did not give sufficient data on their sexual adjustment made statements such as "Sexual adjustment in early marriage would have been easier had we been better informed" or "sexual satisfaction increased considerably after we got some good instruction and reading."

It is evident that lack of knowledge and skill in sexual matters can be ascertained at the time of marriage. By referring persons to sources of information and consultation, difficulties in sexual adjustment arising from this factor can be prevented. If middle-class urban persons have no serious organic or psychological problems, satisfactory sexual adjustment can be secured by remedying their lack of information.

Sexual-Adjustment Problems Due to Organic Factors

Since the research reported here was conducted by nonmedical investigators, no systematic study of organic factors in sexual relations was undertaken. In the interview cases, the subject was routinely asked if physical examinations had revealed any structural or functional deviations in the reproductive system. If there had been no physical examination, one was suggested. Most of those in which some sexual maladjustment was present did seek medical advice.

Only in a small proportion of cases were there reports of any organic difficulties. This was perhaps to be expected, since the couples interviewed were a relatively unselected group. There is, however, considerable evidence to support the contention that difficulties in sex relations are more frequently due to nonorganic than to organic factors. Dickinson and Beam conclude from a medical study of 1,000 marriages that "sexual difficulties are infrequently organic in the woman and, save in exceptional cases, not functional. They are variants of mental and emotional behavior." [3] By the term "mental and emotional behavior" the authors seem to mean the phenomena the social psychologist refers to as attitudes, socially conditioned behavior patterns, and so forth.

Of the 100 couples in this study, only 5 reported organic factors that seemed to affect the sex relation. In some of these cases there was good reason to suspect an attitudinal factor as being more important than the organic condition.

The first case was that of a middle-aged husband who showed a sudden increase of rather intense sexual desire. The symptoms were increased sexual demands upon his wife and increased interest in establishing a sexual relationship with other women. He seemed to desire sexual satisfaction even at the risk of endangering his professional security as well as his marriage and family relationships. A physician diagnosed the case as chronic satyriasis, due to local irritation and congestion which caused excessive activity of the reproductive glandular system. Treatment was not particularly successful, the couple finally separated, and contact with the husband was lost. No psychoanalytic study of the case was possible to determine

---

[3] Dickinson, Robert L., and Beam, Lura, *A Thousand Marriages*, Baltimore, Williams and Wilkins Co., 1931, p. 447.

whether the organic factors were primary or were derivative of unconscious attitudinal factors, such as, for example, the possibility that a situation had arisen in which the man may have been overreacting to a fear of inadequacy or a fear of a homosexual component in his sexual attitudes. There is, however, evidence that conditions indicated in this case may have been produced by purely organic processes.

The second case involved a structural deviation diagnosed as a tipped uterus. The condition was discovered when the wife went to her physician for a physical examination. Her complaints were difficulty in achieving orgasm and failure to become pregnant. A surgical operation corrected the structural condition. The physician's comment was that the condition had nothing to do with satisfactory coitus, but did prevent conception. Following the operation, conception did occur. Satisfactory coitus was not achieved regularly, however, until after psychiatric treatment the wife was able to change some deep-laid attitudes which seemed to be rooted in her early family experiences.

The third case was one in which the wife was infected with gonorrhea by her husband, who had supposed himself cured of an old infection. The pathological condition, of course, complicated the sexual relationship; but the wife, after medical treatment and cure, became frigid for a year or more. The temporary frigidity was apparently due more to attitudes of fear and resentment than to actual organic conditions following the treatment of the disease.

In the fourth case the wife had puerile uterus. There seemed, according to the physician, to be a general lack of maturity of the reproductive system. Intercourse was avoided and was somewhat painful to the wife. The physician recommended tonic and dilational treatment, but the patient's attitude was one of indifference to any attempt to change the condition, and little was done. There was no motivation on her part, since she experienced no sexual desire and seemed to have no appre-

ciation of the amount of deprivation her husband was experiencing. He, for his part, had more or less accepted the situation and was seeking occasional sexual satisfaction in outside
affairs, but was not desirous of a divorce.

The fifth case was that of a wife whose condition was diagnosed by her physician as dyspareunia (local pain in the geni-
talia during coitus), which he attributed to a disproportion
between the sizes of her and her husband's genital organs.
The wife experienced rather intense pain during intercourse
and regarded the difficulty as due to the fact that her husband's
penis was too large for her vagina. In this case there was some
reason for suspecting that the organic factor was secondary to
social-psychological factors. The wife had been strictly reared,
and her mother had inculcated a markedly negative attitude
toward all kinds of sexual behavior. The wife greatly feared
pregnancy. She had been abruptly and clumsily introduced
to sexual relations by her husband, who was devoid of any
sexual art or understanding. Divorce occurred in one year,
and contact with the couple was lost. Hence an adequate analysis of the possible psychological basis of the difficulty is lacking.

The fact that more of the cases did not report organic sexual
difficulties does not necessarily mean they were absent. A complete and systematic physical examination of all the cases would
be necessary before the proportion of physical problems could
be stated with any degree of assurance. It is significant that
of the five cases reporting organic conditions as causes of sexual
maladjustment, all had important social-psychological aspects,
and in two and possibly three of them there is considerable
probability that the social-psychological factors were more important than the organic factors in producing a poor sexual
adjustment. As in the case of other organic defects, the attitudes of human beings toward them are relevant factors that
must also be taken into account.

Since this study did not include a systematic medical examination, no attempt will be made to cover the range of organic conditions affecting sexual adjustment. Readers who are interested in this aspect of the subject may refer to good bibliographies in standard works.[4]

Where organic conditions prejudicial to sexual adjustment are present at the time of marriage, they can be discovered and often corrected if a thorough physical examination is then made by a competent physician.[5]

Sexual-Adjustment Problems Due to Attitudinal Factors

Most of the cases in this study in which sex was a primary problem in marital adjustment seem to classify as psychological or attitudinal problems. There is no doubt that sexual attitude and behavior patterns are in many cases the primary source of maladjustment in marriage. There is evidence, however, to support the contention that frequently, where a sexual problem exists, it has developed because of other problems based on cultural or individual personality factors. In many of the cases dealt with in this study it seemed impossible to determine with any certainty whether sexual or nonsexual factors were primary, so closely were the two interwoven in the case picture. Perhaps the prolonged-interview technique such as that used in Freudian psychoanalysis might reveal the sequence, but this technique was not used on any of the couples studied.

Of the 49 couples with whom sexual matters were discussed, 9 were apparently well adjusted sexually.[6] Of the other 40

---

[4] Examples of works dealing with the physical structure and functional aspects of this problem are: Byford, H. T., *Manual of Gynecology*, 3rd edition, Philadelphia, P. Blakiston's Son & Co., 1903; Dickinson, Robert L., *Topographical Atlas of Human Sex Anatomy;* Dickinson, Robert L., and Beam, Lura, *One Thousand Marriages,* Baltimore, Williams and Wilkins Co., 1931; Hühner, Max, *Disorders of the Sexual Function in the Male and Female,* 3rd edition, Philadelphia, F. A. Davis Co., 1931 (see bibliography in this volume for other useful works).

[5] See Robert L. Dickinson, "Premarital Examination as Routine Preventive Gynecology," *American Journal of Obstetrics and Gynecology,* 16, 1928, pp. 631–641.

[6] The 51 cases which did not furnish sufficient sexual data probably contain a higher proportion of cases with no sexual problems than the 49 cases in which the sexual factor was discussed.

couples, 10 have been classified as cases of lack of knowledge and skill in sexual matters and 5 as cases in which organic factors affect the sexual relationship. Five of the remaining 25 seemed to be fairly clear cases in which specifically sexual attitude problems were primary in the maladjustments of the marriage. In the remaining 20 cases, problems of sexual attitudes, although present, either seemed to be derivatives of maladjustments that had their sources in cultural or individual personality conflicts, or were so interwoven with other aspects of the marriage that it was impossible to say whether the specifically sexual or the nonsexual aspects were primary in the situation.

The 25 cases in which the sexual problem was psychological or attitudinal may be classified into four groups. Under each category cases will be given to illustrate the dynamics underlying some of these surface pictures.

1. In the first group are cases in which there is a general lack of sexual desire on the part of one of the marriage partners. (If both partners have little or no conscious sexual desire, there is usually no particular problem.) In the cases of this class there is considerable avoidance of or actual resistance to sexual activity, with consequent frustration and resentment on the part of the sexually unsatisfied mate. In some of these cases there will be a lack of desire, but a willingness to engage in sex acts as a marital duty for the sake of the spouse. Such "duty" behavior is more likely to be found in the wife than in the husband, partly because of cultural patterns which demand that "wives submit themselves unto their husbands," and partly because of difficulties of intercourse when the male cannot achieve an erection. There are, however, cases in this group in which the husbands have little or no desire, but can manage to achieve a partial erection to perform what they describe as their duty. In either case although a physical sexual act takes place, it is unsatisfactory to the desiring partner, probably because there is no full and free sexual response from the willing but inadequate

mate. The mates of frigid wives or impotent husbands usually give much evidence of a sense of frustration and resentment even though sexual acts take place.

2. The second group is composed of cases in which a person lacks sexual desire for relations with the marriage partner, but has strong sexual desires directed toward other persons either in phantasy or in overt behavior. In some of these cases the person believes himself totally frigid or impotent, but has merely repressed the tabooed extramarital desires.

3. There is a third group of cases which have the common surface characteristics of periods of desire for and indulgence in sexual activity, followed by feelings of revulsion, guilt, disgust, depression, and so on.

4. In a fourth group may be placed cases with the surface characteristics of hypersexual activity. The complaint may be that one partner is making excessive sexual demands on the other or that a partner may feel it is necessary to have several outside sexual affairs because his marital sexual activities are not sufficient. The usual assumption by the persons themselves is that the hypersexual activity indicates an unusually vigorous sex drive and physical energy. With the exception of the few cases actually based on physical factors, these are not excessively vigorous "oversexed" people, but present complex psychological factors to be discussed later.

These four classes are intended to be not basic categories but rather groupings of cases in terms of the surface manifestations or complaints that were immediately presented to the investigator. Very different mechanisms may operate, as will be seen later, in cases of the same groupings. Moreover, these four classes do not exhaust the field; they only represent the range of a limited number of cases.

General Lack of Sexual Desire

In the first class fall cases in which a person has strong conscious and unconscious inhibitory attitudes toward all sexual impulses. The person usually claims to have no sexual impulses or only very mild sexual desire. When the case is that of the wife, she is usually classified as frigid; when the case is that of the husband, he is usually classified as being impotent. Some of these generalized inhibited cases are results of exceedingly strict and thoroughgoing imposition of the cultural taboos on all forms of sexual manifestation. This process starts in the training of the infant and continues unabated throughout adolescence in the typical Puritanic home. The mechanism in others is that the incest desires are repressed by the development of a general repression of all sex desires. In still other cases the repression of incest strivings may operate if the marriage mate too nearly plays the role of a former object of attachment against whom the incest taboos had to be developed.

Another mechanism may be present in the generalized lack of sexual desire. A person's sex drives may have been conditioned homosexually. Strong cultural taboos are imposed which repress conscious and overt homosexuality. There is no desire for intercourse with a heterosexual partner; hence there is no conscious sexual desire.

Still another mechanism found in these cases of weak sex desire is that of a rather complete fixation of the love drives on the self. A person characterized by extreme narcissism may have no specific sexual desires, or the desires may be expressed in considerable autoeroticism.

Another type of case is that of the person who has strong feelings of inferiority or inadequacy and is unable to be assertive and give expression to impulses even in the sexual sphere. Sometimes severe injury to one's social role, one's status, one's security, will produce sexual frigidity or impotence. On the other hand, such damage or feeling of inferiority may result in compensatory excesses in sexual behavior.

A few case excerpts will illustrate some of these mechanisms. It is well to remember that while one mechanism seems to be the significant one, more than one process may be at work to produce the resultant sexual inadequacy.

Mr. B. complained that his wife never wished to have sexual relations with him. She frequently refused on the ground of feeling ill or fatigued, and at other times simply stated she did not desire sexual relations. When sex relations occurred (as they did very rarely), she did not respond. The husband wondered if his wife "really loved" him. He was fairly well informed on sexual anatomy, physiology, and contraceptive methods. He tells of two premarital affairs in which he seemed to demonstrate competence in the art and technique of the sexual act. He takes considerable time in sexual foreplay in an effort to stimulate his wife, but says "her lack of any response to the situation cramps my style."

Mrs. B. thinks her lack of desire is due to her being easily fatigued. "I'm probably not as strong as other women, and do not have the physical energy to want sex." But she adds she can work hard all day and not be too tired to go out to parties or to the theatre. She says she has noticed her feelings of great fatigue will come suddenly just before her husband arrives home at night or just before her usual time for retiring. Her feeling ill or very tired is especially marked on Sundays. At one point in her narrative she told of her husband's being away for a week. She remembers this week particularly for her lack of fatigue, and the Sunday of that week as one of those rare week-ends when she "felt like going places and doing things." She admits that there may be some basis for the suggestion that her feelings of being ill or fatigued might be ways of avoiding sexual intercourse. She adds that the thought of sexual intercourse was sometimes enough to give her these feelings.

Mrs. B. was very closely identified with her strictly religious mother who, she says, "gave me all the facts of sex when I started to ask questions." But it is found that her mother was herself an extremely frigid woman and frequently expressed to her daughter the idea that men are animalistic and women have to submit to the indignity of sexual relations because men could not remain healthy or content if denied such gratification. Mrs. B. says she was nearly twenty-one years of age before she realized (with considerable shock) that there are women who passionately desire sexual intercourse. She thought the woman depraved who expresses such desires.

Mrs. B. relates many instances which reveal the strong repressive training she received from her mother in sexual matters, although the mother evidently gave her accurate information on the anatomy and physiology of sex. Mrs. B. was very religious until after late adolescence, and much of her religious instruction was related to "keeping pure." She has no special desire to change her sexual attitudes, but feels sorry that her husband is not satisfied with the situation. She does not care to seek psychiatric aid. She thinks the solution is for her husband to "exercise will power and restrain his instincts."

Mr. and Mrs. F. present much the same picture as the case just described, but with certain interesting variations. One difference is that Mr. F. not only feels deprived but he takes the situation as an aspersion on his manhood and uses alcohol to bolster his sense of adequacy. Another difference is that Mrs. F. does not have the same resistance to granting her husband sexual access. She does not resist; but she does not respond. In this case, some slight improvement has been noted as a result of Mrs. F.'s reading in sexual-hygiene literature and her attempts to simulate sexual passion. She has been telling her husband she is experiencing more satisfaction, but he states that he thinks "it's just the suggestion from those books and is not real." Mrs. F. wished to go to a psychiatrist, but the family income was inadequate to pay for such treatment.

Mrs. F.'s mother died when she was quite young, and she was brought up by two maiden aunts who were very strict. She was never allowed to play with boys, nor with girls who were likely to have much sexual interest. She was sent to a convent school when she finished elementary school. She said that until she was married she thought people had sex relations only for the purpose of having children. She recalls the horror-struck manner and voice with which her aunts hushed her up when she made inquiries regarding the possibilities of the aunts having any children as other women did. She recalls no sexual episode for which she was punished, but remembers how the aunts would tell her not to have anything to do with boys. She wondered why, but does not remember having asked the aunts. For some time after her childhood she remembers having a vague feeling that any contact with boys or men was somehow dangerous or sinful.

The same generalized repression of sexual drives appeared in the case of Mr. H., who reported that he rarely felt any sexual urges and had had intercourse with his wife only three or four times during the two years of their marriage. He states that with one exception he felt no strong drive nor any satisfaction in the act. His wife made the approaches each time, except once when he was partially intoxicated and "discovered I had some sexual feeling and made love to my wife." Mrs. H. had deserted her husband shortly before contact was made with the case. Hence her side of the story is not available.

Until after he had had several interviews, Mr. H. could report no memories of sex interest or activity as a child. Then he remembered a considerable amount of repressed material which centered around his fifth and sixth years. At that time, according to his memories, he had rather intense curiosity and engaged in exploratory activity with other children. Nearly all of his recollections of sexual investigation at this time were coupled with memories of severe punishment by his parents, especially by his father. When he does not remember punishment, he recalls intense anxiety and fear of discovery. These experiences were apparently followed by a period during which, according to his recollections, there was neither sex activity nor interest. He does remember older boys in school talking of sexual matters and his feeling that they were very sinful. For a short time during early adolescence he masturbated. He recalls acute feelings of guilt. "A great burden seemed to weigh down on me." He was convinced that he had committed "the unpardonable sin." He became very religious after a "revival meeting," joined a church, and became an active leader among the young people. He became locally famous for his piety and for the intensity of his attacks on "the sins of youth."

Mrs. H. was one of the young people he interested in church work during "a campaign for a more Christian community." They married after Mr. H. had been away at college for two years on a scholarship which he received from his church.

Another case of general lack of sex desire is interesting because it offers a more complex etiology than the foregoing cases.

Mr. and Mrs. J. had sought medical advice for their lack of satisfactory sex adjustment. The case turned out, as most cases do, to include many factors, only one of which was sex. Only the sexual problem will be noted here.

Mrs. J. claimed to have no sexual desire and preferred not to have any sexual relations in her marriage. She alternated between avoiding and resisting sexual relations and submitting to them to please her husband. Both asserted a desire to find out the cause of the wife's lack of sexual responsiveness. Mrs. J. had an explanation that the condition was due to a shock which she sustained when she was eight or nine years old. She was sleeping in her room one evening while her parents were visiting with neighbors, and awoke to discover a strange person who was apparently attempting to assault her sexually. She reports,

> I was asleep and was awakened suddenly by someone attempting to unfasten my pajamas and get his hand on me. The first thought in my mind was "This is my brother Bob." I screamed, and people came running in. The man got away before they got there, and the whole thing was hushed up and didn't get in the papers. But ever since I have been afraid; and whenever I think of it, I always remember that I thought it was my oldest brother. [The brother was about sixteen when the episode occurred.]

Mrs. J. states that she avoided hearing or speaking about all sexual matters after this experience. She could produce no memories of sex interest or exploratory activities before the shock experience and none after it. On the face of it, Mrs. J.'s frigidity might be attributed to the shock experience, which "conditioned" her negatively to sexual activity. The psychoanalysts, however, have pointed out that there is some basis for suspecting that shock experiences are frequently pseudo-explanations. In the present case it may perhaps be that the shock experience, while important in itself, gains importance by serving as a convenient way of repressing memories of early sex interests and activities for which there are strong guilt feelings. The contact with this case was not long enough to establish a more reliable interpretation of the factors in the wife's attitudes, but in the interviews certain points came out that are probably significant.

Mrs. J. remembered that as a girl and even at the present time she entertained and entertains a bitter hatred for her brother Bob (the brother she thought of in the assault episode). She states that one of the reasons she married her husband was that he was the exact opposite of her domineering, egocentric brother. But she lets fall statements full of indications that she also has a strong admiration for this brother. As the interviews continued, she finally produced rather vague memories of sexually tinged play with this brother, as "playing doctor," which occurred before the assault experience. These recollections were accompanied by memories of guilt feelings and fears of being discovered.

It is quite possible that Mrs. J.'s feelings of guilt over her incestuous desires made her overreact to the shock experience and that her frigidity is a product of strong repression of early incestuous desires, and possibly repression of anxieties created by sex activities with the brother. The shock memory is for her a more satisfactory, less anxiety-laden explanation for her attitudes.

Sometimes a general lack of sexual desire appears to be the result of what psychoanalysts call a fixation of libidinal drives at pregenital levels.

Mrs. K. had been a model for an exclusive dress shop. She was regarded as a very beautiful woman. Mr. K., a divorced broker, married her after a rather tempestuous and romantic courtship which he remembers now chiefly in terms of the money spent for flowers, jewelry, night-club entertainments, and the like. After a month of marriage, Mrs. K. stated quite frankly to her husband that she had no desire for sex relations with him. She indicated that she would not be adverse to Mr. K.'s having discreet affairs with more congenial sexual companions. Mr. K. was quite certain that there was no other man in the case and that his wife had no sexual desires.

From Mr. K.'s statement (the wife's story could not be obtained), Mrs. K. was happiest and most content when she was physically comfortable and when she was the center of admiring friends.

She was like a cat that had to be petted all the time, but never puts itself out for anybody else. I believe she felt her best when she was being worked on by beauty specialists, masseuses, manicurists, and so on. She spent hours on end on that kind of stuff.

Apparently Mrs. K. spent most of her time on her appearance or her physical comfort. If she had a slight illness, it was a matter of great moment.

She is the most selfish person I ever knew [reports Mr. K.]. I can be dead tired or too sick to hold my head up and it means nothing to her. She even gets sore at me for being sick. But if she is sick or has had some little trouble, if I don't make a fuss over her, she says I am never concerned with anybody but myself.

Mr. K. states that in spite of her "selfishness" he is still very fond of his wife and strongly attracted to her sexually. He feels, however, that the only time she ever yields to him sexually is when she "wants to get something out of me."

Allowing for the possibility that Mr. K. is also a self-centered person, it nevertheless appears that Mrs. K. is probably a highly narcissistic personality. Interpreting the case in this manner amounts to saying that the libidinal drives are turned back upon the self and are expressed through nongenital channels.

Practically nothing is known of Mrs. K.'s early history. It is probably significant that she was an orphan at birth and was reared in an institution until she was six years of age, at which time she was adopted by a childless middle-aged couple. Mr. K. states that she hardly ever refers to her foster parents and seems to have no feeling of affection for them.

Specific Lack of Sexual Desire

The second group of psychological cases is composed of those in which the lack of sexual desire is specific but not general. There are cases in which the frigidity or impotence holds for the marriage situation but not with respect to other possible sexual relations.

Mrs. L. wanted to discuss her marriage because she feared she had made a mistake in marrying Mr. L. After a conventional courtship she married her husband, only to find that she was not responsive to him sexually, although she had regularly enjoyed the mild petting in the courtship. Soon after the marriage, she met a friend of her husband in whom she felt a strong sexual interest. She had never felt the same way toward her husband even during courtship. She avoided the man because she did not wish to get involved in an affair and was afraid he would discover how much she was attracted to him.

She wished especially to discuss the question of whether her fondness for her husband (which persisted) was "just friendship" or "real love," and whether or not she should seek a divorce before sexual problems gave rise to serious maladjustments. She was concerned about her lack of sexual response and wondered if she were "abnormal." This latter question was given point by the fact that two of her friends had remarked that they thought her husband had a good deal of "sex appeal." (He was an athlete, and these friends described him as the quiet, strong-man type.) Moreover, her husband seemed to be sexually attracted to her, was handsome, and knew a good deal about the technique and art of sex.

In describing the husband's personality she used terms such as handsome, intelligent, quiet, reliable, "one you would always go to and expect solid support from," and so on.

In a later interview regarding her family relationships, she gave evidence of strong attachment to her father who was, in turn, very devoted to her (she was an only child). When asked to describe her father's personality, she (apparently unconsciously) used the same kind of phraseology and presented about the same picture she had used in describing her husband.

The man to whom she felt sexually attracted was described as a rather opposite type from her husband. He was pictured as unreliable, assertive, witty, superficial, lacking in principles, and "always in some kind of a jam."

In her dreams she frequently identifies her husband and her father. "I dreamt I was going on a trip, either with my father or my husband; I'm not clear which one." In other ways she shows a tendency to identify the two. Occasionally in the interview she would be speaking of her father and call him by her husband's name, or the slip would be reversed.

Our tentative interpretation, which later appeared to be validated by a partial psychoanalysis, was as follows: Mrs. L. was strongly attached to her father. In this relation, sexual feelings had been completely repressed. She selected as a husband a man who fitted closely the father pattern. She was much attached to him; but the same sexual taboos which operated in her relations with her father partly operated also in her relation with her husband. In relation to a man who was very different from the father-husband pattern, her sexual impulses were freer to become conscious. The marriage mores, however, inhibited her sexual activity in this connection; but the blockage was conscious.

Psychoanalytic efforts gave Mrs. L. sufficient insight and effected shifts in her attitude so that sexual attitudes toward her husband showed some improvement.

For another instance of this discriminative inhibition, the reader may refer to the case of Mr. and Mrs. A. in the chapter on personality factors in marriage adjustment.[7] In this case, while Mrs. A. could not play the adequate mother-sister role sufficiently to satisfy fully a profound need of Mr. A.'s personality, yet she did in part play that role. Certainly whatever satisfaction Mr. A. found in the relationship was due to her efforts to comfort and bolster him. A part of the sexual blockage in Mr. A. appeared to be due to the operation of incest taboos toward the sister role partly played by his wife.

_____

[7] Chapter XI, pp. 192–201.

Alternating Periods of Desire and Aversion

The cases in the third group are similar to other cases of sexual blockage in that there are powerful inhibitory structures against sexual behavior. But in these cases the repression is not complete. The personality alternately shows the predominance of conscious sexual drives followed by a predominance of punishing, condemning, disgust, or other negative reactions. This sequence is illustrated by the following case.

Mrs. M. complained that her husband avoided sex relations and that, when they did occur, they left her unsatisfied. She stated that Mr. M.'s sexual approaches were diffident, embarrassed, and uncertain. Little time was devoted to foreplay, and intercourse was very brief. Consequently she rarely experienced orgasm. After intercourse Mr. M.'s manner seemed to indicate a feeling of embarrassment and disgust. He seemed to feel that a necessary function had been performed, but it was something to get out of mind as soon as possible.

After four years of marriage she had given up any hope for a satisfactory sexual life with her husband and had developed an affair with a friend of the couple, a divorced man-about-town who she said was entirely adequate in his sexual behavior and gave her full satisfaction. She wished to divorce her husband before he discovered her affair.

Mr. M. comes from a well-to-do family in a small Midwestern community. The family is among the leading people of the section and prides itself on its New England background. He stated that sex was a closed question in his family. Even brothers and sisters did not discuss such matters. He has no memories of childhood sexual episodes or punishment.[8] His

---

[8] Since there were only three interviews in this case, it was not possible to obtain a revelation of repressed memories of such experiences.

parents always maintained the attitude of "We know you would never think of doing anything that you couldn't tell your father and mother." He remembers that in his adolescent and youthful sexual experiences the failure to live up to this expectation of his parents caused him acute distress.

Although he lived in a strict family environment, he went around with the smart set of the section, some of whom were quite emancipated in their sexual codes. He participated in their drinking and sexual activity. He felt strong sex urges, but when he engaged in "heavy necking and petting" and later in intercourse with prostitutes he suffered strong feelings of revulsion and a sense of sin.

In his marriage Mr. M. admits having feelings of embarrassment in any intimate activity with his wife. He says, "I'm very modest in my nature and even hate to undress in the same room with my wife. She has no modesty." He says he feels no moral guilt about his sex relations with his wife, but cannot get over the feeling that "there is something nasty about it." He usually feels more or less ill or disgusted after sexual intercourse. He often has a severe headache afterwards. His general comment was "I believe if sex could be eliminated from human nature, we would all be much happier."

Mr. M.'s family relationships had laid down powerful countersexual patterns in his personality, but his life in an outside group enabled him to develop sexual behavior which broke through the inhibitory structures. However, the inhibitory (or superego) patterns still remain strong tendencies. His experience with sex is therefore a kind of see-sawing between indulgence and self-condemnation or disgust reactions.

Surface Evidence of Hypersexual Activity

The fourth group of cases present a surface aspect of excessive sexual need and activity. Doubtless in some of these cases there are genuinely vigorous organic sex drives. In others, however, there are actually undersupplies of sexual energy; or there is a fear of some inadequacy. The excessive activity is in the nature of an attempt to reassure the self against such fears of inadequacy or to keep the self from recognizing strongly tabooed deviate wishes. For example, homosexual components (which according to a widely held theory are present in varying strengths in every personality) in the sexual drives may be repressed by reaction formations which may cause maladjustments in the marriage. The conscious homosexual does not marry, or at least he does not expect to get his libidinal satisfactions in any marriage he may contract. The unconscious homosexual (the personality with strong unconscious homosexual components) may establish a pseudo-heterosexual marriage and be well adjusted to it, as in the passive male-aggressive female combination. In some cases, however, the personality can successfully remain unconscious of its homosexuality only by rather intense preoccupation with heterosexual activity. This may give one the appearance of being "oversexed" or "naturally polygamous."

Mr. and Mrs. I. had been married two years when Mrs. I. came in for an interview. She was very much upset because her husband was frankly interested in another woman. Mr. I. told his wife that he was devoted to her, but that he was naturally oversexed and had a polygamous nature and could not help being attracted to more than one woman. He had several affairs in rapid succession. Mrs. I. had originally decided to tolerate these affairs in the hope that her husband was having a belated adolescent fling and would settle down after he had sown his wild oats. But several months passed with no change except an increase in Mr. I.'s outside interests and a decline in his sexual interest in his wife. She threatened to leave him, and he consented to coöperate in seeking counsel on their problem.

Over a period of time, with some psychiatric encouragement, the following facts emerged. Mr. I. was the only son of a passive father and a very aggressive mother. He identified himself very closely with his father and assumed the same passive role that his father assumed in relation to his mother. He occasionally broke out in rebellion against the mother's dominance, particularly after he joined a gang of adolescent boys who called him a "sissy" for being so obedient to his mother. His few early childhood and adolescent sex experiences included both heterosexual and homosexual activities. However, in the two adolescent heterosexual experiences he played the passive role. The girl in each instance was aggressive.

Mrs. I., the young wife, is a very aggressive, positive type of personality. She is an outstanding leader in the groups in which she participates. In the early stages of the courtship, Mr. I. would come to her for advice and counsel. She played the role of the adequate parent.

After marriage their sex life was intense and highly satisfying. Mrs. I. had had no overt sex experience, but had no serious inhibitions. She assumed a more and more positive and initiatory role in the sex act. Such positive participation is ordinarily highly satisfying to the male, who does not feel his male role threatened by too much aggressiveness on the part of the female. Mr. I., however, did feel threatened. He was apparently not explicitly aware of what was going on, but the history shows that as Mrs. I. became more aggressive in her sexual role, he developed some sexual aversion for her, and it was at this time that he began to develop interests in other women. He reports that homosexual dreams occurred at this time in which his wife was confused with a male. He remembers having transitory anxieties about his "normality" in connection with these dreams.

The interpretation of his seeking other women was that he was seeking to reassure himself of his male heterosexuality. His deep need to get such reassurance intensified as his wife increasingly sought to assert her control over him and to demand that he give up his outside interests. This action on her part doubled Mr. I.'s efforts to escape his passive role, to "assert his manhood," and also to reënact his rebellious pattern against a domineering-mother role. He reports that he "got to the place where he was determined to show her [his wife] who was boss."

It is interesting to note that most of Mr. I.'s paramours were rather aggressive types.

Through the therapeutic interviews Mr. I. gained insight into the dynamics of his behavior. He learned to recognize frankly the homosexual components and to accept them somewhat more casually than had hitherto been possible. The wife was given some "common-sense" insight which enabled her to play down the more obvious aggressive and domineering aspects of her role. The couple made a very good adjustment.

The case excerpts given above are not representative of the entire field of sexual problems; nor is their interpretation offered as a complete analysis of the dynamics of the sexual attitudes in these cases. They do, however, illustrate the point that problems appearing to be similar on the surface may be and frequently are very different when one goes into the patterns of experience of the individual. They also indicate that patterns of love and affection in marriage depend to a large extent on the social interactions of the person throughout his developmental career. They show further that, in practically every case, attitudes toward sex significant for adjustment in marriage are formed in childhood and adolescence and persist in marriage. There is little doubt, therefore, that these attitudes toward sex can be determined in a premarital interview, and that their probable effect upon marriage adjustment can be predicted. In certain cases it may also be feasible to offer information and advice that will prevent or minimize the anticipated marital difficulties.

In conclusion it appears that sexual adjustment in marriage, although complicated by the influence of other factors, is susceptible within certain limits to prediction. The findings of a rather intensive analysis of 49 case histories suggest the importance, for prediction of sexual compatibility in marriage, of (1) a thorough premarital physical examination to detect any organic conditions adverse to sexual adjustment, (2) determining the adequacy of the sexual knowledge of the bride and groom, and (3) a personal interview to discover their attitudes toward sex and the probable influence of past experiences and personal relations upon sexual adjustment in marriage.

CHAPTER XIII

Contingency Factors: Stability and Security

TWELVE questions were included in the Marriage Study Questionnaire referring to postmarital factors which it was assumed might be related to marital adjustment. The items answered at the time the schedule was filled out were the following:

1. Number of years couple has been married.
2. Size of community in which couple lives.
3. Distance of couple's residence from Chicago.
4. Character of neighborhood in which couple resides.
5. (*a*) Type of residence in which couple lives.
   (*b*) Number of rooms in present residence.
   (*c*) Whether or not couple has bought, is buying, or is planning to buy a home.
   (*d*) Amount of rent paid per month.
   (*e*) Changes of residence.
6. Whether or not couple has lived with relatives since marriage.
7. How often couple visits or is visited by relatives.
8. Number of children born to couple.
9. Desire for children expressed by husband and wife.
10. Average time positions have been held by husband and wife since marriage.
11. Amount of unemployment of husband.
12. Financial index of the couple.

These conditions occurring after marriage may be regarded as resultants of factors present at the time of marriage. But they may also be looked upon, in part at least, as new influences which enter into the determination of the present state of adjustment of husband and wife. In this sense they may be termed contingency factors. By contingency factors, then, are meant those conditions which, although occurring after marriage, may be taken into account in predicting before marriage the probabilities of marital adjustment.

Most of the factors listed above can be more or less definitely ascertained before the marriage. Information may be obtained from the engaged couple in regard to the size of the community, the character of neighborhood, and the type of residence in which they plan to live. It is also possible to learn the approximate rent they intend to pay, whether they plan to buy a home, whether or not they will live with relatives, and how often they will visit and be visited by relatives. The couple have also almost without exception decided before marriage whether or not they desire children and, if so, how soon after marriage and how many.[1] The contingency factor of number of years married can of course be readily applied in terms of the given period of time desired.

The four items that cannot be definitely taken into account until at some definite period after marriage are: number of different residences, number of positions held by husband and wife, amount of unemployment experienced by husband, and the financial index of the family. These items can of course be used even before marriage in terms of the hypothetical possibilities as, for example, the possibility of the effect on marital adjustment if the husband be employed three years after marriage, or if he be unemployed, whether less or more than six months.

It must be admitted, however, in regard to every contingency

---

[1] This statement is made on the basis of the findings of a study of engaged couples by E. W. Burgess and Paul Wallin, now in progress.

factor, that the expectation at the time of marriage may not actually be realized. Further research will be necessary to determine the feasibility of the employment of contingency factors in the prediction of marital adjustment.

But whether or not contingency factors may legitimately be used in predicting marriage adjustment, they are highly significant in the study of marital relations, especially in the early years of married life. For of the 16 contingency items listed, all but the first one (the number of years married) are indicative of the important role played by stability and mobility, security and insecurity, in familial life. It is, therefore, according to the bearing of stability and security upon familial integration or, conversely of mobility and insecurity upon familial disintegration, that the contingency items will be mainly considered.

Time and Marriage

What is the effect of time upon marriage? Does marital adjustment (as measured by our indices of agreement on major familial issues, common interests and activities, demonstration of affection and mutual confidences, expressions of dissatisfaction with marriage, and feelings of isolation and personal unhappiness) increase or diminish with the years?

Studies of divorce indicate that the highest percentage of separations of couples who are later divorced occur in the first year of marriage and decline regularly with each successive year.[2] From this fact it might be inferred that marital adjustment is most difficult in the first year of marriage and becomes easier with the passage of time. At any rate, it tends to eliminate from married life those most unsuited for it.

The findings of the present study, while not conclusive on this point, indicate quite the reverse for the first six years of marriage.

---

[2] See United States Census *Bulletin* 96, "Marriage and Divorce," 1887–1906, p. 44. See also E. R. Mowrer, *Family Disorganization,* Chicago, 1927, p. 86.

An examination of Chart 41 shows that of all couples studied in the first year of married life, 55.7 per cent have "good" and only 22.9 per cent "poor" adjustment. On the other hand, of all couples married five and six years, only 29.4 per cent rate "good" and 36.9 per cent "poor" in adjustment. These are both significant differences.[3]

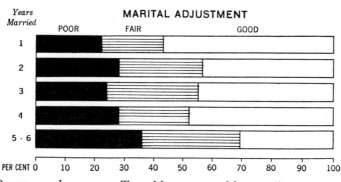

CHART 41.—LENGTH OF TIME MARRIED AND MARITAL ADJUSTMENT.

Couples married two, three, and four years do not differ significantly from each other, all showing proportions with "good" and "poor" adjustment intermediate between those of couples married one year or five and six years.[4]

Fortunately the findings of the study by Lang [5] present data for 7,393 couples showing the relation between length of time married and a rating of the happiness of each marriage by a close acquaintance of the couple. Since there is a high correlation between both the marital-adjustment score and the marital-happiness rating and reports of happiness by either spouse and an outside person, the findings presented in Chart

---

[3] L. M. Terman et al. in their book *Psychological Factors in Marital Happiness*, pp. 177 *ff.*, state that they find very little relation between length of time married and degree of adjustment. However, it is very evident from their data that in the first six years there is a sharp decline in the average adjustment score. This part of their findings agrees with our own.

[4] CR, .445 (combining the percentages with very high scores of those married two, three, and four years) with .557 (married one year), 1.6; and with .294 (married five to six years), 2.8.

[5] *The Rating of Happiness in Marriage,* unpublished M.A. thesis, University of Chicago, 1932.

42 may be taken as indicative of the effect of the passage of time upon reports of marital happiness.

An examination of this chart shows that friends of married couples rate the highest proportion as "very happy and happy" in the first two years of marriage and the lowest proportion in the fifteenth and sixteenth years of marriage. Conversely, the

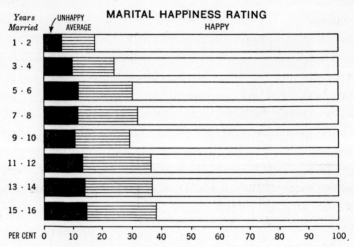

CHART 42.—NUMBER OF YEARS MARRIED AND RATINGS OF MARITAL HAPPINESS BY CLOSE ACQUAINTANCES.

lowest percentages of "unhappy and very unhappy" marriages are found in the first two years of married life, and the highest percentages in the fifteenth and sixteenth years. It may be concluded from the findings presented in this table that marital happiness, at least as reported by friends, tends gradually to decrease and domestic discontent slowly to increase with the number of years married.

Stability and Mobility in Social Relations

In the Orient may be observed in almost complete form the combination of social forces making for the stability of the family. Village life predominates over urban existence. Persons and families are held in abiding bonds to their lands and to their ancestral abodes.   Children are indispensable to the family; their absence is a calamity to be made good by adoption. The status and the career of a person, his marriage and his occupation, are almost entirely controlled by his family.

In contrast to the stability of family life in the Oriental village is the mobility of the modern American metropolitan community.   In Chicago only 29.2 per cent [6] of families own their homes.   Among couples recently married the percentage is much smaller.[7]   In its apartment-house districts 33.4 per cent, and in its rooming-house areas 36.6 per cent, of the families have lived at their present addresses less than one year.[8] Birth control with the approval of the Federal Council of Churches and, at long last, of the American Medical Association accounts in large part for the fact that of all family groups in Chicago barely one-half, or 51.5 per cent, are composed of father, mother, and children.   In an additional 11.0 per cent of the groups children were living with either father or mother, but not with both.[9]

This contrast between stable village life in the Orient and the change and flux of the metropolitan American city suggests the value of analyzing the data in our schedule that provide indices of stability and mobility in community and neighborhood life.   Our problem is to determine, if possible, the effect upon marital adjustment of the location of the couple in terms of the concepts of stability and mobility.

Size of community.   All other things being equal, the larger the community the greater is the mobility of its members.   In this study the communities, all within Illinois, were grouped into three classes: those with a population over 200,000, those

[6] Charles Newcomb and Richard O. Lang, *Census Data of the City of Chicago,* Chicago, 1934.

[7] In our sample of 526 couples, 53 or only 10.1 per cent own their homes.

[8] Adapted from data in Charles Newcomb and Richard O. Lang, *ibid.,* Table 2, pp. 160–264.

[9] E. W. Burgess and Ruth P. Koshuk, unpublished manuscript on *Chicago Family Composition Study.*

with 10,000 to 200,000 inhabitants, and those with less than 10,000. The relation to their marital adjustment of the size of the community in which our couples lived after marriage is presented in Chart 43.

The pattern of distribution of the marital-adjustment scores indicates the validity of the hypothesis that marital adjustment is in inverse relation to the size of the community. Concretely, in the mobile metropolitan community, only 39.2 per cent of the couples in our sample of cases have "good," and as many as

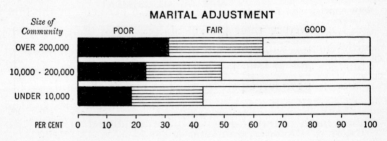

CHART 43.—SIZE OF COMMUNITY AND MARITAL ADJUSTMENT.

31.3 per cent "poor," adjustment. But in the communities of under 10,000 population, 56.6 per cent [10] of the couples are "good" and only 18.9 per cent [11] "poor" in adjustment. These differences are probably significant.[12]

Distance from metropolitan center. If mobility varies inversely with distance from the large city, it may be assumed that couples living within the city limits of Chicago will rate lower in marriage adjustment than couples residing in the suburbs or outside the metropolitan area. The findings of this study are given in Chart 44.

The distribution of cases conforms in general to the hypothesis that the proportion of couples who rate high in "good" adjustment increases with distance from the metropolitan

---

[10] CR, .392 and .566, 2.5.
[11] CR, .313 and .189, 2.0.
[12] CR, .392 and .505 (communities of 10,000 to 200,000), 2.0.

community: in Chicago, 39.8 per cent; in a Chicago suburb, 50.0 per cent; outside the Chicago area, 52.9 per cent.[13] The percentage with "poor" adjustment is higher in Chicago (31.0 per cent) than in the suburbs (20.6 per cent) or outside the Chicago area (23.0 per cent).

Character of neighborhood. The American city is not homogeneous. It is a unity of differentiated areas: neighborhoods of single homes at its periphery succeeded by two-flat districts and apartment-house regions, and, in toward its center,

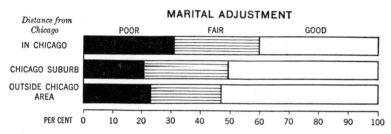

CHART 44.—DISTANCE FROM CHICAGO AND MARITAL ADJUSTMENT.

tenement sections, rooming houses, and lodging houses. The mobility of these areas varies in general inversely with their distance from the business center. The hypothesis to be tested is that the proportion of couples with "good" ratings for marital adjustment will be largest in single-home and suburban areas and smaller in areas of multiple dwellings, such as apartments and rooming houses.

Chart 45 shows a regular decline in the proportion of couples with "good" adjustment from 52.1 per cent in single-home neighborhoods to 32.8 per cent in other multiple-dwelling areas,[14] a difference that is significant.[15] Correspondingly, the proportion with ratings of "poor" adjustment rises consistently from 22.7 per cent in single-home areas to 42.6 per cent [16] in the multiple-dwelling areas.

---

[13] CR, .398 and .529, 2.2.
[14] Rooming-house, two-flat, hotel, etc., areas.
[15] CR, 2.7.
[16] CR, 2.8; CR, .297 (apartment) and .426 (other multiple dwelling), 1.8.

Type of residence. Within any given residential area the family may select a specific type of residence. In an apartment-house area where the majority of residences are in apartment dwellings, the family may live in a single-family or a two-flat dwelling or in a rooming house or hotel. Since it is

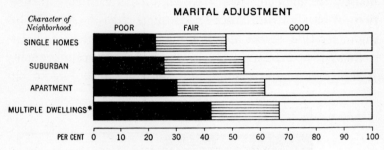

* Rooming-house, two-flat, hotel, etc.

CHART 45.—CHARACTER OF NEIGHBORHOOD AND MARITAL ADJUSTMENT.

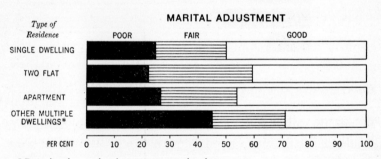

* Rooming house, hotel, or apartment hotel.

CHART 46.—TYPE OF RESIDENCE AND MARITAL ADJUSTMENT.

assumed that the single-home residence represents the extreme of stability and the rooming house and hotel the extreme of mobility, the expectation is that the largest proportion of couples with ratings of "good" adjustment will be found in the former and the smallest proportion in the latter. The findings presented in Chart 46 corroborate this theory.

Of the couples living in single-family dwellings, one-half or 50.4 per cent rate "good" in adjustment as compared with

slightly over one-fourth, or 27.9 per cent, of the couples residing in rooming houses, hotels, or apartment hotels.

In regard to the rating of "poor" adjustment no significant
differences are found between couples living in single-family
houses and those living in two-flat dwellings or apartment
houses, although all these have significantly smaller proportions of families with "poor" adjustment than the families living in rooming houses, hotels, or apartment hotels.

Change of residence.   One of the best measures of mobility
is the frequency of change of residence.   According to our

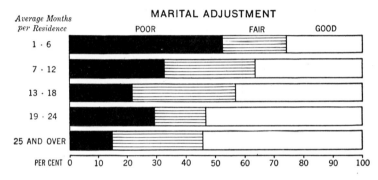

CHART 47.—AVERAGE MONTHS PER RESIDENCE AND MARITAL ADJUSTMENT.

theory, the proportion of couples with the fewest changes of
residence should rate highest in the marriage-adjustment score,
and those with the largest number of changes should rate
lowest.   This theoretical expectation is borne out by the findings presented in Chart 47, which gives the average number of
months per residence since marriage.

The pattern of distribution as shown by the chart is revealing.   It has the distinct general tendency to have greater mobility associated with "poor" adjustment, and less mobility correlated with increasing percentages of "good" adjustment.   High
mobility, as indicated by an average residence of six months
or less, is unfavorable to marital adjustment.   The proportion
of well-adjusted couples whose average length of residence is

six months or less is low, and the difference between this and any other length-of-residence group is statistically reliable.[17] Conversely, average residence of 19 months and over is associated with the highest percentage of "good" adjustment.[18] There can be no doubt that, for the couples in the present study, frequent change of residence is correlated with unhappiness in marriage and continuity of residence with marital happiness.

Home ownership. Significant also as an index of stability is home ownership. The tenant is proverbially mobile; the home owner is rooted locally. The latter has a more vital interest and takes a more active part in neighborhood affairs.

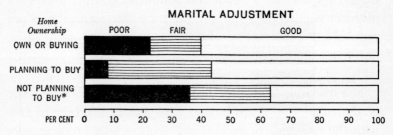

* Including no reply.

CHART 48.—HOME OWNERSHIP AND MARITAL ADJUSTMENT.

He becomes a member of the organizations and institutions of the community. He participates in the formation of public opinion and finds his conduct controlled more and more by the attitudes and opinions of his neighbors. Since in attitudes are found the beginning of acts, a question was also included regarding plans, if any, to buy a home. Our hypothesis was that couples owning, buying, or planning to buy a home would constitute a higher proportion of those with "good" adjustment than couples who were not planning to become home owners.

---

[17] CR, .522 (1 to 6 months) with .324 (7 to 12 months), 2.4; with .217 (13 to 18 months), 3.7; with .291 (19 to 24 months), 2.6; and with .147 (25 months and over), 4.6.
[18] CR, .534 (19 months and more) with .261 (1 to 6 months), 3.7; with .366 (7 to 12 months), 3.1; and with .433 (13 to 18 months), 1.8.

The findings in Chart 48 indicate quite conclusively the significant difference favorable to marital adjustment where the couples are actual or prospective home owners. Six out of 10 couples (60.4 per cent) with an equity in a home, as over against only three and one-half out of 10 (35.6 per cent) who neither own nor plan to buy a home, fall into the group with "good" marital adjustment. Conversely, for these two groups the percentages of "poorly" adjusted couples are, respectively, 22.6 and 36.8.

Most interesting are the findings for the couples who are not yet home owners, but who seriously plan to go into the market for a home. The proportion of these with "good" adjustment is practically the same as for home owners, 56.8 per cent and 60.4 per cent. The per cent "poorly" adjusted is, however, significantly lower—only 8.0 per cent as compared with 22.6 per cent of couples with equity in a dwelling.[19]

The meaning of this finding may lie in the fact that some of the couples who are buying their homes are face to face with the problem of meeting payments, which problem does not as yet confront those who, planning to buy, have all the advantages of anticipation but none of the disillusion of the struggle for realization.

The stabilizing influence of owning, or buying, or planning to acquire a home does not inhere merely in the fact that home ownership roots the married couple in a location and in a neighborhood. Its greater meaning is undoubtedly to be found in the fact that it represents a common objective and a joint project which, in the majority of cases, in its planning and prosecution tends to integrate and unify the young married couple.

Occupational mobility. The number of positions held by husband and by wife since marriage may be taken as a rough index of occupational mobility. The expectation would be

---

[19] CR, 2.4.

that the larger the number of jobs held, the lower would be the ranking of the couple by the marital-adjustment score. This indeed proved to be the case, with differences more marked in the case of the husband than of the wife. The findings are given later in this chapter [20] in connection with the discussion of economic security, since change of jobs is also an index of insecurity as well as of occupational mobility.

Stability and Kinship Relations

In the Orient [21] the stability of the family centered in the lasting bonds of kinship relations. The married career of the young couple was initiated and supervised by the parents and parents-in-law and even by the family council made up of other relatives. The permanence and perpetuity of the family was insured by the presence of children.

In American society today, with the emancipation of the young married couple from the control of the parents and with the apparent decline of the significance of children in family life, interest is keen in the effect upon marital adjustment of different types of relationships with relatives and of the attitude of married couples toward children.

Residence with relatives. One question faced by many married couples is that of living or not living with relatives. Of the 455 couples giving information upon this point, 180 (39.6 per cent) stated that they had lived with relatives. All but 21 of these had lived with the husband's or wife's parents or other relatives as much as two months or more. The findings regarding the couples reporting in this study do not confirm the popular impression of the markedly adverse effect upon marital adjustment of living with parents-in-law or other relatives after marriage. The differences in the proportions with

---

[20] See Chart 56, p. 265.
[21] This paragraph is also applicable to the European peasant family (W. I. Thomas and Florian Znaniecki, *The Polish Peasant in Europe and America*, Boston, Alfred A. Knopf, 1918–20.)

"good" adjustment are only slight and not significant for those who have and those who have not resided with relatives: 42.8 and 45.5 per cent, respectively. A greater difference is to be observed in the "poorly" adjusted couples, 31.7 per cent and 24.7 per cent,[22] respectively. For the limited number of cases in our sample this difference, however, is not large enough to offer reasonable assurance of its significance.

Our tentative conclusion, then, is that living with relatives

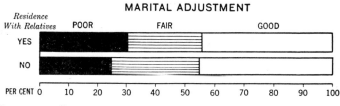

CHART 49.—RESIDENCE WITH RELATIVES AND MARITAL ADJUSTMENT.

after marriage is perhaps only slightly unfavorable to marital adjustment.

In view, however, of the fact that our findings run counter to common-sense observation, further research upon this situation is desirable. It may well be that, in the case of couples for whom the strain of living with relatives would be the greatest, this trial is not adventured. Then, too, our study did not cover a large enough number of cases to differentiate sufficiently between residence of the couple with the husband's and with the wife's relatives.

Frequency of seeing parents and parents-in-law. Another measure of the influence of relatives upon the marital adjustment of the young couple is the number of times during the past year they have seen their parents and parents-in-law. Contrary to our experience with other items correlated with marital adjustment, no consistent picture emerges from the findings, presented in Chart 50.

---

[22] CR, 1.6.

The number of couples who failed to see their parents and parents-in-law during the year is so small that a percentage based upon it cannot be regarded as stable. Disregarding this group, it will be noted that seeing one's parents and parents-in-law 1 to 6 times and 25 to 104 times seems favorable, but seeing them 7 to 24 times and 105 times and over during the year appears to be unfavorable, to marital happiness.

No clear-cut conclusion regarding the relation of contact

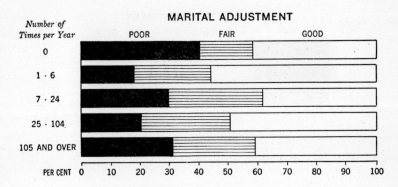

CHART 50.—FREQUENCY OF SEEING PARENTS-IN-LAW AND MARITAL ADJUSTMENT.

with relatives to happiness in marriage emerges from the present study. The relation is evidently not a simple one that could be discovered by the crude methods of the present study. According to our findings, however, it would appear probable that even in a large city parents and parents-in-law still play an important part in the marital adjustment of their children. Moreover, the findings suggest that this part is not always destructive.

Number of children and marital adjustment. Of our 526 couples reporting as to children, the majority, 293, had no children, 174 had one child, and 55 had two or more children. The relation of number of children to marital adjustment is shown in Chart 51.

Apparently in our sample of cases there is no difference in

marriage adjustment between couples with no children and those with one child. There is, however, a marked difference in "good" adjustment between couples with no child or one child and couples with two or three children.[23] The difference between the corresponding groups of "poorly" adjusted couples is perhaps also significant.[24]

Because of the small number of years married that is characteristic of the cases in this study, it would be unwise to draw

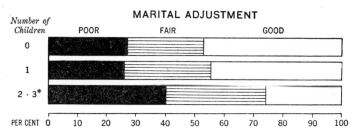

*Including those with four children.

CHART 51.—NUMBER OF CHILDREN AND MARITAL ADJUSTMENT.

hasty conclusions from the data presented. The *Study of Ratings of Marital Happiness* by R. O. Lang furnishes a large number of cases grouped according to number of years married. His data indicate that the effect of the number of children varies with the number of years married. He states,

> In the first two years of marriage those marriages without children were rated happier than those marriages with children. The next two years of marriage showed about the same tendency, but the variation was not so marked. Those marriages of five years and over showed the general tendency to rate marriages with one or two children happier than those marriages with no children or more than two children. There were some variations from this general pattern in a few cases, but the group taken as a whole will warrant this statement.[25]

---

[23] CR, 3.1 and 2.6, for couples with no children and one child, respectively, when compared to those with two or more.
[24] CR, 1.7 and 1.8, for couples with no children and one child, respectively.
[25] *Op. cit.*, pp. 49–50.

Attitude toward having children. The presence or absence of children, or their number, may not be so significant as the attitude of the married couples toward having children. If there are no children, are children desired? If there are children, were they wanted or not wanted? The possible combinations of attitudes, leaving out the question of number of children, are as follows:

Desire for Children	*Children Present*	*Children Absent*
Both husband and wife desire	A	a
Husband does, but wife does not	B	b
Wife does, but husband does not	C	c
Both husband and wife do not	D	d

Because of our small number of cases, it was necessary to combine these eight different groupings into four, as follows:

Desire for Children	*Group*	*No. of Cases*
None, desired by both	a	160
One or more, and desired by both	A	186
None, and not desired by one or both	b, c, d	111
One or more, and not desired by one or both	B, C, D	36
Cases reporting attitude toward having children		493

This simplified classification being used, the relation of the children question to marital adjustment was then obtained. See Chart 52.

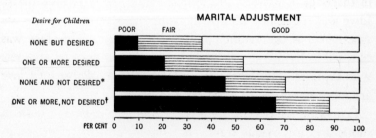

* Not desired by husband or wife, or both.
† Not desired by husband or wife, or both.

CHART 52.—DESIRE FOR CHILDREN AND MARITAL ADJUSTMENT.

These findings regarding attitudes toward having children showed a more marked relationship to marital adjustment than any other item included in our study. It is evident that the child is a potent and vital factor in family life. If companionate marriage be defined as a marital union where children are neither present nor desired, it is one which on the average grades very low in marital happiness. Only those unfortunate marriages that produce unwanted children reach a lower level of marital maladjustment.

The question remains open whether the desire to have or not to have children is a cause or an effect of marital unhappiness. In many marriages it is entirely probable that dissatisfaction with the marriage on the side of one or both partners makes for an aversion to having children. At the same time many marriages are entered upon with a determination on the part of one or both of the couple not to have children. In these cases the disposition against having children may be definitely related to marital maladjustment. The desire not to have children may, for example, be an index of a personality type unwilling to assume responsibility.

Economic Security

In our American mores the affectional and comradely aspect of marriage is stressed and the economic aspect is minimized. Love and romance rather than economic security or status are sanctioned as the "right" basis for marriage. This fact was certified to by the 52 per cent of those filling out our schedule who expressed their conviction that marriages of romantic love are more successful than others.

Economic factors do, however, enter into marriage both in subtle and in obvious ways. It is important, therefore, to attempt to assay the significance of economic factors in making for or against success in marriage. In this study there were several items in the schedule that make possible some evaluation of the role of economics in married life. These were: number of rooms in the home, rent per room per month, employment or unemployment of husband, number of positions held since marriage by husband and wife, and income and savings, which were combined into a financial index.

Number of rooms in the residence. The number of rooms in a couple's residence may be taken as a very rough indication of economic status. In Chart 53 it may be noted that the groups

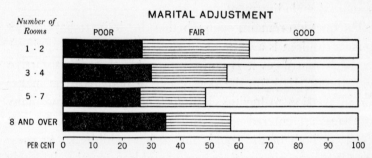

CHART 53.—NUMBER OF ROOMS IN RESIDENCE AND MARITAL ADJUSTMENT.

of couples living in five to seven rooms rate highest on the adjustment score, followed in order by couples living in three and four rooms, by those in eight rooms and over, and by those in one or two rooms.

But the range of difference between these different categories is small, and none of them is statistically significant. On the basis of these findings, then, no great reliance can be put upon number of rooms as a factor in marital adjustment.

Monthly rent per room. Rent has been found in other studies to be a quite reliable index of economic status. In this study it was possible to calculate the monthly rent per room and to correlate this with the marital-adjustment score. An examination of the data reveals no consistent pattern. The only large differences in the proportions of couples with "good" adjustment are: (1) between those paying rent and no rent because of an equity in their home, and (2) between those paying $30 and more rent per room per month and those paying in all other rental categories. The first difference is statistically significant but does not necessarily indicate economic status; the second difference is possibly significant.[26]   The findings of this study do not indicate that the amount of rent paid per room is associated with the degree of adjustment in marriage.

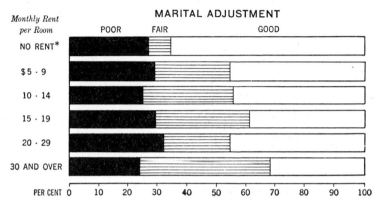

Chart 54.—Monthly Rent per Room and Marital Adjustment.

* No rent because owning or buying home.

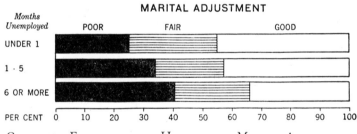

Chart 55.—Employment of Husband and Marital Adjustment.

Employment or unemployment of husband.   Of more significance than number of rooms or rent per room is the employment or unemployment of the husband.   Of the 471 couples reporting, 338 husbands had since their marriage been steadily employed with the loss of less than one month's time; 56 had been unemployed one to five months; and 77 had been without work six months or more (see Chart 55).

The marked difference in marital adjustment is between cases

---

[26] CR, .320 (rent $30 and over) and .432 (rents under $30), 1.6.

in which the husband had been unemployed six or more months (only 33.8 per cent with "good" and 40.2 per cent with "poor" adjustment) and those who had been steadily employed (46.1 per cent with "good" and only 24.6 per cent with "poor" adjustment).[27] For those unemployed from one to five months the number of cases is too small to provide significant differences from the other two groups. Its intermediate position in the two groups of couples with "good" and with "poor" adjustment provides a consistent pattern. Employment and unemployment may be taken, then, as highly satisfactory indicators of economic security and insecurity, and as significantly related to adjustment and maladjustment in marriage.[28]

Changing positions. The average time that positions are held by husband and wife since marriage may serve as an index of occupational mobility. The frequency of changing jobs may also be an indicator of economic insecurity. The data in Chart 56 showing the average number of months positions are held by husbands and wives may be analyzed from this standpoint.

This chart shows in a striking way the association between the average time a position is held and success in marriage. Where the husband averages less than seven months in a position, 65.2 per cent show "poor"[29] and only 8.7 per cent "good" adjustment.[30] But where he has remained 19 months or more in a position, only 23.2 per cent show "poor"[29] and 48.4 per cent "good" adjustment.[30]

In the average time that a position was held by wives the same consistent pattern is to be seen. The significant difference ap-

---

[27] CR, .338 and .461, 2.0; CR, .402 and .246, 2.6.
[28] Calculation was also made of the percentage of time since marriage that the husband was unemployed with even more significant findings than for months unemployed. The percentages with "poor" adjustment are: for no unemployment, 22.2; for less than 30 per cent of time unemployed, 23.6; and for 30 per cent or more of time unemployed, 53.2. The percentages with "good" adjustment are: for no unemployment, 48.8; for less than 30 per cent of time unemployed, 42.7; for 30 per cent or more of time unemployed, 29.8 per cent.
[29] CR, .652 (1 to 6 months) with .293 (7 to 12 months), 3.1; with .302 (13 to 18 months), 3.1; and with .232 (19 months and over), 4.2.
[30] CR, .087 (1 to 6 months) with .379 (7 to 12 months), 3.4; with .382 (13 to 18 months), 3.6; and with .484 (19 months and over), 6.1. CR, .484 and .382, 1.5.

pears to be between those who have remained in a position for an average of 13 months and more and those who have remained only a year or less.   Continuing more than 12 months on the job seems associated with marital happiness.   Our confidence in the significance of this difference is derived largely from the consistency in the pattern because the small number of cases does not provide adequate stability to the figures.[31]

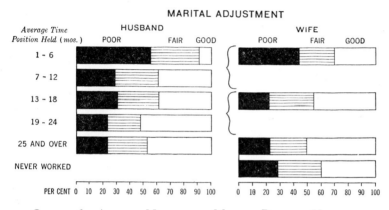

CHART 56.—AVERAGE NUMBER OF MONTHS POSITION HELD BY HUSBAND AND BY WIFE, AND MARITAL ADJUSTMENT.

We may then conclude that in the case of the husband certainly, and in that of the wife probably, frequent changes in positions are correlated with lower percentages in the classification with very high adjustment scores.

For an index of economic security and insecurity, two points should be made in regard to frequent changes of positions.   In many instances changing jobs does mean economic maladjustment, but in others it represents promotion and advancement. Holding one position too long may spell failure and finally result in marital disharmony.   If, then, frequency of changing positions is to be employed as an instrument for the measure-

---

[31] For those with "poor" adjustment CR, .433 (1 to 12 months) with .221 (13 to 24 months), 2.1, and with .228 (25 months and over), 2.1. For those "well" adjusted CR, .300 (1 to 12 months), with .454 (13 to 24 months), 1.5; and with .503 (25 months and over), 2.2.

ment of economic insecurity it needs to be refined in order that adequate account may be taken of the considerations just stated. In the second place, it must be remembered that unemployment and occupational mobility may also indicate personality factors that may affect the marriage quite apart from economic considerations.

Wife working after marriage. A subject of current controversy is whether or not the wife should work after marriage. Our findings indicate that in the first six years of marriage the relation of the wife's working to marital success is one of attitude. It is her attitude toward working, rather than the mere fact of her working, that appears to influence her marital adjustment. Least favorable for adjustment in marriage were those cases in which the wife had planned to work after marriage but had not done so. Favorable to happiness in marriage were those cases in which the wife wanted to work after marriage and had done so, and equally favorable were those cases in which she had not wanted to work after marriage and had not worked. Interestingly, those cases in which the wife before marriage had not planned to work, but had worked after marriage, had a higher proportion than the average of cases of "good" marital adjustment.[32] In general, the conclusion seems justified that the wife's attitude toward working after marriage is what is important for success in marriage rather than the sheer fact of whether or not she works. Further research should also take into account the attitude of the husband toward the wife's working.

The financial index. A significant indication of economic security should be family savings. To use the sheer amount of savings would, however, be obviously unwise, since the security insured by savings lies in their ratio to the family income. Accordingly, the following formula was worked out:

The financial index of a couple is to be ascertained by taking the total savings since marriage divided by the product of the sum

---

[32] See Table 114 in Appendix A.

of present monthly earnings times the length of marriage in years. If the couple is buying or owns a home, allow $1,000 plus $500 for each year married.

In Chart 57 are presented the findings regarding the relation of the ratings upon the financial index to the marital-adjustment score. In the "good" adjustment scores there is a regular

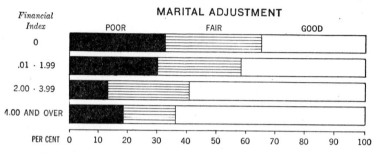

CHART 57.—FINANCIAL INDEX AND MARITAL ADJUSTMENT.

rise with advancing economic status: 34.1, 41.4, 59.1, and 63.0 per cent.[33] The two groups with a higher financial index (2.00 to 3.99 and 4.00 and over) show a low percentage (13.6 and 19.6); of "poorly" adjusted couples, the other two groups show practically the same high percentages (32.6 and 30.3) [34] of "poor" adjustment.

Among all the contingency factors considered in this chapter, the attitude toward having children is the most significant. The desire for children is markedly associated with "good" marital adjustment; the absence of this desire is found in a very high proportion of poorly adjusted couples.

Next in importance to the attitude toward having children is security and stability of employment and income. A high proportion of couples are unhappy where the husband has been unemployed a considerable part of the time since marriage.

---

[33] CR, .341 with .591, 3.4; and with .630, 3.5. CR, .414 with .591, 2.5; and with .630, 2.6.

[34] CR, .136 with .326, 3.1; with .303, 3.0.

Frequent changing of jobs, particularly in the case of the husband, is correlated with lessened probabilities of success in marriage. Savings taken in ratio to income and corrected for the factor of time married are positively associated with higher adjustment scores. In the case of the wife, both planning to work after marriage and working, and not planning to work and not working, are correlated with marital success.

Other factors that are probably correlated, but to a lesser extent, with success in marriage are shortness of time married, living in a smaller rather than a larger city, residence in a neighborhood of single- rather than multiple-family dwellings, buying or planning to buy a home, and infrequent seeing of parents-in-law. Contingency factors not found significant for marriage adjustment were residence after marriage with relatives, number of rooms in residence, and monthly rent per room. Taken together, the contingency factors show a relatively high correlation with adjustment in marriage. They are as important as all of the premarital items of the present study. It is therefore important to determine to what extent contingency items can be determined before marriage, because through such determination the efficiency of prediction would be increased. The crucial problem is whether or not acts after marriage are the result of attitudes present before marriage and, if so, whether or not these attitudes can be ascertained previous to marriage.

CHAPTER XIV

The Prediction of Marital Adjustment

T HE CENTRAL objective of this study is to determine to
what extent adjustments in marriage can be predicted
from a knowledge of a limited number of easily obtainable
items in the premarital backgrounds of husbands and wives.
A numerical index of present adjustment in marriage was developed, as already described in Chapters IV and V. Our purpose now is to show how selected premarital-background items
were used to determine the possibility of predicting before marriage the marital-adjustment scores of the couples.

The schedules in the study called for information upon such
points as age; place in the family; health; education; occupation; employment history; earnings; amount saved at time of
marriage; religious affiliation and activity; participation in organized social groups; friendships with men and women;
length of courtship and engagement; attachments to and conflicts with parents; happiness of parents' marriage; and certain
items on the occupation, religion, education, and the social-
economic status of the parents.

In dealing with the data it was first necessary to devise a
method whereby the information about each of the items could
be combined into single numerical expressions whose variations
would correlate as closely as possible with the variations in the
marriage-adjustment scores. The procedure followed in constructing such a prediction score was similar to the procedure
used in constructing the marital-adjustment index.[1] Since the

---

[1] See Chapter V, "Constructing an Index of Marital Adjustment."

problem was to predict the adjustment score, that score was utilized as a guide in assigning numerical values to replies to questions regarding premarital factors. Just as the happiness ratings of the 526 couples were used as a guide in assigning score points to the different possible answers to the questions selected in constructing the adjustment index, so the adjustment scores of the sample of 526 couples were employed as a guide in assigning score points to the different possible answers to the questions on background items. The object was to get a single prediction score which would correlate as closely as possible with the adjustment score.

Each item of information about the premarital background of husband and of wife was correlated with the adjustment score. Those items which showed a significant relationship were selected for use in constructing the prediction score. Twenty-one items in the husband's background material, 17 items in the wife's background, and 3 items common to both were selected for this purpose. Each type of reply was then given a numerical value in accordance with its frequency in the "very high" adjustment-score group.[2] A few tables will serve to illustrate the procedure.

Table 42 shows the relationship between level of educational achievement at the time of marriage and the present marriage-adjustment score. The data in this table indicate that, in our sample, the higher the educational level at the time of marriage, the greater the chances are that the marriage-adjustment score will be high. It also seems that, contrary to certain pronouncements regarding the college girl as a poor marriage risk, the wife's educational achievement makes more difference in the chances for a high adjustment score in marriage than does the husband's.

The numerical values assigned to the different educational levels were determined (with certain minor variations to be

---

[2] See pp. 275–283 for items used.

indicated later) by the procedure already described in the discussion of the adjustment score. In the case of the husbands, 20 points were given to replies stating that the husband was at a graduate level of educational achievement at the time of marriage; 15 if he was in, or had completed, college; 0 if he was in

TABLE 42

PERCENTAGE DISTRIBUTION OF MARRIAGE-ADJUSTMENT SCORES AT
DIFFERENT EDUCATIONAL LEVELS

Educational Level	Marital-Adjustment Score*				No. of Cases
	Very Low	Low	High	Very High	
Husband's education:					
Graduate work	3.8	8.6	36.2	51.4	105
College	9.8	15.1	26.8	48.3	205
High school	15.1	24.3	27.0	33.6	152
Grades only	21.6	19.6	21.6	37.2	51
No reply	30.8	7.7	30.8	30.7	13
Total					526
Wife's education:					
Graduate work	0.0	4.8	38.7	56.5	62
College	9.2	18.9	22.9	48.9	227
High school	14.4	16.3	32.2	37.1	202
Grades only	33.3	25.9	25.9	14.8	27
No reply	37.5	25.0	12.5	25.0	8
Total					526
All cases	11.8	16.7	28.3	43.2	

* For convenience in presentation, the adjustment scores were grouped as follows: very low, 20–79; low, 80–119; high, 120–159; very high, 160–199.

or had completed high school; 5 if his education did not exceed the grades; and 0 if no reply was given to the question.

In the case of the wife's schedule, 40 points were given for the graduate level at time of marriage; 30 for the collegiate level; 20 for the high-school level; 0 for the grade-school level; 10 if no reply was given to the question.

Table 43 shows the relation between the number of social organizations the persons belonged to at the time of marriage and the marriage-adjustment scores. This table seems to suggest that persons with proclivities for joining organized social groups are better risks for marriage adjustment than those who lack such tendencies. This item seems to be more discriminating for husbands than for wives. Scores assigned husbands' answers were: 20 for membership in three or more organizations; 10 for membership in two; 5 for one; 0 for none; and 0

TABLE 43

RELATION BETWEEN MEMBERSHIP IN SOCIAL ORGANIZATIONS AT
TIME OF MARRIAGE AND MARRIAGE-ADJUSTMENT SCORE
(Percentage Distribution)

Number of Organizations	Marriage-Adjustment Score				No. of Cases
	Very Low	Low	High	Very High	
Husband:					
Three or more	8.6	9.9	27.2	54.3	81
Two	8.7	16.3	27.9	47.1	104
One........................	11.9	18.1	27.1	42.9	210
None	13.3	17.3	37.3	32.0	75
No reply	19.6	21.4	23.2	35.8	56
Total					526
Wife:					
Three or more	4.2	18.9	22.1	54.7	95
Two	13.3	15.9	25.7	45.1	113
One........................	13.0	14.3	34.2	38.5	161
None	12.5	17.0	28.4	42.0	88
No reply	16.0	20.2	27.6	36.2	69
Total					526
All cases	11.8	16.7	28.3	43.2	

for no reply. For the wives' answers the scores were: 15 for membership in three or more organizations; 5 each for two and none; 0 for membership in one; and 0 for no reply.

Table 44 shows the relation between the marriage-adjustment score and the number of persons of the opposite sex that husbands and wives went with steadily before marriage. Scores assigned to the husbands' answers to the question were as follows: 10 points if he went with none but his wife; 5 if he went with one other; 5 for two or three others; 5 for four or five others; 0 if he went with six or more; and 0 for no reply to the question.   For the wives' answers the scores were: 5 points for none but husband; 0 for one; 5 for two or three; 0 for four or five; 10 for six or more; and 0 for no reply.

TABLE 44

RELATION BETWEEN NUMBER OF PERSONS OF OPPOSITE SEX HUSBANDS
AND WIVES WENT WITH STEADILY BEFORE MARRIAGE
AND MARRIAGE-ADJUSTMENT SCORE
(Percentage Distribution)

Number of women husband went with steadily before marriage:	Marriage-Adjustment Score				No. of Cases
	Very Low	Low	High	Very High	
None but wife	7.8	15.6	27.3	49.2	128
One	10.0	21.3	25.0	43.8	80
2 to 3	12.2	14.4	28.1	45.3	139
4 to 5	13.8	11.3	28.7	46.3	80
6 or more	9.5	19.0	35.7	35.7	42
No reply	21.0	24.6	29.8	24.6	57
Total					526
Number of men wife went with steadily before marriage:					
None but husband ...	9.8	16.1	27.7	46.4	112
One	7.1	15.5	34.5	42.9	84
2 to 3	14.8	17.4	21.5	46.3	149
4 to 5	11.7	20.0	29.4	38.8	85
6 or more	5.0	12.5	32.5	50.0	40
No reply	19.6	16.1	34.0	30.4	56
Total					526
All cases	11.8	16.7	28.3	43.2	

These illustrative tables serve to show that the number of score points assigned to different answers to a question corresponds roughly to the proportions of persons with "very high" adjustment scores who gave the answers.   In the case of any given question, the answer given by the highest proportion of couples with a "very high" adjustment score (160 to 199 points) received the maximum score points; the answers given by the smallest proportion of "very high" adjustment-score couples received o points.

The size of the maximum score for the "best" answer for each question is always approximately equal to the difference between the highest and lowest proportions in the "very high" adjustment-score column of the tables (disregarding always the "no reply" group).

As an illustration Table 43, on membership in social organizations, may be selected. Note the percentages in the "very high" adjustment-score column. In the section on the husband the highest percentage (54.3) is for the reply "three or more." That answer is, therefore, given the maximum score (20). The lowest percentage is for the answer "none." That answer is, therefore, given the lowest score (o). The maximum score is arrived at by getting the difference between the highest and lowest percentages in the column (disregarding "no replies"). In this instance the difference between 54.3 and 32.0 is approximately 20 points.[3]

The intermediate score values are assigned by inspection roughly, in accordance with the relative size of the percentages for intermediate answers. Thus in the same table cited above, the intermediate answers of "two" and "one" were given 10 and 5 points, respectively. The score for "no reply" was assigned in the same manner in which the intermediate scores were assigned.

This procedure used for determining the size of maximum score points allows for a rough evaluation of items upon the basis of their relative value in discriminating between good or poor chances of adjustment. Compare, for example, the difference between the highest and lowest percentage in the "very high" adjustment column in Table 43 above with the differ-

---

[3] In each case the score assigned is that multiple of five which is nearest the actual difference.

ence between the highest and lowest percentage in the corresponding column of Table 44 (husbands' section). Whereas the difference in the former case is over 20 points, the corresponding difference in the latter case is about 13 points (49.2 minus 35.7). This would suggest that the item of membership in social organizations before marriage is more valuable as a predictive item than the item regarding the number of women the husband went with steadily before marriage. Hence there is justification for giving the latter item less score weight. The maximum score in this instance was 10 points for the answer "none but wife."

Thus this procedure makes it possible to give the higher score weights to those items which seem to discriminate most sharply between couples who had very high adjustment scores and those who did not.[4]

The procedure outlined above being used, the 21 most significant items in the husband's background, the 17 most significant items in the wife's background, and the 3 most significant common to both were selected, and appropriate score values were assigned to all possible answers to questions on these items. These values are given in Table 45.

TABLE 45

WEIGHTING KEY FOR PREDICTION SCORE *

	Score Value Assigned
I. *Items Used in Husband's Background:*	
1. Place in family:	
Only child	0
Oldest	15
Middle	20
Youngest	15
No reply	0

* Tables on which these scores are based are in Appendix A.

---

[4] That the procedure for assigning score weights is extremely crude there is no doubt. But in view of the crudity of the basic data, it was felt that more refined methods of weighting and scoring would not add greatly to the precision of the score and would not be justified so far as the present study is concerned.

TABLE 45 (*Continued*)

Score Value
Assigned

2. Most attached to which sibling:
   Only child 0
   No special attachment but has sibling 20
   Older brother 20
   Older sister 10
   Younger brother 15
   Younger sister 15
   No reply 10

3. Area of residence at time of marriage:
   Chicago: rooming-house area 0
   Chicago: area of "first settlement" 15
   Chicago: area of "second settlement" 20
   Chicago: hotel area 0
   Chicago: apartment and apartment hotel 10
   Chicago: private homes of "better class" 20
   Chicago: suburbs 30
   Other city 10
   Small town (not Chicago suburb) 20
   Rural 15
   No reply 5

4. Education at marriage:
   Grades only 5
   High school 0
   Professional school (not collegiate grade) 0
   College 15
   Graduate or professional work (beyond college) 20
   No reply 0

5. Occupation at marriage:
   None 0
   Unskilled industrial 0
   Clerical and semiskilled 0
   Farmer 20
   Small trades and skilled 0
   Sales and semiprofessional 5
   Professional—teaching 20
   Professional—ministry 20
   Professional—law, medicine, etc. 5
   Large business management 20
   Other—student, etc. 0
   No reply 0

TABLE 45 (*Continued*)

Score Value
Assigned

6. How long held position at time of marriage:
   Less than one year 10
   One to less than three years 0
   Three to less than five years 10
   Five to less than seven years 5
   Seven years or more 0
   No reply 0

7. Work record before marriage:
   Never worked because in school, or worked only
      at school vacation time 15
   Irregularly employed or continually changing jobs   0
   Regularly employed 20
   No reply 0

8. Monthly income at marriage:
   None 10
   Under $150 0
   $150 to under $250 10
   $250 to under $350 5
   $350 or more 0
   No reply 0

9. Amount saved at marriage:
   None 0
   Under $1,000 10
   $1,000 to under $2,000 20
   $2,000 to under $3,000 15
   $3,000 and over 10
   No reply 0

10. Financial index at marriage (obtained by dividing
    total savings at marriage by the product of his age at
    marriage and his monthly earnings at time of mar-
    riage):
    0 (no savings) 0
    .01 to .29 15
    .30 or over 20
    No reply 5

11. Family-background index:
    Under 70 0
    70 to   89 5
    90 to 119 25

TABLE 45 (*Continued*)

Score Value
Assigned

12. Religious activity at marriage (attendance):
    Member, but amount of church attendance not
    stated 5
    No attendance at church affairs 0
    Attends no more than once a month 10
    Attends two or three times per month 20
    Attends four or more times per month 15
    No reply 0

13. Age when stopped going to Sunday School:
    Never went 10
    Stopped at 10 years or younger 0
    11 to 18 years of age 25
    19 8 years of age and over 30
    No reply 10

14. Number of social organizations of which a member
    at marriage:
    None 0
    One 10
    Two 15
    Three or more 20
    No reply 0

15. Childhood and adolescence spent chiefly in:
    City 0
    Small town 10
    Country 30
    No reply 0

16. Number of women went with steadily before
    marriage:
    None but wife 10
    One 5
    Two to three 5
    Four to five 5
    Six or more 0
    No reply 0

17. Number of men friends at marriage:
    Almost none 0
    A few 5
    Several 20
    Many 20
    No reply 0

TABLE 45 (*Continued*)

Score Value
Assigned

18. Marital status of husband's parents:
    Married, both living 5
    Separated or divorced 0
    Both dead 5
    Father dead 15
    Mother dead 20
    No reply 5
19. Rating of happiness of husband's parents' marriage:
    Very happy 40
    Happy 20
    Average 10
    Unhappy 20
    Very unhappy 0
    No reply 20
20. Husband's conflict with father:
    None 40
    Very little 30
    Moderate 30
    A good deal 15
    Almost continuous 0
    No reply 20
21. Did husband's parents favor his marriage?
    Both "yes" 20
    One "yes"; the other "no" 0
    Both "no" 5
    No reply 5

II. *Items Used in Wife's Background:* *
    1. Wife's place in her family:
       Only child 0
       Oldest 10
       Middle 10
       Youngest 0
       No reply 0
    2. Area of residence at time of marriage:
       Chicago: rooming-house area 5
       Chicago: area of "first settlement" 10

---

* Some of the items parallel those in the husband's background; some do not. The items selected were those that showed some discrimination whether or not they were parallel to the husband's items.

TABLE 45 (*Continued*)

	Score Value Assigned
Chicago: area of "second settlement"	5
Chicago: hotel area	5
Chicago: apartment area and hotel apartments	0
Chicago: private homes ("better class")	15
Chicago: suburbs	15
Other city	10
Small town (not Chicago suburb)	20
Rural	15
No reply	5

3. Education at marriage:

Grades only	0
High school	20
Professional school (not collegiate in grade)	20
College	30
Graduate or professional work	40
No reply	10

4. Occupation at marriage:

None	5
Domestic service	0
Unskilled industrial	0
Clerical and office, semiskilled operators, etc.	0
Skilled office secretaries, stenographers	10
Nursing	5
Professional—teaching	20
Professional—social work	5
Professional—law, medicine, etc.	0
"Business women" (higher-paid)	10
Other—student, etc.	5
No reply	10

5. How long held position at time of marriage:

Less than one year	0
One to less than three years	5
Three to less than five years	10
Five to less than seven years	10
Seven years or more	20
No reply	0

6. Was wife in occupation in harmony with her stated vocational ambitions?

No vocational ambition	0
Same	20

TABLE 45 (*Continued*)

	Score Value Assigned
Slightly different	20
Great difference	5
No reply	15
7. Wife's work record at marriage:	
Never worked	0
Occasionally employed	5
Regularly employed	15
Housekeeper at home	10
Outside interest activity (not gainful employment)	20
No reply	10
8. Income at marriage:	
None	10
Under $100	0
$100 to under $150	15
$150 to under $200	20
$200 and over	20
No reply	0
9. Amount saved at marriage:	
None	15
Under $500	5
$500 to under $1,500	15
$1,500 to under $2,500	0
$2,500 and over	20
No reply	5
10. Family-background index:	
Under 55	0
55 to 64	15
66 and over	25
11. Religious activity (attendance) at marriage:	
Member; no church attendance stated	5
Never attended	0
Attended not more than once per month	5
Attended two to three times per month	5
Attended four or more times per month	10
No reply	5
12. Age when stopped attending Sunday school:	
Never went	0
Ten years of age or younger	0
Eleven to eighteen years of age	10
Nineteen years of age or over	20
No reply	0

TABLE 45 (*Continued*)

Score Value
Assigned

13. Number of social organizations of which a member
at marriage:

None	5
One	0
Two	10
Three or more	20
No reply	0

14. Number of women friends at marriage:

Almost none	0
A few	20
Several	10
Many	30
No reply	20

15. Rating of wife's parents' marriage:

Very happy	20
Happy	20
Average	10
Unhappy	0
Very unhappy	0
No reply	0

16. Wife's conflict with her father:

None	10
Very little	0
Moderate	0
A good deal	5
Almost continuous	5
No reply	5

17. Did parents favor wife's marriage?

Both "yes"	20
Father "yes"; mother "no"	15
Father "no"; mother "yes"	0
Both "no"	5
No reply	5

III. *Items Common to Husband and Wife:*
   1. How long they have known each other:

Under six months	0
Six months to less than two years	10
Two years to less than five years	20
Five years to less than ten years	25

TABLE 45 (*Continued*)

	Score Value Assigned
Ten years or more	30
No reply	20
2. How long were they "keeping company"?	
Under one year	0
One year to under three years	5
Three years and over	20
No reply	5
3. Difference in age between husband and wife:	
Same age	5
Husband older by one to three years	5
Husband older by four to seven years	0
Husband older by eight or more years	10
Wife older by one to three years	10
Wife older by four or more years	30
No reply	0

A study of the score values in the above key and of the tables in the appendix from which these weights were obtained will reveal that the empirical procedure of weighting yielded values which, in some instances, seem quite inconsistent and which frequently run counter to what common observation would lead one to expect. Take, for example, such apparent inconsistencies as giving more score points to wives who were members of no organizations than to those who were members of one; or, to take another instance, that of giving more value to a grade-school level of education of the husband than to a high-school level. The differences in score values cited, although not great, violate one's feeling for consistency. But it seemed preferable to be consistent in empirical procedure rather than to violate that procedure for the sake of consistent weightings in some of our items.

The items listed in the above key were scored for each of the 526 couples, and the resulting scores were correlated with the adjustment scores of the sample.

The Pearsonian coefficient of correlation between the two scores was $+.51$.

Table 46 gives some idea of the distribution of the two scores with reference to each other. Since the adjustment score was used as a guide in weighting the items in the premarital or prediction score, some fairly close relation between the two scores would be expected. It is reassuring to find that some correspondence exists. But it is desirable to look a little more closely at the evidence regarding the reliability and validity of the prediction score.

TABLE 46

RELATION BETWEEN THE PREDICTION SCORES AND
MARRIAGE-ADJUSTMENT SCORES
(Percentage Distribution)

Premarital Prediction Score	Marriage-Adjustment Score				No. of Cases
	Very Low	Low	High	Very High	
700 to 779	0.0	10.0	10.0	80.0	10
620 to 699	1.5	12.1	25.8	60.6	66
540 to 619	5.8	21.9	29.2	43.1	137
460 to 539	27.6	29.4	25.9	17.1	170
380 to 459	39.8	31.1	15.1	14.0	93
300 to 379	57.2	25.7	11.4	5.7	35
220 to 299	75.0	25.0	0.0	0.0	8
Total					519*

* Seven cases were thrown out because subjects failed to answer a sufficient number of background questions for computation of their scores.
Mean prediction score = 516.0.   σ = 98.8.

Reliability of Background Score

Table 47 shows the relation between the prediction scores computed from 70 pairs of schedules filled out independently by husbands and wives.[5] The reliability coefficient of +.88 is satisfactory, although our sample of 70 pairs is too small to be entirely conclusive.

[5] In each case the husband and the wife answered all questions on both own and mate's background.

TABLE 47

CORRELATION OF PREDICTION SCORES COMPUTED FROM SCHEDULES FILLED OUT SEPARATELY BY HUSBANDS AND WIVES

	Scores from Wives' Schedules													
Scores from Husbands' Schedules	220–259	260–299	300–339	340–379	380–419	420–459	460–499	500–539	540–579	580–619	620–659	660–699	700–739	No. of Cases
740 to 779	....	....	....	....	....	....	....	....	....	....	....	....	1	1
700 to 739	....	....	....	....	....	....	....	....	....	....	....	....	1	1
660 to 699	....	....	....	....	....	....	....	....	....	....	....	2	....	2
620 to 659	....	....	....	....	....	....	....	....	1	3	7	4	....	15
580 to 619	....	....	....	....	....	....	....	....	3	5	....	1	....	9
540 to 579	....	....	....	....	....	....	....	2	4	2	....	....	....	8
500 to 539	....	....	....	....	1	....	3	1	....	....	....	....	....	5
460 to 499	....	....	....	....	2	3	8	....	....	....	....	....	....	15
420 to 459	....	....	....	1	....	3	3	....	....	....	....	....	....	7
380 to 419	....	....	....	....	2	2	....	....	....	....	....	....	....	5
340 to 379	....	....	....	1	....	....	....	....	....	....	....	....	....	2
300 to 339	....	....	....	....	....	....	....	....	....	....	....	....	....	0
260 to 299	....	....	....	....	....	....	....	....	....	....	....	....	....	0
220 to 259	1	....	....	....	....	....	....	....	....	....	....	....	....	1
No. of Cases	1	0	0	2	5	8	14	3	10	11	7	7	2	70

$r = +.884$ $\sigma_r = .026$.

Table 48 shows the correlation between pairs of prediction scores computed from pairs of schedules filled out by the same persons at different times. The time interval between the filling out of the first and the second schedule ranged from eight months to two years. Here again the evidence indicates a reasonable degree of reliability of the background score.

Validity of the Background Score

It has been shown above that the background score is correlated with the marriage-adjustment score. But since the adjustment score was used in determining the score values for the various items in the prediction score, the correlation found between the two scores is not of any particular value for demonstrating the validity of the prediction score.

More convincing is the relation found between the prediction score and the answers to the question of whether the couples are separated, divorced, have contemplated separation or divorce, or have not contemplated such a step.

Table 49 shows the relation between the answers to this question and the prediction score. The distribution in the table indicates that the background score does discriminate on the one hand between couples whose marriages have resulted in either separation or divorce or a serious consideration of such a step, and on the other hand those couples for whom such a condition has not resulted.

A much more exacting test of the validity of the score is to try it on a new sample of cases which was not used in constructing the score. For this purpose schedules were collected from a new sample of 155 couples in the same general social-economic level from which the first group was drawn. Their replies were scored in the manner described above. Notwithstanding the fact that the ranges in the adjustment and prediction scores were narrower than those of the original sample, the correlation coefficient was +.48.

TABLE 48

Correlation Between Prediction or Background Scores Computed from First and Second Schedules Filled Out by Same Persons at Different Times (Time Interval: Eight Months to Two Years)

Score on First Schedule	Score on Second Schedule																f
	300–324	325–349	350–374	375–399	400–424	425–449	450–474	475–499	500–524	525–549	550–574	575–599	600–624	625–649	650–674	675–700	
700 to 725																1	1
675 to 699												2					2
650 to 674													1	1			2
625 to 649												1	1		1		3
600 to 624												1	1				2
575 to 599									1								1
550 to 574										1		1		1			3
525 to 549										1	1	1					3
500 to 524							1		2	1			1				5
475 to 499							1	3		1							5
450 to 474							1	1									2
425 to 449						1		1									2
400 to 424																	0
375 to 399			1	1		1	1										4
350 to 374		1															1
325 to 349						1											1
300 to 324	1																1
f	1	1	1	1	0	3	4	5	3	4	1	6	4	2	1	1	38

r = .88. σ_r = .037.

287

TABLE 49

PERCENTAGE DISTRIBUTION OF PREDICTION SCORES FOR THOSE WHO:
ARE DIVORCED, ARE SEPARATED, HAVE CONTEMPLATED DIVORCE
OR SEPARATION, AND HAVE NOT CONTEMPLATED DIVORCE
OR SEPARATION

Prediction Score	Marital Status				No. of Cases
	Divorced	Separated	Have Contemplated Divorce or Separation	Have Not Contemplated Divorce or Separation	
700 to 779	0.0	0.0	9.1	90.9	11
620 to 699	2.9	0.0	5.9	91.2	68
540 to 619	2.9	4.3	6.5	86.3	139
460 to 539	13.9	15.0	13.9	57.2	173
380 to 459	25.0	17.0	16.0	42.0	100
300 to 379	34.2	21.9	21.9	21.9	41
220 to 299	50.0	37.5	12.5	0.0	8
No. of cases	73	61	64	342	540*

* Twenty-one additional cases added to the sample of 519 used in Table 46.

This completes the statistical evidence on the reliability and validity of the prediction score. It is evident that there is a relationship between the prediction score and the score upon the adjustment index. This relationship, although quite satisfactory particularly for an exploratory study, is not so high as might be desired. In the next chapter evidence from case studies will be presented that will enable us to appraise better the validity of the adjustment and prediction scores and to understand the reason for the relatively low correspondence between them.

The procedure used to determine how far adjustment in marriage can be predicted from a knowledge of certain premarital-background items regarding husband and wife may be summarized as follows:

1. The answers to each item about the premarital backgrounds of husband and wife were correlated with the adjustment score.

2. Each background item that showed a significant relation to the adjustment score was selected for use in construction of the prediction score.

3. The answers given to each selected item by husbands and wives were given the weights indicated by their association with the adjustment score.

4. The background score for each couple was obtained by the sum total of the weights of the appropriate answers to all the background items of husband and wife.

5. The background scores thus derived for the 526 couples were correlated with the adjustment scores, and a Pearsonian coefficient of correlation of $+.51$ was obtained.

6. The reliability of the background score was estimated by determining the association between the prediction scores computed from schedules independently filled out by husbands and by wives and from schedules filled out by the same persons at different times.

7. The validity of the background score was first tested by determining its relation to answers to the question whether the couples were divorced, separated, had contemplated divorce or separation, or had not contemplated such a step. The validity of the score was also tested by applying to it a new sample of cases that had not been used in the construction of the score, with a resultant correlation of $+.48$.

CHAPTER XV

Five Case Studies of Marital Adjustment

THE PURPOSE of this chapter is to present five cases [1] that illustrate differing degrees of adjustment and to show the extent to which the adjustment scores and the prediction scores correspond to the subjective estimate one gets from the case picture itself. These cases will also serve to illustrate how premarital factors in the schedule operate to yield high or low prediction scores and, in general, to test the validity of the adjustment and prediction scores.

Case I.—An Unadjusted Couple with Low Prediction and Poor Adjustment Scores: William and Laura A. [2]

Both Mr. and Mrs. A. agree in rating their marriage as unhappy, and Mr. A. regards it as a hopeless failure. He complained bitterly to his physician, in whom he confided his troubles, that his marriage was a tragic mistake. He felt that he was not "cut out" for marriage and its responsibilities; he felt that his freedom was seriously curtailed. He was now disgusted with his wife's personality and appearance. He complained that she was too dependent on him, and that everything she did irritated him, beyond endurance.

Mrs. A. felt that the marriage was highly unsuccessful, but

---

[1] Two of the following cases were presented in the chapter on personality factors. The three remaining cases are presented in such a way as to give an idea of both the schedule and the interview data.

[2] See pp. 192–201 for a fuller description of this case.

still had hopes that she and her husband could find some basis of adjustment. She felt that her husband was not doing his share in trying to make the marriage a success. He was not a "sturdy oak" that she could depend on and that she thought a man should be. He was too dependent on her. He was unreasonable in his antagonism toward her family. He did not appreciate her efforts to work and support the two of them when he was out of work. He was grouchy and unsympathetic. Her attitude was, however, that almost anything was preferable to breaking the marriage.

Since the important personality and sexual factors in this case have already been discussed,[3] it will be necessary only to indicate what the schedule items showed regarding the degree of adjustment and the premarital factors that indicated favorable or unfavorable chances for adjustment.

The schedule that was sent in when the case was referred by the physician had been filled out by Mr. A. The adjustment score was 111. For our sample of 526 couples, the adjustment scores had a possible range of 0 to 194 points. Actually, the range was from 20 to 194, with a mean score of 140.8. The score of 111 on the A.'s schedule has a percentile rank of .232, which places the marriage in the lowest quartile. The answers that brought the score down were: checking "occasionally disagree" on seven of the eleven items in the agreement table;[4] checking "would not marry at all if had life to live over"; listing four complaints on questions regarding complaints and annoyances with marriage and spouse. In the interviews, Mrs. A.'s answers did not always conform to the schedule replies of her husband, but her answers, too, were sufficiently unfavorable to give the marriage a low score.

The premarital score for this couple, based on the answers concerning the premarital backgrounds of husband and wife, was 400. For our sample of 526 couples the background score

---

[3] Pp. 192–201, 290–293.
[4] See the schedule in Appendix B.

had a possible range of o to 890.   Actually the range was from 220 to 780, with a mean score of 516.   The A. score of 400 has a percentile rank of .132, which places the couple in the least hopeful quartile of the sample.

Some of the items which lowered the score may be briefly indicated.   By referring to the scoring key for the prediction score, the reader may see to what extent the indicated background items were unfavorable.

The economic items for the most part were unfavorable. Before his marriage, Mr. A. had worked quite irregularly and had held the job he had at marriage about one year.   He was earning $100 per month and had saved less than $200 before marriage.   Mrs. A. had worked about two years before marriage.   She was earning $50 a month and had saved nothing. Moreover, her occupation was very different from what she wanted as a career: she wanted to teach kindergarten, but was working as a clerk in a store.   After marriage Mr. A. lost his job, and Mrs. A. supported the two on her very low income. They lived in a cheap rooming house for most of the two years of their marriage.

As to education, both had finished high school.   Mr. A. had taken a little extra training in drafting, but not enough to equip him for a position as a trained draftsman.

The religious items also were scored low.   Both Mr. and Mrs. A. were of the same religious denomination but had stopped attending religious school in early adolescence and at present hardly ever attended church.

Neither of the A.'s belonged to any organized social group. They had very few friends of either sex.

Although both came from families containing several children (a favorable item), the relationships in the families were only fair in Mr. A.'s case and rather poor in Mrs. A.'s case. Mr. A.'s parents were rated as only average in their marital happiness.   There was some conflict between the father and Mr. A., and only moderate attachment.   Mr. A. was quite closely attached to his mother and his sisters and was very dependent upon them, as the personality material shows.

Mrs. A.'s parents were rated as average in the success of their marriage. There was only moderate attachment between Mrs. A. and her father. She was, however, quite attached to her mother. As indicated in the case-study materials, there was strong conflict in her relations with her oldest brother and a feeling of keen disappointment in her father.

While superficially the two families belonged to the same social, religious, and economic class, there were some significant differences in the backgrounds. The families were of different national origins. The wife's father was better educated than the husband's father. The husband's parents were very regular attendants at church and participated in community life to a considerable extent. The wife's parents never attended church and were more or less isolated with respect to organized social activities in the community. The general atmosphere and family relationship patterns were very different in the two families, as one can see from the case-study materials.

Hence it can be said that, in addition to the very serious problems of personality adjustment in this case, the economic, vocational, religious, social, and general family background factors were such as to make it extremely unlikely that this would be a satisfactory marriage.

Case II.—A Well-Adjusted Couple with High Prediction and Good Adjustment Scores: James and Mary O.[5]

The following case stands in rather sharp contrast to that of the A.'s. Mr. and Mrs. O. volunteered their assistance in this study and stated that they had no problems in their marital relationships. They agreed in rating the marriage as very

---

[5] See pp. 178–191 for a fuller description of this case.

happy and confidently regarded it as a permanent success. The adjustment score is 175, which gives the couple a percentile rank of .790; hence they are well within the upper quartile of the sample. The score on the premarital items is 640, which has a percentile rank of .896. They are thus practically in the most favorable tenth of the sample so far as the schedule items are concerned. The case-study materials on the personality patterns in this marriage are given on pages 178–191. What follows is a brief statement of the important schedule items which account for the relatively high prediction score.

In this case the economic and vocational items are quite favorable. Both husband and wife had worked regularly in professional vocations for which they had had professional training. At the time of marriage the husband was earning $180 per month and the wife $125. Although neither had saved any money, they had both taken out insurance and had paid college and graduate expenses.

The O.'s belonged to the same religious denomination and were moderately regular in church attendance. Both had attended Sunday school until their early twenties.

Both were members of two or three organized social groups and participated in community activities. Each had many friends of both sexes.

The couple came from families in which the relationships were quite close and affectionate. The parents of both are rated as very happy in their marriages. While he was rather strongly attached to his parents, Mr. O. had some history of conflict with his father and mother during childhood and adolescence. However, he had achieved a rather good adjustment with them later. Mrs. O. reported consistently positive relations with her parents. Like her husband, she came from a fairly large family.

The family backgrounds of the two are very similar. Both are from old families of the same state, with rural background. The fathers of the couple are professional men, and the families have a superior status in their communities. Both families are active in religious and other social organizations in their communities. The atmosphere and affectional patterns of the two families are quite similar, especially in the relationships between men and women.

The personality materials and the schedule items all point to a marriage relationship that is satisfactory and likely to be permanent.

Case III.—A Couple Changing from Poorly to Well Adjusted with Low Prediction and Poor Adjustment Scores: Charles and Virginia C.

Mr. and Mrs. C. have been married two years. When they were interviewed, they agreed in their statements that their marriage had been quite unhappy, but was now beginning to be very happy. They had separated for several months by mutual agreement (after having been married 16 months) in order, as they put it, to give themselves a chance to make up their minds about whether or not to continue the marriage. Mr. C. feels that he never had any doubt about his own desire to continue, but felt a separation would be desirable for Mrs. C.'s sake. Mrs. C. feels that she was the one who was really in doubt about the permanence of her affection for her husband.

Mr. C. complained of the fact that the nature of his work made it impossible for him to give his wife the amount of attention she desired and also did not allow time to cultivate common recreational and cultural interests. In the one year they had known each other before marriage, they had had little opportunity to discover how similar or divergent their fundamental interests were. After marriage it appeared that he was very ambitious and interested in his career, while she had little drive to accomplish anything and enjoyed a rather purposeless existence. They also found their tastes in friends to be somewhat divergent.

The husband complained that his wife lacked sufficient decisiveness of character. She was too easily influenced by friends. She had no specific goals, and her studies suffered (they were both in school at the time of marriage) from her interest in friends, bridge, movies, and so on. Moreover, her choice of girl friends and her occasional mild interest in other men seemed at times to have the character of spiteful activities to annoy her husband.

Virginia C. said she was "weak-willed" and too easily influenced by friends who had no "purpose in life," but complained also that she was very much disappointed in not having a settled home life in which her husband would be the chief support of the home and the manager of their mutual affairs. She felt her husband ought to take charge of situations more decisively. She particularly objected to her husband's allowing her father to interfere and manage their affairs for them. The reconciliation did, as a matter of fact, date from the time the husband assumed a more decisive role, particularly at a point where he was called on to challenge the right of Mrs. C.'s father to interfere in their affairs.

The adjustment score, computed on the schedules that were filled out by the couple while they were still separated, is 137. This gives them a percentile ranking of .392 in the sample of 526. They are thus in the second lowest quartile of adjustment scores. The premarital items, when scored, yield an index of 490. This gives the couple a percentile rank of .350 in the 526.

Mr. C. is the oldest of four children in a second-generation German-American family. His parents lived for most of their lives before marriage in a very stable, conservative, and religious neighborhood in a large city, but soon after their marriage moved to another section of the city. They continued some active connections, however, particularly religious connections. The father, especially, is described as a very religious person. He was quite stern and very strict in his requirements of the children, although as the children grew up his overt discipline relaxed considerably. The mother is not nearly so strict, and Charles has always felt himself much closer to her than to his father.

The father is the owner of a business concern and is fairly prosperous. He has been able to give his children good educational and cultural advantages, and was partially supporting Charles in his graduate study of law at the time he and Virginia married. Both the father and the mother have had some training at the collegiate level. The members of the family have participated quite fully in the social, religious, and civic activities of their community, and have considerable status in their social groups.

Charles's parents are rated as very happily married, and are proud of the fact that there are no records of open domestic breaks in the family on either side of the house. The parents were doubtful of the wisdom of their son's marriage on the score that his wife's family had a history of a good deal of domestic strife and of several divorces among near relatives as well as in her immediate family.

Charles has always been very much the favorite of his mother, and has always been the object of considerable solicitude on her part. He says that he has always felt quite close to her, but he claims that he has emancipated himself from her and feels more amused than otherwise at her expressions of concern about his welfare. He has always been afraid of his father, and there has been some conflict in this relationship. He has usually relied on his mother to deal with his father for him. Early in his life he adopted a policy of passive resistance and avoidance of conflict without ever openly rebelling.

At the time of his marriage he was living with his parents and pursuing his study of law. He was active in church and community social life, although he was gradually shifting his social life away from home and community. He tends to play a passive rather than an aggressive or leadership role in his social relationships. But his friendly and interested manner plus his alertness and responsiveness have made him very well liked by those who know him socially or professionally. He is ambitious and hard-working, and is already receiving recognition for his very evident ability. In discussing himself, he tends to assume a rather self-minimizing attitude.

Mrs. C. is the only child of native-born American parents. Her mother is of Norwegian parentage; her father's parents are native-born and of German descent. Her mother had only a grade-school education, but did much in the way of self-education. Mrs. C. is a member of a Protestant denomination but has never been active in the church. Her father has had college and law-school training, and has a good law practice in a small city. (One reason Mrs. C. gave for her original attraction to Mr. C. is that he was in law.) Having always been antagonistic toward religion, he has no religious affiliation. He is very active in politics and dominates the groups with which he works.

With the exception of the father's political activity, the family has participated very little in the community life, and the father is said to have had no intimate friends. He is admitted by everyone, however, to be the dominant personality in the political life of the town. He tried to dominate and order the lives of his wife and daughter just as he did his political groups. His marriage was unhappy, and his wife divorced him while Virginia was in the grades. Both parents remarried, the father almost immediately and the mother some years later.

Virginia was devoted to her father as a child, but was deeply hurt and disillusioned when she learned that her father was unfaithful to her mother. She is still quite attached to him, but shows strong hostility toward him at times, especially when he is particularly insistent about planning her life for her. She resentfully attributes her "weak will" to the fact that her father did things for her and planned for her all her life, and never allowed her to think and act for herself. The father's actions with regard to her were never of a disciplinary character, nor were they of the indulgent, spoiling type.   They always had the character of planning for her, deciding for her, and so on, until, as Mrs. C. puts it, she had no mind or will of her own.   He decided she should go into his vocation, what school she should attend, what she should do during vacations, and so forth, and was very much disappointed when she decided she could not go on with law.   She felt guilty over disappointing him.   It is interesting that, although she felt she could not do the work for a law degree, she could not decide on any alternate vocation.

When she married, Mrs. C. had no particular career in view, she had no business experience, nor was she connected with any community or religious organization.   She did engage in considerable social activity of a rather aimless sort with friends whose organization of life was very similar to her own.

The couple married while they were both in school: Charles was 24 and Virginia was 19.   Sexual adjustment, satisfactory to both, was achieved very quickly.   Mr. C. was able to continue his school work and make enough to support himself.   Mrs. C. continued to draw her regular income from her father. There was some friction over friends, but more serious tensions seemed to center around the fact that the husband was not decisive enough and left too much for his wife to decide. Moreover, he would, as she puts it, allow her father to run over him.   Her accumulated irritation at his passive attitude turned into disgust, and in conflict situations she began to belittle him. She began to wonder if they were "suited," if she really loved him, and the like, and they finally decided on a "trial" separation.

Reconciliation was expedited by two things: (1) the realization on the part of Mrs. C. of the necessity for more independence and definiteness on her part; (2) the realization on the part of Mr. C. of the necessity for, and actual demonstration to himself and wife of, a new role—a more assertive, decisive, and aggressive role.   When he was able to tell his father-in-law to "keep hands off," and to take other decisive action about matters concerning himself and his wife, he says that his "stock went up" immediately. It is interesting to note in this connection, too, that the wife claims that her sexual satisfaction was much more intense after the assumption of the new role by her husband than it had been in the first year of marriage.

Apparently what happened in the husband's case was that the crisis produced a shift from his overawed and passive position as a son to the assumption of the dominant-father role, which in turn fitted in better with the role configuration expected by his wife. The shift did not, however, produce enough of a tendency to domineer so that the wife's attitudes of hostility and rebellion toward her father would be animated.

Case IV.—A Fairly Well Adjusted Couple with Low Prediction and Good Adjustment Scores: Robert and Helen D.

Mr. and Mrs. D. have been married three years, and both rated their marriage as happy. They intimated that they desired an interview "just to see what it was like."

Their schedules yielded an adjustment score of 177, which has a percentile rank of .815. Thus they are in the highest quartile of the sample. Their premarital score, however, is 460, which has a percentile rank of .272, and is barely in the second quartile. The case has, therefore, a special interest in that the high adjustment score is associated with a prediction score which indicates only moderate chances of their being in the satisfactorily adjusted groups.

Robert D. came from a fairly wealthy family of a small Midwestern city. His father, a self-educated and successful business man, was never active in the social, religious, or civic life of the community, preferring to remain somewhat aloof from his neighbors. He was, however, fairly liberal in his contributions of money to religious and community affairs. The mother, on the other hand, was quite religiously inclined and active in all kinds of church life. The parents were happily married, and Robert remembers little or no domestic conflict. The father was a rather quiet person and had little to do with the running of the home or disciplining of the children.

There were four children. Robert was the youngest, ten years younger than the next oldest sibling, a sister. He says he thinks he was an unexpected baby, but adds that he always felt that his mother was pleased at having a baby in her middle age. He had little contact with the two oldest boys, but his sister was a special nurse for him. He enjoys relating how he could manage his sister and wheedle her into doing things for him. He tells with much merriment how she would get mad at him and "bawl hell out of me," but "I knew all the while she was fond of me and would do what I wanted sooner or later." He tells of instances in which he would exasperate her just for the fun of a "row" with her.

He describes himself as shy and not very sociable with other children during school days. Even in college he preferred solitary recreations; his wife says it was because he was still shy, and did not know how to act with other people. He has always been somewhat solitary and, in group life, tended to play a rather passive role. He is friendly and agreeable with outsiders, especially in situations in which he can rely on his wife to manage matters. His wife complains half angrily and half indulgently that she has to do all the fighting with trades-men and landlords, and that anybody can run over him.

He states that his relations with his parents were always satis-factory for him. He was closer to his mother during childhood and early adolescence, but had some conflict with her over whether or not he was to continue his activity in Sunday school and church. During this latter period he felt himself to be on more sympathetic and understanding terms with his father than with his mother.

At the time of his marriage, Robert had been working steadily for a year and a half in a position in which he could use to con-

siderable advantage the special preparation in mathematics
and statistics he had received in an Eastern university. He was
26 years of age at the time, had dropped his religious connections, and had become rather antagonistic toward organized
religion. He was a member of no organized groups and had
relatively few friends of either sex.

He met his wife in the office, where she had a rather responsible secretarial position. Almost their first contact was one
in which he sought advice and counsel from her on business
matters, which advice she seemed quite ready to give and capable of giving.

Helen D. came from a fairly successful middle-class American family. Neither of her parents had more than a grade-
school education, but the family had many cultural advantages
by reason of the father's success as a merchant. The family
lived in a large city and participated little in social, religious,
and civic activities.

The parents were quite unhappy the first 18 years of their
married life and several times contemplated separation. They
have reached only a moderate adjustment more recently. Helen
describes a childhood of much tension and insecurity. She still
has strong feelings of hostility toward her family. She was
much attached to her father as a child, but learned to hate him
when her mother began to use her as a confidante and tell her
of real or fancied abuses at the hands of her husband. At
present she has turned against her mother and sides more with
her father. She blames her mother for much of the unhappiness in her home and for "poisoning her mind" against her
father. During her 'teens she was at odds with her father most
of the time, and ran away from home twice, each time taking
a room with some family friends.

She is the younger of two children, the older being a boy.
According to Helen, the mother doted on the son, "spoiled
him rotten," so that even now, when he is nearly 30, he cannot
hold a job and depends on his parents, although he has mar-

ried and has a home of his own. Helen tells of how she used to fight her brother's battles for him, take care of him, assume most of the responsibilities, boss him about, and so on. She describes a markedly ambivalent attitude of affection and hostility toward him. As she puts it, she would love him one minute and be willing to do anything for him, and the next minute would feel like "murdering" him. Her present attitude is that he is "no good," and that his wife, who is ten years older than he, will always have to support him when he can no longer depend upon his mother.

When she married, Mrs. D. had been working regularly in one business office since her graduation from high school. She had refused to go to college. She had a few friends of both sexes, but none of them seem to have been very permanent. She had had a good deal of mental conflict over religious matters and had withdrawn from her church. Her husband says that he was attracted by her efficient, businesslike manner, her readiness to assume responsibility, and her rather sharp, "bossy" attitude in the office.

In their married life the D.'s reached an adjustment only after some difficulty. Satisfactory sexual adjustment was difficult to achieve, partly because of rather strong mental inhibitions on the part of Mrs. D., and partly on account of a condition calling for a minor surgical operation. This aspect of the marriage is still somewhat problematical, although considerable progress has been made and the relationship is now a great deal more satisfactory to both than it was before. Another center of some tension was Mr. D.'s insistence upon using most of his leisure time to devote to his work and to his study. The couple's very limited contacts in the city in which they settled did not provide Mrs. D. with enough interests and outlets of her own, and, since she was not working, she resented having almost no attention from her husband. Mrs. D.'s sudden spells of sarcasm and criticism were hard for her husband to understand and interpret at first. But now, when he tells of her outbursts, he shows the same sort of merriment that he showed in his description of the way he and his sister got along.

They have reached a fairly satisfactory adjustment, and the marriage seems to be permanent in spite of the rather poor prognosis derived from the schedule data, particularly the data on the wife's background. The fact that the brother-sister configurations of both are complementary is perhaps very important. Even when Mrs. D.'s hostility is aroused toward Mr. D., who stands to her in a relation similar to that of her brother in earlier years, he gets a satisfaction from the situation similar to that he used to get from his sister's temper displays. Moreover, he is fitted by his earlier role patterns to be the passive and dominated and protected person that he is in many ways in his relations with Mrs. D.

Here again it is seen that the more external factors which serve as bases for a statistical classification of the case according to chances for adjustment do not provide a picture of the personality factors which are more immediate in the situation. The case should, however, still be classed as problematical both because of the factors indicated by the low prediction score and because of the ambivalence in personality adjustment revealed by the case study.

Case V.—A Couple with Doubtful Adjustment with High Prediction and Poor Adjustment Scores: Howard and Eleanor E.

Mr. and Mrs. E. heard of this study and came to the writers for advice in their attempt to solve their marriage problems. They had been married two years. Both agreed that the first eight months or year had been ideally happy. They dated their difficulties from the time Mr. E. had begun to show some interest in other women. There had been no overt sexual activity, but he had showed considerable curiosity about several women with whom the couple had contact, and had interested himself in what he regarded as harmless friendships with them. Mrs. E.'s reaction had been a strong hostility and overweening jealousy.

Mr. E.'s response to his wife's jealous sulking was a strong assertion of his philosophy that in marriage persons should be free, that neither should interfere with the other's friendships, and so on. They would argue, come to an agreement, be happy for a while, and then fall into the same conflict again. The tensions increased until the couple agreed to separate and get a divorce; but they decided first to see whether some advice from an outsider would help. Both were quite bitter and miserable when they came in.

They agreed in rating their marriage as very unhappy, but insisted on adding that at times it was very happy. They were doubtful about a successful outcome, but both seemed to have a strong desire to stay together if possible.

The adjustment score is 121, which gives them a percentile rank of .280 in the sample of 526. The background or prediction score is 690, which has a percentile rank of .966. There is, then, considerable disparity between the predicted adjustment and the actual adjustment score.

Mr. and Mrs. E.'s families lived in small towns and had been quite well known to one another for two generations. Mr. E.'s father had had several different jobs and was frequently out of work. At the time of Howard's marriage, his father was a clerk in a small grain elevator and had a small share in the business. The family were always in rather poor condition financially. They were looked down upon by the upper clique in the town, and Howard tells of the feeling of inferiority he endured throughout his life in that town. The family were active in religious affairs, especially the mother. When Howard went to high school, he participated more fully in the social life of the community. He always felt himself something of an outsider in his social group, and he compensated by emphasizing peculiarities of manner and dress. He early adopted ideas radical enough to shock his fellows. When he went to college, he embraced radical, artistic, and philosophic interests.

Howard's father was a rather kindly, passive, and somewhat inadequate sort of person toward whom the son had a very sentimental and affectionate attitude. The father had little to do in disciplining the children and left most of the running of the home to the mother. The mother is somewhat more aggressive, and was very definitely the head of the house.

In his interviews, Howard shows a striking ambivalence in his attitude toward his mother. He is quite attached to her and was very dependent upon her. Illnesses all had pleasant memories for him, for they were times when he received a great amount of tender attention and solicitude from his mother. On the other hand, he remembers his intense hatred of her when she punished him, or when in his late 'teens she would object to his plans or assert an opinion different from his own. He would become particularly angry if she criticized what he was doing or tried to change his plans or nag at him. At such times his antagonism would, he says, "blaze out," and he would do something to show her he was angry with her. Then he would feel very guilty and try to make amends.

Howard was the oldest of three children, and there was a difference of several years between himself and his two sisters. He seems to have been quite attached to them and they to him. In spite of the occasional conflicts between himself and his mother, Howard felt rather close to his family. The whole family seemed to have a good deal of attachment for one another, and the parents seemed to be very happy in their marriage. In spite of their inferior status, to which Howard was especially sensitive, there was a fairly full social life and participation in the community.

Mrs. E. was the only child in a family of fairly comfortably situated farmers who lived in a small town not far from Mr.

E.'s home town.   Her family possessed a slightly higher status in their community than Mr. E.'s family did in theirs.   They felt somewhat superior to the E.'s, and Eleanor's mother objected to the marriage because she felt Howard was not good enough for her daughter.   This attitude of her mother was also a basis of some conflict between Howard and Eleanor before they married.

Eleanor's family had the same general religious and cultural background as her husband's family.   They were active in church and community organizations.   They had a fuller social life than did Howard's family.   Eleanor was her mother's pride and joy; moreover, the family and neighbors impressed Eleanor with the fact that she had great ability as a leader—and she was a popular leader in her social groups.

The family relations were not quite so happy as those in Howard's family.   The parents were not so happily married, and at times the situation was rather tense.   Eleanor sided with her mother and was quite antagonistic toward her father.   She felt that her father did not appreciate her mother enough and at times did not pay her sufficient attention.   Her mother appears to have been a rather decisive person and was inclined to be very critical of her husband and of other male relatives. However, relations were not seriously strained, and Eleanor remembers her family life as rather happy.

When Howard and Eleanor were married, they had both had some college experience.   They were both in good positions, earning money with which to return to school.   Both were active in social, religious, and civic organizations, were quite popular in their groups, and were idealistic about their marriage.   They planned that Mr. E. should do part-time work and finish working for his college degree while Mrs. E. continued her full-time work and carried the major part of the financial burden.

It is interesting to note that at the beginning, and throughout the courtship, Mr. E. tended to take a dependent role and Mrs.

E. played something of an indulgent "mothering" role. Before Howard and Eleanor considered themselves as seriously interested in one another, he used to go to her for advice and counsel about his affairs and for long confidential chats about ideals, ambitions, and plans. She was a sympathetic confidante and encouraged what was to her a flattering dependence. The same general patterns continued in courtship and for almost a year after marriage, and it is this period that Mr. E. describes in almost idyllic terms. Their quarrels came when she assumed a critical attitude and did not agree with his plans.

Although both date their major problems from Mr. E.'s interest in mildly Bohemian friendships with women, it is evident from the history that friction had begun some time before, when Mrs. E. attempted to criticize or offer suggestions that ran counter to Mr. E.'s wishes. At such times he would develop a bad case of blues, wonder whether they were happy, and, in general, sulk.

As these instances increased, Mrs. E. became more aggressively hostile and critical. She suggested that she had given up a bright future to marry him against the best advice of her mother and friends. She began to feel unappreciated, and was jealous of the attention and time Mr. E. devoted to activities, friends, study, and so forth. She began to nag and to criticize. Mr. E. reacted by telling her that neither party to a marriage should take a possessive attitude toward the other —that a marriage should not be forced.

His rebellion against his wife took the form of drinking and a sally into liaisons with other women, both of which activities hurt his wife deeply. She criticized and complained; but the more she did so, the more intensely did Mr. E. assert his independence.

Sexual adjustment was very satisfactory to both. It is interesting to note, however, that about the time Mr. E.'s "affairs" began Mrs. E. had begun to take a more aggressive role in the sex act. They had discovered certain variations in sex play in which the wife was the more active and the husband the more passive member. On checking, it was found that this particular procedure occurred with increasing frequency during the period in which Mr. E. was most intense in his assertions of his right to have liaisons with other women. Moreover, in telling of his sex life, Mr. E. asked several times if he were "normal," by which he meant to ask if he had homosexual tendencies.

In the interviews Mr. E. discovered that he was motivated in his drinking and extramarital interests by: (1) a desire to revenge himself on his wife when she took the role of a critical or punishing mother; (2) a desire to demonstrate his emancipation from a rather infantile dependence; and (3) a fear of a homosexual component, which fear had been aroused by his wife's behavior, not only in sex relations but in other aspects of the marriage as well.

Mrs. E. discovered that her antagonism had been occasioned by the fact that her desire to be the unquestioned center of the attention of her husband was thwarted by what to him, at least in the first stages, were harmless friendly attentions to other women. She also learned that her aggressive, critical, and hostile actions caused her husband to react by more serious assertions of his right to extramarital friendships. These more pronounced efforts to assert his rights intensified her feeling of insecurity, and she became more positive in her condemnations and criticisms. Thus the breach widened.

She also felt that she had made a mistake when she brought up the old question of his inferior status as compared with her own, since by so doing she made herself the object of all the hostility her husband felt toward those who used to regard him as an inferior.

Any interpretation of this case should take into account the fact that the schedule was filled out at a time of acute conflict between Mr. and Mrs. E. At that particular moment the adjustment score is quite appropriately "very low." Nevertheless both the prediction score and the analysis of personality factors through the case study indicate the possibilities of satisfactory marital adjustment. The case study also suggests that marital difficulties may recur in the future.

The Adjustment Score as a Fair Index of Marital Adjustment

These five cases throw much light upon the value and the limitations of the adjustment index and the prediction score. They indicate that the adjustment index is a fairly reliable and valid indicator of marriage adjustment at the time of the filling out of the schedule. These cases further suggest that the prediction score is a fairly reliable and valid instrument except in those instances in which the personality factors are operating in a direction contrary to that of the other background factors.

Table 50 shows the adjustment score, percentile rank in the adjustment-score range of our sample, the prediction score, and the corresponding percentile ranking of the latter, for each of the five couples, and also their actual adjustment as revealed by the case studies.

By reviewing the cases the reader can check his impressions of the case with the figures shown in the table. It will be noted that in cases A and C the background items are such that low prediction scores result. In O, the background items yield a high prediction score. In all three there is a fair correspondence between the percentile ranks of the prediction and adjustment scores.

Cases D and E, however, show wide discrepancies between the two scores. In D, the background items were such that the prediction score was quite low. In spite of such a score, the present adjustment is fair. The case summary indicates that a major factor in the adjustment is the compatibility of personality or psychological characteristics. In E, the background materials gave a prediction of high degree of adjustment, but in this instance there were serious psychological or personality difficulties which at least temporarily interfered with marital adjustment.

These two negative cases point to a fundamental fact regarding the prediction score; namely, that it does not include items upon relevant personality characteristics.

TABLE 50

ADJUSTMENT AND PREDICTION SCORES WITH PERCENTILE RANKING
AND ACTUAL ADJUSTMENT FOR FIVE SELECTED COUPLES

Name of Couple	Adjustment Score	Percentile Rank of Adjustment Score	Prediction Score	Percentile Rank of Prediction Score	Actual Adjustment*
William & Laura A.	111	.232	400	.132	Very low
James & Mary O.	175	.790	640	.896	Very high
Charles & Virginia C.	137	.392	480	.350	Low
Robert & Helen D. ...	177	.815	460	.272	Problematic; high at present
Howard & Eleanor E.	121	.280	690	.966	Problematic; acute conflict at present

* As indicated by the case studies.

The Need for Supplementing the Prediction Score by Case Studies

The most significant point emerging from this comparison of schedule data and case-study evidence is the hypothesis that a discrepancy between the expected adjustment indicated by the prediction score and the actual finding of the adjustment index indicates the probable presence of personality factors operating in a direction contrary to the other factors.   If further research corroborates this conclusion, then it becomes important either to employ personality tests or to make use of case studies to locate and to attempt to measure the significance of these differences between the prediction score and adjustment-index findings.   In all probability it will be desirable to use both personality tests and case studies, since the cases of divergence between adjustment index and prediction score are those most important both for future research and for the practical application of prediction technique.   If to the present scoring of social and economic factors could be added scorings on personality characteristics and data from case studies, the precision of the predictions would be considerably increased.

The study of the foregoing cases suggests the following summary remarks:

1.   The adjustment index is fairly sensitive to the degree of adjustment in marriage.

2.   The prediction score taken by itself is a very crude index of the probabilities for good adjustment.

3.   Personality factors are extremely important and need to be taken into account if we are to understand the relationships in any marriage.

4.   If some measure of personality factors can be included in the prediction score, the precision of the predictions will be greatly increased.

5.   In cases in which there is a marked divergence between the prediction score and the adjustment index, case studies should be made to reveal the role of personality factors in marital adjustment.

CHAPTER XVI

Basic Problems in Prediction

SO FAR only the results of simple statistical procedures have been presented in this book. They have been quite sufficient to show: (1) that prediction of marital adjustment is feasible, at least within certain limits; and (2) that an expectancy table of probabilities of success and failure in marriage can be devised.

Three important questions still remain to be considered:

1. How much more improvement in prediction can come from the refinement and perfection of statistical techniques?

2. What are the limitations of prediction by statistical methods?

3. How may statistical methods be supplemented by case studies in order to improve the prevision of marital adjustment?

No final answer to these questions can be given here. The most that can be done is to submit to the reader certain data and ideas derived from working with these problems. These will be taken up under the following heads: (1) refinement in methods of weighting items that go into the adjustment and prediction scores; (2) the search for basic factors; (3) the unexpected disappearance of the economic factor; (4) the relative importance in adjustment of husband's and wife's background score; (5) the significance of multiple correlations; (6) limitations of statistical method; (7) the distinctive value of the case-study method; and (8) problems of the case-study method.

313

Adjustment and Prediction Scores

The items in the adjustment score were originally selected as representative of agreement upon vital issues, satisfaction with marriage and one's spouse, common interests, degree of demonstration of affection, amount of confiding in partner, and absence of feelings of unhappiness and lonesomeness. A simple system of weighting of items was adopted.[1] The different replies possible for each item were given a weight according to their association with the rating of marital happiness given by husband or wife.

As we have already reported, this method of weighting the items was checked by assigning arbitrary weights to each possible reply by common-sense judgment of its relation to marital success. The high correlation between the two methods of weighting ($+.96$) warrants confidence in the reliability of the scale.

Professor Terman used practically the same items to determine his scale of marital happiness. He, however, weighted his test items by a more refined statistical procedure.[2] The difference between the procedures in the two studies makes it possible to determine the extent and the significance for prediction of the difference between adjustment scores arrived at by simple and by more complex statistical methods.

The most practical way of making this comparison was to score our sample of cases by the weights which Terman had given to each subcategory of the items in his marital-happiness scale on the basis of the replies of his couples. Then a correlation was obtained between the adjustment scores arrived at in the two ways. The high correlation, $+.90$, is gratifying because it indicates how stable is the adjustment score derived

---

[1] For fuller explanation, see pp. 58–68.
[2] L. M. Terman *et al.*, *Psychological Factors in Marital Happiness*, New York, McGraw-Hill Book Co., 1938, pp. 54–59.

from groups of married couples in two different sections of the country. It does not, moreover, indicate any great discrepancy in scores the weights of which are determined by simple as compared with more refined methods.

A further question remained: that of the relative efficiency for prediction of our adjustment score and Terman's marital-happiness scale. Accordingly, the prediction scores for our 526 couples were correlated with the adjustment scores derived by using Terman's weights, and were then compared with the correlation already obtained by the use of our own adjustment scores. The respective Pearsonian coefficients were +.50 (Terman's scale) and +.51 (our adjustment scores), showing no reliable difference.

In Chapter XIV is described the simple method of weighting the different possible replies for the items making up the prediction score. This was the method originally used in this study. In the attempt to discover the effect upon prediction of using more refined methods, two other procedures were tried. The first was to assign weights to the subcategories of each item according to the ratio of the mean adjustment score of the subcategory to that of the sample.[3] The second was to allocate weights according to the critical ratio of the difference between the mean of a selected subcategory and that of each of the other subcategories in the item. This latter method was used by Terman. The correlations of prediction scores with adjustment scores by these three methods were:

Original method, simple weights........................ +.51
Weights assigned by deviation from the mean +.52
Weights assigned by critical ratio of the difference between means... +.49

---

[3] The mean adjustment score (M) for the entire 526 cases was 140.1. For each item, such as years married, the mean adjustment score (M_1) for each subcategory such as one year, two years, three years, etc., was computed. For example, the mean adjustment score for persons married one year at the time of filling out the schedules was 147.5. The weight assigned to a subcategory was computed from the formula $[(M_1/M)-1]100$. For the subcategory "married one year," the weight assigned is 5.3.

None of the differences between any pair of these coefficients is large enough to be statistically significant. The differences can be easily accounted for by chance. It is apparent that the more refined methods of weighting did not improve the efficiency of prediction.

It may be well at this point to raise the question of why a refinement of statistical procedure in weighting adjustment and prediction items does not result in at least a small significant rise in the coefficient of correlation between the prediction and the adjustment scores. The question is not easily answered, but certain suggestions may be offered. Let it be assumed that marital adjustment is correlated with a certain limited number of basic factors. Then it could be further assumed that precise measures of these factors would yield composite values that would correlate closely with a precise measure of marital adjustment. Now our composite prediction score correlates only approximately with the adjustment score. If we assume that the adjustment score is fairly valid, we must conclude that: (1) we have not included items in our schedule that serve as measures of all the basic factors affecting adjustment; or (2) the schedule items are very imperfect measures of the basic factors affecting adjustment in marriage; or (3) there is a combination of deficiencies 1 and 2. The probabilities are that our items do crudely indicate some basic factors and leave others out of account. It is also probable that our schedule items are not precise measures of the factors they do take into account. Obviously, by using different weighting methods we do not improve the correlation between our schedule items and the assumed basic factors they indicate, nor do we thus extend the number of basic factors taken into account. Hence the correlation between the adjustment score and the prediction score based upon our present items must remain fairly low.

The Search for Basic Factors

In the present state of our knowledge of marital adjustment, any discussion of basic factors must necessarily be tentative and approximate. A simple first attempt at stating them was to draw upon our familiarity with the case materials of this study and from this knowledge to list the categories which emerged in our attempts to systematize the case materials. In this attempt five general groupings of factors which influenced marital adjustment appeared: (1) basic personality factors, (2) cultural patterns, (3) social status and participation, (4) economic factors, (5) affectional or response factors. These five groupings we have called (1) psychogenetic, (2) cultural-impress, (3) social-type, (4) economic-role, and (5) response-pattern factors.

After the data were collected it was found feasible to classify the items in the schedule under the five categories. Not all of the categories are adequately represented in the schedule items. It is clear, moreover, that the schedule questions are not so sharply focused as they might have been upon the five areas.

One way, however, to test these categories set up on the basis of informal analyses of cases would be to see whether the schedule items, when treated by some intercorrelational procedure, group themselves into clusters more or less analogous to the above categories. The statistical method adapted to this problem is that developed by L. L. Thurstone [4] and called by him the method of multiple-factor analysis. This is not the place to describe the procedure involved in Thurstone's method. In brief, it is a procedure by which a whole complex of intercorrelated items may be treated to show: (1) the minimum number of independent (uncorrelated) basic factors that need to be assumed to account for all the covariation in the

---

[4] See his *Vectors of Mind,* Chicago, University of Chicago Press, 1935, and *Primary Mental Abilities,* Chicago, University of Chicago Press, 1938.

complex of intercorrelations; (2) the amount or loading of each basic factor in each of the items in the complex. The procedure is essentially that of discovering the number of general factors by isolating the various clusters of the variables in the matrix and then rotating the system of clusters so as to describe most completely the system in terms of the loadings of each item in uncorrelated or orthogonal factors.

We did not perform a complete multiple-factor analysis of our data. To begin with, the method calls for the coefficient of correlation between each variable and every other variable in the complex to be treated. We had 97 variables in our schedule (including the items in the backgrounds of husband and wife, the common items, and postmarital items). The amount of time and money necessary for an analysis of all these variables was prohibitive, and it was not warranted, because many of our items were not given in precise enough form. It was decided to experiment with the method by applying it to 28 items in the husband's premarital background. The items selected are listed below. Their code numbers are given for convenience in identifying them in Chart 58.

HUSBAND'S PREMARITAL ITEMS INCLUDED IN THE FACTOR ANALYSIS
(Each item refers to conditions at time of the husband's marriage)

19 Age of husband
24 Size of husband's family
28 Health of husband
29 Husband living with parents
30 Residence in a stable community
31 Education of husband
32 Husband's occupation
33 Length of time he held position
34 Regularity of employment
35 Amount of income
36 Amount of savings
38 Religious affiliation
39 Regularity of church attendance
40 Age when husband stopped attending Sunday school
41 Number of organizations of which husband is a member

42 Raised in rural or urban environment
43 Number of women he went with steadily
44 Number of men friends
45 Number of women friends
46 Husband's father native- or foreign-born
47 Family background score
49 Husband's mother living or dead
50 Happiness rating of husband's parents' marriage
51 Amount of conflict between husband and his father
52 Amount of attachment to father
53 Amount of conflict between husband and his mother
54 Amount of attachment to mother
55 Approval of marriage by husband's parents

The matrix showing the intercorrelations among the above items, when treated by the multiple-factor method, yielded certain fairly distinct clusters. These are indicated graphically in Chart 58. In this chart the items are represented by their code numbers. Those items whose intercorrelation [5] is

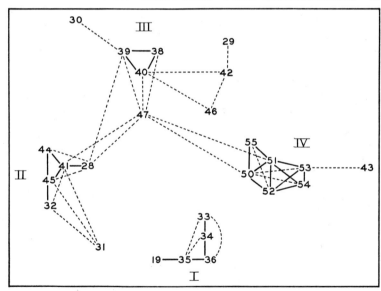

CHART 58.—GRAPHIC REPRESENTATION OF CLUSTERS OF SELECTED ITEMS IN HUSBAND'S PREMARITAL BACKGROUND AS INDICATED BY INTERCORRELATIONS OF THESE ITEMS BY THE MULTIPLE-FACTOR METHOD.

---

[5] These correlation coefficients are corrected for communality and are consequently higher in many instances than the uncorrected coefficients.

±.80 or more are joined by solid lines. Those whose inter-correlation is ±.70 to ±.79 are joined by a dotted line.[6] No relationship of less than ±.70 is shown. In the cluster marked I are the following items:

33 Length of time husband held position
34 Regularity of employment
35 Amount of income
36 Amount of savings
19 Age of husband

Clearly this is a cluster of economic factors.
    In cluster II are the following items:

28 Health of husband
31 Education of husband
32 Husband's occupation
41 Number of organizations of which husband is a member
44 Number of men friends
45 Number of women friends

These items for the most part can be thought of as connected with social status, social contacts, and participation. It will be noted that cluster II has a twofold connection with item 47 (the family-background index belonging to cluster III), which is correlated +.71 with 28 (husband's health) and +.77 with 41 (number of organizations). Cluster II is again connected with cluster III through a correlation of +.71 between 28 (husband's health) and 39 (regularity of church attendance).
    In cluster III are the following items:

38 Religious affiliation
39 Regularity of church attendance
40 Age when husband stopped attending Sunday school

---

[6] For convenience in illustrating the clusters, we have taken account of the magnitude and not the sign of the coefficients. In the few instances in which the correlation was negative, it was possible to invert the statement of the variable so the relation could be regarded as positive. For example, there is a correlation of −.78 between urban background and age at which husband stopped attending Sunday school. This statement can be reversed to say there is a correlation of +.78 between rural background and age at which husband stopped attending Sunday school. This inversion was done with items 42, 51 and 53.

Note that this cluster is also associated with item 47. In addition, item 39 is correlated with item 30 (residence in stable community). Item 40 is correlated with 42 (rural or urban background) and with 46 (nationality of husband's father). The items in this cluster are indexes of a religious factor. They probably indicate the degree to which the person has been inculcated with the mores of his culture.

In cluster IV are the following items:

50 Rating of happiness of husband's parents' marriage
51 Amount of conflict between husband and his father
52 Amount of attachment to father
53 Amount of conflict between husband and his mother
54 Amount of attachment to mother
55 Approval of marriage by husband's parents

These items indicate the kind of family interrelationships existing in the background of the person, and hence are probably closely associated with basic personality factors. It will be seen that items 50 and 51 are loosely correlated with item 47. Item 53 (amount of conflict with mother) is correlated with item 43 (the number of women husband went with steadily before marriage).

It has been noted that all the clusters except I are loosely correlated with item 47 (family-background index). The reason for this apparently wide relationship of 47 with the others is that this index is a rough measure of the degree to which the parental family background approximated that of a stable, educated, religious, middle-class family of "standing" in the community. This index is specifically based on the following information about the husband's parents: (1) religious preference and activity; (2) education; (3) size of family; (4) economic status; (5) social status in the community; (6) marital happiness; and (7) father's occupation. Since many of these items indicate social patterns that are likely to be transmitted in a middle-class family, it was to be expected that a score based on them would be somewhat correlated with corresponding items in the background history of children from such families.

Two items, 24 (size of husband's family) and 49 (mother living or dead), did not correlate closely with any other item in the complex. The closest relation between 24 and any other was with item 28 (health of husband). The closest relation of 49 (mother living or dead) was with 55 (approval of husband's marriage).

We did not carry the factor analysis to completion with these items and hence are not able to state the extent to which the clusters represent independent (uncorrelated) factors. However, for our present purposes it is sufficient to indicate the approximate clustering of the items. It is now possible to compare the groupings of our schedule items with the categories derived from reflection on case-study material. Cluster I clearly corresponds to our economic category (economic role). Cluster II corresponds to our category of social status and participation (social type). Cluster III taken together with item 47, with which it is more closely associated than are the other clusters, corresponds to our category of cultural patterning (cultural impress). Cluster IV corresponds to the category of personality factors (psychogenetic).

Since there were no items on affectional or response patterns in the list selected for statistical treatment, no cluster emerged that corresponds to the category of response patterns.

In a sense this partial factor analysis is merely pulling the same rabbit out of the hat that we put in it to begin with. It does, however, give a certain confirmation to our informally determined categories.

These tentative factor categories having been established, it was then possible to classify all the schedule items into these groupings and to get a score for each of the five categories by adding the score points of all of the items classified in a given category. These five separate scores could then be dealt with by usual methods of partial and multiple correlation to determine the independent contribution each category made to the prediction of marital adjustment. First the five factors were intercorrelated with results, as shown in Table 51.

TABLE 51

INTERCORRELATIONS OF THE FIVE FACTORS

Five Factors	Psycho-genetic	Cultural Impress	Social Type	Economic Role	Response Pattern
Psychogenetic					
Cultural impress	+.30				
Social type	+.45	+.47			
Economic role	+.29	+.32	+.53		
Response patterns	+.30	+.32	+.42	+.34	

An inspection of this table shows for the most part only moderate intercorrelations. There are, however, two exceptions to this general conclusion. The factor "social type" correlates over +.40 with all of the other factors, going as high as +.53 with the economic score. None of the intercorrelations of other factors exceeds +.34.

The next step was to get zero-order correlations of each of the five factors with the adjustment score and then, by the method of partial correlation, to find the correlation of each factor with the adjustment score, holding the other four factors constant. The results of these calculations are presented in Table 52.

The considerable drop in the correlations of each factor with the adjustment score when the other factors are held constant was to have been expected, since Table 51 shows some intercorrelation among all of them. The most surprising finding is the low partial correlation, +.04, obtained for the economic-role factor, which will be discussed shortly. So far as the items contained in this study are significant, they indicate that psycho-

TABLE 52

ZERO-ORDER AND PARTIAL CORRELATIONS OF THE FIVE FACTORS WITH ADJUSTMENT SCORE

	Correlations with Adjustment Score	
The Five Factors	Zero-Order Correlations	Other Factors Held Constant
Psychogenetic	+.39	+.20
Cultural impress	+.36	+.14
Social type	+.46	+.18
Economic role	+.32	+.04
Response patterns	+.40	+.20

genetic, social-type, and response-pattern factors have about equal importance for the prediction of marital adjustment, with cultural impress as a slightly less important fourth factor.

Economic role as a negligible factor in this sample. Quite unexpected was the virtual disappearance of economic role as an independent factor. The low partial correlation with the adjustment score indicates that the apparent effect of this factor is actually almost entirely the effect of the other four factors.

The first reaction of the reader to this finding is likely to be, as was that of the writers, one of surprise and incredulity. The individual premarital items included under the economic grouping were significantly related to the adjustment score. These included occupation of husband and wife at time of marriage, their income, length of time they had held positions, and savings. The explanation for the disappearance of this group of economic items seems to inhere in the fact that they do not constitute an independent variable, but are correlated with items included under the other four groupings.

Three objections may be raised. The first is that the significant economic items may have been omitted. This may be correct, but it is rather difficult to suggest items that would be as important as those included.

The second objection is that economic factors may operate indirectly rather than directly upon marriage through the as-

sumed effect of the economic status of parents upon the psychogenetic traits, cultural impress, social type, and response patterns of their children.   That, however, remains to be proved,
and is probably negligible.   The items regarding the economic
and social status of the parents had the lowest significance for
the marital adjustment of young people among all the items in
the cultural-background index.[7]

In the third place it must be remembered that our sample is
essentially one economic class.   We have a few cases from the
upper and very few from the lower strata of the economic
pyramid.   Hence all we can conclude from the above results
is that in this urban middle-class sample the premarital economic items had little independent effect on the marriage-
adjustment scores.

The observation should be made, moreover, that even if the
premarital economic factor in itself be unimportant for adjustment in marriage, postmarital economic conditions may be of
first-rate importance.   But it may turn out that these can also
be fully accounted for by the four noneconomic premarital
factors.

Relative Significance of Husbands' and Wives' Premarital Prediction Items

An interesting and significant question is the relative importance of the background items of husband and of wife for
the prediction of adjustment in marriage.   One way of measuring this was to take the zero-order and partial correlations of
items that could be classified as husband's background items,
wife's background items, and premarital items common to
both with the marital-adjustment score.   These are presented
in Table 53.

The zero-order correlations of predictive scores (husbands',
wives', and common) show little difference from each other,

---

[7] See p. 78.

TABLE 53

ZERO-ORDER AND PARTIAL CORRELATIONS OF HUSBANDS', WIVES', AND
COMMON SCORES WITH THE ADJUSTMENT SCORES

	Correlation with Adjustment Scores	
Groups of Predictive Items	Zero-Order Correlation	Other Groups Held Constant
Husbands' scores	+.47	+.30
Wives' scores	+.40	+.16
Common scores	+.43	+.19

The correlation of the wives' scores, +.40, is only slightly lower than that of the husbands' scores, +.47. But when each grouping of predictive items is taken with the others held constant, considerable difference is found. The partial correlations with the adjustment scores are: husbands' score, +.30; wives' score, +.16; and common score, +.19. The important discovery here is that the partial correlation of the husbands' scores with the adjustment scores is almost twice that of the correlation between the wives' background scores and marital adjustment.

The magnitude of the difference was unexpected, although other evidence for the greater significance of the husbands' background items had not been wanting. First, in this and other studies of prediction of success in marriage, it was evident that in general there was a wider range of variation in relation to adjustment scores between subcategories of the husbands' than of the wives' items. Secondly, in the correlation figures available for comparison between husbands' and wives' background scores with the adjustment scores, the differences are always in favor of the husbands' scores, as shown in Table 54.

The point, then, seems well established that the husband's background items are more significant for the marital adjustment of the couple than are those of the wife. The only apparent explanation of this fact seems to be that, for the most part, the wife must, or does, make the major adjustment in marriage. The husband, according to this interpretation, makes on

TABLE 54

ZERO-ORDER CORRELATIONS BETWEEN THE ADJUSTMENT SCORES (OR
MARITAL-HAPPINESS SCALE) AND HUSBANDS' AND WIVES' SCORES

Studies of Marital Adjustment	Correlation of Adjustment Scores with Background Scores	
	Husbands	Wives
Present study, 526 cases: background items (omitting items common to both)	.47	.40
Terman's study: background items	.35	.29
Present study: using 105 schedules filled out entirely by husbands and 226 schedules filled out entirely by wives: all background items *	.56	.43

* These schedules were selected from the 526 schedules of the present study. The background scores of husbands and wives were correlated separately with the adjustment scores of husbands and wives. Consequently, the correlation is with the background score of the husband and his adjustment score, and similarly in the case of the wife.

the average less effort to adjust. This theory assumes that the husband is either less adjustable than the wife in the marriage relationship, or that in the United States he still plays the superordinate role in marriage and consequently does not have to adjust so much as the wife. At any rate, the traits which he manifests before marriage apparently play a more significant role for good or for ill in the adjustment process than do those of the wife.

Multiple Correlation

The total score for the premarital items correlated with adjustment scores gave a zero-order coefficient of +.51. How much would this coefficient be raised by classifying the items in basic-factor categories and computing their separate scores so that partial and multiple correlation might be employed? To test the value of this procedure, multiple correlations were calculated.

With the partial correlations determined for the grouping of items under "psychogenetic," "cultural impress," "social type," "economic role," and "response patterns," it was possible to obtain a multiple correlation of these five factors with the adjustment score. The coefficient of multiple correlation was found to be +.56. With the addition of the contingency score, based on postmarital items, the coefficient of multiple correlation was increased to +.61.

Employing 26 background items, Professor Terman [8] obtained correlations of +.35 for husbands and +.29 for wives. Ten of Terman's background items were the same as those used in the present study; 16 were different. He obtained a multiple correlation of background items and combined personality items of +.54 for husbands and +.47 for wives. There is some question as to whether personality items obtained after marriage should be included in prediction, because it has not yet been demonstrated that they are unaffected by marriage or by other events occurring after marriage.

Our multiple correlation of +.61 (including the contingency items), and that of Terman of +.54 for husbands (including personality items), indicate the highest correlations presumably obtainable before marriage with the items employed in these two exploratory studies. For it is feasible to ask questions before marriage covering many of the contingency items of this study and all of the personality items used by Terman.

It is evident, however, that a law of diminishing returns is operating here. The inclusion of new items or new groupings of items beyond a certain point seems to add very little to the efficiency of prediction. This is probably due to the fact (1) that the individual items used are only roughly correlated with basic factors in marriage adjustment, and (2) that the scores did not include all the basic factors.

In the writers' judgment, the combination of premarital and

---

8 L. M. Terman, *Psychological Factors in Marital Happiness,* Chapter 13.

personality items taken from these two studies (by Terman and the authors) would yield a correlation of around +.60, and the guess is hazarded that the highest correlation to be secured by present statistical methods will be around +.70.

Limitations of Statistical Methods

We have shown that it is possible to obtain correlation co-efficients of +.50 to +.60 between a composite score on items that either are or could to some degree be included in a pre-marital history, and a score indicating approximate degrees of adjustment in marriage. An approximate estimate of the amount of variation in the marriage-adjustment score accounted for by the prediction score may be obtained by squaring the coefficient of correlation between them. This means that our present prediction score and the combined prediction and con-tingency score account for only 25 to 36 per cent of the varia-tion found in the marriage-adjustment score. If our guess is right that with present methods of investigation and measure-ment we shall not obtain a correlation much better than +.70, then only about half of the variation in adjustment scores will be accounted for.

The question arises as to why statistical prediction in the present and the near future is so limited in precision. One answer may be that the underlying factors determining adjust-ment in marriage have not been isolated and given proper weight.[9] Another is that the items used are imperfect indexes of the factors determining adjustment. If these answers are correct, and there is little doubt that they are, at least in part, then precision of statistical prediction can be somewhat in-creased by more complete isolation, more nearly perfect measur-ing, and more appropriate weighting of the assumed basic fac-tors.

----

[9] We are assuming for purposes of discussion that the measure of adjustment in marriage at any given time can be made reasonably precise.

Even if the indicated improvements were pushed to their upper practicable limits, the precision of statistical prediction would still be considerably short of approximate perfection. The reason for this decided limitation lies in the difficulties inherent in applying statistical procedures to the phenomena of marital interaction.

In the first place, statistical methods require that the phenomena studied be broken down—atomized—into manageable units. While methods are available for reintegrating the results of such analytical or atomistic treatment, they can only approximate the various dynamic syntheses actually realized in the concrete instances of marriage relationships.

In the second place, statistical analysis is based on observations taken at a moment in time and hence necessarily has a static character. The factors determining marital adjustment are dynamic, and marital adjustment itself is a moving equilibrium which escapes static analysis. Thus while statistical prediction may be valid for averages and for stated probabilities that results will fall within certain defined limits, it can only be approximate.

Implied in the above-noted limitations is the fact that present statistical methods deal with averages and probabilities and not with specific, dynamic combinations of factors. Under these conditions the method cannot state precisely the course of an individual sequence. This is a strength as well as a weakness in that the method makes possible the comprehension of a multitude of concrete instances which otherwise could not be grasped by any observer. This means, however, that statistical prediction is quite limited in its applicability to individual instances. For, as any careful observer knows, every marriage is a unique configuration of factors that cannot be stated in terms of statistical description, which is necessarily based on central tendencies and probabilities of masses of instances.

The crucial question arising from the above considerations is: To what extent can statistical methods in the future surmount some of these limitations? Are these limitations inherent in statistical methods, or do they only characterize the present stage of their use? May they not, to a great extent, represent a condition of too few numbers to permit the full freedom of operation of statistical method?

There can be no doubt that large numbers of cases greatly facilitate statistical manipulation of data. For example, assume that 10 items are relevant to adjustment in marriage. It may be assumed for purposes of argument that their significance for the marital relationship inheres in the conjunction of each one of these items with the other 9. The simplest expression of the relation of each item to adjustment in marriage is two-fold: (1) in the form favorable, and (2) in the form unfavorable. For example, a church wedding appears to be favorable and marriage elsewhere unfavorable to marital happiness. Or, if the item is happiness of a parent's marriage, a report of "happy" is favorable to marital adjustment of a son or daughter, but a report of "unhappy" is unfavorable. If it be desired to set up a mammoth table that would provide groupings for all the positive and negative categories of 10 selected items, it is evident that the total groupings would be 2 to the 10th power, or 1,024. An average of 100 couples to a group would make necessary a sum total of 102,400 couples for this statistical procedure. Even this large number would undoubtedly be too few to provide an adequate number of cases for certain combinations. There is no doubt, however, that many of these theoretical 1,024 combinations would be found highly significant for the understanding of adjustment in marriage.

Until such an aggregate of data is available, the chief reliance must be upon case studies for the indication of important configurations of dynamic factors.

The Distinctive Value of the Case Study

It is in revealing the dynamic factors in human relationships that the distinctive value of the case study exists. An intimate personal document discloses the organic relationship between factors which, more than the mere presence of the factors, is often significant for marital adjustment.

In order, therefore, to improve prediction, case-study analysis should be employed in combination with statistical procedure. In large part, case-study and statistical methods can be profitably used in close interrelation, but in considerable part the case-study method must be employed in relative independence of statistical procedure in order to derive from it its highest value for prevision.

The interdependent use of case studies and statistics should be mutually advantageous to the further development of the efficiency of the two methods. The fact is that they are closely and inextricably interrelated. Obviously all statistics ultimately come from "cases." A schedule is constructed upon the basis of data derived from the examination of individual cases. From the examination and analysis of cases come insights, clues, and leads on the basis of which new items may be introduced into the schedule and their average significance determined. Correspondingly, an unexpected statistical finding may require exploration by interview to determine its meaning and dynamic significance for adjustment. Furthermore, the analysis of ideal types of dynamic and organic relationships derived from case studies may suggest reorganization of predictive items under more significant categories. On the other hand, the relative importance for prediction of the many possible typologies may be determined by statistical procedures. The method of factor analysis will probably be very useful in determining significant categories. The present study of 526 cases exemplifies in an exploratory way certain of the advantages of this interdependence and interaction between statistical and case-study methods.

Only one illustration will be given of the way in which discoveries by analysis of case-study materials may enrich the items of the predictive index. Thus far we have not been able to reduce personality items and their combinations in marriage, as revealed by case studies, to any form that would allow a quantitative correlation with adjustment in marriage. If certain forms of relationships such as the dominant-submissive be isolated for study, something of the sort may be possible. An exploratory attempt to correlate various combinations of "strong" and "weak" personalities with happiness ratings has been attempted.[10] Space does not allow a description of the rating methods and the computation of "strong" and "weak" scores. Suffice it to say that strong persons were assertive, dominant, leading, responsibility-assuming in their behavior; and weak persons were nonassertive, passive, dependent in their behavior. Table 55 gives the percentages of differing combinations according to the ratings of happiness in marriage.

TABLE 55

PERCENTAGE DISTRIBUTION OF HAPPINESS RATINGS FOR DIFFERENT
MARITAL COMBINATIONS OF STRONG AND WEAK PERSONALITIES

Personality Combinations	Very Happy	Happy	Average	Unhappy or Very Unhappy	No. of Cases
Husband much stronger......	23.6	21.4	24.7	30.3	89
Husband somewhat stronger	34.6	28.8	17.3	19.2	104
Husband and wife equal....	34.4	24.5	23.2	17.9	151
Husband somewhat weaker	20.8	25.0	29.2	25.0	120
Husband much weaker......	4.4	24.4	32.2	38.9	90
Whole sample	24.9	24.9	25.1	25.1	554

According to this table it might be assumed that, in the relationships involving dominance and submission, the predictions

10 Unpublished study by Leonard S. Cottrell, Jr.

are more favorable where the couple have equally strong personalities or where the husband is "somewhat stronger" than are the predictions where the husband is too dominant or is weaker than the wife. This item incorporated in the prediction index may possibly improve prediction. Yet the fact remains that these abstracted forms of relations give no hint of the specific patterns of relationship in a given case. But from the case materials we get the impression that the specific patterns and their shifts are the important things, and they may best be estimated in their effect upon marital adjustment by the case-study method.

The conclusions drawn from a detailed study of an individual case are drawn largely, it is true, on the basis of what is called insight. This method, if it may be called a method, is that of empathy, of sympathetically entering into the experiences and attitudes of another person through the medium of an interview or a personal document and thus, for the time, identifying oneself with the other and taking his role.[11] By this procedure the student of human behavior is able both to appreciate the attitudes and acts of the subject from the subject's point of view and to understand them in the perspective of knowledge of other cases.

Our studies indicate that trends in the personality that are not fully in consciousness often exert a profound influence upon the interpersonal relations of marriage. The psychiatrist has developed methods of probing beneath the conscious attitudes of the person into his unconscious motivations and forgotten experiences. For this reason and because of his medical background he is disposed to make an intensive study of each indi-

---

[11] This method is to be partially distinguished from the method of sympathetic introspection proposed by C. H. Cooley in his *Social Organization* and his article "The Roots of Social Knowledge," *American Journal of Sociology*, 32, 1926, pp. 59–79 (Chapter 9 in *Sociological Theory and Social Research*, New York, Henry Holt and Co., 1930) in that with this method the investigator attempts to assume the role position of the subject as he responds to his life situations, and does not stop with mere sympathetic reproduction of his acts, gestures, and emotional states. See also J. L. Moreno, "Interpersonal Therapy and the Psychopathology of Interpersonal Relations," *Sociometry*, Vol. 1, 1937, pp. 9–76.

vidual case as a basis of diagnosis and prognosis. Since a large and essential part of success or failure in marital adjustment seems to depend upon the operation of unconscious factors, the participation of the psychiatrist in research in marital adjustment is indispensable.

Problems of the Case-Study Method

The case-study method presents, however, many methodological difficulties. It is, as already stated, the method of empathy, which means that the observer must partially identify himself with the subjects studied. He must attempt to take their roles and assume their attitudes, and to see and react to situations as he imagines they have done or do. This must be done for the subject's earlier experiences as well as for contemporary relationships. At the same time that the investigator is identifying himself with the subject, a part of his personality system must be reserved to observe and note what has been going on, and to state the probable future resultants of the interactional processes observed in this manner. It is difficult to see how such a complex observational process can be put into mensurable form so as to reduce relevant aspects of the phenomena to statistical description.

But for the fact that they are so frequently overlooked, it should hardly be necessary to stress the difficulties of communicating this kind of knowledge or understanding to other persons. The difficulty is particularly noticeable when an attempt is made to communicate such insight to persons who for one reason or another are unable to identify themselves with the subjects under discussion. This latter point might be the basis for a discussion that could lead to exceedingly complex problems of personality organization and interaction, but these problems must wait for the moment.[12]

---

[12] See Harry Stack Sullivan, "Psychiatry: Introduction to the Study of Interpersonal Relations," *Psychiatry*, Vol. 1, February 1938, pp. 121–134.

Another complicating feature of the case-study method follows from what has been said: it is the problem of the observer himself.[13] In the first place, there is the rather obvious and least difficult question of theoretical orientation. That is, a person who formulates reality in terms of a Freudian conceptualization will use a vocabulary that differs considerably from that used by a physiological psychologist. If, however, the two observers are sufficiently sensitized to the actual events studied and have somewhat similar individual and cultural personality organizations, their formulations of what they see may be translated from one vocabulary to another. Far more difficult is the problem of the unconscious observational orientation of the observer. This will be affected by many things, ranging from his class position in society to his childhood relationships with his family. In the study of interpersonal relations such as marriage, the latter biographical fact is more obviously relevant to the manner in which the student will interpret or even describe what he sees in a given marriage situation.

For example, let us assume that an observer is still naïve about himself. Let us further assume that this observer has had a very domineering mother, against whom he has reacted intensely with rebellious behavior of one sort or another. In technical language let us say that he overreacts to any slight indication of aggression from a female. As he identifies himself with members in a marriage situation in which there is conflict, he may interpret even slight aggression by the wife as domineering behavior, and the wayward behavior of the husband may be seen by him as a reaction against this dominance. Another observer might see the situation as one in which the husband desires more aggressive behavior from the wife and uses wayward behavior as a way to provoke it. Either one of the observers may be correct, or both may be partially correct.

---

[13] John Dollard has pointed out the sources of observer bias in his study of racial relations in a Southern community. The same problems are encountered here. See Dollard's *Class and Caste in a Southern Town*, New Haven, Yale University Press, 1938.

The point here is that relational patterns in one's own career give one an observational perspective. If the case-study method is ever to achieve any stability and reliability, there must be a more self-conscious effort at making explicit the observational perspectives of observers when these observers report their observations. This is something more than mere linear calibration of human observational instruments. A psychological positional or perspective factor is introduced.[14]

We do not go far in this discussion before we seem to be entangled in an almost hopeless jungle of social-psychological relativity. Some observers are rendered so insecure by the difficulties that they tend to dismiss the problem as of no importance or to discard the method as a scientific technique (not without sneaking it in through the back door, however, when they seek to interpret findings made by "objective" techniques). The problem is not hopeless. After all, in practical affairs we carry on and communicate and act from common reference points. What we need is a research effort to make more explicit the relation between reported observations and known perspectives of observers. This will enable us to state the nature of the deviations that occur from known perspectives. Moreover, it should be pointed out that case documents taken by recording instruments may be analyzed and interpreted by other observers who may, in part, correct "subjectivity." Even here, however, the material in the document will reflect the questions, points of emphasis, and perspective of the observer who has taken the case interview.

If the difficulties of the method of empathic introspection and the problems of communication and of observer perspective are left aside, there is still the difficulty of using this method for prediction. This difficulty may be indicated thus: In projecting himself into the developmental experiences of two subjects, the observer is forced to make estimates of the strength of the

---

[14] Harry Stack Sullivan, *op. cit.*

attitude and motivation components of role patterns developed in the relationships experienced by these subjects. He has to determine the likelihood that what appears to be a most probable relational pattern will continue into the marriage or will give way to other patterns that express other traits or roles developed in the given personalities. He needs to specify the marriage situations in which a relational pattern which now appears to be the most probable will be maintained, and the situations in which radical shifts of role may take place.

In conclusion, the fact must be faced that the interpretation of case studies by the empathic method is not standardized and that its virtue and weakness inhere in the lack of standardization. There can be no guarantee that any two persons using this method on the same cases will arrive at the same results. By comparison the great advantage of the statistical method is that any two or more investigators employing the same procedure will, if they are accurate, come out with absolutely the same results.

What the student of the case study must be on his guard against is, as we have seen, the pitfall of the personal equation, especially a tendency to overemphasize certain factors. Here it is that the findings of statistical prediction can be of real assistance to him. By charting out in a given case the average weight that factors and items may be assumed to have in the mass of cases, the student will perhaps be enabled the better to assess and to indicate the minimum or maximum importance in the given case of certain items and factors, especially in their dynamic configuration. In this way he will not disregard or overlook the examination of items and factors that in the mass are proved to be of importance, and, on the other hand, he will give full recognition to the items and factors that make this case significantly different from all others.

In other words, he will behave like the physician who, to be sure, brings to his diagnosis and prognosis of an individual case of illness all the medical science he has learned, but who at the same time applies the wisdom of his past experience and his intimate acquaintance with the individual characteristics—physical, mental, and social—of a particular patient.

Prospects for the considerable improvement of the prediction of adjustment in marriage appear bright, especially if a practical working relation can be established between the methods of statistics and those of case study. Each method has values and limitations that are distinctive and important. It is feasible, the writers believe, to use them in combination so that each complements and strengthens the other.

The study of basic problems of prediction considered in this chapter may now be summarized:

1. The reason that refinement of statistical procedure and the inclusion of additional items do not result in any significant rise in the coefficient of correlation between the prediction and adjustment scores may be (a) the non-inclusion of certain items in the adjustment score which would improve its reliability and validity as a measure of adjustment in marriage or (b) the non-inclusion of background items that would be better indicators (than those employed) of the basic factors actually making for adjustment in marriage.

2. The five fundamental factors in marital adjustment that appear to emerge from our case studies and from Thurstone's method of factor analysis have been tentatively named (a) psychogenetic characteristics, (b) impress of cultural background, (c) social type, (d) economic role, and (e) response patterns.

3. When the background items are grouped under these five basic headings and treated by the method of partial correlation, three basic background factors—namely, psychogenetic characteristics, response patterns, and social type—appear to have approximately equal weight in their association with the adjustment score. The fourth factor, impress of cultural background, seems to have somewhat less weight, and the fifth fac-

tor, economic role, is shown to exert only a negligible influence.

4. A comparison by partial correlation showed that the correlation between the background score of the husband with the adjustment score was nearly twice that of the wife.

5. By present statistical methods of prediction it is feasible to account for only about half of the variation in adjustment scores by the items included in the background score. Further improvement in prediction may be made by statistical analysis of significant combinations of items if it is possible to obtain tens of thousands of cases.

6. The case-study method is to be relied upon for the discovery of the dynamic factors in marriage adjustment.

7. The limitations of the statistical method as at present employed in prediction is that it applies averages from the universe studied to the particular case for which the prediction is made. The limitation of the case-study method lies in the subjectivity of its findings, in the difficulties of communicating to others the insights and understanding that it furnishes the investigators, in the theoretical and unconscious orientation of the observers, and in the present lack of standardization of the method.

8. The establishment of a practical working relation between the methods of statistics and those of case study is essential for further research in the improvement of the prediction of adjustment in marriage.

CHAPTER XVII

Major Findings and Their Interpretation

AT THE conclusion of a study the three following questions are almost always asked, and they are always well worth attention:

1. What, if any, contributions have been made to knowledge?
2. What is the significance of these contributions?
3. What further research is indicated?

The discussion of the third question upon further research will be reserved for the next and final chapter. An attempt will be made in this chapter to answer the first two questions by summarizing briefly the major findings of the study and by indicating their significance for an understanding of the way in which men and women adjust to each other in marriage.

Wives make the major adjustment in marriage. An outstanding, if not the most significant, finding of this study is that the background items of the husbands are much more important for adjustment in marriage than are the background items of the wives.

Why should the premarital characteristics of the husband be so much more closely correlated with marital adjustment than those of the wife? Perhaps in marriage the wife, on the average, makes much more of an adjustment to the husband than he makes to her.

On first thought the explanation that wives in the United States make the major adjustment in marriage is directly in contradiction to the American conception that marriage is a "fifty-fifty proposition" in which husband and wife make equal adaptations to one another.   It might have been assumed that husbands in this country more than anywhere else in the world are disposed to cater to and comply with the wishes, attitudes, and even whims of their wives.   European visitors to the United States are quick to point out the dominant position of the American wife in the home and the subservient or secondary role of her husband.

The findings of this study regarding the relatively greater weight of the characteristics of the husband in determining marital adjustment suggest that too much emphasis has been placed upon the superficial aspects of the American marital relationship.   These aspects appear greater by contrast with the obvious and definite subordination of woman to man in Old-World marriages.   Where the mores decree that the wife shall be submissive to the husband, as in Germany and to a lesser extent in England, all couples manifest a uniform pattern of behavior which corresponds to the approved forms.

In the United States, where the mores sanction equality in the marriage relation, the superficial forms of the husband's behavior may hide the actual situation.   Since the mores do not demand the obvious display of the husband's dominance, wide individual differences in the marital relation are apparent.   In many unions the wife is in fact, and not merely seemingly, superordinate.   The domineering wife and the "henpecked" husband, to mention an extreme illustration, are much more evident in the United States than in Europe.   The dictatorship of wives, however, is undoubtedly limited to a relatively small proportion of marriages.   The majority of wives must still achieve their aims in subtle and indirect ways which evidence the dominant position of their husbands.

The statistical findings of this study deal with averages and obscure individual differences.   Our problem is, then, to explain why so great an average discrepancy exists between the greater inferred adaptability of the wife than of the husband.

Two explanations are at hand which may operate independently or in conjunction. First, it may be assumed that the new mores emphasizing equality of the sexes in marriage have not as yet entirely displaced the old attitude that the husband should be dominant. Second, it may be asserted that the trait of dominance is, on the average, more marked in the male, and that of submission in the female. To the extent that this is true, the wife would be disposed to be subordinate and the husband superordinate.

To state that at present in American society dominance is in general a male, and submission a female, trait is not to imply that this difference is necessarily biological. It may, in fact, be social, not in the sense that it is commanded by the mores, but in that it persists in the attitudes arising out of our self-consciousness of sex differences and our conception of what is expected in the behavior of boys and girls, men and women.

Further research will be necessary to clarify the points raised by the discussion of these findings. If they actually measure present differences in the amount of adjustment made by man and woman in marriage, then it should be possible to determine the varying differences in adjustment between the husbands and wives in different sections of the United States. Comparative studies might be made to verify assumed differences between the East and the West, the North and the South, or between different districts within the city, as between equalitarian-family areas, semipatriarchal immigrant districts, and the matricentric suburban neighborhoods. It would be assumed, for example, that the Southern wife makes a greater adjustment in marriage than the Western wife, and that the immigrant wife living in the semipatriarchal-family neighborhood is more submissive to her husband than is the wife who is herself gainfully employed and residing in the apartment-house area with its equalitarian standards of family life.

The affectional relationships of childhood condition the love life of the adult. The response patterns of relationships established in childhood appear to be the dynamic factor determining the expression of affection in adult life. This finding is derived from the examination of 100 case studies in this investigation. It corresponds more or less closely to the conclusions reached by other workers in their clinical analysis of material obtained over a prolonged period by intensive psychiatric interviews. It is corroborated by the statistical evidence provided by this study.

Two general effects of the familial affectional environment upon the adjustment in marriage of young people have been independently established by Terman's study and by the present research:

1. Happy marriages of parents are correlated with happiness in the marriage of their children. This relationship is the outstanding association noticed in the study of the relation between background items of both husbands and wives and their adjustment in marriage.

2. Close attachment in childhood to father and mother and absence of conflict with them is positively correlated with the person's adjustment in marriage.

These two conclusions indicate the general correlation that obtains between a happy family relationship in childhood, with close attachment between parents and children, and a satisfactory adjustment as an adult in the marriage relationship itself.

Our case-study data enable us to proceed a step further and to make a specific formulation of a theory of childhood affectional attachment in relation to marital adjustment, as follows:

1. In childhood the person builds up a response relationship to the parent of the opposite sex which markedly influences his response to and selection of a love object in adult life.

2. If the childhood affectional relation to the parent of the opposite sex has been a satisfying one, the person will tend to

fall in love with someone possessing temperamental and personality characteristics similar to those of the loved parent.

3. If the childhood affectional relation has been unsatisfactory, he is more likely to fall in love with a person of opposite temperamental and personality characteristics. An exception occurs where the relation in childhood has been one of frustration rather than of conflict, so that as a consequence of idealization the person seeks all the more in a loved one the personality type of the parent of the opposite sex. Where the attitude is ambivalent, then there may develop alternating attitudes of love and hatred toward the affectional object.

4. The childhood response fixation is generally, but not always, upon the parent of the opposite sex. It may under certain conditions be centered upon the parent of the same sex or upon a brother or sister.

5. The actual complex of attitudes in affectional relationships in adult life tends to reproduce all the significant response patterns of childhood. Thus the adult unconsciously strives to act in his love life not only his childhood role with regard to his sex-opposite parent but also his childhood roles with regard to his parent of the same sex, to his older brother or sister, and to his younger brother or sister. Where the relation has been ambivalent, as in the case of submissive and rebellious behavior, this pattern also tends to be expressed in the marital relation.

This theory of the nature of early childhood affectional relationships as determining the dynamics of adjustment in marriage is of such great significance, if correct, that systematic effort should be made to verify or disprove it by objective methods. Its validation would greatly simplify the understanding of a great field of behavior that otherwise seems to be hopelessly complex, complicated, and often contradictory.

Socialization of the person is significant for adjustment in marriage. A group of background items constituting what may be called the social factor in marital adjustment is found to be significantly related to success in marriage. Among these items are: higher level of education; objective evidence of religious activity, such as duration and frequency of attendance at Sunday school and church; the number and sex of friends; participation in social organizations; and residence in neighborhoods of single-family dwellings. These items taken together may be regarded as an index of sociability, or of socialization in respect to the degree of participation and achievement of the person in the activities of the community and its chief cultural institutions—the family, the school, and the church.

The impress of social institutions upon a person may be measured in terms of his conformity to social rules, his respect for conventions, and his stability of character. The socialization of the person which results prepares him for adjustment in marriage.

The economic factor, in itself, is not significant for adjustment in marriage. A finding quite unexpected by the writers, and almost certain to be surprising to the public, is the virtual disappearance of the premarital economic items from the group of items significant in marital adjustment. It is true that several economic items such as moderate income, savings, occupations characterized by stability and social control, and regularity and continuity of employment are positively correlated with adjustment in marriage. But all these combined add very little to the effectiveness of the prediction that can be made without them. In fact, by the method of partial correlation whereby other factors are held constant, the discovery is made that the correlation of the economic factor with the prediction score is only .04 in comparison with .20 for the psychogenetic factor and the response factor, respectively; .18 for the socialization factor; and .14 for the cultural-impress factor.[1]

The explanation for the very low weight to be assigned to the economic items in marital adjustment is that they add very little to the items included under psychogenetic, cultural-im-

---

[1] See partial correlations of these factors, pp. 323–324.

press, social-type, and response factors. It may, indeed, be argued that the economic behavior of the person, at least so far as it affects adjustment in marriage, is an expression of these noneconomic factors. Economic items such as moderate income, savings, occupations characterized by stability and social control, regularity and continuity of employment, may all be taken as indicating a stabilized and socialized personality which readily adjusts to the marriage situation. But this is a type of personality which is also strongly indicated by psychogenetic, cultural-impress, social-type, and response factors. The economic behavior of the person may therefore be thought of as the resultant of these noneconomic influences. In fact, the trait of personality which all our items are measuring may turn out to be *adjustability* or *socialization* that makes for adjustment in society, in industry, and in marriage. However, it must be remembered that the sample on which this study is based does not cover the entire range of economic groups in our culture.

With the majority of couples, sexual adjustment in marriage appears to be a resultant not so much of biological factors as of psychogenetic development and of cultural conditioning of attitudes toward sex. This finding is derived from case studies and, while rather clearly indicated, should not be taken as conclusively established. It is in harmony with the obvious generalization that the biological growth and maturation of the individual takes place in association and interaction with his emotional, intellectual, and social development. The understanding of any one of these aspects of human growth is necessarily to be arrived at in the context of the others.

Prediction before marriage of marital adjustment is feasible, and should and can be further developed through statistical and case-study techniques. This study has demonstrated the feasibility of predicting adjustment in marriage and has indicated the course of future research to improve the accuracy and significance of prediction.

With present methods it is entirely practicable to indicate the risk group into which any engaged person will fall, with a definite statement regarding the statistical probabilities of success or failure in marriage. This is, however, group prediction, as with life-expectancy tables which are used by life-insurance companies. But the prediction of marital adjustment has one advantage over that of a life-expectancy table: our study indicates that statistical prediction for all practical purposes can be applied to particular individuals at the two extremes where all, or at least 99 out of 100, persons assigned to the highest and to the lowest risk group will either succeed or fail in marriage, according to the predictions.

The most practical use of prediction will, however, undoubtedly be with individual cases. It is, therefore, the aim of research to increase the precision, reliability, and significance of prediction in individual cases.

Promising leads for investigators who want to achieve this objective lie in two opposite directions. One is the intensive study of relatively few cases to identify the chief dynamic factors operating in marriage relationships. An example of a dynamic factor which has already been isolated is that of the persistence in adult life of an affectional pattern which determines the object of the love response. Such a discovery may later be subjected to test by statistical procedure. Intensive studies of individual cases will, however, generally be necessary in order to identify the particular configuration of dynamic factors in the interpersonal relationships of a given couple.

A second direction of research will involve dealings with not hundreds and thousands but tens and hundreds of thousands of cases, so that significant groupings of items may be identified by statistical methods. Although the obtaining of such large numbers of cases may not be feasible at the present time, there is no reason why research in this field should not ultimately aspire to the amassing of the hundreds of thousands of cases that are necessary to achieve the most significant results possible with statistical procedures.

In conclusion, a recapitulation of the findings of this study shows the following:

1.   Contrary to prevailing opinion, American wives make the major adjustment in marriage.

2.   Affectional relationships in childhood, typically of the son for the mother and the daughter for the father, condition the love-object choice of the adult.

3.   The socialization of the person, as indicated by his participation in social life and social institutions, is significant for adjustment in marriage.

4.   The economic factor in itself is not significant for adjustment in marriage, since it is apparently fully accounted for by the other factors (impress of cultural background, psychogenetic characteristics, social type, and response patterns).

5.   With the majority of couples, problems of sexual adjustment in marriage appear to be a resultant not so much of biological factors as of psychological characteristics and of cultural conditioning of attitudes toward sex.

6.   Prediction before marriage of marital adjustment is feasible, and should and can be further developed through statistical and case-study methods.

In short, the outstanding factors in marital adjustment seem to be those of affection, temperamental compatibility, and social adaptability.   The biological and economic factors are of less importance and appear to be largely determined by these other factors.

These six major findings represent the outstanding contributions which the present study makes to our knowledge of marital adjustment, particularly as adjustment may be predicted before marriage.   In this study, as in many others, the most significant contribution is not to be found in any one finding, nor even in the sum total of findings, but in the degree to which the study opens up a new field to further research.   The next and final chapter deals with this challenge.

CHAPTER XVIII

The Future of Research in
Marriage Adjustment

THE PRESENT study of prediction of marital adjustment
should first be seen in the perspective of previous and
contemporary investigations before its implications for future
inquiries are considered. A significant research project in the
social as well as in the physical and the biological sciences is
Janus-faced. It looks back to the investigations which preceded
it and it looks forward to the studies which it may germinate.

Review of Studies of Prediction
of Marital Adjustment

The first investigator relying upon inductive evidence who
state a relationship between a premarital factor and marital
success was Hornell Hart,[1] in a study in which he was assisted
by Wilmer Shields. Their study was statistical, and the criterion of marital failure was divorce. They found that marriages of men under 24 years and of women under 19 years
included a much higher proportion of unhappy unions than
marriages of older couples, and that 29 years for bridegrooms
and 24 for brides were the optimum ages for entering marriage
with the highest probability of happiness. These findings were

---

[1] It is of historical interest to note that Hornell Hart was also the first to call
attention to the feasibility of the prediction of violation of parole. See his article
"Predicting Parole Success," *American Journal of Criminal Law and Criminology*,
14, 1923, pp. 405–413.

based upon a comparison of cases from the Philadelphia Marriage License Bureau with cases from the Domestic Relations Court of the same city.[2]

In 1929 the reports of two important studies were published, both of which concentrated upon the sexual factor in marriage but included items upon other factors.

The study by Katharine B. Davis of factors in the sex life of 2,200 college women relied upon statistical analysis of questionnaire data, and the criterion of marital success was the reported happiness or unhappiness of the marriage. She found the following premarital items of wives significantly associated with their happiness after marriage: amount of formal education, health, general sex instruction, absence of "spooning," and no sex intercourse before marriage.[3]

Gilbert V. Hamilton, M.D., made an intensive psychiatric study of 100 married men and 100 married women.[4] He, too, analyzed his data by statistical and not by case-study methods. His criterion of success in marriage was a high score upon a list of satisfactions with marriage.

In his book he sets forth the association of many premarital factors with marital happiness. Because of the small number of cases included, only one correlation may be accepted with some certainty that it is statistically significant; namely, the positive correlation between marital satisfaction and the husband's report that his wife is physically like his mother. In the case of three other factors, there is considerable probability that the association is a reliable one; namely, a positive correlation between marital satisfaction and (1) same degree of formal education, (2) virginity of wife at marriage, and (3) the wife's having brothers. It must be borne in mind, however, that Hamilton's sample of cases was rather highly selected, so that

---

2 "Early Marriage and Happiness," *Journal of Social Hygiene,* 12, 1926, pp. 544–549. See pp. 115–117 for a discussion of this study.

3 Katharine B. Davis, *Factors in the Sex Life of Twenty-two Hundred Women,* New York, 1929, p. 59.

4 Gilbert V. Hamilton, *A Research in Marriage,* New York, Boni, 1929.

his findings apply, not to the general population, but to an urban group of relatively high income composed of rather sophisticated persons, probably with a disproportionately high percentage of those with problems of marital adjustment.

Jessie Bernard,[5] using an instrument of marital satisfaction which she devised, and by statistical methods, finds one pre-marital factor to be positively associated with success in marriage; namely, an age difference between spouses of zero to five years with the wife's happiness and of zero to ten years with the husband's happiness.

In a statistical study of factors in marital adjustment for 104 well-adjusted and 70 poorly adjusted couples, Clifford Kirkpatrick reports only two positive findings: (1) "in the case of women there is a marked tendency for greater intimacy with one or the other parent to be unfavorable to marital adjustment," and (2) "in the case of the males an excess or deficiency of friendship with the opposite sex is unfavorable to marital adjustment."[6] The couples were rated as well adjusted or poorly adjusted by students securing answers to the questionnaire.

With the assistance of his students, Paul Popenoe made a statistical study of the marital happiness of over 2,000 couples as related to the happiness of their parents' marriages[7] and found a positive correlation. Another study of 738 elopements of couples of approximately the same economic and social status as the larger group just mentioned showed elopement as unfavorable to marital adjustment.[8]

Clarence W. Schroeder included in his study of *Divorce in a City of* 100,000 *Population*[9] a statistical comparison of certain

[5] "Factors in the Distribution of Success in Marriage," *American Journal of Sociology,* 40, 1934, pp. 56–59, and "Some Biological Factors in Personality and Marriage," *Human Biology,* 7, 1935, pp. 430–436.
[6] "Factors in Marital Adjustment," *American Journal of Sociology,* 43, 1937–38, pp. 270–283.
[7] "Marital Happiness in Two Generations," *Mental Hygiene,* 21, 1937, pp. 218–222.
[8] "Study of 738 Elopements," *American Sociological Review,* 3, 1938, pp. 47–53.
[9] Doctoral dissertation, University of Chicago Libraries, 1938.

premarital factors for married and divorced couples of similar economic status. His criterion of marital failure was divorce. He found seven premarital items positively correlated with marital success; namely, parents' marriage reported happier than average; parents not divorced or separated; sex instruction from mother or from books; education beyond high school; attendance at church three or more times a month; attendance at Sunday school beyond 18 years; and being reared in country or small town.

L. M. Terman has recently published a statistical study of schedules filled out by 792 California couples.[10] The criterion of marital success was the score of husband and wife upon a scale of marital happiness, the items of which are practically the same as those of the marital-adjustment index used in this study. He found 26 background factors significant for prediction. Factors having the highest positive correlation with marital happiness are: rated marital happiness of the parents;[11] rated happiness of childhood;[12] no conflict with mother; firm but not harsh discipline in the home; amount of attachment to father and mother; no conflict with father; frank attitude of parents toward early sex curiosity; relative mental ability where the husband is not inferior (with the wife's happiness) and where the husband is not much superior (with the husband's happiness); absence of severe and frequent childhood punishment; absence of disgust and aversion toward sex in premarital attitude of the subject, and, in the case of the wife, absence of passionate longing.

Other background factors having a moderately high positive correlation with marital happiness are: age at marriage of husband, 22 and over, and 20 and over for wife; schooling of husband beyond high-school graduation, and one or more years of

10 *Psychological Factors in Marital Happiness,* New York, McGraw-Hill Book Co., 1938, pp. 167–266.
11 Above average or happier for the wife; decidedly more happy than average for the husband.
12 Above average for husband; average or above for wife.

college for wife; first meeting of spouses was not a "pick-up" or at a place of private or public recreation; premarital acquaint-ance of three years or more for husband's happiness and one year or more for wife's happiness; length of engagement, six months or longer for husband's happiness and three months or longer for wife's happiness; the wife not being an only child; rating by husband of his mother as average or above in general attractiveness; some or no physical resemblance of wife to hus-band's mother and no, some, or close physical resemblance of husband to wife's father; sex instruction, even if rather inade-quate (or even very inadequate in the case of the wife); chief source of sex information before 18 from parents or teachers; wife learning origin of babies between 6 and 16 years; no sex shock experienced by wife between 10 and 15 years; wife 12 years or older at first menstruation; wife never "petted" at high-school age; and wife never desired to be of opposite sex.

The present study based upon a sample of 526 couples finds a correlation of success in marriage with premarital factors as follows:

1. Certain factors at the time of marriage show a rather high positive correlation with adjustment in marriage; namely, the marriage of the parents of both husband and wife reported as happy; approval of marriage by parents of the couple; supe-rior family background of husband and wife; similarity of their family backgrounds; husband and wife not only children; hus-band closely attached to, and having little or no conflict with, his father and mother; wife's close attachment to mother; hus-band and wife reared in country; both attended Sunday school beyond 18 years of age; church attendance by husband two or more times a month; husband with graduate or professional education, and wife with college, graduate, or professional education; certain occupations for husband, and teaching for wife; wife employed at occupation the same as or similar to the one she prefers; income of wife $150 to $200 a month;

husband had several or many men friends and several women friends; wife did not lack men friends and had many women friends; wife 15 or more pounds underweight; at time of marriage husband resided in suburbs; couple acquainted with each other two or more years; husband and wife kept company three years and were engaged three years and over; husband and wife 22 to 30 years old at time of marriage; couple married by minister, priest or rabbi.

Certain factors at the time of marriage show a moderate positive association with adjustment in marriage; namely, husband not attached to any brother or sister; wife not attached to any sibling except younger brother; wife closely attached to, and having no conflict with, her father; both regularly employed; husband with moderate income; husband and wife a member of three or more organizations; husband healthy; husband living at college dormitory or fraternity; wife had moderate income; wife employed seven or more years; husband had savings; wife's residence in small town or city suburb; couple married in church or in parsonage.

Comparing the Findings of the Different Studies

These various studies have used different indexes of marital success and different background items. Assuming the validity and general comparability of the indexes of success in marriage employed by the different research workers, Chart 59 has been prepared showing the premarital or background items found to be associated with adjustment in marriage.

In considering the findings of the studies as reported in Chart 59, it is well to keep in mind the fact that the samples investigated were drawn from different sections of the country and from different socio-economic groups. The study by Katherine B. Davis of factors in the sex life of 1,000 married women was the most extensive inquiry both in number of cases and in their geographical distribution over the country;

her group was the most homogeneous culturally, since three-fourths of them had more than high-school education. The groups investigated in all the other studies were definitely localized and were less homogeneous. Bernard's group in St. Louis was culturally on much the same level as the Davis group, 72.4 per cent of them having more than high-school education. Hamilton's cases were largely from New York City, higher than the average in socio-economic status, and probably heavily weighted with intellectuals and with those with marital problems. Hart and Shields compared a random sample of couples married from 1905 to 1922 in Philadelphia and cases of unhappy marriages appearing in the Domestic Relations Court in May and June, 1924, a group undoubtedly of much lower socio-economic status.

Schroeder in his comparison of divorced and non-divorced couples chose a Midwestern city of 100,000 (Peoria, Illinois), and selected non-divorced couples to match his divorced group, which was predominantly of low economic and social status. The remaining studies are somewhat scattered geographically, those of Terman and of Popenoe being made in southern California, that of Kirkpatrick in Minneapolis, and that of Burgess and Cottrell in Illinois, but they all are predominantly concerned with urban couples of the middle class, largely of high-school and college education and engaged in white-collar jobs. All in all, these studies represent soundings in representative strata of American life. It will be interesting to discover how close together or wide apart the findings of the different studies proved to be.

An analysis of this chart shows that investigators have found 55 different premarital items associated with marital success. Of these items, 18 have been reported by two or more studies, while 35 have been found in only one study. The fact that two-thirds of the items were found to have some significance by only one investigator is due in only two or three instances to conflicting findings. It can be attributed rather to the fact that different students selected different premarital items.

CHART 59

PREMARITAL ITEMS FAVORABLE TO ADJUSTMENT IN MARRIAGE: A COMPARISON OF FINDINGS OF ALL STUDIES

(H, husband; W, wife)

Premarital Items	Studies by Bernard, Davis, Hamilton, Hart Kirkpatrick, Popenoe, and Schroeder	Terman's Study (792 Couples)	This Study (526 Couples)
Acquaintance, length of	....	H, three years or more W, one year or more	Two or more years
Age at marriage.......	H, 24 and over........ W, 20 and over (Hart)	H, 22 and over....... W, 20 and over.......	H, 22 to 30 W, 22 and over
Age difference.........	H, o to 10 years older W, o to 5 years younger (Bernard)	....	H, older by one to three years or same age as wife
Attachment to father.	....	Good deal or very close	H, close W, close
Attachment to mother	....	Good deal or very close	H, close W, close
Attachment to parents, degrees of preference	W, absence of greater intimacy with one parent (Kirkpatrick)	W, absence of markedly greater attachment	....
Attachment to siblings	....	....	H, none W, none or younger brother
Babies, learned origin of	....	W, 6 to 16 years.......	....
Brother or brothers....	W has (Hamilton).....	....	....
Church attendance.....	Three times a month (Schroeder)	....	H, two or more times a month W, four times a month
Conflict with father....	....	None or very little.....	H, little or none W, little or none
Conflict with mother...	....	H, none............. W, none or very little	H, little or none
Courtship, length of...	....	....	Three or more years
Discipline in home.....	....	Firm but not harsh....	....
Education............	W, beyond high school (Davis) Spouses have equal education (Hamilton) beyond high school (Schroeder)	Beyond high school....	H, college graduate or professional W, college, post-graduate, or professional
Employment, length of	....	....	W employed seven or more years
Employment, regularity	....	....	Regularly
Employment, type....	....	....	W, same as or similar to what she wants
Engagement, length of	Did not elope (Popenoe)	H, six months or longer W, three months or longer	Nine months and more
Family background, level	....	....	Superior level
Family background, similarity	....	....	Similar

CHART 59 (*Continued*)

Premarital Items	Studies by Bernard, Davis, Hamilton, Hart, Kirkpatrick, Popenoe, and Schroeder	Terman's Study (792 Couples)	This Study (526 Couples)
Friends, men..........	....	....	H, several or many W, does not lack
Friends, women.......	H, excess or deficiency (Kirkpatrick)	....	H, several or many W, many
Happiness in childhood	....	Above average........	....
Health..............	W, healthy (Davis)....	....	H, healthy
Height-weight deviation	....	....	W, 15 or more pounds underweight
H physically resembles W's father	....	W, none, some, or close	....
Income..............	....	....	H, moderate W, moderate
Married by..........	Minister or priest (Schroeder)	....	Minister, priest, or rabbi
Married where........	....	....	At church or parsonage
Meeting place, first...	....	Other than "pickup" or a place of private or public recreation	....
Membership in organizations	....	....	H, two or more W, three or more
Menstruation, age at first	....	W, not before 12 years	....
Mental ability, relative	....	W, husband not inferior H, husband not much superior	....
Mother's (H's) attractiveness as rated by H	....	H, average or above...	....
Occupation..........	....	....	H, certain occupations W, teaching
Order of birth........	....	W, not only child.....	H, not only child; if only and youngest, do not marry only and youngest
Parents' approval of marriage	....	....	Approved by both
Parents' marital happiness	Rated happy (Popenoe, Schroeder)	W, about average or happier Rated (happy) H, rated decidedly happier than average	Rated happy
Parents' marital status.	Not divorced or separated (Schroeder)	....	....
Petting (or spooning)..	W, none (Davis)......	W, never.............	....
Rearing, urban or rural.	Country and small town (Schroeder)	....	Reared in country
Punishment in childhood	....	None, rare, or occasional	....
Religious home training	....	H, considerable.......	....

CHART 59 *(Concluded)*

Premarital Items	*Studies by Bernard, Davis, Hamilton, Hart, Kirkpatrick, Popenoe, and Schroeder*	*Terman's Study* (792 Couples)	*This Study* (526 Couples)
Residence,neighborhood	....	....	H, in suburbs W, small town or city suburb
Savings.............	....	....	H has
Sex — response of parents to child's early curiosity	....	Frank................	....
Sex, attitude toward...	....	H, indifference or interest and pleasant anticipation	....
Sex information, source of	....	Parents or teachers....	....
Sex, desire to be of opposite	....	W, never desired......	....
Sex instruction........	W, some (Davis) from mother or books (Schroeder)	H, more than very inadequate W, not entirely lacking	....
Sex shock.............	....	W, none from 10 to 15 years	....
Sexual intercourse.....	W, none (Davis)...... W, none (Hamilton)	None, or with future spouse only	....
Sunday-school attendance	Beyond 18 years (Schroeder)	....	Beyond 18 years
Wife physically resembles H's mother	H, wife resembles (Hamilton)	H, some or none.......	....

Premarital Items Found to Be Significant by Two or More Studies

Of the 18 items, two were reported by four of the investigators. These are:

1. Report of parents' marital happiness.
2. High level of formal education.

Three items were reported by three of the investigators. These are:

1. Later age at marriage.
2. Some sex instruction in childhood.
3. No premarital sexual intercourse by wife.

Thirteen items are asked in practically the same way in two of the studies. They are:

1. Acquaintance, length of.
2. Attachment to father.
3. Attachment to mother.
4. Attachment, degrees of preference.
5. Church attendance.
6. No conflict with father.
7. No conflict with mother.
8. Engagement, length of.
9. Friends, women (of husband).
10. Married by minister, priest, or rabbi.
11. Petting or spooning (wife, never).
12. Rearing in country.
13. Sunday-school attendance beyond 18 years.

Where the same questions have been asked in the various studies, the findings are with few exceptions the same. Hamilton finds the same educational level correlated with marital happiness, a finding not supported by the results of other studies. Then, in several instances, particularly in the studies by Hamilton and by Kirkpatrick, the number of couples studied was too small to yield statistically reliable findings upon certain items which were found to be statistically significant in inquiries that sampled larger groups.

In general, however, it may be said that the findings of these studies substantiate each other. This fact is all the more significant because of the wide diversity in geographical distribution and in the socio-economic status of the samples. It is in accordance with one of the major findings of the study; namely, that personality and cultural factors outweigh the economic factor in making for or against happiness in marriage.

The research to date is promising in regard to the prospects of rich returns in future research. These pioneer investigations have defined the objective of this field of inquiry as the discovery of the items and factors associated with success in marriage; they have demonstrated that it is feasible to devise criteria of marital success, and they have indicated the practicability, within certain limits, of the prediction of adjustment in marriage. All these studies are exploratory. They have blazed a trail in a region of human relationships that had previously seemed almost impenetrable; they have opened up leads that should be followed. On the basis of their methods and findings it is now feasible to outline a plan for further research.

A Plan for Further Research

In outlining a research program in a new field attention should always be called to its tentative character and to the necessity for its continuous revision in the light of subsequent research developments.

Only the projects of first importance for the increase of our knowledge of marital adjustment will be suggested here, with a brief indication of what their contribution would be to an integrated program.

1. Of vital significance to further research is the problem of devising a more satisfactory criterion of adjustment in marriage.[13] One task to be faced is that of further testing the assumptions[14] upon which the adjustment score is based. A second problem is to determine, if possible, the explanation for those cases in which there is considerable divergence between the adjustment scores of the husband and the wife. A third task is to increase the precision with which the scoring device discriminates among varying degrees of adjustment. The construction of adjustment tests that are discriminative and reasonably resistant to distortions due to the tendency to "put

---

[13] One such study is now being made by Paul Wallin, University of Chicago.
[14] See pp. 47–56.

the best foot forward" should prove a fertile field for experimentation. In addition to meeting these requirements, the test should if possible be diagnostic. If the adjustment test itself cannot also be diagnostic, then a procedure must be devised that is specifically aimed at locating the major strengths and weaknesses in a given marriage. Since every relationship has its unique qualities, no general test can fully obviate the necessity for case study where counseling or full analysis of the situation is required. But granting such limitations, a valid diagnostic test is needed to carry forward extensive studies of different types of marital adjustments and maladjustments.

Another objective in connection with criteria and tests of adjustment is to discover to what extent we can trust the general application of a given adjustment test to various groupings by age, by socio-economic status, and so forth. It has been found in this study as well as in a similar one [15] that the proportion of very high adjustment scores declines with the increase in number of years married. This fact raises the question whether couples, on the average, actually become less well adjusted as the duration of their marriage increases, or whether we have run upon the fact that the basis of good adjustment itself varies through time and, therefore, requires different criteria of measurement. To what extent are the adjustment scores, constructed for middle-class urban people for the most part, applicable to other socio-economic groups in the population, and to what extent do different criteria and different tests need to be used? Obviously this is a highly significant problem for study.

2. Studies similar to the present one should be repeated both on the same and different types of populations for purposes of testing further the validity of individual predictive items and the validity of the prediction scale as a whole. It is important to establish whether or not samples similar to the

---

[15] Edith Webb Williams, *Factors in Adjustment of Rural Marriages,* unpublished Ph.D. thesis, Cornell University, 1938.

one in this study would yield the same results. It is also important to discover how similar or divergent the findings will be in populations different from that of the previous studies. All those items found to be significant in the investigations already made should be included in new studies and additional promising items should be added.

L. S. C. Smythe [16] adapted the schedule used in this study to a similar study of young Chinese married couples living in southern China. They were urban, college, middle-class people. With a few exceptions, he obtained results rather closely conforming to those of the present work. Edith Webb Williams,[17] using the same kind of schedule in a study of 200 rural couples, has obtained closely similar results with some of the items and interesting differences with others. Lewis M. Terman, in a study of over 700 couples in southern California, obtained findings on items comparable to those of this study.[18] Ernest W. Burgess and Paul Wallin [19] at the University of Chicago are carrying on a study of engaged couples in a metropolitan region. In this last study, data are being accumulated to be related in time to the degree of adjustment realized in the marriages of the engaged couples studied.

In addition to what is being done, it is necessary to sample more systematically the different cultural and socio-economic groups in the general population. Not only should results of such efforts indicate the extent to which certain items and factors hold for all groups, but divergence between groups and regions will throw light on the situations making for these variations. Divergence of findings should also yield a basis for evaluating properly the significance of items that vary from class to class. Thus, for example, in the present study

---

[16] L. S. C. Smythe, *Marriage Study,* a preliminary report (mimeographed) of a study by a seminar on the Chinese family at the University of Nanking, 1936.

[17] Edith Webb Williams, *op. cit.*

[18] Lewis M. Terman, *Psychological Factors in Marital Happiness,* New York, McGraw-Hill Book Co., 1938.

[19] E. W. Burgess and Paul Wallin, unpublished study of engaged couples.

the proportion of couples having very high adjustment scores increased with increasing numbers of common interests. Mrs. Williams [20] found with a rural sample that the same rule held up to a certain point. After a high degree of community of interests had been achieved, the proportion of high adjustment scores increased only with the addition of divergent interests. The tentative interpretation was that, in urban marriages, vocational activities are disparate and need to be counterbalanced by a large amount of common activity in leisure time, whereas in rural life the economic activity is communal and there is an apparent need for some divergence of interests on the part of the marriage mates.

Another illustration of possible differences from class to class may be found in the income levels of different groups that are associated with optimum probabilities of good adjustment. Given a minimum economic security to begin with, the absolute amounts of income may not prove to be significant apart from the expectations regarding the plane of living that mates bring to the marriage.

3. The present study is a pioneer inquiry and, therefore, has the limitations which are likely to characterize exploratory research. For the most part the data obtained are in rather crude form, and the number of cases is small. These limitations excluded certain types of statistical treatment. The statistical treatment of the present data, however, with more funds and time could have been carried much further. These considerations suggest the necessity for constructing more precise instruments for getting more significant information from larger samples of cases to correlate with marriage adjustment. When this is done, more refined statistical methods may be used, with more assurance, to extract as much as possible from the data.

4. More research is needed to discover the actual relation

---

[20] Edith Webb Williams, *op. cit.*

between the background factors and adjustment in marriage. Two general questions suggest themselves. One is the problem of the direct effect of a given factor upon the marriage relationship. The other is the problem of what the item indicates about the kind of personality involved and the effect of the personality, rather than the factor itself operating directly, on the relationship. For example, it was found that when the premarital-work history of the husband was irregular, the probabilities that his marriage would have a high adjustment score were less than if he had a history of regular employment. The question arises as to how much the probable economic and social insecurity indicated by the fact of irregular employment affects the adjustment; and, on the other hand, what does irregularity of employment of a young, urban, middle-class man in 1929 and 1930 indicate about the young man's personality, which in itself may affect his marriage relationship? This kind of question has to be asked about many, if not all, of the background factors. Even such a factor as differences in cultural and social background exhibits both aspects. What types of personality are most likely to marry socially superior, inferior, or culturally different mates? Quite apart from socio-economic factors, are such personalities more likely or less likely to make good marriage adjustments?

In addition to the possible relation of any factor to personality, there is always the question of the extent to which it is significant in itself or is an index of other factors. For example, in the present study increasing education is positively correlated with chances of good adjustment. To what extent is education in itself a factor in adjustment, and to what extent does it indicate greater economic security, greater maturity, higher intelligence quotients, and so on, which may or may not affect the probabilities of marital adjustment?

Closely connected with these questions are many special research problems raised by our data, two of which may be mentioned. Conflict with and attachment to parents is more significant for husbands than for wives in regard to adjustment in marriage.[21] The same differences appear in the rural study.[22] Such findings raise important points for further study in the social psychology of marriage. Interesting questions regarding the effect of children on marriage relations are raised by our results. A positive attitude toward having children seems to be associated with increased probabilities for good adjustment; but the actual having of children in the first four or five years seems to be associated with reduced chances of good adjustment. These findings suggest such questions as: How does the birth of the first child affect marriage relationships? What kinds of personalities are helped and what kinds are hindered in their marital adjustments by the presence of a child?

5. A possibly important background factor quite neglected in this study is that of the preparation of husband and wife for marriage. In the schedule the only item relevant to this factor was the request that the couple name books that had influenced their conception of marriage. With the increase of the literature of advice in regard to matters of sex and marriage, and with the recent growth of academic courses in preparation for marriage and of marital-counseling centers, it is possible to obtain data from schedules and interviews that would show the degree of efficacy of present methods of education for marriage.

The knowledge of young women regarding the different activities involved in housekeeping, and their training in home economics, constitute a factor which should be studied in relation to marital success. The questions of whether or not the wife is to have an allowance or there is to be a joint bank account, or whether the household is to be run upon a budget, should be included in any comprehensive future study.

---

[21] See pp. 93–97.
[22] Edith Webb Williams, *op. cit.*

6. One of the most intriguing fields of research that this study has helped to open up is that of the relation between personality patterns and marriage adjustment. While much has been discovered in clinical work, particularly by psychoanalytic workers, little if any systematic application of clinical insights to the general problem of marriage adjustment has been made.

The seven propositions regarding role patterns in marriage relations which were stated in Chapter XI [23] may be regarded as hypotheses upon which further research might be based.

The following questions may also be considered:

1. Is it possible to develop a useful system of classification of personality traits or of role patterns for work in this field? Any classification may have to be in terms of behavior patterns in specified situations rather than a classification by abstract "trait" names, since "role" implies a specific situational field. There is evidence that the roles significant for the marriage situation are those that develop in relation to parents and siblings. [24]

2. Is it possible to measure the adjustment probabilities for the various type combinations of personality or of role types? Terman [25] and his associates, using standard test forms, attempted to measure the relation of individual traits to marital adjustment and found certain ones to be significant. These were, however, for couples who had been married for varying numbers of years; hence their predictive value is questionable. The same tests are being used by Cottrell and Williams at Cornell, but results are not yet available. Another effort is being made at Cornell to get comparative ratings of husbands and wives on a number of characteristics with the hope that

[23] Pp. 174–177.
[24] See case studies in Chapters XI and XII, and L. S. Cottrell, Jr., "Roles and Marital Adjustment," *Publications of the American Sociological Society*, 27, 1933, pp. 107–115.
[25] L. M. Terman, *op. cit.*

certain personality combinations related to good and poor adjustment will be discovered.

The most thoroughgoing use of standardized psychological tests is being made by E. Lowell Kelley [26] at Connecticut State College in a study of 500 engaged couples. Burgess and Wallin at Chicago are attempting to determine, by the extensive use of case-history material, the significance of a limited number of personality traits for adjustment in engagement and marriage. Harriet R. Mowrer, in her clinical studies of marital discord, has found classification by role types valuable for diagnosis and treatment. [27]

Great need exists for systematic and intensive case studies with a view to getting clear descriptions of personality patterns and their dynamic role in specific situations in marital relations. Without them the "test" and "rating" studies are likely to prove sterile or misleading.

3. Is it possible to give quantitative expression to personality factors, and thus make it possible to include them in the prediction score? Judging from the case studies of the present research, precision in prediction will be greatly increased by the inclusion of personality factors.

4. Granted that the more significant personality patterns that operate in marital adjustment can be isolated, is it possible to isolate the childhood and adolescent family relationships that are most likely to produce the patterns in question? If this can be done, a beginning can be made in defining the family conditions under which good and poor marital personalities are being produced.

5. Inextricably involved in the study of individual personality, and yet of sufficient special interest to warrant underscoring it for research, is the matter of varying family patterns and their influence on marital success. Even in relatively

---

26 Unpublished study.
27 *Personality Adjustment and Marital Discord*, New York, American Book Company, 1935.

homogeneous cultural milieus, families as well as individuals
vary in their patterns of action. Some families are voluble,
expressive; others are reticent, inhibited. These general attitudes frequently seem to characterize the entire field of family
interaction. Mates who come from two such families will
have deeply imbedded patterns that may complicate their
adjustment to one another. One mate may be disgusted by
the "gushing" of the other; the second may feel highly insecure
in not receiving accustomed expressions of intimate appreciation from the first. Families differ in their values, relations
to the community, familism, indulgence-repression patterns,
intimacy, and demonstration of affection. Many hypotheses
bearing on these differences could be set up. For example,
persons from families in which most of the social, economic,
and affectional security is furnished in and by the family are
likely to emphasize the maintenance of strong family relations
in seeking their major satisfactions in life; and persons from
families that are not the chief source of such satisfactions are
likely to emphasize nonfamilial values and relationships. Mates
from such opposite backgrounds may have serious adjustment
problems.

6. While sex relations have received more attention than
any other aspect of marital problems in recent literature, we
are yet far from a satisfactory coördination of our understanding of the problems of sexual adjustment with our knowledge of
other aspects of the marriage relation. The psychoanalysts have
done more than any other group to show the sexual processes in
relation to other activities of the personality. Even in their
studies, however, there is no systematic analysis of the processes
of marital adjustment with the sexual patterns placed in the
total context of the relationship.

There is need for some psychiatric investigations of couples
representing various patterns of personality relationships to
give us some conception of the varying sexual activities and
attitudes and the intertwining of sexual factors with other fac-

tors in the marriage. On the basis of a number of such intensive studies, certain schedule items might be developed by which to obtain some important sexual indexes for use in prediction studies.

7. The studies in this field already completed have been restricted to married couples. The findings of these investigations have, it is true, indicated the association between premarital factors and success in marriage and the feasibility of predicting at the time of marriage the probabilities of marital adjustment. But they are all open to the objection that the data upon which they are based were secured after, rather than before, marriage. While the answers to certain of the questions would not be changed if the answers were obtained at the time of marriage, there can be no certainty that this would be so with all the questions. Therefore it is highly essential that research be directed to securing data from young people before marriage and that, periodically after marriage, information be obtained from the married couples regarding their adjustment.

Such a study of couples before and after marriage entails, of course, much more in time and funds than do studies limited to married couples, but the results should be correspondingly more valuable. Fortunately two studies of engaged couples are now in progress to which reference has earlier been made,[28] and the findings of which will be awaited with interest.

8. Most significant from both a practical and a theoretical viewpoint would be research in marital adjustment carried on by means of an experimental and a control group of engaged couples. The experimental group of young people not only would be interviewed but would also be given advice upon problems—sexual, psychological, economic, and regarding household management, and so on—that presumably could make for improvement in marital adjustment. The control group, which in other respects would not differ from the ex-

[28] See p. 368.

perimental group, would be given no advice. At a certain time after marriage, for instance three years, the two groups would again be interviewed, and material would be obtained by which differences in marital adjustment, if any, could be determined. Only by some such method will it be possible to find out what are the general and specific effects of premarital education and counseling regarding marriage adjustment. And there is no doubt that investigations of this kind are entirely feasible.[29]

An Institute for Research in Marriage Adjustment

From this brief survey of needed future research it is evident that the problems calling for solution and the opportunities for fruitful investigation are manifold and extensive. It is evident that they cannot adequately be carried on by the isolated research worker. Research in the dynamic factors making for marital success requires planning and organization. The establishment of an institute for research in marriage adjustment would offer the facilities commensurate with the magnitude of the research task.

The argument for the creation of a research institute can be simply and briefly stated. If research in this field is to provide the knowledge imperatively needed and urgently demanded, it must be carried on (1) systematically, (2) continuously, and (3) in an integrated fashion. If the research were carried on in this way, there is every assurance that significant and consistent additions would be made to knowledge. An institute would make it possible to plan research systematically and to take up the different problems for investigation in their logical order and in fruitful relation to each other.

The most significant research in factors making for marital success must be carried on with continuity not only of projects but also of the human material. Couples should be revisited

---

[29] A judgment based upon experience in a study of engaged couples now in progress.

not only three years after marriage but six, nine, twelve, and fifteen years thereafter, to observe the effect of the changes in adjustment that come with time. Continuous studies of this type would be extremely difficult, if not impossible, except under the auspices of an institute or some other permanent research organization.

Research in this field to be significant must be increasingly integrated research involving two or more of the life sciences. The present study clearly indicates the different aspects of marital adjustment—sexual, medical, psychogenetic, economic, cultural, and social—that require investigation with the methods of the pertinent biological, psychological, and social sciences. A research institute with a well-rounded program should have upon its staff specialists from these different disciplines who are interested and equipped to work in this field. Study of difficulties in sexual adjustment would be carried on in its various aspects, biological, psychological, and cultural. Research in heredity through a study of family histories would determine the probable inheritance in each given union of cancer, diabetes, mental disorder, epilepsy, Huntington's chorea, and other inherited physical or mental defects. The social psychologist and the psychiatrist would be called upon to study the role of psychogenetic traits in marital adjustment. The sociologist would be primarily concerned with the cultural aspects of marriage. The economist and the home economist would conduct research in the economic and homemaking areas of married life.

Working together upon aspects of a common problem and upon interrelated projects, the specialists from different disciplines would progressively become aware of their part of the project in the context of the research enterprise as a whole. This should mean the conduct of research upon a higher level of integration and efficiency than has heretofore been attained.

An Institute for Research in Marriage Adjustment so organized and oriented would undoubtedly become a center for training for research in this field. As soon as research personnel were trained, new research centers would be opened and marriage-consultation bureaus would add research workers to their staffs. The knowledge obtained from research would thus be made rapidly available to the public.

The studies in marital adjustment already made or now in progress demonstrate the willingness and eagerness of young people, unmarried and married, to coöperate in this type of research. They realize keenly the importance of the findings for themselves and for others. They are willing to make their contribution to the pooling of experience which is a necessary precondition to the advancement of knowledge.

Prediction in the Psychological and the Social Sciences

The value of the findings and the methods developed in this investigation transcends their applications, important as they are, to the field of adjustment in marriage. Their scientific significance is to be measured by their contribution to the basic methodology of the prediction of human behavior. Two general conclusions emerging from this study are, in the judgment of its writers, relevant to further research in the field of human relations. These may be briefly stated.

Further significant research in the understanding of human behavior and its prediction requires the setting up of projects which combine the viewpoints and the techniques of the biological, the psychological, and the social sciences. The conceptual systems and methods of any one of these disciplines alone is inadequate because man's behavior in society is a resultant of the constant interplay of constitutional, psychogenetic, cultural, and social influences. Research that uses one method to the exclusion or partial representation of the others is likely to end in one-sided and limited conclusions.

The other main finding of this study, undoubtedly applicable to a wider range of subject matter than the area of this project, is that the prediction of human behavior is likely to be imperfect and highly contingent unless it relies upon the methods and data both of statistics and of case study. Each method has its own values and limitations; the unique merit of their combined use is that they not only are supplementary and complementary but, when brought into working relation with each other, increase the efficiency of both methods.

Further studies in the dynamics and prediction of human behavior should, if the findings of this study are valid, employ points of view and methods of the biological, the psychological, and the social sciences and of case study and statistics. As a result of careful case studies which reveal the processes of the action of persons in social situations, and as a result of the statistical analysis made possible by the accumulation of mass data, we are now able to formulate more searching hypotheses concerning the basic mechanisms and underlying factors in human conduct which, when they are sufficiently tested and verified, may be applied to other fields. Areas of human behavior ripe for prediction studies which call for a combination of these methods include those of school achievement, occupational success, and recidivism of criminal behavior. These fields invite intensive and systematic cultivation not only because of exploratory predictive studies already made but because in school, employment, and penological situations records are available and can be further developed to meet the requirements of significant research.

Whereas in school, in employment, and in crime, prediction is concerned with but one actor in a social situation, in marriage the attempt is made to predict in a situation involving the interaction of two personalities. This makes the study of marriage more complicated but also more promising for revealing the dynamics of behavior.

Continuous, systematic, and integrated research upon factors making for adjustment in marriage should be instituted not alone for its further contributions to scientific knowledge but because of its great potential practical value for the prevention of much marital maladjustment and for the enhancement of human happiness.

APPENDIX A

Tables Not Included in the Text

TABLE 56 (CHART 3)[1]

CULTURAL BACKGROUNDS OF HUSBAND AND WIFE AND ADJUSTMENT

Marital Adjustment

Family-Back-ground Index	Poor (per cent)	Fair (per cent)	Good (per cent)	No. of Cases	Mean Ad-justment[2]	CR
Husband: [3]						
Under 70	40.6	26.8	32.5	123	128.6	—5.1
70 to 89	32.2	29.8	38.0	242	136.1	—4.4
90 to 119	13.7	27.3	59.0	161	154.0*	
Total				526		
Wife: [3]						
Under 55	35.0	36.8	28.2	117	129.2	—4.4
55 to 64	30.1	26.7	43.2	273	139.0	—3.1
65 and over	19.9	24.2	55.9	136	151.9*	
Total				526		
All cases	28.5	28.3	43.2			

* In this Appendix the figure is starred which is taken as the point of origin for determining the critical ratio (CR) of the differences between the means.

[1] In parenthesis after the table number is given the corresponding number of the chart. Charts 3 to 57 in the text were prepared on the basis of the data appearing in Tables 56 to 110 in this appendix.

[2] The marital-adjustment score has a range of from 20 to 200 points. The mean adjustment score of our couples is 140.8, σ 38.8. Under the column "Mean Adjustment" is entered the mean of the adjustment scores of the cases falling in each subcategory.

[3] It will be noted that the wives' background scores are lower than those of the husband and that the range is not so great. This is due to the fact that different weight values were used on the items in the two background scores. The possible range of scores on the husbands' backgrounds was from 36 to 120, inclusive. The possible range for the wives' scores was from 38 to 73, inclusive. The difference in weightings resulted from the fact that the individual items in the husbands' family backgrounds correlated higher with the adjustment score than did the same items in the wives' backgrounds. They were thus given higher weights. See pp. 78–79.

TABLE 57 (CHART 4)

RURAL OR URBAN RESIDENCE IN CHILDHOOD AND ADOLESCENCE AND ADJUSTMENT

Place of Residence	Marital Adjustment			No. of Cases	Mean Adjustment	CR
	Poor (per cent)	Fair (per cent)	Good (per cent)			
Husband:						
City	32.5	28.3	39.2	286	136.8	—3.2
Small town	25.9	29.3	44.8	174	142.5	—2.2
Country	10.4	25.0	64.6	48	156.2*	
No reply	......	......	......	18		
Total				526		
Wife:						
City	29.5	27.0	43.5	322	140.6	—2.2
Small town	29.7	33.1	37.2	145	136.2	—2.7
Country	12.5	25.0	62.5	40	155.0*	
No reply	......	......	......	19		
Total				526		
All cases	28.5	28.3	43.2			

TABLE 58 (CHART 5)

HUSBAND'S ATTACHMENT TO PARENTS AND ADJUSTMENT

Degree of Attachment	Marital Adjustment			No. of Cases	Mean Adjustment	CR
	Poor (per cent)	Fair (per cent)	Good (per cent)			
To father:						
Little or none	42.7	37.3	20.0	75	120.3*	
Moderate	26.2	29.9	43.9	157	142.0	+3.5
A good deal	20.3	32.0	47.7	128	146.5	+4.2
Very close	25.7	20.2	54.1	109	145.4	+3.9
No reply	......	......	......	57		
Total				526		
To mother:						
Little or none	51.7	17.2	31.1	29	116.2*	
Moderate	24.8	41.3	33.9	109	139.4	+2.2
A good deal	28.8	26.2	45.0	149	139.7	+2.2
Very close	24.7	24.7	50.5	186	145.9	+2.9
No reply	......	......	......	53		
Total				526		
All cases	28.5	28.3	43.2			

TABLE 59 (CHART 6)

Husband's Conflict with Parents and Adjustment

Degree of Conflict	Marital Adjustment			No. of Cases	Mean Adjustment	CR
	Poor (per cent)	Fair (per cent)	Good (per cent)			
With father:						
None	22.0	26.6	51.4	218	147.2*	
Very little	28.6	28.7	42.6	136	138.5	—1.8
Moderate	31.4	27.1	41.4	70	136.8	—1.7
A good deal	38.2	35.7	26.2	42	132.2	—2.3
Almost constant	26.7	66.7	6.7	15	124.9	—2.1
No reply	......	......	......	45		
Total				526		
With mother:						
None	24.2	26.8	49.0	257	144.4	+2.9
Very little	31.3	25.7	43.1	144 ⎱	138.1	+1.9
Moderate	27.9	34.9	37.2	43 ⎰		
A good deal	44.9	37.9	17.2	29 ⎱	124.5*	
Almost constant	42.9	42.9	14.3	7 ⎰		
No reply	......	......	......	46		
Total				526		
All cases	28.5	28.3	43.2			

378

TABLE 60 (CHART 7)

Wife's Attachment to Parents and Adjustment

Marital Adjustment

Degree of Attachment	Poor (per cent)	Fair (per cent)	Good (per cent)	No. of Cases	Mean Adjustment	CR
To father:						
Little or none	31.3	32.8	35.9	64	134.1*	
Moderate	27.6	29.5	42.9	105	140.1	
A good deal	27.3	27.9	44.8	154	142.2	+1.2
Very close	26.0	27.8	46.2	158	142.6	+1.3
No reply	......	......	......	45		
Total				526		
To mother:						
Little or none	50.0	20.6	29.4	34	120.0*	
Moderate	29.7	29.7	40.6	101	138.3	+1.9
A good deal	20.0	32.0	48.0	125	147.6	+3.1
Very close	26.9	26.5	46.6	219	141.9	+2.5
No reply	......	......	......	47		
Total				526		
All cases	28.5	28.3	43.2			

TABLE 61 (CHART 8)

WIFE'S CONFLICT WITH PARENTS AND ADJUSTMENT

Marital Adjustment

Degree of Conflict	Poor (per cent)	Fair (per cent)	Good (per cent)	No. of Cases	Mean Adjustment	CR
With father:						
None	26.3	26.0	47.7	258	144.0*	
Very little	35.2	28.1	36.7	128		
Moderate	27.7	33.8	38.5	65	135.7	—2.1
A good deal [1]	21.8	36.9	41.3	46		
No reply	......	......	......	29		
Total				526		
With mother:						
None	26.6	28.4	45.0	211	143.4*	
Very little	28.6	26.7	44.7	150	140.0	
Moderate	27.5	36.2	36.2	69	138.1	
A good deal [2]	26.7	25.0	48.3	60	141.2	
No reply	......	......	......	36		
Total				526		
All cases	28.5	28.3	43.2			

[1] Includes 12 cases of "almost continuous" conflict.
[2] Includes 8 cases of "almost continuous" conflict.

TABLE 62 (CHART 9)

APPRAISAL OF THE HAPPINESS OF PARENTS' MARRIAGE AND ADJUSTMENT

Appraisal of Parents' Marriage	Marital Adjustment			No. of Cases	Mean Adjustment	CR
	Poor (per cent)	Fair (per cent)	Good (per cent)			
Husband's parents:						
Very happy	19.9	19.8	60.3	136	151.0*	
Happy	25.0	33.1	41.9	172	141.4	—2.0
Average	39.7	28.4	31.9	141	130.8	—4.2
Unhappy and very unhappy	25.9	38.7	35.4	54	137.2	—2.0
No reply	......	......	......	23		
Total				526		
Wife's parents:						
Very happy	26.4	24.3	49.3	148	144.3	+1.5
Happy	27.8	25.8	46.4	151	141.7	
Average	32.8	27.0	40.1	137	137.4*	
Unhappy and very unhappy	20.8	45.9	33.3	72		
No reply	......	......	......	18		
Total				526		
All cases	28.5	28.3	43.2			

TABLE 63 (CHART 10)

APPRAISAL OF HAPPINESS OF PARENTS' MARRIAGE
(COMBINED RATINGS) AND ADJUSTMENT

Appraisal of Parents' Marriage	Marital Adjustment			No. of Cases	Mean Adjustment	CR
	Poor (per cent)	Fair (per cent)	Good (per cent)			
Very happy with very happy	11.9	15.2	72.9	59	160.8*	
Happy with happy	23.7	23.6	52.7	55	144.5	—2.1
Very happy with all others	28.2	27.5	44.3	149	138.0	—3.8
Happy with others [1]	25.7	34.5	39.8	113	138.0	—3.7
Average, unhappy and very unhappy with same	37.8	34.3	27.9	111	124.7	—5.7
Either or both, no reply	......	......	......	39		
Total				526		
All cases	28.5	28.3	43.2			

[1] Except with "very happy."

TABLE 64 (CHART 11)

PARENTAL STATUS AND ADJUSTMENT

Marital Adjustment

Parental Status	Poor (per cent)	Fair (per cent)	Good (per cent)	No. of Cases	Mean Adjustment	CR
Husband's parents:						
Married, both living	27.1	32.5	40.4	302	140.1	—1.5
Separated or divorced	37.6	31.2	31.2	16	124.7	—1.6
Both dead	39.6	20.8	39.6	48	133.3	—1.7
Father dead	25.8	23.6	50.6	89 }	146.5*	
Mother dead	23.0	21.2	55.8	52 }		
No reply	......	......	......	19		
Total				526		
Wife's parents:						
Married, both living	27.4	26.8	45.8	358	141.7	
Separated or divorced	28.1	37.5	34.4	32	136.9	
Both dead	23.0	30.8	46.2	26	146.5*	
Father dead	25.9	30.6	43.5	62 }	137.1	—1.1
Mother dead	38.2	32.4	29.4	34 }		
No reply	......	......	......	14		
Total				526		
All cases	28.5	28.3	43.2			

TABLE 65 (CHART 12)

Size of Family and Adjustment

Marital Adjustment

Size of Family	Poor (per cent)	Fair (per cent)	Good (per cent)	No. of Cases	Mean Adjustment	CR
Husband's family:						
One child	49.1	20.0	30.9	55	124.4*	
Two to three children	23.2	36.0	40.8	164	142.0	+2.5
Four to five children	26.6	22.3	51.1	139	144.9	+2.8
Six or more children	24.0	29.5	46.5	129	144.6	+2.8
No reply	......	......	......	39		
Total				526		
Wife's family:						
One child	38.1	23.8	38.1	63	133.5*	
Two to three children	26.7	30.6	42.7	206	140.4	+1.0
Four to five children	25.6	25.6	48.8	125	144.7	+1.6
Six or more children	22.7	29.9	47.4	97	146.1	+1.8
No reply	......	......	......	35		
Total				526		
All cases	28.5	28.3	43.2			

384

TABLE 66 (CHART 13)

Place in Family and Adjustment

Place in Family	Marital Adjustment			No. of Cases	Mean Adjustment	CR
	Poor (per cent)	Fair (per cent)	Good (per cent)			
Husband:						
Only child	49.1	20.0	30.9	55	124.4*	
Oldest child	19.7	33.3	47.0	132	146.3	+3.0
Middle child	22.7	28.4	48.9	176	145.7	+3.0
Youngest child	28.4	25.5	46.1	102	142.0	+2.3
No reply	......	......	......	61		
Total				526		
Wife:						
Only child	38.1	23.8	38.1	63	133.5*	
Oldest child	22.7	28.1	49.2	128	144.9	+1.7
Middle child	24.9	26.1	49.0	157	144.8	+1.7
Youngest child	30.1	34.1	35.8	123	137.0	
No reply	......	......	......	55		
Total				526		
All cases	28.5	28.3	43.2			

385

TABLE 67 (CHART 14)

PLACE IN FAMILY OF HUSBAND AND WIFE AND OF THEIR PARENTS AND MARITAL-HAPPINESS RATINGS

Marital-Happiness Rating

Place in Family of Husband, Wife, and Parents	Unhappy (per cent)	Average (per cent)	Happy (per cent)	Very Happy (per cent)	No. of Cases	CR[1]
Oldest and oldest	11.3	18.6	23.0	47.1*	291	
Oldest and middle	10.6	19.7	31.4	38.3	765	—2.6
Oldest and youngest	13.7	18.9	27.6	39.8	387	—1.9
Oldest and only	11.1	14.8	32.4	41.7	108	
Middle and middle	8.5	22.4	31.6	37.5	841	—2.8
Middle and youngest	11.4	20.8	30.8	37.0	649	—2.9
Middle and only	16.4	18.0	25.4	40.2	189	
Youngest and youngest	17.3	17.9	29.1	35.7	179	—2.4
Youngest and only	22.5	18.0	30.6	28.8	111	—3.6
Only and only	21.8	17.4	34.8	26.0	46	—3.0
Total	422	711	1,065	1,368	3,566	
All cases	11.8	19.9	29.9	38.4		

[1] CR's are for the percentages in the "very happy" category.

TABLE 68 (CHART 15)

SIBLING ATTACHMENT AND ADJUSTMENT

Attached to Which Sibling	Marital Adjustment			No. of Cases	Mean Adjustment	CR
	Poor (per cent)	Fair (per cent)	Good (per cent)			
Husband:						
None	16.9	33.8	49.3	148	149.4	+2.1
Older brother ..	23.2	25.6	51.2	43	146.9	+1.5
Older sister	37.5	22.9	39.6	48	133.4*	
Younger brother	24.2	32.3	43.5	62 [2]	144.0	+1.3
Younger sister	22.8	33.3	43.9	66 [2]	142.9	+1.1
No reply, or not applicable [1] ..	......	......	......	159		
Total				526		
Wife:						
None	19.0	32.0	49.0	100	148.2*	
Older brother	30.2	27.9	41.9	43	135.4	—1.5
Older sister	32.4	38.2	29.4	68	133.7	—2.3
Younger brother	20.4	25.9	53.7	54	148.8	
Younger sister	28.9	25.0	46.1	76	142.0	—1.8
No reply, or not applicable [1]	......	......	......	185		
Total				526		
All cases	28.5	28.3	43.2			

[1] Includes only children and those cases of attachment to more than one sibling.
[2] Combining categories "younger brother" and "younger sister," mean adjustment is 143.8, and CR 2.8.

TABLE 69 (CHART 16)

AGE AT MARRIAGE OF HUSBAND AND WIFE AND ADJUSTMENT

Age at Marriage	Marital Adjustment			No. of Cases	Mean Adjustment	CR
	Poor (per cent)	Fair (per cent)	Good (per cent)			
Husband:						
17 to 21	38.5	32.7	28.8	52	129.5*	
22 to 24	17.3	33.9	48.8	127	148.4	+3.2
25 to 27	24.6	29.5	45.9	122	143.3	+2.2
28 to 30	18.8	20.3	60.9	69	151.8	+3.3
31 and over	28.8	24.2	47.0	66	141.3	+1.7
No reply	......	......	......	90		
Total				526		
Wife:						
16 to 18	46.9	34.4	18.7	32	121.2*	
19 to 21	28.5	29.2	42.3	123	139.8	+2.7
22 to 24	20.9	29.1	50.0	148	146.8	+3.8
25 to 27	22.5	27.5	50.0	80	145.9	+3.2
28 and over	17.7	24.2	58.1	62	151.4	+3.9
No reply	......	......	......	81		
Total				526		
All cases	28.5	28.3	43.2			

TABLE 70 (CHART 17)

HEALTH PREVIOUS TO MARRIAGE AND ADJUSTMENT

Health Before Marriage	Marital Adjustment			No. of Cases	Mean Adjustment	CR
	Poor (per cent)	Fair (per cent)	Good (per cent)			
Husband:						
Sickly	72.7	9.1	18.2	11	111.2	—2.5
Average	31.4	30.5	38.1	118	136.9	—1.3
Healthy	25.8	28.1	46.1	384	142.6*	
No reply	......	......	......	13		
Total				526		
Wife:						
Sickly	45.0	25.0	30.0	20 ⎱	137.5	—1.1
Average	29.8	27.0	43.2	148 ⎰		
Healthy	25.9	30.0	44.1	347	142.2*	
No reply	......	......	......	11		
Total				526		
All cases	28.5	28.3	43.2			

TABLE 71 (CHART 18)

WEIGHT DEVIATION AND ADJUSTMENT

Marital Adjustment

Weight Deviation	Poor (per cent)	Fair (per cent)	Good (per cent)	No. of Cases	Mean Adjustment	CR
Husband:						
15 lbs. or more overweight	28.7	24.5	46.8	94	140.5	—1.2
5 to 14 lbs. overweight	33.0	20.7	46.3	82	139.7	—1.3
4 lbs. overweight to 4 lbs. underweight	22.3	34.1	43.6	94	144.0	
5 to 14 lbs. underweight	22.2	36.4	41.4	99	142.7	
15 lbs. or more underweight ..	22.7	26.7	50.6	75	148.1*	
No reply	......	......	......	82		
Total				526		
Wife:						
15 lbs. or more overweight	50.0	22.7	27.3	22	123.5	—2.5
5 to 14 lbs. overweight	28.1	25.0	46.9	32	143.7	
4 lbs. overweight to 4 lbs. underweight	24.7	30.4	44.9	69	143.5	—1.0
5 to 14 lbs. underweight	32.7	30.1	37.2	156	134.2	—3.2
15 lbs. or more underweight ..	20.0	27.4	52.6	175	149.2*	
No reply	......	......	......	72		
Total				526		
All cases	28.5	28.3	43.2			

TABLE 72 (CHART 19)

EDUCATIONAL STATUS AND ADJUSTMENT

Educational Status	Marital Adjustment			No. of Cases	Mean Adjustment	CR
	Poor (per cent)	Fair (per cent)	Good (per cent)			
Husband:						
Grades only	41.2	21.6	37.2	51	129.1	—3.0
High school [1]	39.4	27.0	33.6	152	131.2	—4.4
College	24.9	26.8	48.3	205	144.1	—1.9
Graduate or professional	12.4	36.2	51.4	105	152.6*	
No reply	......	......	......	13		
Total				526		
Wife:						
Grades only	59.3	25.9	14.8	27	109.5	—3.6
High school [1]	30.7	32.2	37.1	202	136.1	—1.7
College	28.2	22.9	48.9	227	143.3*	
Graduate or professional	4.8	38.7	56.5	62	158.9	+1.6
No reply	......	......	......	8		
Total				526		
All cases	28.5	28.3	43.2			

[1] Or professional school not of collegiate grade.

TABLE 73 (CHART 20)

Age at Which Stopped Attending Sunday School and Adjustment

Age Stopped Attending Sunday School	Marital Adjustment			No. of Cases	Mean Adjustment	CR
	Poor (per cent)	Fair (per cent)	Good (per cent)			
Husband:						
Never went	34.6	34.5	30.9	55	131.6	—2.8
10 years or under	47.0	32.4	20.6	34	120.3	—3.6
11 to 18 years	29.1	25.4	45.5	244	141.1	—2.3
19 to 25 years [1]	15.5	31.7	52.8	142	150.8*	
No reply	......	......	......	51		
Total				526		
Wife:						
Never went	30.0	37.5	32.5	40	136.5	—2.0
10 years or under	44.8	24.2	31.0	29	124.5	—2.7
11 to 18 years	31.4	27.3	41.2	245	136.8	—3.3
19 to 25 years [1]	18.4	29.3	52.3	174	150.2*	
No reply	......	......	......	38		
Total				526		
All cases	28.5	28.3	43.2			

[1] Includes those still attending at time of marriage.

TABLE 74 (CHART 21)

Church Attendance and Adjustment

Average Monthly Attendance	Marital Adjustment			No. of Cases	Mean Adjustment	CR
	Poor (per cent)	Fair (per cent)	Good (per cent)			
Husband:						
None	39.7	27.8	32.5	126	136.9	—1.8
None checked [1]..	32.4	27.0	40.5	37	130.6	—3.3
Once or less	27.1	27.7	45.2	166	140.5	—1.9
Two or three times	11.9	31.0	57.1	42	153.5*	
Four times [2]	17.6	30.4	52.0	125	150.3	
No reply	......	......	......	30		
Total				526		
Wife:						
None	37.1	27.4	35.5	62 ⎫	134.2	—2.2
None checked [1]..	37.5	17.9	44.6	56 ⎭		
Once or less	28.1	29.6	42.3	142	139.9	—1.2
Two or three times	25.0	33.3	41.7	60	139.1	—1.0
Four times	22.3	30.8	46.9	175	145.5*	
No reply	......	......	......	31		
Total				526		
All cases	28.5	28.3	43.2			

[1] But a church member.
[2] Includes cases which indicate other church activity if attendance is not checked.

TABLE 75 (CHART 22)

PLACE IN WHICH MARRIED AND ADJUSTMENT

Marital Adjustment

Place Married	Poor (per cent)	Fair (per cent)	Good (per cent)	No. of Cases	Mean Adjustment	CR
Church or parsonage	22.5	28.1	49.4	253	145.7*	
Home	34.3	26.1	39.5	157	135.4	—2.3
Elsewhere	34.6	29.9	35.5	107	134.1	—2.3
No reply	......	......	......	9		
Total	28.5	28.3	43.2	526		

TABLE 76 (CHART 23)

MEMBERSHIP IN ORGANIZATIONS AND ADJUSTMENT

Marital Adjustment

No. of Organizations	Poor (per cent)	Fair (per cent)	Good (per cent)	No. of Cases	Mean Adjustment	CR
Husband:						
None	30.7	37.3	32.0	75	134.8*	
One	30.0	27.1	42.9	210	139.4	
Two	25.0	27.9	47.1	104	144.1	+1.5
Three or more	18.5	27.2	54.3	81	149.3	+2.2
No reply	......	......	......	56		
Total				526		
Wife:						
None	29.6	28.4	42.0	88	138.7*	
One	27.3	34.2	38.5	161		
Two	29.2	25.7	45.1	113		
Three or more	23.2	22.1	54.7	95	150.5	+2.6
No reply	......	......	......	69		
Total				526		
All cases	28.5	28.3	42.3			

TABLE 77 (CHART 24)

Number of Husband's Friends and Adjustment

	Marital Adjustment					
Number of Friends	Poor (per cent)	Fair (per cent)	Good (per cent)	No. of Cases	Mean Adjustment	CR
Men friends:						
A few [1]	40.0	29.2	30.8	120	129.7*	
Several	21.2	31.8	47.0	151	145.1	+3.0
Many	26.9	24.8	48.3	242	142.8	+2.7
No reply	......	......	......	13		
				—		
Total				526		
Women friends:						
Almost none	48.2	18.5	33.3	54	128.3*	
A few	28.4	29.7	41.9	155	139.3	+1.6
Several	22.0	26.2	51.8	141	146.2	+2.5
Many	26.9	30.8	42.3	156	141.3	+1.9
No reply	......	......	......	20		
				—		
Total				526		
All cases	28.5	28.3	43.2			

[1] Includes eight cases who reported "almost none."

TABLE 78 (CHART 25)

NUMBER OF WIFE'S FRIENDS AND ADJUSTMENT

Number of Friends	Marital Adjustment			No. of Cases	Mean Adjustment	CR
	Poor (per cent)	Fair (per cent)	Good (per cent)			
Men friends:						
Almost none	45.0	37.5	17.5	40	122.3*	
A few	26.0	25.9	48.1	135	142.8	+2.7
Several	24.8	29.6	45.6	169	142.7	+2.8
Many	28.2	28.1	43.7	167	141.3	+2.6
No reply	......	......	......	15		
Total	·			526		
Women friends:						
Almost none	52.9	23.5	23.5	17	116.6	—2.4
A few	29.8	27.3	42.9	55	139.8	
Several	34.7	36.3	29.0	124	130.7	—3.2
Many	23.7	26.5	49.8	317	145.7*	
No reply	......	......	......	13		
Total				526		
All cases	28.5	28.3	43.2			

TABLE 79 (CHART 26)

NUMBER OF INTIMATE ASSOCIATIONS WITH OTHER SEX BEFORE MARRIAGE
AND ADJUSTMENT

Intimate Associations with other Sex	Marital Adjustment			No. of Cases	Mean Adjustment	CR
	Poor (per cent)	Fair (per cent)	Good (per cent)			
Husband:						
None	23.5	27.3	49.2	128	145.8*	
One	31.2	25.0	43.8	80	139.9	—1.0
Two or three	26.6	28.1	45.3	139	141.5	
Four or five	25.0	28.7	46.3	80	141.8	
Six or more	28.6	35.7	35.7	42	138.4	—1.0
No reply	......	......	......	57		
				—		
Total				526		
Wife:						
None	25.9	27.7	46.4	112	143.1	
One	22.6	34.5	42.9	84	144.2	
Two or three	32.2	21.5	46.3	149	138.6	—1.6
Four or five	31.8	29.4	38.8	85	137.3	—1.7
Six or more	17.5	32.5	50.0	40	149.6*	
No reply	......	......	......	56		
				—		
Total				526		
All cases	28.5	28.3	43.2			

TABLE 80 (CHART 27)

OCCUPATION OF HUSBAND AT MARRIAGE AND ADJUSTMENT

Husband's Occupation	Marital Adjustment			No. of Cases	Mean Adjustment	CR
	Poor (per cent)	Fair (per cent)	Good (per cent)			
Clerical or semi-skilled	30.6	32.7	36.7	49	137.6	
Small trades and skilled	32.8	28.7	38.5	122	136.9*	
Sales and semi-professional	30.2	26.9	42.9	119	139.3	
Teaching	21.7	17.4	60.9	46	149.3	+1.6
Medicine, law, and other professions [1] (except teaching)	22.2	30.9	46.9	81	145.6	+1.5
Large business, management, entrepreneur	26.7	13.3	60.0	30	147.4	+1.2
All others [2]	......	......	......	55	139.5	
No reply	......	......	......	24		
Total	28.5	28.3	43.2	526		

[1] Including the ministry.
[2] Including farmers.

398

TABLE 81 (CHART 28)

OCCUPATIONS OF 17,533 HUSBANDS AND HAPPINESS RATINGS BY
FRIENDS OR ACQUAINTANCES

	Marital-Happiness Rating				
Occupation	Unhappy (per cent)	Average (per cent)	Happy (per cent)	No. of Cases	CR[1]
Laborers	40.5	24.6	34.9	605	14.9
Traveling salesmen	35.9	24.3	39.9	198	9.1
Mechanics	24.5	29.9	45.7	278	8.5
Carpenters	24.7	28.6	46.7	105	5.6
Auto mechanics	31.9	19.4	48.6	144	6.0
Plumbers	23.9	27.3	48.8	88	4.8
Real-estate salesmen	27.7	22.7	49.6	141	7.0
Musicians	31.1	19.2	49.7	167	6.1
Truck drivers	27.4	22.9	49.8	223	6.8
Gas-station employees	22.8	26.4	51.0	110	4.9
Barbers	22.0	26.5	51.5	132	5.2
Skilled workers	22.2	25.9	51.9	405	7.7
Bond salesmen	27.3	19.4	53.3	139	4.9
Farmers	21.1	25.6	53.3	1230	9.4
Railroad workers	24.4	21.5	54.2	205	5.5
Meat-market owners	24.1	21.3	54.6	108	4.2
Railroad office workers	19.8	23.3	57.0	116	3.9
Salesmen, unclassified	26.6	16.3	57.1	857	7.4
Automobile salesmen	29.0	13.0	58.0	200	4.6
Clerks	20.3	21.2	58.5	354	5.4
Druggists	16.1	24.1	59.8	174	3.9
Electricians	18.7	21.4	59.9	182	4.0
Brokers	23.1	16.9	59.9	242	4.4
Insurance salesmen	23.4	16.0	60.6	655	5.7
Mail clerks	19.6	19.6	60.8	158	3.6
Garage owners	19.6	18.9	61.5	143	3.3
Factory foremen	13.8	24.4	61.8	123	3.0

[1] CR's are for percentages in the "happy" category. CR's are negative unless otherwise indicated.

(Continued on the following page)

TABLE 81 (CHART 28) (*Continued*)

Marital-Happiness Rating

Occupation	Unhappy (per cent)	Average (per cent)	Happy (per cent)	No. of Cases	CR
Small-store owners	15.7	21.9	62.3	948	5.5
Bank employees	14.3	23.3	62.4	210	3.6
Dentists	17.5	20.1	62.5	309	4.1
Bookkeepers	18.2	19.3	62.5	192	3.5
Printers	13.4	24.1	62.6	187	3.4
Contractors	19.7	17.3	63.0	162	3.1
Clothing-store owners	16.2	20.5	63.3	117	2.7
Store salesmen	21.3	15.3	63.4	483	4.4
Lawyers	18.8	17.1	64.1	771	4.7
Owners, large business	19.9	15.6	64.5	231	3.2
Advertising	17.7	17.7	64.6	130	2.5
Grocery-store owners	16.8	18.4	64.8	125	2.5
Architects	15.7	19.5	64.8	179	2.8
Corporation officials	21.9	13.1	65.0	183	2.8
Government workers	15.9	18.4	65.7	201	2.7
Newspaper workers	16.9	16.5	66.5	248	2.7
Bankers	17.5	15.4	67.1	292	2.7
Physicians	18.4	14.5	67.2	654	3.4
Office workers	12.8	19.2	68.0	390	2.7
Civil engineers	12.9	18.3	68.8	93	1.5
Accountants	13.9	16.3	69.7	294	2.0
Managers	13.0	16.1	70.9	578	2.0
Educational administrators	07.2	21.7	71.1	166	1.3
Wholesale salesmen	08.1	20.5	71.4	161	1.2
Electrical engineers	09.5	18.1	72.4	105	
Teachers	11.9	15.4	72.7	707	1.4
Engineers	11.5	15.8	72.7	304	1.1
High-school teachers	10.8	15.3	73.9	111	
Students	15.9	09.1	75.0	629	
Athletic coaches	14.9	09.7	75.4	134	
College professors	09.8	13.8	76.4*	450	
Ministers	11.2	09.3	79.5	174	
Chemical engineers	07.5	09.8	82.7	133	+1.6

TABLE 82 (CHART 29)

OCCUPATION OF WIFE AT MARRIAGE AND ADJUSTMENT

	Marital Adjustment					
Wife's Occupation	Poor (per cent)	Fair (per cent)	Good (per cent)	No. of Cases	Mean Adjustment	CR
None	34.2	27.6	38.2	76	136.6	—2.7
Domestic and un-skilled work	55.6	33.3	11.1	18	105.6	—4.2
Clerical and semi-clerical work	41.9	27.4	30.6	62	126.1	—3.8
Skilled office positions	28.3	26.0	45.7	127	141.1	—2.3
Teaching	16.3	28.7	55.0	129	152.2*	
Other professions [1]	19.5	41.5	39.0	41	145.4	—1.1
Other [2]	28.1	31.3	40.6	32	139.1	—1.6
No reply	......	......	......	41		
Total	28.5	28.3	43.2	526		

[1] Including women in medicine, law, social work, and business women in higher-paid positions and nursing.
[2] Includes students.

TABLE 83 (CHART 30)

LENGTH OF TIME HELD POSITION AND ADJUSTMENT

Marital Adjustment

Years Held Position	Poor (per cent)	Fair (per cent)	Good (per cent)	No. of Cases	Mean Adjustment	CR
Husband:						
Less than one	28.1	22.8	49.1	57	143.5	+1.0
One to two	29.6	28.1	42.2	135	138.1	
Three to four	22.2	26.9	50.9	108	146.3	+1.6
Five to six	20.7	31.0	48.3	58	146.3	+1.4
Seven and over ..	34.1	25.3	40.6	91	136.0*	
No reply	......	......	......	77		
				—		
Total				526		
Wife:						
Less than one	31.8	31.8	36.4	44	133.9	—2.8
One to two	28.4	30.9	40.7	123	139.1	—3.1
Three to four	26.9	27.9	45.2	93	141.5	—2.6
Five to six	26.8	25.0	48.2	56	143.7	—1.9
Seven and over ..	13.5	26.9	59.6	52	157.5*	
No reply	......	......	......	158		
				—		
Total				526		
All cases	28.5	28.3	43.2			

TABLE 84 (CHART 31)

WORK RECORD BEFORE MARRIAGE AND ADJUSTMENT

Work Record	Marital Adjustment					
	Poor (per cent)	Fair (per cent)	Good (per cent)	No. of Cases	Mean Adjustment	CR
Husband:						
None	26.4	31.0	42.5	87	141.7	+2.0
Irregular [1]	42.7	25.6	31.7	82	127.9*	
Regular	24.8	27.9	47.4	323	143.8	+2.8
No reply	......	......	......	34		
Total				526		
Wife:						
None	41.3	28.0	30.7	75	128.5	—2.7
Irregular [2]	29.0	34.2	36.8	76	136.1	—1.4
Regular	24.4	28.2	47.3	319	144.0*	
No reply [3]	......	......	......	56		
Total				526		
All cases	28.5	28.3	42.3			

[1] Includes cases of continually changing positions.
[2] Denotes occasional more than irregular employment.
[3] Includes 34 cases of housekeeping at home and other nonremunerative work.

TABLE 85 (CHART 32)

INCOME AT MARRIAGE AND ADJUSTMENT

Marital Adjustment

Monthly Income at Marriage	Poor (per cent)	Fair (per cent)	Good (per cent)	No. of Cases	Mean Adjustment	CR
Husband:						
None	16.0	36.0	48.0	25	148.3	+1.5
Under $150	34.1	27.1	38.8	129	134.9*	
$150 to $249	21.3	29.4	49.2	197	146.6	+2.3
$250 and over	36.5	22.1	41.4	104	136.6	
No reply	......	......	......	71		
Total				526		
Wife:						
None	28.4	26.9	44.8	67	141.8	+1.5
Under $100	34.8	31.3	33.9	112	131.3*	
$100 to $149	25.9	26.6	47.5	143	143.8	+2.2
$150 and over [1]	21.1	28.1	50.8	128	149.5	+3.3
No reply	......	......	......	76		
Total				526		
All cases	28.5	28.3	43.2			

[1] Includes 44 cases with incomes of $200 and over.

TABLE 86 (CHART 33)

SAVINGS OF HUSBAND AND ADJUSTMENT

Marital Adjustment

Savings at Marriage	Poor (per cent)	Fair (per cent)	Good (per cent)	No. of Cases	Mean Adjustment	CR
None	35.3	28.7	36.0	136	134.0*	
Under $1,000	22.9	30.0	47.1	140	145.2	+2.2
$1,000 and over	26.1	23.9	50.0	142	143.2	+1.7
No reply	......	......	......	108		
Total	28.5	28.3	43.2	526		

TABLE 87 (CHART 34)

Savings of Wife at Marriage and Adjustment

Marital Adjustment

Savings at Marriage	Poor (per cent)	Fair (per cent)	Good (per cent)	No. of Cases	Mean Adjustment	CR
None	27.8	22.6	49.6	115	142.4	
Under $500	29.0	31.8	39.2	107	138.1*	
$500 and over	24.4	26.8	48.8	123	146.1	+1.4
No reply	......	......	......	181		
Total	28.5	28.3	43.2	526		

TABLE 88 (CHART 35)

Husband's Financial Index at Marriage and Adjustment

Marital Adjustment

Financial Index	Poor (per cent)	Fair (per cent)	Good (per cent)	No. of Cases	Mean Adjustment	CR
Zero	35.6	28.9	35.5	135	133.7*	
.01 to .29	22.7	28.5	48.8	172	145.6	+2.4
.30 to .59	30.4	17.4	52.2	46	141.2	
.60 and over	18.2	31.8	50.0	22	147.7	+1.5
No reply	......	......	......	151		
Total	28.5	28.3	43.2	526		

TABLE 89 (CHART 36)

DIFFERENCE IN AGE OF HUSBAND AND WIFE AND ADJUSTMENT

Marital Adjustment

Difference in Age	Poor (per cent)	Fair (per cent)	Good (per cent)	No. of Cases	Mean Adjustment	CR
Same age	13.1	39.1	47.8	46	149.1	+2.0
Husband older:						
One to three years	21.4	31.0	47.6	168	146.3	+2.1
Four to seven years	35.4	26.4	38.2	110	135.3*	
Eight years or more	31.1	17.8	51.1	45	142.1	
Wife older	23.2	23.2	53.6	56	148.6	+1.9
One or both, no reply	......	......	......	101		
Total	28.5	28.3	43.2	526		

TABLE 90 (CHART 37)

DURATION OF ACQUAINTANCE BEFORE MARRIAGE AND ADJUSTMENT

Marital Adjustment

Period of Acquaintance Before Marriage	Poor (per cent)	Fair (per cent)	Good (per cent)	No. of Cases	Mean Adjustment	CR
Under six months	47.0	30.6	22.4	49	120.5	—4.5
Six to 23 months	37.7	24.6	37.7	122	132.4	—4.0
Two to four years	27.8	28.4	43.8	194	141.4	—2.8
Five years and more	14.7	32.0	53.3	150	153.1*	
No reply	......	......	......	11		
Total	28.5	28.3	43.2	526		

TABLE 91 (CHART 38)

DURATION OF KEEPING COMPANY AND ADJUSTMENT

| Duration of Courtship | Marital Adjustment | | | No. of Cases | Mean Adjustment | CR |
	Poor (per cent)	Fair (per cent)	Good (per cent)			
Under three months	39.3	28.6	32.1	28	129.5	—2.7
Three to 11 months	42.9	23.8	33.3	105	126.6	—4.8
One year to three years	28.9	31.8	39.3	201	139.2	—3.5
Three to five years	12.6	30.6	56.8	111	154.4*	
Five years and over	17.2	27.6	55.2	58	152.1	
No reply	......	......	......	23		
Total	28.5	28.3	43.2	526		

TABLE 92 (CHART 39)

DURATION OF ENGAGEMENT AND ADJUSTMENT

| Duration of Engagement | Marital Adjustment | | | No. of Cases | Mean Adjustment | CR |
	Poor (per cent)	Fair (per cent)	Good (per cent)			
Under three months	50.0	24.3	25.7	70	121.7	—5.6
Three to eight months	33.0	26.8	40.2	179	136.6	—4.5
Nine to 23 months	18.0	35.9	46.1	128	147.5	—2.3
24 months and over	11.0	26.4	62.6	91	158.5*	
Not engaged	37.0	25.9	37.0	27	134.8	·—2.6
No reply	......	......	......	31		
All cases	28.5	28.3	43.2	526		

TABLE 93 (CHART 40)

ATTITUDE OF PARENTS TOWARD THE MARRIAGE AND ADJUSTMENT

Attitude of Parents	Marital Adjustment			No. of Cases	Mean Adjustment	CR
	Poor (per cent)	Fair (per cent)	Good (per cent)			
Husband's parents:						
Both approve [1] ..	23.6	27.7	48.7	382	144.8*	
One disapproves [2]	44.0	32.0	24.0	50	125.9	—3.8
Both disapprove [3]	40.8	28.6	30.6	49		
No reply	......	......	......	45		
Total				526		
Wife's parents:						
Both approve [1] ..	23.1	29.5	47.4	363	144.4*	
One disapproves [2]	43.5	21.0	35.5	62	128.6	—3.3
Both disapprove [3]	42.9	23.2	33.9	56		
No reply	......	......	......	45		
Total				526		
All cases	28.5	28.3	43.2			

[1] Includes a few cases in which one parent approves and the other is dead or no reply was made for him or her.

[2] Includes a few cases in which one parent may be dead.

[3] Includes a few cases in which there is no reply for one parent, although he or she is living.

TABLE 94 (CHART 41)

LENGTH OF TIME MARRIED AND ADJUSTMENT

Marital Adjustment

Years Married	Poor (per cent)	Fair (per cent)	Good (per cent)	No. of Cases	Mean Adjustment	CR
One	22.9	21.3	55.7	61	147.5	+2.4
Two	28.3	28.9	42.8	159 ⎫		
Three	24.5	31.1	44.4	106 ⎬ 140.0		+1.5
Four	28.7	24.1	47.2	108 ⎭		
Five to six	36.9	33.7	29.4	92	131.0*	
Total	28.5	28.3	43.2	526		

TABLE 95 (CHART 42)

NUMBER OF YEARS MARRIED AND RATINGS OF MARITAL HAPPINESS BY CLOSE ACQUAINTANCES

Marital-Happiness Rating

Years Married	Unhappy (per cent)	Average (per cent)	Happy (per cent)	No. of Cases	CR[1]
One to two	6.4	11.0	82.6*	1,732	
Three to four	8.3	14.9	76.8	1,384	—4.0
Five to six	11.1	18.8	70.2	1,086	—7.5
Seven to eight	11.1	20.9	68.0	837	—7.9
Nine to ten	10.2	19.6	70.2	857	—6.9
Eleven to twelve	13.0	23.7	63.3	668	—9.3
Thirteen to fourteen	14.3	23.3	62.4	502	—8.6
Fifteen to sixteen	14.4	24.8	60.9	327	—7.6
Total				7,393	

[1] CR's are for percentages in "happy" category.

TABLE 96 (CHART 43)

SIZE OF COMMUNITY AND ADJUSTMENT

Marital Adjustment

Size of Community	Poor (per cent)	Fair (per cent)	Good (per cent)	No. of Cases	Mean Adjustment	CR
Over 200,000	31.3	29.5	39.2	370	137.1*	
10,000 to 200,000	23.7	25.8	50.5	97	146.4	+2.0
Under 10,000	18.9	24.5	56.6	53	149.4	+1.9
No reply	......	......	......	6		
Total	28.5	28.3	43.2	526		

TABLE 97 (CHART 44)

DISTANCE FROM CHICAGO AND ADJUSTMENT

Marital Adjustment

Distance from Chicago	Poor (per cent)	Fair (per cent)	Good (per cent)	No. of Cases	Mean Adjustment	CR
In Chicago	31.0	29.1	39.8	364	137.6*	
Chicago suburb	20.6	29.4	50.0	68	146.8	+1.7
Outside Chicago area	23.0	24.1	52.9	87	146.3	+1.7
No reply	......	......	......	7		
Total	28.5	28.3	43.2	526		

TABLE 98 (CHART 45)

CHARACTER OF NEIGHBORHOOD AND ADJUSTMENT

Marital Adjustment

Character of Neighborhood	Poor (per cent)	Fair (per cent)	Good (per cent)	No. of Cases	Mean Adjustment	CR
Single homes	22.7	25.2	52.1	163	147.5*	
Suburban	25.0	28.1	46.9	64	143.2	
Apartment	29.7	31.4	38.9	226	137.6	—2.3
Multiple dwellings [1]	42.6	24.6	32.8	61	124.6	—3.2
No reply	......	......	......	12		
Total	28.5	28.3	43.2	526		

[1] Rooming house, two-flat, hotel, etc.

TABLE 99 (CHART 46)

TYPE OF RESIDENCE AND ADJUSTMENT

Marital Adjustment

Type of Residence	Poor (per cent)	Fair (per cent)	Good (per cent)	No. of Cases	Mean Adjustment	CR
Single dwelling	24.0	25.6	50.4	129	144.8	+3.2
Two flat	22.4	37.9	39.7	58	143.9	+2.9
Apartment	27.8	27.8	44.4	263	141.6	+3.0
Other multiple dwellings [1]	45.6	26.5	27.9	68	121.7*	
No reply	......	......	......	8		
Total	28.5	28.3	43.2	526		

[1] Rooming house, hotel, or apartment hotel.

TABLE 100 (CHART 47)

AVERAGE MONTHS PER RESIDENCE AND ADJUSTMENT

Marital Adjustment

Average Months per Residence	Poor (per cent)	Fair (per cent)	Good (per cent)	No. of Cases	Mean Adjustment	CR
One to six	52.2	21.7	26.1	46	113.9	—4.7
Seven to twelve	32.4	31.0	36.6	142	132.0	—3.7
Thirteen to eighteen	21.7	35.0	43.3	120	142.2	—1.7
Nineteen to twenty-four	29.1	17.4	53.5	86	141.0	—1.6
Twenty-five and over	14.7	31.9	53.4	116	151.1*	
No reply	......	......	......	16		
Total	28.5	28.3	43.2	526		

TABLE 101 (CHART 48)

HOME OWNERSHIP AND ADJUSTMENT

Marital Adjustment

Home Ownership	Poor (per cent)	Fair (per cent)	Good (per cent)	No. of Cases	Mean Adjustment	CR
Own or buying	22.6	17.0	60.4	53	148.7	+2.6
Planning to buy	8.0	35.2	56.8	125	156.7	+6.7
Not planning to buy [1]	36.8	27.6	35.6	348	132.8*	
Total	28.5	28.3	43.2	526		

[1] Including no reply.

TABLE 102 (CHART 49)

RESIDENCE WITH RELATIVES AND ADJUSTMENT

Marital Adjustment

Residence with Relatives	Poor (per cent)	Fair (per cent)	Good (per cent)	No. of Cases	Mean Adjustment	CR
Yes	31.7	25.5	42.8	180	137.5	—1.4
No	24.7	29.8	45.5	275	143.3*	
No reply	......	......	......	71		
Total	28.5	28.3	43.2	526		

TABLE 103 (CHART 50)

FREQUENCY OF SEEING PARENTS-IN-LAW AND ADJUSTMENT

Marital Adjustment

Number of Times a Year	Poor (per cent)	Fair (per cent)	Good (per cent)	No. of Cases	Mean Adjustment	CR
None	40.7	18.5	40.7	27	134.6	
One to six	18.1	26.7	55.2	105	149.0	+1.9
Seven to 24	30.9	32.7	36.4	55	135.0*	
25 to 104	20.0	30.4	49.6	115	148.3	+1.9
105 and over	31.4	28.8	39.7	156	137.8	
No reply	......	......	......	68		
Total	28.5	28.3	43.2	526		

TABLE 104 (CHART 51)

NUMBER OF CHILDREN AND ADJUSTMENT

Marital Adjustment

Number of Children	Poor (per cent)	Fair (per cent)	Good (per cent)	No. of Cases	Mean Adjustment	CR
None	27.7	26.6	45.7	293	141.5*	
One	26.4	29.9	43.7	174	140.8	
Two to three [1]	40.0	34.5	25.5	55	127.8	—2.2
No reply	......	......	......	4		
Total	28.5	28.3	43.2	526		

[1] Including those with four children.

413

TABLE 105 (CHART 52)

DESIRE FOR CHILDREN AND ADJUSTMENT

Marital Adjustment

Children Desired	Poor (per cent)	Fair (per cent)	Good (per cent)	No. of Cases	Mean Adjustment	CR
None, but desired	9.4	26.9	63.7	160	158.6*	
One or more and desired	20.4	32.8	46.8	186	146.5	—3.3
None and not desired [1]	55.0	24.3	20.7	111	116.0	—8.5
One or more not desired [2]	66.7	22.2	11.1	36	106.3	—7.0
No reply	......	......	......	33		
Total	28.5	28.3	43.2	526		

[1] Not desired by husband, or wife, or both.
[2] Not desired by husband, or wife, or both.

TABLE 106 (CHART 53)

NUMBER OF ROOMS IN RESIDENCE AND ADJUSTMENT

Marital Adjustment

No. of Rooms	Poor (per cent)	Fair (per cent)	Good (per cent)	No. of Cases	Mean Adjustment	CR
One to two	27.0	36.5	36.5	74	137.7	
Three to four	30.1	26.6	43.3	203	138.3	—1.0
Five to seven	26.6	26.7	46.7	195	142.9*	
Eight and over	35.5	22.6	41.9	31	137.7	
No reply	......	......	......	23		
Total	28.5	28.3	43.2	526		

TABLE 107 (CHART 54)

MONTHLY RENT PER ROOM AND ADJUSTMENT

Marital Adjustment

Monthly Rent Per Room	Poor (per cent)	Fair (per cent)	Good (per cent)	No. of Cases	Mean Adjustment	CR
No rent [1]	27.5	7.5	65.0	40	146.9*	
$ 5 to 9	29.3	25.6	45.1	82	142.1	
10 to 14	25.2	31.1	43.7	103		
15 to 19	30.2	29.4	40.4	109		
20 to 29	32.2	22.6	45.2	62	137.6	—1.1
30 and over	24.0	44.0	32.0	50		
No reply	......	......	......	80		
Total	28.5	28.3	43.2	526		

[1] No rent, because owning or buying home.

TABLE 108 (CHART 55)

EMPLOYMENT OF HUSBAND AND ADJUSTMENT

Marital Adjustment

Months Unemployed	Poor (per cent)	Fair (per cent)	Good (per cent)	No. of Cases	Mean Adjustment	CR
Under one	24.6	29.3	46.1	338	143.9*	
One to five	34.0	23.2	42.8	56	136.1	—1.2
Six or more	40.2	26.0	33.8	77	131.7	—2.2
No reply	......	......	......	55		
Total	28.5	28.3	43.2	526		

415

TABLE 109 (CHART 56)

AVERAGE NUMBER OF MONTHS POSITION HELD BY HUSBAND AND BY WIFE, AND ADJUSTMENT

Marital Adjustment

Average Number of Months Position Held	Poor (per cent)	Fair (per cent)	Good (per cent)	No. of Cases	Mean Adjustment	CR
Husband:						
One to 6	65.2	26.1	8.7	23 }	124.2	—2.9
Seven to 12	29.3	32.8	37.9	58 }		
13 to 18	30.2	31.6	38.2	76	134.1	—1.5
19 to 24	23.2	24.4	52.4	82	144.8*	
25 and over	23.2	29.6	47.2	267	142.6	
No reply				20		
				—		
Total				526		
Wife:						
One to 12	43.3	26.7	30.0	30 }	136.8	—1.3
13 to 24	22.1	32.5	45.4	77 }		
25 and over	22.8	26.9	50.3	171	144.2*	
Never worked ..	28.9	31.2	39.8	221	135.7	—1.9
No reply				27		
				—		
Total				526		
All cases	28.5	28.3	43.2			

TABLE 110 (CHART 57)

FINANCIAL INDEX AND ADJUSTMENT

Marital Adjustment

Financial Index	Poor (per cent)	Fair (per cent)	Good (per cent)	No. of Cases	Mean Adjustment	CR
Zero	32.6	33.3	34.1	126	134.0	—3.7
.01 to 1.99	30.3	28.3	41.4	152	138.5	—3.1
2.00 to 3.99	13.6	27.3	59.1	66	155.1*	
4.00 and over	19.6	17.4	63.0	46	154.4	
No reply	......	......	......	136		
				—		
Total	28.5	28.3	43.2	526		

TABLE 111 [1]

By Whom Married and Adjustment

Marital Adjustment

By Whom Married	Poor (per cent)	Fair (per cent)	Good (per cent)	No. of Cases	Mean Adjustment	CR
Minister, priest, or rabbi	25.7	28.3	46.0	467	142.8*	
Other	54.9	25.5	19.6	51	116.0	—4.0
No reply	......	......	......	8		
Total	28.5	28.3	43.2	526		

[1] Tables 111 to 114 are without corresponding charts in the text.

TABLE 112

RESIDENCE AT TIME OF MARRIAGE AND ADJUSTMENT

	Marital Adjustment					
Character of Neighborhood	Poor (per cent)	Fair (per cent)	Good (per cent)	No. of Cases	Mean Adjustment	CR
Husband:						
Small town [1]	17.3	32.7	50.0	52	148.6	—1.0
Other city	25.3	33.3	41.4	99	142.2	—2.2
Chicago suburb	10.0	32.0	58.0	50	155.7*	
Single homes	29.3	24.1	46.6	58	141.6	—2.0
Second immigrant settlement	25.0	26.8	48.2	56	145.8	—1.5
First immigrant settlement	25.0	31.3	43.7	16	141.5	—1.2
Apartment [2]	37.8	25.4	36.8	114	131.6	—3.8
Rooming house..	40.9	27.3	31.8	22	132.2	—2.4
No reply [3]	......	......	......	59		
Total				526		
Wife:						
Small town [1]	19.0	25.4	55.6	63	150.0*	
Other city	24.0	32.2	43.8	121	143.2	—1.1
Chicago suburb	21.1	30.8	48.1	52	142.7	
Single homes	34.7	16.3	49.0	49	138.7	—1.0
Second immigrant settlement	26.0	34.0	40.0	50	141.5	—1.1
First immigrant settlement	25.0	31.2	43.8	16	144.1	
Apartment [2]	35.6	28.8	35.6	104	134.4	—2.3
Rooming house..	36.4	22.7	40.9	22	135.5	—1.3
No reply [4]	......	....	..	49		
Total				526		
All cases	28.5	28.3	43.2			

[1] Not a Chicago suburb.
[2] Including apartment hotels.
[3] Including seven with rural residence.
[4] Including three with rural residence.

TABLE 113

WIFE'S VOCATIONAL AMBITION COMPARED WITH OCCUPATION BEFORE
MARRIAGE AND ADJUSTMENT

Marital Adjustment

Vocational Ambition and Occupation Before Marriage	Poor (per cent)	Fair (per cent)	Good (per cent)	No. of Cases	Mean Adjustment	CR
No difference	21.3	33.8	44.9	136	} 148.0*	
Slight difference	13.9	16.7	69.4	36		
Great difference	40.2	23.4	36.4	77	130.5	—2.8
No vocational ambition	39.2	30.4	30.4	46	128.3	—2.6
No reply				231		
Total	28.5	28.3	43.2	526		

TABLE 114

WIFE'S INTENTION BEFORE MARRIAGE REGARDING WORK COMPARED WITH
WORKING AFTER MARRIAGE AND ADJUSTMENT

Marital Adjustment

Did Wife Intend to Work after Marriage?	Poor (per cent)	Fair (per cent)	Good (per cent)	No. of Cases	Mean Adjustment	CR
Yes, and has worked	24.5	29.6	45.9	233	144.3*	
Yes, and has not worked	37.5	33.3	29.2	24	129.7	—1.53
No, and has worked	35.4	22.9	41.7	48	134.1	—1.35
No, and has not worked	28.8	28.3	42.9	184	139.8	—1.07
No reply				37		
Total	28.5	28.3	43.2	526		

APPENDIX B

Schedule Form Used In This Study

Schedule secured by...   Date filled out...........................
Date given out..

MARRIAGE STUDY

We are trying to learn more about factors which make for happy and unhappy marriages. To do this we need the coöperation and assistance of a great many married people, people whose marriages are very happy or whose marriages are only moderately satisfactory, as well as people whose marriages are unsatisfactory.

You can help us a great deal by filling out the attached questionnaire as frankly and as carefully as possible. Please do not hesitate to be perfectly frank in your answers.

You will note that the questionnaire does not call for any mark of identification. Thus your answers as well as the many others we get will be absolutely anonymous. Moreover, all of the material will be treated confidentially.

We are very desirous of having the coöperation of a number of people who are willing to discuss their marriages more fully than is possible in the questionnaire. If you are a person who is happily married, you can help us by telling us about what makes for your happiness. If you are only moderately happy, you can help us by telling us the things which seem to interfere with complete happiness. If your marriage is unsatisfactory or has perhaps resulted in separation or divorce, you can be of great assistance by discussing with us the difficulties. No matter what your situation is, you will render great aid by allowing us to talk with you. You can be assured that you will talk with a mature person who is experienced in these matters and who above all will strictly preserve your confidence.

If you will grant a personal interview, you may write your name, address, and telephone number on the last page of the questionnaire after you have answered the questions. Please see that you have given some answer to every question.

E. W. BURGESS, University of Chicago

I. THE MARRIAGE PERIOD (Selected cases where a period of from two to five years has elapsed after the marriage). If couple is separated or divorced, answer questions in this section as of time of the separation.

    1. Date of marriage: (by month and year) ....

    2. Where married: (check) at home............... at church...............; elsewhere (specify)........................

    3. Married by whom...................; minister...................; other person (specify) ....

    4. Number of different residences since marriage................

420

5. Please give following facts about your present residence: Number of rooms...................
Do you own or rent your present home?.......... If rent, what rent per month?............
Type of dwelling: (check) rooming house........; hotel........; apartment hotel........; large apartment........; small apartment.......; two flat........; house.........
Character of neighborhood: (check) rooming house........; immigrant........ workingmen's homes ....; hotel........; apartment........; private homes........; suburban........; other (specify)...................
Size of community: (check) over 200,000........; 25,000 to 200,000 ....; 10,000 to 25,000........; 2,500 to 10,000.......; 1,000 to 2,500........; under 1,000........; rural......... How far do you live from Chicago?......................

6. Since marriage has couple ever lived with any of following, and if so, for how long? Husband's parents .... wife's parents ....; husband's relatives.................; wife's relatives.................; other (specify)................ ....; always lived alone.........

7. How far does couple live from husband's parents?.................; wife's parents?..................

8. How many times a year does couple see husband's parents?..........; wife's parents?...........

9. Is couple buying a home?........; planning to buy a home?.........

10. Number of children born to couple.......... Did husband want children?..........; did wife?................. If no children, does husband want children?.................; does wife?............

11. Number of different positions held by husband *since marriage*......................
Husband's present occupation.................... Present monthly earnings...........
Amount saved by couple since marriage..............
Number of months husband was out of work since marriage...........
Unemployment due to ....

12. Number of different positions held by wife *since marriage*.....................
Wife's present occupation........ .... Present monthly earnings............

13. Husband's church attendance since marriage: (check) none.......; less than once a month........; once a month......... twice ....; three times ....; four times.........

14. Wife's church attendance since marriage: (check) none........; less than once a month........; once a month.......; twice ......; three times ......; four times......... Does husband go to same church as wife or to a different one?....................

15. Chief interests (other than vocation) of husband: politics..........; theatre..........; religious activity............; reading............; movies...........; social life............; friends..........; sports (specify)...................; hobbies (specify)...................; other (specify)................; none ....

16. Chief interests (other than vocation) of wife: politics..........; theatre.......... religious activity..........; reading.........; movies..........; social life..........; friends..........; sports (specify)...................; hobbies (specify)...................; other (specify)....................... none...........

17. Do husband and wife engage in outside interests together? (check) all of them..........; some of them..........; very few of them..........; none of them..........

18. In leisure time husband prefers (check); to be "on the go"..........; to stay at home..............
Wife prefers: to be "on the go"..........; to stay at home..........

19. Husband's state of health since marriage (check): very sickly...........; sickly...........; average health............; healthy............; very healthy............

20. Wife's state of health since marriage (check): very sickly..........; sickly..........; average health..........; healthy..........; very healthy..........。

21. State approximate extent of agreement or disagreement on following items: *(Please place a check opposite every item.)*

Check One Column for Each Item Below	Always Agree	Almost Always Agree	Occasionally Disagree
Handling family finances.........	....	....	....
Matters of recreation	....	....	....
Religious matters	....	....	....
Demonstrations of affection	....	....	....
Friends	....	....	....
Intimate relations	....	....	....
Caring for the baby	....	....	....
Table manners	....	....	....
Matters of conventionality	....	....	....
Philosophy of life	....	....	....
Ways of dealing with in-laws ...	....	....	....

Check One Column For Each Item Below	Frequently Disagree	Almost Always Disagree	Always Disagree
Handling family finances.........	....	....	....
Matters of recreation	....	....	....
Religious matters	....	....	....
Demonstrations of affection	....	....	....
Friends	....	....	....
Intimate relations	....	....	....
Caring for the baby	....	....	....
Table manners	....	....	....
Matters of conventionality	....	....	....
Philosophy of life	....	....	....
Ways of dealing with in-laws....	....	....	....

Specify other matters of disagreement...。
When disagreements arise, they usually result in: husband giving in ....;
wife giving in ....; agreement by mutual give and take..........。

22. Do you kiss your husband (wife) every day?..........; occasionally?.........;
almost never?..........。

23. Do you ever wish you had not married? frequently..........; occasionally..........; rarely..........; never..........。

24. If you had your life to live over, do you think you would: (check) marry the same person..............; marry a different person..............; not marry at all..........?

25. Do you confide in your husband (wife)? almost never..........; rarely..........; in most things..........; in everything..........。

26. Check which of the following were *your two main* reasons for marrying: to please parents..........; to escape your own family..........; for money..........; for business reasons..........; social custom..........; loneliness..........; to have a home..........; romantic love..........; other..........。

28. Give the title and authors of three or four books or articles which you read before marriage and which were important in influencing your conception of marriage (if you cannot remember any, please say so)...............
....

29. Couple separated (year)............. Reasons..
Couple divorced (year)............. Reasons..

30. What things annoy and dissatisfy you most about your marriage?...............
....
31. What things does your husband (wife) do that you don't like?..............
32. Have you ever contemplated separation?.......... Divorce?..........
33. Appraisal of marriage: very unhappy..........; unhappy..........; average.........
happy..........; very happy...........
This section filled out by: husband..........; wife..........; other person
(specify).......................................

II. THE HUSBAND (All information on this page refers to the husband at *the time of marriage or previous to marriage*).

1. Enter following information for each brother and sister of husband in order from oldest to youngest. *Place circle around number which indicates husband's place in order of birth.* Be sure to give year of birth of *all*, including husband.

Order of Birth	1st Child	2nd Child	3rd Child	4th Child	5th Child	6th Child
Year of birth						
Sex M or F						
Year of death						

Order of Birth	7th Child	8th Child	9th Child	10th Child	11th Child
Year of birth					
Sex M or F					
Year of death					

Which one (1st, 2nd, 3rd, etc.) in above table was husband *most attached to?*.......... (If he was not especially attached to any brother or sister, please state that he was not.).......................
Height at marriage.................... Weight..........

2. State of health before marriage: very sickly..........; sickly..........; average health..........; healthy.......... very healthy..........

3. Marital status before this marriage: single........; widowed........; divorced........
If married before, state how many times..................

4. Residence at time of marriage: name of city or town..................
Approximate address (such as "near 4900 South Western Avenue")..........
....
Living with parents..........; with relatives..........; rooming with private family..........; in rooming house..........; in hotel..........; elsewhere (specify)
....
If away from home, did you have a roommate? always..........; usually..........; never..........

5. Total number of years of schooling completed at time of marriage (check):

Grades

0........; 1........; 2........; 3........; 4........; 5........; 6........; 7........; 8........

High School College

1..........; 2..........; 3..........; 4..........; 1..........; 2..........; 3..........; 4..........;

Number of years beyond college in graduate or professional work?..........
Training for what profession?..................

6. In what occupation did husband classify himself at marriage? (specify).................
In what work was he actually employed?.................... How long had he held this position?............
Work record *before* marriage: none because in school.........; worked only at vacations.........; never worked.........; irregularly employed.........; always employed but continually changing jobs.........; regularly employed........
Monthly income at time of marriage.......... Amount saved before marriage................

7. Religious affiliation at marriage: church preference (specify)......................
Activity in church *before* marriage: (check) member.........; never attended.........; less than once per month.........; once per month.........; twice.........; three times.........; four times.........; held office.........; sang in choir.........; attended prayer meetings.........; member of young people's society in church.........; other activity......................

8. Sunday school: at what age stopped going to Sunday school or other religious school for children? never went.........; 10 years or younger.........; 11–14 years.........; 15–18 years.........; 19–25 years.........; still going at time of marriage..........

9. Membership in organizations at time of marriage: (check those husband belonged to or attended regularly). Church club.........; athletic club.........; social club.........; Kiwanis.........; Rotary.........; luncheon club.........; fraternal order........; labor union.........; farmer's organization.........; grange.........; other organizations (specify)......................; none at all......... . Did husband ever serve in the Army or Navy?....................

10. Husband's childhood and adolescence was spent mainly in: (check) city.........; small town.........; country..........

11. Before he was married, how many women had husband gone with steadily?
....

12. Husband's men friends before marriage (check): almost none.........; a few.........; several.........; many..........
Husband's women friends before marriage (check): almost none.........; a few.........; several.........; many............
This section filled out by: husband.........; wife.........; other person (specify)
....

III. THE PARENTS OF THE HUSBAND (The following information should be given *as if at the time of the marriage of son*.)

	Mother of Husband	Father of Husband
1. State or country of birth............................	....	....
2. Racial or national stock............................	....	....
3. Religious preference: give the church or denomination............................	....	....
4. How active in church: member, regular attendant, held office, sometimes attended, never attended............................	....	....
5. Education: give last year of schooling completed............................	....	....
6. Place in order of birth among brothers and sisters (only child, oldest, youngest, middle)	....	....
7. Number of brothers and sisters parents had	....	....
8. Occupation of parents............................	....	....

9. Economic status of husband's parents: (check) very wealthy.........; wealthy ....; well-to-do.........; comfortable.........; meager.........; poor..........

10. Social status of husband's parents in their own community (check): leading family.........; upper class.........; reputable.........; inferior.........; very inferior ....; uncertain..........

11. Marital status of husband's parents at time of husband's marriage (check): married (both living).........; separated.........; divorced.........; both dead ....; one dead (specify which)..................... If parents have been divorced or widowed state if married again...

12. Appraisal of parent's marriage: very happy.........; happy.........; average ....; unhappy.........; very unhappy..........

13. Amount of conflict between father and son (check): none.........; very little.........; moderate.........; a good deal.........; almost continuous conflict.......... Reason for conflict...
Amount of attachment between father and son (check): none.........; very little.........; moderate.........; a good deal.........; very close.......... Reason for attachment ....

14. Amount of conflict between mother and son (check): none.........; very little.........; moderate.........; a good deal.........; almost continuous conflict.......... . Reason for conflict ....
Amount of attachment between mother and son (check): none.........; very little ....; moderate .... ; a good deal.........; very close..........
Reason for attachment ....

15. Did his father favor son's marriage.........; his mother.........?
This section filled out by: husband.........; wife; ....; other person (specify) ....

IV. THE WIFE (The information asked for on this page refers to the wife at *the time of marriage or previous to marriage*).

1. Enter following information for each brother and sister of wife in order from oldest to youngest. *Place circle around number which indicates wife's place in order of birth.* Be sure to give year of birth of *all* including wife.

Order of Birth	1st Child	2nd Child	3rd Child	4th Child	5th Child	6th Child
Year of birth..........	....	....	....	....	....	....
Sex M or F..............	....	....	....	....	....	....
Year of death........	....	....	....	....	....	....

Order of Birth	7th Child	8th Child	9th Child	10th Child	11th Child
Year of birth..........	....	....	....	....	....
Sex M or F..............	....	....	....	....	....
Year of death	....	....	....	....	....

Which in above table (1st, 2nd, 3rd, etc.) was wife most attached to?.................... (If she was not especially attached to any brother or sister, please state she was not.)....................
Height at marriage.................... Weight at marriage................

2. State of health before marriage: very sickly.........; sickly.........; average health.........; healthy.........; very healthy..........

3. Marital status before this marriage: single........; widowed.......; divorced........
If married before, state how many times....................

4. Residence at time of marriage: name of city or town.................................
Approximate address (such as "near 4900 South Western Avenue")...........
....

Living with parents..........; with relatives..........; rooming in private
family..........; in rooming house..........; in hotel..........; elsewhere
(specify)............................ If living away from home, did wife have
roommate? always..........; usually..........; never..........

5. Education: check number of years of schooling completed at time of
marriage:

Grades

0........; 1........; 2........; 3........; 4........; 5........; 6........; 7........; 8........;

High School   College

1..........; 2..........; 3..........; 4..........; 1..........; 2..........; 3..........; 4..........;

Number of years beyond college in graduate or professional work?...............
Training for what profession?....................................

6. In what occupation did wife classify herself at marriage? (specify)...............
In what work was she actually employed?....................................
How long had she held this position?............................ Vocational ambition before marriage............................ Preparation for it............................
Work record before marriage: never worked outside the home........; occasionally employed........; regularly employed for............ years; occupied at
home as main housekeeper........; as helper to her mother or other person........;
engaged in one of the following: music............; art............; social life............;
volunteer social work............; other (specify)....................................
Monthly income at time of marriage..................... Amount saved before
marriage............................
Did wife plan to work after marriage?...............................

7. Religious affiliation at marriage: church preferred (specify)............................
Activity in church before marriage (check): member..........; never attended..........; attended less than once a month..........; attended once a
month........; twice........; three times........; four times........; held office........;
sang in choir..........; attended prayer meetings..........; member of young
people's society in church....................; other activity....................................

8. Sunday school: at what age stopped going to Sunday school or other
religious school for children? never went..........; 10 years or younger..........;
11–14 years..........; 15–18 years..........; 19–25 years..........; still going at
time of marriage..........

9. Membership in organizations at time of marriage (check those wife belonged to or attended regularly): church club..........; social club..........;
bridge club..........; woman's club..........; home bureau..........; lecture
course..........; parent-teacher's association..........; other organization (name)
....................; none at all....................

10. Wife's childhood and adolescence was spent mainly in (check): city..........;
small town..........; country..........

11. How long before marriage had wife known her husband?............................
How long before marriage were they keeping company?............................
How long before marriage were they engaged?............................
Before she was married, how many men had wife gone with steadily?..........

12. Wife's men friends before marriage (check): almost none..........; a few..........;
several..........; many..........
Wife's women friends before marriage (check): almost none..........; a
few..........; several..........; many..........

This section filled out by: husband..........; wife..........; other person (specify)..

V. THE PARENTS OF THE WIFE (The following information should be given *as if at the time of marriage of the wife*).

	Mother of Wife	*Father of Wife*
1. State or country of birth.............................	....	....
2. Racial or national stock.............................	....	....
3. Religious preference: give the church or denomination.............................	....	....
4. How active in church: member, regular attendant, held office, sometimes attended, never attended.............................	....	....
5. Education: give last year of schooling completed.............................	....	....
6. Place in order of birth among brothers and sisters (only child, oldest, youngest, middle)	....	....
7. Number of brothers and sisters parents had	....	....
8. Occupation of parents	....	....

9. Economic status of wife's parents (check): very wealthy..........; wealthy..........; well-to-do..........; comfortable..........; meager..........; poor..........

10. Social status of wife's parents in their own community (check): leading family..........; upper class..........; reputable..........; inferior..........; very inferior..........; uncertain..........

11. Marital status of wife's parents at time of wife's marriage (check): married (both living)..........; separated..........; divorced..........; both dead..........; one dead (specify which)..........................
    If parents have been divorced or widowed, state if married again..................

12. Appraisal of parent's marriage: very happy..........; happy..........; average..........; unhappy..........; very unhappy..........

13. Amount of conflict between father and daughter (check): none..........; very little..........; moderate..........; a good deal..........; almost continuous conflict.......... Reason for conflict ....
    Amount of attachment between father and daughter (check): none..........; very little..........; moderate..........; a good deal..........; very close..........
    Reasons for attachment..................................

14. Amount of conflict between mother and daughter (check): none..........; very little..........; moderate..........; a good deal..........; almost continuous conflict.......... Reason for conflict ....
    Amount of attachment between mother and daughter (check): none..........; very little..........; moderate..........; a good deal..........; very close..........
    Reason for attachment..................................

15. Did her father favor daughter's marriage?..........; her mother?..........
    This section filled out by: husband..........; wife..........; (other person specify)..

VI. Please answer the following questions as truthfully as you can for yourself *at the present time.* They represent our way of becoming acquainted with you. In front of each question, you will find: Yes No ? Cross out the correct answer for each question. Try to answer by Yes or No, if it is possible. If you are entirely unable to give even a tentative Yes or No, then cross out the question mark.

Yes   No   ?   Do you get stage fright?
Yes   No   ?   Do you take responsibility for introducing people at a party?
Yes   No   ?   Do you worry too long over humiliating experiences?
Yes   No   ?   Do you often feel lonesome, even when you are with other people?
Yes   No   ?   Do you consider yourself a rather nervous person?
Yes   No   ?   Are your feelings easily hurt?
Yes   No   ?   Are you sometimes the leader at a social affair?
Yes   No   ?   Do ideas often run through your head so that you cannot sleep?
Yes   No   ?   Are you frequently burdened by a sense of remorse?
Yes   No   ?   Do you worry over possible misfortunes?
Yes   No   ?   Are you usually even-tempered and happy in your outlook on life?
Yes   No   ?   Are you troubled with shyness?
Yes   No   ?   Do you daydream frequently?
Yes   No   ?   Have you ever had spells of dizziness?
Yes   No   ?   Do you get discouraged easily?
Yes   No   ?   Do your interests change quickly?
Yes   No   ?   Is it difficult to move you to tears?
Yes   No   ?   Does it bother you to have people watch you at work even when you do it well?
Yes   No   ?   Can you stand criticism without feeling hurt?
Yes   No   ?   Do you make friends easily and quickly?
Yes   No   ?   Are you troubled with the idea that people are watching you on the street?
Yes   No   ?   Does your mind often wander badly so that you lose track of what you are doing?
Yes   No   ?   Have you ever been depressed because of low marks in school?
Yes   No   ?   Are you touchy on various subjects?
Yes   No   ?   Are you often in a state of excitement?
Yes   No   ?   Do you frequently feel grouchy?
Yes   No   ?   When you were in school did you feel at ease and self-confident when you recited in class?
Yes   No   ?   Do you often feel just miserable?
Yes   No   ?   Does some particular useless thought keep coming into your mind to bother you?
Yes   No   ?   When you were in school did you hesitate to volunteer in a class recitation?
Yes   No   ?   Are you usually in good spirits?
Yes   No   ?   Do you often experience periods of loneliness?
Yes   No   ?   Do you often feel self-conscious in the presence of superiors?
Yes   No   ?   Do you lack self-confidence?
Yes   No   ?   Do you find it easy to speak in public?
Yes   No   ?   Do you usually feel that you are well-dressed and make a good appearance?
Yes   No   ?   Do you feel that you must do a thing over several times before you leave it?
Yes   No   ?   If you see an accident are you quick to take an active part in giving help?
Yes   No   ?   Are you troubled with feelings of inferiority?
Yes   No   ?   Is it is easy for you to make up your mind and act on your decision?
Yes   No   ?   Do you have ups and downs in mood without apparent cause?
Yes   No   ?   Are you in general self-confident about your abilities?

Yes No ? Do you think that a person should ever marry one whom he does
              not love?
Yes No ? Do you think marriages of romantic love are more successful than
              others?
Yes No ? Do you think divorce is ever justifiable?
Yes No ? Do you think divorce is ever justifiable for any other reason than
              unfaithfulness on the part of a mate?

*(Adapted from L. L. Thurstone, Personality Schedule (1930). Used by permission
of the author and of the University of Chicago Press.)*

Give what appear to you to be the three most important factors making for success
in marriage...
....

Give what appear to you to be the three most important factors making for failure
in marriage...
....

Remarks:
....
....

If you are willing to coöperate further in this study by granting us an interview, will
you please sign your name and give your address and telephone number below.

Name ....
Address ....
Telephone ....

APPENDIX C

Case-Study Outline Used in This Study

RESEARCH OUTLINE FOR MARRIAGE HISTORY

Confidential Outline. Please return this outline with your paper.

(Please read entire outline carefully before beginning to write.)

The following outline is prepared to assist persons interested in coöperating in a scientific study of marriage and family relationships. The points suggested below are to help you organize your thoughts and memories. *Do not be bound* by them, but tell freely about your background and experience and that of your spouse as it comes to your mind. Do not simply answer questions in the outline, but write fully, using descriptions of concrete experiences. Include incidents not specifically called for but which seem to you to be significant. Above all, be perfectly frank about all of your experiences. You may feel sure that what you tell will be kept in strictest confidence. You, of course, may not be able to give all the material regarding your spouse that this outline suggests, but give what you can. If you so desire, you may use assumed names. In giving a full and detailed account of your marriage you are aiding us in a very fundamental way in our study of this field of human experience, and we assure you of our very sincere appreciation of your coöperation in this matter.

A. Couple
  I. Courtship
    1. Tell about your courtship—the time, place and manner of meeting. Describe the situation in which each of you were, where each of you were living, occupation of each. How long had you known each other, what precipitated the love affair? How long was the courtship, how long the engagement? Under what circumstances did you see each other? Were they realistic or romantic; did the courtship allow you to know all sides of each other's personalities?
    2. Technique of courtship: What methods of attraction

430

were used by each? What attractions did each hold for the other? Was courtship warm and ardent or matter-of-fact? What were the points of conflict or disagreement during courtship and engagement? Who really took the initiative or aggressive role, and who the passive?

3. Knowledge of the affair by parents of husband and of wife. Part they took in the courtship and engagement. Their attitude toward it.

4. Matters discussed by couple and how freely and intimately discussed: e.g., past experiences and attitudes toward life, finances, children, sex, home, ambitions, etc.

5. Preparation for marriage in the form of reading, seeking counsel, etc. What was read and whose counsel was sought?

6. What were the expectations that each had of marriage— glamorous and romantic, matter-of-fact and realistic, limiting of freedom, etc.? How much hesitation did you have about marrying?

7. Where married, by whom? Did couple marry in home town of bride or groom, at home, at own church, other place? Did couple elope?

II. Marital life

1. Honeymoon: Happiness, new discoveries about mate, good times, etc.

2. Where couple lived after marriage. How far from parents' homes. Moves; number of moves; reasons for moving.

3. What was the economic and financial situation of couple? Were there debts; was there preparation financially for economic needs of marriage? Was there outside financial aid from family of either? Did wife have to work; did she plan to work after marriage? Financial arrangements between husband and wife. Were there conflicts over spending, over sharing funds, over wife's having or not having an account herself or with husband? In what manner were these conflicts adjusted?

4. Religious situation, same or different denominations, degree of interest of each in religious activities, conflicts about religious matters? How conflicts were adjusted?

5. Recreation: Interests, activities, common or divergent interests and activities. Were there differences of opinion on these matters, and if so, how were differences adjusted?

6. Friends: Did both have many or few friends; was one popular and the other not popular; did couple have

different tastes in friends? Were husband's friends mainly men or women? Were wife's friends men or women?

7. Health: sickness, chronic ailments—effect that health conditions had on relationships.

8. In-laws: How far do you live from the families of husband and wife? How often does couple see the two families? How much contact is maintained? What is the nature of relationships? Do the in-laws interfere or force counsel on the couple? Does either of couple seek and depend on counsel and aid from any of the relatives? General attitude toward relatives held by each of the couple.

9. Sex: How satisfactory or how difficult was early sex adjustment? How much sex knowledge did husband and wife have at time of marriage? Attitudes toward sex held by each. Relative intensity of desire on part of each. Degree of satisfaction in sex life for each. Techniques of sex life. Is husband considerate in sex demands; is wife? Is husband skilled in the art of love? What are the things about your sex life that are unsatisfactory to wife; to husband?

10. Demonstration of affection: Ways and frequency of demonstration of affection. Which is the more demonstrative? Are there irritations or frictions on account of the difference in degree of demonstrativeness?

11. Children: Do you have children? If so, give ages and sex. Number of miscarriages or abortions? Did husband wish the children? Did wife? Basis of objection, if there were objections. Did wife become pregnant as result of deliberate planning or otherwise? Did both know that pregnancy was planned? If one mate wished children and the other did not, how were the objections of the one overcome? When child came, were both satisfied with the sex of the child? Which of the couple was disappointed? If there are no children, does husband want children; does wife? State fully the present attitude about having children. Have you tried to have children and find that you cannot? If this is true, how much of a dissatisfaction is this? How satisfactory to each are the methods of contraception used?

12. Main factors of dissatisfaction: Discuss fully the special points about your marriage which are unsatisfactory to you. Discuss fully the special points about your spouse

that are irritating to you or that you dislike in him or her. Tell what you can of what in the marriage and in you annoys and irritates your spouse.

To what degree is your marriage a disappointment? How nearly does it accord with your expectations?

13. In matters of conflict in your marriage, how are they settled or adjusted? To what extent is there freedom of discussion of issues between husband and wife? Do either or both have other persons that they prefer "opening up" to and talking over problems with? How satisfactory are the mates as confidantes? What matters does husband not discuss with wife? What secrets does wife keep from husband?

14. General role that each plays with reference to the other. Does husband tend to be dominant, to "lord it over" the wife? Does he take a "fatherly" attitude at times? Is he contemptuous and does he look down on wife's abilities? Does he take an attitude of equality with wife? Does he look up to the wife? Does wife tend to be dominant, take a motherly attitude, be contemptuous, hold an attitude of equality, look up to husband, etc.? Does your mate play the role to you that you prefer him or her to play? If not, what role would you prefer him or her to play?

15. What superiorities or inferiorities do you feel with reference to your mate? Is husband's status and relationship outside the home satisfactory to the wife or unsatisfactory? Is wife's status and relationship outside the home satisfactory or unsatisfactory to the husband?

16. Ways by which each attempts to "get his way": reasoning and discussion, demonstrating affection, flattery, reference to example of others, nagging, cajoling, weeping, playing sick, etc.

17. To what extent have common interests in the children drawn or held husband and wife together? Have husband and wife preferred certain children to the others? What have been the chief points of conflict between husband and wife in rearing and controlling the children?

18. Have relationships between the two changed from what they were in the earlier part of the marriage? Is the changed relationship more satisfactory or less so?

To what extent have interests of the two converged; diverged?

To what extent have common interests developed?

Write fully in chronological order the history of the
marriage up to the present time, describing crises in
family life and how they were met.

B. Background of the Husband
   I. His family: nationality, race, and religion of his parents.
      The cultural and educational status and background of each
      parent.
      1. Notable or interesting or significant features about the
         history of either or both of the families of his parents.
         Social and economic status of husband's family.   Where
         did husband's family live?
      2. Describe fully the relationships in husband's family; be-
         tween his parents.   What role each played with respect
         to the other, extent of affection demonstrated, conflicts
         between them, etc.   Relation between each parent and
         the children, especially between parents and the husband
         himself.   Relations between husband and his brothers
         and sisters.   Did parents have favorites; which were the
         favorites?   Were there perceptible divisions of the family
         into little alliances?   Describe.   Tell of husband's special
         attachments and special antagonisms to members of his
         family during his childhood, adolescence, and young
         adulthood.   Demonstrations of affection in the family
         and degree of participation in this by the husband.

      General participation (or lack of it) by the husband.
      3. Way in which husband's family dealt with the follow-
         ing matters:
         a. Finances: arrangement between husband's father and
            mother, between his parents and their children.
            Were there allowances, rewards, etc.?   Conflicts over
            finances; dissatisfaction over finances in husband's
            family.   Ways these were adjusted in his family.
         b. Religion: attitude of his parents, their religious hab-
            its, their requirements of their children concerning
            religion.   How important did religion appear to be
            in husband's family?
         c. Recreation: kinds family engaged in together.
            Forms approved and disapproved by family.   Con-
            flicts and how settled, e.g., over such things as danc-
            ing, drinking, etc.
         d. Social contacts: friends, social activity.   Encouraged
            or discouraged by family.   Conflicts in family over
            such matters and how adjusted.

    e. Sex: attitudes toward; how dealt with by the family?

    f. Any other matters of conflict? How were conflicts met?

II. Husband's own history
1. Place and time of birth.
2. Education.
3. Type of community in which he spent childhood and adolescence.
4. Health history.
5. What sort of friendships and attachments did he have at different times of his life (childhood, adolescence, early adulthood)? His usual role with other persons (timid, shy, retiring, submissive, aggressive, frank and open, friendly, etc.). His sex preferences in friends. Did he associate with and prefer boys more or girls more?
6. Personal appearance, temperament, disposition, peculiarities, idiosyncrasies. Relate at least one outstanding childhood event that reveals personality traits.
7. Special feelings of inferiority. Was he self-reliant or dependent? Upon whom did he depend or fall back upon when he met hard situations?
8. Sociability: interests that he had; organizations to which he belonged. Role in his activities.
9. Ambitions, occupations, and work record: did he shift his ambitions readily, give up easily; did he shift occupations readily? Did he stick at one thing in spite of difficulties?
10. Sexual development: early sex experiences, adolescent experiences. How did he get his sex information? Attitudes and conflicts regarding sex. How completely informed on sex?
11. Previous courtships and love affairs. What sort of women or girls? Why did they not continue or result in marriage? Present attitude toward "old flames."
12. Attitudes regarding marriage; expectation of marriage. His conception of man's role with respect to women.

C. Background of the Wife: (Same material for wife as for husband)
  I. Wife's family, . . . etc.
  II. Wife's own history, ...

If you are willing to answer questions on specific points in your history upon which we may need more information, will you write your name, address, and telephone number at the end of your paper.

Bibliography

CHAPTER I

Adjustment in Marriage

Bosanquet, Helen, *The Family,* London, Macmillan and Co., 1906.

Buck, Pearl, *The Good Earth,* New York, The John Day Co., 1931.

Calhoun, A. W., *A Social History of the American Family from Colonial Times to the Present,* Cleveland, Arthur H. Clark Co., 1917–19.

Canby, Henry Seidel, "Sex and Marriage in the Nineties," *Harpers Magazine,* 169, 1934, pp. 427–436.

Chapin, F. Stuart, *Cultural Change,* New York, The Century Co., 1928. Chapter 10, "Cultural Lag in the Family."

Dell, Floyd, *Love in the Machine Age,* New York, Farrar and Rinehart, 1930.

Ellis, Havelock, *Marriage Today and Tomorrow,* San Francisco, Westgate Press, 1929.

Elmer, Manuel C., *Family Adjustment and Social Change,* New York, Long and Smith, 1932.

Frank, Lawrence K., "Social Change and the Family," *Annals of the American Academy of Political and Social Science,* 160, 1932, pp. 94–102.

Goodsell, Willystine, *A History of Marriage and the Family* (rev. ed.), New York, The Macmillan Co., 1934.

Groves, Ernest R., *The Marriage Crisis,* New York, Longmans, Green and Co., 1928.

Groves, E. R., and Ogburn, W. F., *American Marriage and Family Relationships,* New York, Henry Holt and Co., 1928.

Howard, George E., *A History of Matrimonial Institutions,* Chicago, University of Chicago Press, 1904.

Kulp, Daniel H., *Country Life in South China: The Sociology of Familism,* New York, Teachers College, Columbia University, 1925.

Lippmann, Walter, *A Preface to Morals,* New York, The Macmillan Co., 1929.

Lunn, Hugh Kingsmill, *Made on Earth, a Panorama of Marriage,* Harper and Brothers, 1938.

Martindale, Cyril C., *Wedlock,* New York, Sheed and Ward, 1937.

Mowrer, Ernest R., *Family Disorganization,* Chicago, University of Chicago Press, 1927. Chapter 1, "Confused Ideals of the Modern Family."

Newcomb, Theodore, "Recent Changes in Attitudes Toward Sex and Marriage," *American Sociological Review,* 2, 1937, pp. 659–667.

Ogburn, William F., "The Family and Its Functions," in *Recent Social Trends,* New York, McGraw-Hill Book Co., Inc., 1933, pp. 661–708.

Ogburn, William F., "Recent Changes in Marriage," *American Journal of Sociology,* 41, 1935, pp. 285–298.

Sait, Una M., *New Horizons for the Family,* New York, The Macmillan Co., 1938.

Sapir, Edward, "Observations on the Sex Problem in America," *American Journal of Psychiatry,* 8, 1928, pp. 519–534.

Stekel, Wilhelm, *Marriage at the Crossroads,* New York, W. Godwin, 1931.

Stern, Bernhard J., *The Family, Past and Present,* New York, D. Appleton-Century Co., 1938.

Stouffer, S. A., and Spencer, L. M., "Recent Increases in Marriage and Divorce," *American Journal of Sociology,* 44, 1939, pp. 551–554.

Sugimoto, E. I., *A Daughter of the Samurai,* New York, Doubleday, Page and Co., 1925.

Sumner, William G., "The Family and Social Change," *American Journal of Sociology,* 14, 1909, pp. 577–591.

Thomas, W. I., "Older and Newer Ideals of Marriage," *American Magazine,* 67, 1909, 548–552.

Westermarck, Edward, *The Future of Marriage in Western Civilization,* New York, The Macmillan Co., 1936.

CHAPTER II

Social Characteristics of the Couples Studied

Bernard, L. L., editor, *The Fields and Methods of Sociology,* New York, R. Long and R. R. Smith, 1934. Chapter 14, "Family Study."

Bingham, Walter V., and Moore, Bruce V., *How to Interview,* New York, Harper and Brothers, 1931.

Cavan, Ruth Shonle, "The Questionnaire in a Sociological Research Project," *American Journal of Sociology,* 38, 1933, pp. 721–727.

Chapin, F. Stuart, *Field Work and Social Research,* New York, The Century Co., 1920.

Cooley, C. H., *Sociological Theory and Social Research,* New York, Henry Holt and Co., 1930.

Davis, Katharine B., *Factors in the Sex Life of Twenty-Two Hundred Women,* New York, Harper and Brothers, 1929. Chapters 3–4,

"The Happiness of Married Life," and Appendix 2, "Comparative Study of Methodology."

Dickinson, Robert L., and Beam, Lura, *A Thousand Marriages, a Medical Study of Sex Adjustment*, Baltimore, Williams and Wilkins Co., 1931. Chapter 1, "The Sources"; Chapter 2, "The Patient."

Foster, R. G., "Study of Early Marriage Adjustments," *Journal of Educational Sociology*, 9, 1935, pp. 119–123.

Hamilton, Gilbert V., *A Research in Marriage*, New York, A. and C. Boni, 1929.

Harvey, O. L., "The Questionnaire as Used in Recent Studies of Human Sexual Behavior," *Journal of Abnormal and Social Psychology*, 26, 1932, pp. 379–389.

Jocher, Katharine, "Methods of Research in Studying the Family, *Family*, 9, 1928, pp. 80–85.

Lasswell, Harold D., *Psychopathology and Politics*, Chicago, University of Chicago Press, 1930. Chapter 9, "The Prolonged Interview and Its Objectification."

Lundberg, George A., *Social Research: a Study in Methods of Gathering Data*, New York, Longmans, Green and Co., 1929.

Monroe, Day, *Chicago Families; a Study of Unpublished Census Data*, Chicago, University of Chicago Press, 1932.

Mowrer, Harriet R., *Personality Adjustment and Domestic Discord*, New York, American Book Co., 1935. Chapter 2, "The Interview."

Rice, Stuart, A. (ed.), *Methods in Social Science*, Chicago, University of Chicago Press, 1931.

Robinson, Virginia P., "Case Studies of the Family for Research Purposes," *Family*, 6, 1926, pp. 298–300.

Shaw, Clifford R., "Case Study Method," *Publications of the American Sociological Society*, 21, 1927, pp. 149–157.

Terman, L. M., *Psychological Factors in Marital Happiness*, New York, McGraw-Hill Book Co., 1938. Chapter 3, "The Present Investigation: Information Secured, Populations Studied, and Treatment of Data."

Webb, Sidney and Beatrice, *Methods of Social Study*, London, Longmans, Green and Co., 1932.

Young, Pauline V., *Interviewing in Social Work*, New York, McGraw-Hill Book Co., Inc., 1935.

CHAPTER III

Happiness as a Criterion of Success in Marriage

Bentham, Jeremy, *An Introduction to the Principles of Morals and Legislation*, Oxford, The Clarendon Press, 1879 (1st ed., 1780).

Bernard, Jessie, "Distribution of Success in Marriage," *American Journal of Sociology*, 39, 1933, pp. 194–203.

Brinton, Daniel G., *The Pursuit of Happiness*, Philadelphia, D. McKay, 1893. Part 4, Chapter 5, "Love, Marriage and Family Relations."

Eliot, Thomas D., "Why Family Harmony," *Mental Hygiene*, 16, 1932, pp. 85–100.

Ferguson, Leonard, "Correlates of Marital Happiness," *Journal of Psychology*, 6, 1938, pp. 285–294.

Hartmann, George W., "Personality Traits Associated with Variations in Happiness," *Journal of Abnormal and Social Psychology*, 29, 1934, pp. 202–212.

Hellmann, Kurt E., *Die Psychologie des Glücks*, Vienna, R. Lányi, 1930.

Lang, Richard O., *A Study of the Degree of Happiness or Unhappiness in Marriage as Rated by Acquaintances of the Married Couples*, unpublished M. A. thesis, University of Chicago, 1932.

Mill, J. S., *Utilitarianism*, London, Parker, Son, and Bourn, 1863. Chapter 2.

Pitkin, Walter B., *The Psychology of Happiness*, New York, Simon and Schuster, 1929.

Russell, Bertrand, *The Conquest of Happiness*, New York, H. Liveright, 1930.

Russell, Dora (Mrs. Bertrand Russell), *The Right to Be Happy*, New York, Harper and Brothers, 1927.

Sailer, Randolph C., *Happiness Self-Estimates of Young Men*, New York, Teachers College, Columbia University, 1931.

Souriau, Paul, *Les Conditions du bonheur*, Librairie Armand Colin, 1908. 2me partie, "La vie de famille," pp. 143–223.

Watson, Goodwin B., "Happiness Among Adult Students of Education," *Journal of Educational Psychology*, 21, 1930, pp. 79–109.

Woodhouse, Mrs. C. G., "A Study of 250 Successful Families," *Social Forces*, 8, 1930, pp. 511–532.

CHAPTER IV

MEASURING ADJUSTMENT IN MARRIAGE

Foster, Robert G., "Methods for Studying Early Marriage Adjustment," *Sociology and Social Research*, 20, 1935, pp. 58–62.

Heft, G., "Das Problem der Ehevermittlung," *Archiv für Rassen- und Gesellschaftbiologie*, 28, 1934, pp. 178–202.

Kern, Marjorie D., *Getting Along Together, for Husbands and Wives*, New York, R. M. McBride and Co., 1937.

Keyserling, Count Hermann, *The Book of Marriage*, New York, Harcourt, Brace and Co., 1926. "The Correct Statement of the Marriage Problem," pp. 3–49.

Kirkpatrick, C., "Factors in Marital Adjustment," *American Journal of Sociology*, 43, 1937, pp. 270–283.

Mowrer, Harriet R., *Personality Adjustment and Domestic Discord*, New York, The American Book Co., 1935. Chapter 3, "Personality Adjustment and Domestic Discord."

Mowrer, Ernest R., and Harriet R., *Domestic Discord*, Chicago, University of Chicago Press, 1928.

Nimkoff, M. F., *The Family*, Boston, Houghton Mifflin Co., 1934. "Marriage Adjustment," pp. 373–388.

Simmel, Georg, "Ehe als Vergesellschaftung zu Zweien," *Soziologie*, Leipzig, Duncker und Humblot, 1908, pp. 86 ff.

Toops, Laura C., "The Measurement of Success in Marriage and in Parenthood," *Teachers College Record*, 30, 1929, pp. 579–588.

Waller, Willard, *The Family, a Dynamic Interpretation*, New York, The Cordon Co., 1938. Chapter 17, "Marriage Adjustment."

Wile, Ira S., *The Man Takes a Wife; a Study of Man's Problems In and Through Marriage*, New York, Greenberg, 1937.

Young, Kimball, "Adjustment," *Encyclopedia of the Social Sciences*, The Macmillan Co., New York, 1930, Vol. 1, pp. 438–439.

CHAPTER V

CONSTRUCTING AN INDEX OF MARITAL ADJUSTMENT

Bernard, Jessie, "An Instrument for Measurement of Success in Marriage," *Publications of the American Sociological Society*, 27, 1933, pp. 94–106.

Cottrell, Leonard S., Jr., *The Reliability and Validity of a Marriage Study Schedule*, Ph.D. thesis, University of Chicago, 1933.

Hamilton, Gilbert V., *A Research in Marriage*, New York, A. and C. Boni, 1929. Chapter 3, "Kinds and Degrees of Spousal Satisfaction and Dissatisfaction."

Hamilton, G. V., and Macgowan, K., *What is Wrong with Marriage*, A and C. Boni, 1929. Chapter 2, "Measuring Marriage and Other Things."

Kirkpatrick, Clifford, "Community of Interest and the Measurement of Marriage Adjustment," *Family*, 18, 1937, pp. 133–137.

Terman, L. M., *Psychological Factors in Marital Happiness*, New York, McGraw-Hill Book Co., Inc., 1938. Chapter 4, "The Index of Marital Happiness."

CHAPTER VI

The Impress of Cultural Backgrounds

Baber, Ray, "A Study of 325 Mixed Marriages," *American Sociological Review*, 2, 1937, pp. 705–716.

Benedict, Ruth, *Patterns of Culture*, Boston, Houghton Mifflin Co., 1934.

Brown, L. Guy, "The Development of Diverse Patterns of Behavior among Children in the Same Family," *Family*, 9, 1928, pp. 35–39.

Burgess, Ernest W., "The Cultural Approach to the Study of Personality," *Mental Hygiene*, 14, 1930, pp. 307–325.

Burgess, Ernest W., "The Family and the Person," *Publications of the American Sociological Society*, 22, 1927, pp. 133–143; also Chapter 10 in *Personality and the Social Group*, Chicago, University of Chicago Press, 1927.

Drachsler, Julius, *Intermarriage in New York City, a Statistical Study of the Amalgamation of European Peoples*, New York, Columbia University Press, 1921.

Faris, Ellsworth, *The Nature of Human Nature*, New York, McGraw-Hill Book Co., Inc., 1937. Chapter 3, "The Subjective Aspect of Culture."

Frank, L. K., "The Concept of Inviolability in Culture," *American Journal of Sociology*, 36, 1931, pp. 607–615.

Frazier, E. F., *The Negro Family in the United States*, Chicago, University of Chicago Press, 1939.

Jones, Mary C., and Burks, Barbara S., "Personality Development in Childhood," *Monographs of the Society for Research in Child Development*, 1, 1936. No. 4, Part 5, "Cultural Influences upon Personality," pp. 104–126.

Linton, Ralph, *The Study of Man*, New York, D. Appleton-Century Co., 1936. Chapter 26, "Culture and Personality."

Mead, Margaret, *Coming of Age in Samoa*, New York, W. Morrow and Co., 1928.

Mead, Margaret, *Growing Up in New Guinea*, New York, W. Morrow and Co., 1930.

Sanderson, Dwight, and Foster, Robert G., "A Sociological Case Study of Farm Families," *Family*, 11, 1930, pp. 107–114.

Shand, Alexander F., *The Foundations of Character*, London, Macmillan and Co., 1914.

Terman, L. M., *Psychological Factors in Marital Happiness*, New York, McGraw-Hill Book Co., Inc., 1938. Chapter 9, "Background Factors: The Family."

Thomas, William I., *Primitive Behavior*, New York, McGraw-Hill Book Co., Inc., 1937. Chapter 17, "Exemplifications of Bantu Culture."

Young, Kimball, "The Projection of Parents' Ambitions upon Their Children," *Source Book for Social Psychology,* New York, A. A. Knopf, 1927, pp. 374–378.
Young, Kimball, editor, *Social Attitudes,* New York, Henry Holt and Co., 1931. Chapter 8, "Family Tradition and Personality."

CHAPTER VII

PSYCHOGENETIC CHARACTERISTICS

Adler, Alfred, *The Practice and Theory of Individual Psychology,* New York, Harcourt, Brace and Co., 1932.
Baruch, D. W., "A Study of Reported Tension in Interparental Relationships as Co-existent with Behavior Adjustment in Young Children," *Journal of Experimental Education,* 6, 1937, pp. 187–204.
Brill, A. A., *Psychoanalysis, Its Theories and Applications,* Philadelphia, W. B. Saunders Co., 1914. Chapter 10, "Oedipus Complex." Chapter 11, "The Only or Favorite Child in Adult Life."
Carpenter, J., and Eisenberg, P., "Some Relations between Family Background and Personality," *Journal of Psychology,* 6, 1938, pp. 115–136.
Carter, W. Paul, *The Only Child in the Family: a Comparison with Other Orders of Birth,* Ph.D. thesis, University of Chicago, 1937.
Cavan, Ruth S., "The Relation of Home Background and Social Relations to Personality Adjustment," *American Journal of Sociology,* 40, 1934, pp. 143–154.
Ciocco, Antonio, "On Human Social Biology. III. Elements Affecting the Formation of the Marital Group," *Human Biology,* 11, 1939, pp. 234–247.
Eliot, Thomas D., "The Bereaved Family," *Annals of the American Academy of Political and Social Science,* 160, 1932, pp. 184–190.
Fluegel, J. C., *The Psychoanalytic Study of the Family,* 4th edition, London, Hogarth Press, 1931.
Horney, Karen, "Zur Problematik der Ehe," *Psychoanalytische Bewegung,* 4, 1932, pp. 213–223.
Horney, Karen, *The Neurotic Personality of Our Time,* New York, W. W. Norton and Co., 1937. Chapter 8, "Ways of Getting Affection and Sensitivity to Rejection."
Jones, H. E., "The Influence of Family Constellation, Personality Development in Childhood," *Monographs of the Society for Research in Child Development,* 1, 1936, No. 4, pp. 120–126.
Jung, C. G., *Psychological Types,* New York, Harcourt, Brace and Co., 1923.

Levy, David, "Hostility Patterns in Sibling Rivalry Experiments," *American Journal of Orthopsychiatry,* 6, 1936, pp. 183–257.

Lewin, Kurt, *Dynamic Theory of Personality,* New York, McGraw-Hill Book Co., Inc., 1935.

Myerson, Abraham, *The Nervous Housewife,* Boston, Little, Brown and Co., 1920.

Neumann, Frederika, "The Effects on the Child of an Unstable Home Situation," *Mental Hygiene,* 12, 1928, pp. 742–750.

Popenoe, Paul, and Wicks, D., "Marital Happiness in Two Generations," *Mental Hygiene,* 21, 1937, pp. 218–223.

Sapir, Edward, "Personality," *Encyclopedia of the Social Sciences,* New York, The Macmillan Co., Vol. 12, 1934, pp. 85–87.

Spencer, D. M., "The Composition of the Family as a Factor in the Behavior of Children in Fijian Society," *Sociometry,* 2, 1939, pp. 47–55.

Spranger, E., *Types of Men; the Psychology and Ethics of Personality,* translated from the 5th German edition, Halle, M. Niemeyer, 1928.

Stagner, R., "The Role of Parents in the Development of Emotional Instability," *American Journal of Orthopsychiatry,* 8, 1938, pp. 122–129.

Stagner, R., and Katzoff, E. T., "Personality as Related to Birth Order and Family Size," *Journal of Applied Sociology,* 20, 1936, pp. 340–346.

Waller, Willard, *The Family, A Dynamic Interpretation,* New York, The Cordon Co., 1938, especially Chapters 1–6.

Watson, John B., *Behaviorism,* New York, W. W. Norton and Co., 1925. Chapter 12, "Personality."

Weill, Blanche, *The Behavior of Young Children of the Same Family,* Cambridge, Harvard University Press, 1928.

White, William A., *Mechanisms of Character Formation,* New York, The Macmillan Co., 1916.

Witmer, Helen L., "The Influence of Parental Attitudes on the Social Adjustment of the Individual," *American Sociological Review,* 2, 1937, pp. 756–763.

Woods, F. A., "Successful Men Have Larger Families," *Journal of Heredity,* 19, 1928, pp. 271–279.

CHAPTER VIII

THE SOCIAL TYPE

A. *General*

Allport, Floyd H., *Institutional Behavior,* Chapel Hill, University of North Carolina Press, 1933. Chapter 17, "Adult Institutions and Children's Personalities."

Bolin, J. S., and Holmes, S. J., "Marriage Selection and Scholarship," *Journal of Heredity*, 18, 1927, pp. 253–255.

Bossard, J. H. S., "Residential Propinquity as a Factor in Marriage Selection," *American Journal of Sociology*, 38, 1932, pp. 219–224.

Crux, J., and Haeger, F., "Körperbau und Gattenwahl," *Zeitschrift für Sexualwissenschaft und Sexualpolitik*, 17, 1930, pp. 337–348.

Davie, M. R., and Reeves, R. J., "Propinquity of Residence before Marriage," *American Journal of Sociology*, 44, 1939, pp. 510–517.

Folsom, Joseph K., "Changing Values in Sex and Family Relations," *American Sociological Review*, 2, 1937, pp. 717–726.

Goodenough, Florence, "The Social Status Scale, 1933," in F. S. Chapin, *The Measurement of Social Status, Minneapolis, University of Minnesota Press*, 1933.

Harris, D., "Age and Occupational Factors in the Residential Propinquity of Marriage Partners," *Journal of Social Psychology*, 6, 1935, pp. 257–261.

Hart, Hornell and Ella B., *Personality and the Family*, D. C. Heath and Co., 1935.

Jones, H. E., "Homogamy in Intellectual Abilities," *American Journal of Sociology*, 35, 1929, pp. 369–382.

Kretschmer, E., "Physical and Spiritual Harmony in Marriage," *The Book of Marriage*, Count Hermann Keyserling, editor, New York, Harcourt, Brace and Co., 1926, pp. 305–328.

Lumpkin, Katherine D., *The Family: A Study of Member Rôles*, Chapel Hill, University of North Carolina Press, 1933.

McKenzie, Roderick D., *The Metropolitan Community*, New York, McGraw-Hill Book Co., Inc., 1933.

Mead, George H., *Mind, Self and Society*, Chicago, University of Chicago Press, 1934.

Mowrer, E. R., *Family Disorganization*, Chicago, University of Chicago Press, 1927. Chapter 5, "The Ecology of Family Disorganization."

Park, R. E., *The City*, Chicago, University of Chicago, 1925.

Plant, James S., *Personality and the Cultural Pattern*, New York, Commonwealth Fund, 1937, especially Chapters 7–8.

Popenoe, P., "Divorce and Remarriage from a Eugenic Point of View," *Social Forces*, 12, 1932, pp. 48–50.

Strong, Samuel M., *Social Type Method; Social Types in the Negro Community*, Ph.D. thesis in progress, University of Chicago, Department of Sociology, 1939.

Waller, Willard, *The Old Love and the New; Divorce and Readjustment*, New York, H. Liveright, 1930.

Wirth, Louis, *The Ghetto*, Chicago, University of Chicago Press, 1928. "The Social Type," pp. 71–83.

Wirth, Louis, "Some Jewish Types of Personality," *Publications of the American Sociological Society*, 20, 1926, pp. 90–96.

Zorbaugh, H. W., *The Gold Coast and the Slum,* Chicago, University of Chicago Press, 1929.

B. *The Age Factor*

Bossard, J. H. S., "The Age Factor in Marriage; A Philadelphia Study, 1931," *American Journal of Sociology,* 38, 1933, pp. 536–547.

Commins, W. D., "The Marriage-Age of Oldest Sons," *Journal of Social Psychology,* 3, 1932, pp. 487–490.

Duncan, Otis D., with McClure, J. H., Salisbury, J., and Simmons, R. H., "The Factor of Age in Marriage," *American Journal of Sociology,* 39, 1933, pp. 469–482.

Fetscher, R., "Zur Frage der Altersdifferenz der Gatten," *Zeitschrift für Sexualwissenschaft und Sexualpolitik,* 15, 1928, pp. 103–108.

Harris, J. Arthur, and Vivian, Roxana H., "Variation and Correlation in the Mean Age at Marriage of Men and Women," *American Naturalist,* 48, 1914, pp. 635–637.

Hart, Hornell, "Age Combinations at Marriage as a Partial Index of Probable Success in Marriage," *Marriage Hygiene,* 1, 1935, pp. 361–370. See also Hart, Hornell and Ella B., *Personality and the Family,* New York, D. C. Heath and Co., 1935. "At What Age Is It Best to Marry," pp. 96–104.

Hart, Hornell, and Shields, W., "Happiness in Relation to Age at Marriage," *Journal of Social Hygiene,* 12, 1926, pp. 403–407.

Notestein, F. W., "Differential Age at Marriage According to Social Class," *American Journal of Sociology,* 37, 1931, pp. 22–48.

Rogers, Ethel, "One Hundred Juvenile Marriages," *Social Forces,* 13, 1935, pp. 400–409.

Ungern-Sternberg, R. v., "Heiratsalter und Häufigkeit der Ehescheidung," *Zeitschrift für Rassenkunde,* 7, 1938, pp. 297–298.

CHAPTER IX

The Economic Role

Bell, Howard M., *Youth Tell Their Story,* Washington, D. C., American Council on Education, 1938. Chapter 2, "Youth and the Home."

Bingham, Walter V. D., *Aptitudes and Aptitude Testing,* New York, Harper and Brothers, 1937.

Bossard, J. H. S., and Weaver, W. W., "The Prospect for Youth," *Annals of the American Academy for Political and Social Science,* 194, 1937, pp. 1–216.

Donovan, Frances, *The Saleslady,* Chicago, University of Chicago Press, 1929.

Donovan, Frances, *The School Ma'am*, New York, Frederick A. Stokes Co., 1938.

Donovan, Frances, *The Woman Who Waits*, Boston, Badger, 1920.

Hughes, Everett C., "Personality Types and the Division of Labor," *American Journal of Sociology*, 33, 1928, pp. 754–768.

Lang, Richard O., *A Study of the Degree of Happiness or Unhappiness in Marriage*, unpublished M.A. thesis, University of Chicago, 1932.

Lynd, R. S. and Helen M., *Middletown in Transition*, New York, Harcourt, Brace and Co., 1937. Chapter 4, "Making a Home."

McKain, Walter C., Jr., and Anderson, C. A., "Assortative Mating in Prosperity and Depression," *Sociology and Social Research*, 21, 1937, pp. 411–418.

Marvin, Donald M., "Occupational Propinquity as a Factor in Marriage Selection," *Publications of the American Statistical Association*, 16, 1918, pp. 131–151.

Popenoe, Paul, "Assortative Mating for Occupational Level," *Journal of Social Psychology*, 8, 1937, pp. 270–274.

Stouffer, Samuel A., and Lazarsfeld, Paul F., *Research Memorandum on the Family in the Depression*, New York, Social Science Research Council, Bulletin 29, 1937.

Wile, Ira S., *The Man Takes a Wife; a Study of Man's Problems In and Through Marriage*, New York, Greenberg, Publisher, 1937.

CHAPTER X

RESPONSE PATTERNS: ROMANCE AND COMPANIONSHIP

A. *General*

Allport, Floyd H., *Institutional Behavior*, Chapel Hill, University of North Carolina Press, 1933. Chapter 18, "Seeing Women As They Are."

Blumer, Herbert, *Movies and Conduct*, New York, The Macmillan Co., 1933. Chapter 7, "Emotional Possessive Love and Passion"; Chapter 10, "Schemes of Life."

Burgess, E. W., "The Romantic Impulse and Family Disorganization," *Survey*, 57, 1926, pp. 290–294. Also in Reuter, E. B., and Runner, Jessie F., *The Family*, New York, McGraw-Hill Book Co., Inc., 1931, pp. 117–127.

Burton, Robert, *The Anatomy of Melancholy*, edited by Floyd Dell and Paul Jordan-Smith, New York, Farrar and Rinehart, 1929. Part 3, "Love Melancholy."

Carpenter, Niles, "Courtship Practices and Contemporary Social Change in America," *Annals of the American Academy of Political and Social Science*, 160, 1932, pp. 38–44.

Dreikurs, R., "The Choice of a Mate," *International Journal of Individual Psychology*, 1, 1935, pp. 99–112.

Dunlap, Knight, *Civilized Life; the Principles and Applications of Social Psychology*, Baltimore, Williams and Wilkins Co., 1934.

Finck, Henry T., *Primitive Love and Love Stories*, New York, C. Scribner's Sons, 1899.

Finck, Henry T., *Romantic Love and Personal Beauty*, New York, C. Scribner's Sons, 1887.

Groves, E. R., "Courtship and Marriage," *Mental Hygiene*, 18, 1934, pp. 26–39.

Horney, Karen, "The Overvaluation of Love," *Psychoanalytic Quarterly*, 3, 1934, pp. 605–638.

Horney, Karen, "The Problem of the Monogamous Ideal," *International Journal of Psycho-Analysis*, 9, 1928, pp. 318–331.

Huch, Ricarda, "Romantic Marriage," *The Book of Marriage*, Count Hermann Keyserling, editor, New York, Harcourt, Brace and Co., 1926, pp. 168–196.

Iovetz-Tereshchenko, N. M., *Friendship-Love in Adolescence*, London, G. Allen and Unwin, 1936.

Jones, E., "Jealousy," *Psyche*, 11, 1930, pp. 41–55.

Key, Ellen, *Love and Marriage*, New York, G. P. Putnam's Sons, 1911.

Landis, P. H., "Control of the Romantic Impulse Through Education," *School and Society*, 44, 1936, pp. 212–215.

Lewisohn, Ludwig, "Is Love Enough," *Harper's Magazine*, 166, 1933, pp. 544–553.

Mangus, Arthur R., "Relationships between the Young Woman's Conception of Her Intimate Male Associates and of Her Ideal Husband," *Journal of Social Psychology*, 7, 1936, pp. 403–420.

Mather, W. K., Jr., "The Courtship Ideals of High School Youth," *Journal of Sociology and Social Research*, 19, 1934, pp. 166–172.

Mayo, Elton, "Should Marriage Be Monotonous?" *Harper's Magazine*, 151, 1925, pp. 420–427.

Mowrer, Ernest R., *Family Disorganization*, Chicago, University of Chicago Press, 1927. "The Romantic Complex," pp. 158–165.

Popenoe, Paul, and Neptune, D. W., "Acquaintance and Betrothal," *Social Forces*, 16, 1938, pp. 552–555.

Popenoe, Paul, "A Study of 738 Elopements," *American Sociological Review*, 3, 1938, pp. 47–53.

Pruette, Lorine, "The Family and the Modern Novel," *Family*, 9, 1928, pp. 46–50.

Riviere, J., "Jealousy as a Mechanism of Defense," *International Journal of Psycho-Analysis*, 13, 1932, pp. 414–424.

Timmons, B. F., "The Cost of Weddings," *American Sociological Review*, 4, 1939, pp. 224–233.

Waller, Willard, "The Rating and Dating Complex," *American Sociological Review*, 2, 1937, pp. 727–734.

Waller, Willard, *The Family, a Dynamic Interpretation*, New York, The Cordon Co., 1938. Part 2, "Courtship Interaction."

Wembridge, Eleanor, "Why Jennie Gets Her Man," *Survey*, 67, 1932, pp. 364–367.

Wile, Ira S., "Love at First Sight as Manifest in 'The Tempest,' " *American Journal of Orthopsychiatry*, 8, 1938, pp. 341–356.

Wile, Ira S., and Winn, Mary D., "Romance Outside the Pale," *Survey*, 61, 1929, pp. 716–717.

B. *Factors in Marriage Selection*

Dunlap, Knight, *Personal Beauty and Racial Betterment*, St. Louis, C. V. Mosby Co., 1920.

Gini, C., "Un nuovo fattore di selezione matrimoniale? L'ordine de generazione," *Metron*, 11, 1933, 117–132.

Hoffeditz, E. L., "Family Resemblance in Personality Traits," *Journal of Social Psychology*, 5, 1934, 214–227.

Hoffstätter, R., "Ähnlichkeit, Gattenwahl und Ehe," *Zeitschrift für Sexualwissenschaft und Sexualpolitik*, 16, 1929, pp. 242–257.

Hoffstätter, R., "Beziehungen zwischen physiognomischer Ähnlichkeit und Ehe," *Zeitschrift für angewandte Psychologie*, 52, 1937, pp. 107–122.

Jones, D. F., "Like Father Like Son-in-Law," *Scientific Monthly*, 26, 1928, 557–560.

Jones, H. E., "Homogamy in Intellectual Abilities," *American Journal of Sociology*, 35, 1929, pp. 369–382.

Kelly, E. L., "A Preliminary Report on Psychological Factors in Assortative Mating," *Psychological Bulletin*, 34, 1937, p. 749.

Kretschmer, Ernst, "Physical and Spiritual Harmony in Marriage," *The Book of Marriage*, Hermann Keyserling, editor, New York, Harcourt, Brace and Co., 1926, pp. 305–308.

Marvin, Donald M., *Occupational Propinquity as a Factor in Marriage Selection*, Ph.D. Thesis, University of Pennsylvania, 1918.

Müller-Freienfels, R., "Zur Psychologie der erotischen Selektion," *Zeitschrift für Sexualwissenschaft und Sexualpolitik*, 15, 1928, pp. 81–103.

Popenoe, Paul, "Mate Selection," *American Sociological Review*, 2, 1937, pp. 735–743.

Richardson, Helen M., "Studies of Mental Resemblance Between Husbands and Wives and Between Friends," *Psychological Bulletin*, 36, 1939, pp. 104–20. (Bibliography.)

Schiller, Belle, "A Quantitative Analysis of Marriage Selection in a Small Group," *Journal of Social Psychology*, 3, 1932, pp. 297–319.

Schmich, G., "Die Auslesewirkung der Ehe," *Neue Generation*, 27, 1931, pp. 82–89.

Schooley, M., "Personality Resemblances Among Married Couples," *Journal of Abnormal and Social Psychology*, 31, 1936, pp. 340–347.

Schulze-Naumburg, B., "In welchen Eigenschaften ergängen Eheleute einander?" *Umschau*, 34, 1935, pp. 670–674.

Szondi, L., "Contributions to 'Fate Analysis.' An Attempt at a Theory of Choice in Love," *Acta Psychologica*, Vol. 3, No. 1, The Hague, M. Nijhoff, 1937.

Willoughby, R. R., "Neuroticism in Marriage: IV, Homogany; V, Summary and Conclusions," *Journal of Social Psychology*, 7, 1936, pp. 19–48.

CHAPTER XI

PERSONALITY FACTORS IN MARRIAGE ADJUSTMENT

Allport, Gordon, *Personality, a Psychological Interpretation*, New York, Henry Holt and Co., 1937.

Bernreuter, R. G., "The Theory and Construction of the Personality Inventory," *Journal of Social Psychology*, 4, 1933, 387–405.

Cottrell, Leonard S., Jr., "Roles and Marital Adjustment," *Publications of the American Sociological Society*, 27, 1933, pp. 107–115.

Fluegel, J. C., *The Psycho-analytic Study of the Family*, London, Hogarth Press, 5th edition, 1935.

Folsom, Joseph K., *The Family*, New York, John Wiley and Sons, 1934. Chapter 15, "Marital Roles, Frustrations, and Interaction."

Glueck, Bernard, "Some of the Sources of Marital Discontent," *Family*, 16, 1935, pp. 3–9.

Hart, Hornell and Ella, *Personality and the Family*, Boston, D. C. Heath and Co., 1935.

Hartmann, G. W., "Personality Traits Associated with Variations in Happiness," *Journal of Abnormal and Social Psychology*, 29, 1934, pp. 202–212.

Johnson, W. B., and Terman, L. M., "Personality Characteristics of Happily Married, Unhappily Married, and Divorced Persons," *Character and Personality*, 3, 1935, pp. 290–311.

Jung, C. G., "Marriage as a Psychological Relationship," in *The Book of Marriage*, Hermann Keyserling, editor, New York, Harcourt, Brace and Co., 1926, pp. 348–362.

Mowrer, Harriet R., *Personality Adjustment and Domestic Discord*,

New York, American Book Co., 1935. Chapter 1, "The Clinical Approach to Domestic Discord."

Oberndorf, C. P., "Psychoanalysis of Married Couples," *Psychoanalytic Review*, 25, 1938, pp. 453–475.

Plant, James S., *Personality and the Cultural Pattern*, New York, The Commonwealth Fund, 1937.

Pratt, G. K., "Some of the Psychopathology of Marriage Adjustment," *American Journal of Psychiatry*, 9, 1930, pp. 861–870.

Stagner, R., "Marital Similarity in Socio-Economic Attitudes," *Journal of Applied Psychology*, 22, 1938, pp. 340–346.

Terhune, W. B., "Marital Maladjustments," *Yale Journal of Biology and Medicine*, 4, 1931, pp. 149–165.

Terman, L. M., *Psychological Factors in Marital Happiness*, New York, McGraw-Hill Book Co., Inc., 1938. Chapter 2, "An Exploratory Search for Psychological Factors in Marital Compatibility"; Chapter 6, "Personality Correlates of Marital Happiness"; Chapter 7, "The Personalities of Happily Married and of Unhappily Married Persons."

Terman, L. M., and Buttenwieser, Paul, "Personality Factors in Marital Compatibility," *Journal of Social Psychology*, 6, 1935, pp. 143–171, 267–289.

Wellisch, S., "Korrelation zwischen Ähnlichkeit und Eheglück," *Zeitschrift für Sexualwissenschaft und Sexualpolitik*, 16, 1930, pp. 508–509.

Wile, Ira S., "The Dynamics of Marriage," *Urologic and Cutaneous Review*, 33, 1929, pp. 537–542.

Willoughby, R. R., "Neuroticism in Marriage," *Journal of Social Psychology*, 5, 1934, pp. 3–36, 467–499; 6, 1935, pp. 397–436; 7, 1936, pp. 19–48.

Willoughby, R. R., "Spousal Estimation of Emotionality," *Human Biology*, 10, 1938, pp. 417–425.

CHAPTER XII

THE SEXUAL FACTOR

Bromley, Dorothy, and Britten, Florence H., *Youth and Sex*, New York, Harper and Brothers, 1938.

Davis, Katharine B., *Factors in the Sex Life of Twenty-two Hundred Women*, New York, Harper and Brothers, 1929.

Dickinson, Robert L., *The Single Woman*, Baltimore, Williams and Wilkins Co., 1934.

Dickinson, Robert L., and Beam, Lura, *A Thousand Marriages; a Medical Study of Sex Adjustment,* Baltimore, Williams and Wilkins Co., 1931.

Ellis, Havelock, *Sex in Relation to Society,* Philadelphia, F. A. Davis Co., 1913.

Ellis, Havelock, *Studies in the Psychology of Sex,* 7 volumes, Philadelphia, F. A. Davis Co., 1910–1928.

Ellis, Havelock, "Sex in Contemporary Life," *Marriage Hygiene,* 3, 1937, pp. 275–278.

Ernst, J. R., "Causes of Divorce from the Viewpoint of a Psychiatrist," *Medical Journal and Record,* 129, 1929, pp. 263–266.

Freud, Sigmund, *Three Contributions to the Theory of Sex,* 3rd revised edition, New York, Nervous and Mental Diseases Publishing Co., 1918. Also Book 3 in *The Basic Writings of Sigmund Freud,* edited by A. A. Brill, New York, Random House, 1938.

Groves, Ernest R., "Sex Adjustment of College Men and Women," *Journal of Educational Sociology,* 8, 1935, pp. 353–360.

Groves, Ernest R., "Courtship and Marriage," *Mental Hygiene,* 18, 1934, pp. 26–39.

Hamilton, Gilbert V., *A Research in Marriage,* New York, A. & C. Boni, 1929.

Harvey, O. L., "Some Statistics Derived from Recent Questionnaire Studies Relative to Human Sexual Behavior," *Journal of Social Psychology,* 3, 1932, pp. 97–100.

Harvey, O. L., "The Scientific Study of Human Sexual Behavior," *Journal of Social Psychology,* 3, 1932, pp. 161–188.

Horney, Karen, *New Ways in Psychoanalysis,* New York, W. W. Norton and Co., 1939.

Hühner, Max, *Practical Treatise on Disorders of the Sexual Function in the Male and Female,* 3rd edition, Philadelphia, F. A. Davis Co., 1929.

Malinowski, Bronislaw, *Sex and Repression in Savage Society,* New York, Harcourt, Brace and Co., 1927.

Margold, Charles W., *Sex Freedom and Social Control,* Chicago, University of Chicago Press, 1926.

May, Geoffrey, *The Social Control of Sex Expression,* New York, William Morrow and Co., 1931.

Mayo, Elton, "Sin with a Capital S," *Harper's Magazine,* 154, 1927, pp. 537–545.

Mead, Margaret, *Coming of Age in Samoa,* New York, W. Morrow and Co., 1928.

Mead, Margaret, *Sex and Temperament in Three Primitive Societies,* New York, W. Morrow and Co., 1935.

Mowrer, Harriet R., "Sex as a Factor in Domestic Discord," *American Sociological Review,* 1, 1936, pp. 252–263.

Peck, M. W., and Wells, F. L., "On the Psycho-sexuality of College Graduate Men," *Mental Hygiene*, 7, 1923, pp. 697–714; 9, 1925, pp. 502–520.

Sapir, Edward, "The Discipline of Sex," *American Mercury*, 16, 1929, pp. 413–420.

Sapir, Edward, "Observations on the Sex Problem in America," *American Journal of Psychiatry*, 8, 1928, pp. 519–534.

Smith, Edith L., and Cabot, Hugh, "A Study in Sexual Morality," *Journal of Social Hygiene*, 2, 1916, pp. 527–548.

Stekel, W., *Bi-Sexual Love*, New York, Emerson Books, 1933.

Stekel, W., *Frigidity in Woman in Relation to Her Love Life*, New York, Boni and Liveright, 1925.

Terman, L. M., *Psychological Factors in Marital Happiness*, New York, McGraw-Hill Book Co., Inc. Chapter 10, "Background Factors: Sex Education and Sex Attitudes"; Chapters 11–12, "Specific Sexual Adjustments and Their Relation to Marital Happiness"; Appendix I, "Correlates of Orgasm Adequacy in Women."

Terman, L. M., and Miles, C., *Sex and Personality*, New York, McGraw-Hill Book Co., Inc., 1936.

Thomas, William I., *Primitive Behavior*, New York, McGraw-Hill Book Co., Inc., 1937. Chapter X, "Sexual Behavior."

Thomas, William I., "Sex and Society," *Studies in the Social Psychology of Sex*, Chicago, University of Chicago Press, 1907.

Velde, Th. H. Van de, *Ideal Marriage; Its Physiology and Technique*, New York, Covici-Friede, 1933.

Velde, Th. H. Van de, *Sex Hostility in Marriage*, New York, Covici-Friede, 1931.

Watson, Goodwin, and Green, G., "Scientific Studies and Personal Opinion on Sex Questions," *Journal of Abnormal and Social Psychology*, 27, 1932, pp. 130–146.

Wells, F. L., "General Personality and Certain Features of the Sex Life," *Mental Hygiene*, 10, 1926, pp. 345–354.

Wile, Ira S., *The Sex Life of the Unmarried Adult*, New York, The Vanguard Press, 1934.

CHAPTER XIII

Contingency Factors

Andrews, Benjamin R., *Economics of the Household*, New York, The Macmillan Co., 1935.

Angell, Robert C., *The Family Encounters the Depression*, New York, C. Scribner's Sons, 1936.

Cavan, Ruth S., and Ranck, Katherine H., *The Family and the Depres-*

sion; a Study of One Hundred Chicago Families, Chicago, University of Chicago Press, 1938.

Ciocco, A., "On Human Social Biology. II. Disruptive and Cohesive Factors in the Marital Group," *Human Biology,* 10, 1938, pp. 555–574.

Hamilton, Gilbert V., and MacGowan, K., *What Is Wrong with Marriage?* New York, A. and C. Boni, 1929. Chapter 5, "Marriage and Money."

Kaplan, A. D. H., and Williams, Faith M., *Income and Expenditure in Chicago,* 1935–1936. Vol. 1, "Family Income," United States Department of Labor, Bureau of Labor Statistics, Washington, D. C., 1939; Vol. 2, "Family Expenditures in Chicago," in press.

Kyrk, Hazel, *Economic Problems of the Family,* New York, Harper and Brothers, 1933.

LaFollette, Cecile T., "A Study of the Problems of Six Hundred Fifty-Two Gainfully Employed Married Women Homemakers," New York, *Teachers College Contributions to Education,* 619, 1934, pp. 1–219.

Le Play, F., *Les Ouvriers Européens,* second edition, six volumes, Paris, 1879. Volume I, *La Méthode d'observation,* translated in an abridged adaptation, constitutes Chapters 19–30 of C. C. Zimmerman and M. E. Frampton, *Family and Society.*

Lundberg, George A., and Komarovsky, Mirra, *Leisure; a Suburban Study,* New York, Columbia University Press, 1934. Chapter 6, "The Suburban Family and Leisure Time."

Lynd, Robert S. and Helen M., *Middletown, a Study in Contemporary American Culture,* New York, Harcourt, Brace and Co., 1929. Chapters 4–12.

Mowrer, Ernest R. and Harriet R., *Domestic Discord,* Chicago, University of Chicago Press, 1928.

Ogburn, W. F., and Thomas, D. S., "The Influence of the Business Cycle on Certain Social Conditions," *Journal of the American Statistical Association,* 18, 1922, pp. 324–340.

Peixotto, Jessica, *Getting and Spending at the Professional Standard of Living,* New York, The Macmillan Co., 1927.

Popenoe, Paul, "Motivation of Childless Marriages," *Journal of Heredity,* 27, 1936, pp. 469–472.

Smiedler, Edgar, *The Industrial Revolution and the Home,* Ph.D. thesis, Catholic University of America, 1927.

Sorokin, P. A., *Contemporary Sociological Theories,* New York and London, Harper and Brothers, 1928, pp. 551–554.

Stouffer, S. A., and Lazarsfeld, P. F., *Research Memorandum on the Family in the Depression,* New York, Social Science Research Council, 1937.

Sturgis, Laura L., "The First Year of Marriage," *Harper's Magazine*, 168, 1933-34, pp. 405-413.

Terman, L. M., *Psychological Factors in Marital Happiness*, New York, McGraw-Hill Book Co., Inc., 1938. Chapter V, "The Interpretation of Domestic Grievances."

Thomas, Dorothy S., *Social Aspects of the Business Cycle*, London, G. Routledge and Sons, 1925.

Waller, Willard, *The Old Love and the New; Divorce and Readjustment*, New York, H. Liveright, 1930.

Williams, Faith M., and Zimmerman, Carle C., *Studies of Families Living in the United States and Other Countries*, Washington, D. C., United States Department of Agriculture, 1935.

Williams, James M., *Human Aspects of Unemployment and Relief*, Chapel Hill, University of North Carolina Press, 1933.

Woodhouse, Mrs. Chase G., "Does Money Make the Marriage Go?" *Survey*, 67, 1932, pp. 355-358.

Young, Kimball, and Dedrick, C. L., "Variation in the Duration of Marriages Which End in Divorce," *Journal of the American Statistical Association*, 27, 1932, pp. 160-167.

Zimmerman, Carle C., *Consumption and Standards of Living*, New York, D. Van Nostrand Co., 1936.

Zimmerman, C. C., and Frampton, M. E., *Family and Society*, New York, D. Van Nostrand Co., 1935.

CHAPTER XIV

THE PREDICTION OF MARITAL ADJUSTMENT

A. *Studies of Prediction of Adjustment in Engagement and Marriage*

Burgess, E. W., and Cottrell, L. S., Jr., "The Prediction of Adjustment in Marriage," *American Sociological Review*, 1, 1936, pp. 737-751.

Burgess, E. W., and Wallin, Paul, *Predicting the Adjustment of Engaged Couples* (a study in progress), University of Chicago.

Kelly, E. Lowell, *Study of Engaged Couples* (a study in progress), Connecticut State College.

Terman, L. M., *Psychological Factors in Marital Happiness*, New York, McGraw-Hill Book Co., Inc., 1938. Chapter 13, "The Relative Contributions of Personality Factors, Background Factors, and Sexual Factors to Happiness in Marriage."

Winch, Robert, *The Relation of Neurotic Tendency to Adjustment in Engagement*, M. A. thesis, University of Chicago, 1939.

B. *Studies of Prediction of Adjustment in Other Fields of Behavior*

Bingham, Walter V. D., *Aptitudes and Aptitude Testing,* New York, Harper and Brothers, 1937. Especially Chapter 19, "Interpreting Test Performance."

Bruce, A. A., Harno, A. J., Burgess, E. W., and Landesco, John, *The Workings of the Indeterminate Sentence Law in Illinois,* Springfield, Illinois, Division of Pardons and Paroles, 1928. Part 4, "Factors Determining Success or Failure on Parole, pp. 205–249.

Charters, W. W., "Predictive Measures," *Journal of Higher Education,* 9, 1938, pp. 167–168.

Fleming, J. W., "Predicting Trade-school Success," *Independent Arts and Vocational Education,* 27, 1938, pp. 315–318, 365–367, 422–426; 28, 1939, pp. 15–17, 62–64, 142–146.

Deputy, E. C., *Predicting First Grade Reading Achievement,* New York, Teachers College, Columbia University, 1930.

Glueck, Sheldon and Eleanor T., *Five Hundred Criminal Careers,* New York, 1930. Chapter 18, "Predictability in the Administration of Criminal Justice."

Glueck, S. and E. T., *Five Hundred Delinquent Women,* New York, A. A. Knopf, 1934. Chapter 17, "Predicting Recidivism and Appropriate Treatment."

Glueck, S. and E. T., *Later Criminal Careers,* New York, Commonwealth Fund, 1937. Chapter 12, "Prediction of Criminal Conduct Following Expiration of Sentence."

Glueck, S. and E., *One Thousand Juvenile Delinquents,* Cambridge, Harvard University Press, 1934. Chapter 11, "Predicting the Behavior of Delinquents."

Hart, Hornell, "Predicting Parole Success," *Journal of Criminal Law and Criminology,* 14, 1923, pp. 405–413.

Lanne, W. F., "Parole Prediction as Science," *Journal of Criminal Law and Criminology,* 26, 1935, pp. 377–400.

Laune, F. F., *Predicting Criminology: Forecasting Behavior on Parole,* Evanston, Northwestern University Press, 1936.

Monachesi, Elio D., *Prediction Factors in Probation,* Minneapolis, Sociological Press, 1932.

Odenweller, A. L., *Predicting the Quality of Teaching,* New York, Teachers College, Columbia University, 1936.

Perry, Robert D., *Prediction Equations for Success in College Mathematics,* Nashville, George Peabody College, 1935.

Redden, Elizabeth A., *Embezzlement, a Study of One Kind of Criminal Behavior with Prediction Tables Based on Fidelity Insurance Records,* Ph.D. thesis, University of Chicago, 1939.

Segel, David, *Predication of Success in College,* Washington, U. S. Government Printing Office, 1934, bibliography.

Somers, Grover T., *Pedagogical Prognosis: Predicting the Success of Prospective Teachers,* New York, Teachers College, Columbia University, 1923.

Stanger, Margaret A., and Donohue, Ellen K., *Prediction and Prevention of Reading Difficulties,* New York, Oxford Univ. Press, 1937.

Stouffer, S. A., and Tibbitts, Clark, "Tests of Significance in Applying Westergaard's Method of Expected Cases to Sociological Data," *Journal of the American Statistical Association,* 28, 1933, pp. 293–302.

Thorndike, E. L., and others, *Prediction of Vocational Success,* New York, The Commonwealth Fund, 1934.

Tibbitts, Clark, "Reliability of Factors Used in Predicting Success or Failure in Parole," *Journal of Criminal Law and Criminology,* 22, 1932, pp. 844–853.

Tibbitts, C., "Success or Failure on Parole Can Be Predicted," *Journal of Criminal Law and Criminology,* 22, 1931, pp. 11–50.

Van Vechten, Courtlandt C., *Study of Success and Failure of One Thousand Delinquents Committed to a Boys' Republic,* Ph.D. thesis, University of Chicago, 1935.

Vold, G. B., "Do Parole Prediction Tables Work in Practice?" *Publications of the American Sociological Society,* 25, 1931, pp. 136–138.

Vold, G. B., *Prediction Methods and Parole,* Hanover, Sociological Press, 1931.

CHAPTER XV

Case Studies of Marital Adjustment

Cottrell, Leonard S., Jr., "Roles and Marital Adjustment," *Publications of the American Sociological Society,* 27, 1933, pp. 107–115.

Krueger, E. T., "A Study of Marriage Incompatibility," *Family,* 9, 1928, pp. 53–60.

Mudd, Emily H., "An Analysis of One Hundred Consecutive Cases in the Marriage Counsel of Philadelphia," *Mental Hygiene,* 21, 1937, pp. 198–217.

Mowrer, Ernest R., *Family Disorganization,* Chicago, University of Chicago Press, 1927. Chapter 10, "Behavior Sequences in Family Disorganization." Chapter 12, "Socio-analysis of a Case of Family Disorganization."

Mowrer, Harriet R., *Personality Adjustment and Domestic Discord,* American Book Co., 1935. Chapter 12, "Analysis and Treatment."

Taft, Jessie, "The Effect of an Unsatisfactory Mother-Daughter Relationship upon the Development of a Personality," *Family*, 7, 1927, 10–17.

Waller, Willard, *The Family, a Dynamic Interpretation*, New York, Cordon Co., 1938. "Forty Years of Conflict," pp. 363–379.

CHAPTER XVI

BASIC PROBLEMS IN PREDICTION

Angell, Robert C., *The Family Encounters the Depression*, New York, C. Scribner's Sons, 1936. Appendix A, "Notes on the Logic of Generalizations on Family Case Studies."

Blumer, Herbert, "Science without Concepts," *American Journal of Sociology*, 36, 1931, pp. 515–533.

Burgess, Ernest W., "Statistics and Case Studies," *Sociology and Social Research*, 12, 1927, pp. 103–120.

Cavan, Ruth S., Hauser, P. M., and Stouffer, S. A., "Note on the Statistical Treatment of Life-history Material," *Social Forces*, 9, 1930, 200–203.

Cohen, Morris R., *Reason and Nature; an Essay on the Meaning of Scientific Method*, New York, Harcourt, Brace and Co., 1931. Book III, Chapter 1, "The Social and the Natural Sciences."

Cottrell, L. S., Jr., "Roles and Marital Adjustment," *Publications of the American Sociological Society*, 27, 1936, pp. 107–115.

Dollard, John, *Criteria for the Life History*, New Haven, Yale University Press, 1935.

Furfey, P. H., and Daly, J. E., "A Criticism of Factor Analysis as a Technique of Sociological Research," *American Sociological Review*, 2, 1937, pp. 178–186.

Hanks, Lucien M., "Prediction from Case Material to Personality Test Data; a Methodological Study of Types," *Archives of Psychology*, No. 207, 1936.

Hollingworth, H. L., "Psychological Factors in Marital Happiness," *Psychological Bulletin*, 36, 1939, pp. 191–197.

Kelly, E. L., "Concerning the Validity of Terman's Weights for Predicting Marital Happiness," *Psychological Bulletin*, 36, 1939, 202–203.

Kirkpatrick, Clifford, "Statistical Investigation of the Psychoanalytic Theory of Mate Selection," *Journal of Abnormal and Social Psychology*, 32, 1937, pp. 427–430.

Lundberg, George, "Quantitative Methods in Social Psychology," and "Discussion," by Willard Waller, *American Sociological Review*, 1, 1936, pp. 38–60.

Lundberg, George, *Social Research, a Study in Methods of Gathering*

Data, New York, Longmans, Green and Co., 1929. Chapter 8, "Case Studies and the Statistical Method."

Moreno, J. L., "Interpersonal Therapy and the Psychopathology of Interpersonal Relations," *Sociometry*, 1, 1937, pp. 9–76.

Murray, H. A., editor, *Explorations in Personality, a Clinical and Experimental Study of Fifty Men of College Age*, New York, Oxford University Press, 1938.

Pearson, Karl, *The Grammar of Science*, 3rd revised edition, London, A. and C. Black, 1911.

Peirce, Charles S., *Chance, Love and Logic*, New York, Harcourt, Brace and Co., 1923.

Poincaré, Henri, *The Foundations of Science*, New York, Science Press, 1921.

Rice, Stuart A., "Hypotheses and Verifications in Clifford R. Shaw's Studies of Juvenile Delinquency, in *Methods in Social Science*, Rice, S. A., editor, Chicago, University of Chicago Press, 1931.

Sheffield, Ada E., "The Situation as the Unit of Family Case Study," *Social Forces*, 9, 1931, pp. 465–474.

Stouffer, Samuel A., *An Experimental Comparison of Statistical and Case History Methods of Attitude Research*, Ph.D. thesis, University of Chicago, 1930.

Stouffer, S. A., and Lazarsfeld, Paul F., *Research Memorandum on the Family in the Depression*, New York, Social Science Research Council, 1937. Appendix A, "Notes on the Logic of Generalizations in Family Case Studies."

Sullivan, Harry S., "Psychiatry: Introduction to the Study of Interpersonal Relations," *Psychiatry*, 1, 1938, pp. 121–134.

Symonds, P. M., *Diagnosing Personality and Conduct*, New York, Century Co., 1931.

Terman, L. M., *Psychological Factors in Marital Happiness*, New York, McGraw-Hill Book Co., Inc., 1938. Chapter 13, "The Relative Contributions of Personality Factors, Background Factors, and Sexual Factors to Happiness in Marriage."

Terman, L. M., "The Effect of Happiness or Unhappiness of Self-report Regarding Attitudes, Reaction Patterns and Facts of Personal History," *Psychological Bulletin*, 36, 1939, pp. 197–202.

Thomas, William I., and Thomas, Dorothy S., *The Child in America*, New York, A. A. Knopf, 1928. Chapter 12, "The Sociological Approach," especially pp. 571–575.

Thurstone, L. L., and Chave, E. J., *The Measurement of Attitude*, Chicago, University of Chicago Press, 1929.

Thurstone, L. L., "Measurement of Opinion," *Journal of Abnormal and Social Psychology*, 22, 1928, pp. 415–430.

Thurstone, L. L. and T. G., "A Neurotic Inventory," *Journal of Social Psychology*, 1, 1930, pp. 1–30.

Thurstone, L. L., *The Vectors of Mind; Multiple-Factor Analysis for the Isolation of Primary Traits,* Chicago, University of Chicago Press, 1935.

Uexküll, Jakob, *Theoretical Biology,* London, K. Paul, Trench, Trubner and Co., 1926.

Waller, Willard, "Insight and Scientific Method," *American Journal of Sociology,* 40, 1934, pp. 285–297.

Young, Kimball, "Method, Generalization, and Prediction in Social Psychology," *Publications of the American Sociological Society,* 27, 1933, pp. 23–34.

Znaniecki, F., *The Method of Sociology,* New York, Farrar and Rinehart, 1934.

CHAPTER XVII

Major Findings and Their Interpretation

Burgess, Ernest W., *The Function of Socialization in Social Evolution,* Chicago, University of Chicago Press, 1916. Part 3, "The Role of Socialization in Personal Development."

Dewey, John, *Human Nature and Conduct,* New York, Henry Holt and Co., 1922.

Faris, Ellsworth, *The Nature of Human Nature,* New York, McGraw-Hill Book Co., Inc., 1937. Part 3, "Sociology and Education."

Groves, Ernest R., *The American Woman; the Feminine Side of a Masculine Civilization,* New York, Greenberg, 1937.

Horkheimer, Max, editor, *Autorität und Familie,* Paris, Alcan, 1936.

Horney, Karen, "The Flight from Womanhood: the Masculinity Complex in Women as Viewed by Men and Women," *International Journal of Psychoanalysis,* 7, 1926, pp. 324–339.

Kirkpatrick, Clifford, "A Methodological Analysis of Feminism in Relation to Marital Adjustment," *American Sociological Review,* 4, 1939, pp. 325–334.

Mead, Margaret, *Sex and Temperament in Three Primitive Societies,* New York, W. Morrow and Co., 1935.

Popenoe, Paul, "Can the Family Have Two Heads?" *Sociology and Social Research,* 18, 1933, pp. 12–17.

Schulze-Naumburg, B., "In welchen Eigenschaften ergänzen Eheleute einander?" *Umschau,* 34, 1935, pp. 670–674.

Simmel, Georg, *Soziologie,* 3rd edition, Munich, 1923, pp. 101–185, 250–256. Chapter 3 translated by A. W. Small as "Superiority and Subordination" in *American Journal of Sociology,* 2, 1896, pp. 167–189, 392–415.

Terman, L. M., *Psychological Factors in Marital Happiness,* New York,

McGraw-Hill Book Co., Inc., 1938. Chapter 14, "Summary and Conclusions."

Williams, James M., *Principles of Social Psychology*, New York, A. A. Knopf, 1922. Book 5, "The Conflict of Interests in Family Relations."

CHAPTER XVIII

THE FUTURE OF RESEARCH IN MARRIAGE ADJUSTMENT

A. *Reports of Research in Marriage Adjustment*

Bernard J., "Factors in the Distribution of Success in Marriage," *American Journal of Sociology*, 40, 1934, pp. 49–60.

Bernard, J., "Some Biological Factors in Personality and Marriage," *Human Biology*, 7, 1935, pp. 430–436.

Burgess, E. W., and Cottrell, L. S., Jr., "The Prediction of Adjustment in Marriage," *American Sociological Review*, 1, 1936, pp. 737–751.

Davis, Katharine B., *Factors in the Sex Life of Twenty-two Hundred Women*, New York, Harper and Brothers, 1929.

Dickinson, R. L., and Beam, Lura, *A Thousand Marriages*, Baltimore, Williams and Wilkins Co., 1931.

Hamilton, Gilbert V., *A Research in Marriage*, New York, A. and C. Boni, 1929.

Hart, Hornell, and Shields, Wilmer, "Happiness in Relation to Age at Marriage," *Journal of Social Hygiene*, 12, 1926, pp. 403–407.

Kirkpatrick, C., "Factors in Marital Adjustment," *American Journal of Sociology*, 43, 1937, pp. 270–283.

Popenoe, Paul, "A Study of 738 Elopements," *American Sociological Review*, 3, 1938, pp. 47–53.

Popenoe, Paul, and Wicks, D., "Marital Happiness in Two Generations," *Mental Hygiene*, 21, 1937, pp. 218–223.

Schroeder, C. W., *Divorce in a City of One Hundred Thousand Population*, Peoria, Illinois, Bradley Polytechnic Library, 1939. Chapter 11, "Personal Factors in Divorce."

Terman, L. M., *Psychological Factors in Marital Happiness*, New York, McGraw-Hill Book Co., Inc., 1938.

Terman, L. M., and Buttenwieser, Paul, "Personality Factors in Marital Compatibility," *Journal of Social Psychology*, 6, 1935, pp. 143–171, 267–289.

Williams, Edith W., *Factors in Adjustment in Rural Marriages*, Ph.D. thesis, Cornell University, 1938.

Winch, Robert, *The Relation of Neurotic Tendency to Adjustment in Marriage*, M. A. thesis, University of Chicago, 1939.

B. *Marriage Counseling*

Bernard, William S., "Student Attitudes on Marriage and the Family," *American Sociological Review,* 3, 1938, pp. 354–361.

Bridgman, Ralph P., "Guidance for Marriage and Family Life," *Annals of the American Academy of Political and Social Science,* 160, 1932, pp. 144–164.

Clark, Le Mon, *Emotional Adjustment in Marriage,* St. Louis, C. V. Mosby Co., 1937.

Exner, M. J., *The Sexual Side of Marriage,* New York, W. W. Norton and Co., 1932.

Fetscher, P., "Die Entwickelung der Eheberatung im Deutschen Reich," *Deutsche medizinische Wochenschaft,* 56, 1939, pp. 2138–2140.

Fetscher, P., "Probleme der Eheberatung," *Zeitschrift für öffentliche Gesundheitspflege,* 5, 1929, pp. 238–248.

Folsom, Joseph K., editor, *Plan for Marriage,* New York, Harper and Brothers, 1938.

Foster, Robert G., "A National Survey of Family Consultation Centers," *Journal of Social Hygiene,* 19, 1933, pp. 355–366.

Groves, Ernest R., *Preparation for Marriage,* New York, Greenberg, 1936.

Hixenbaugh, Elinor R., "Reconciliation of Marital Maladjustment; an Analysis of 101 Cases," *Social Forces,* 10, 1931, pp. 230–236.

Hixenbaugh, E. R., "Marriage Consultation in a Domestic Relations Court," *Journal of Social Hygiene,* 19, 1933, pp. 534–536.

Hutton, Isobel, *The Sex Technique in Marriage,* New York, Emerson Books, 1932.

Kirkpatrick, Clifford, "Techniques of Marital Adjustment," *Annals of the American Academy of Political and Social Science,* 160, 1932, pp. 178–183.

Kirkpatrick, C., "Student Attitudes Toward Marriage and Sex," *Journal of Educational Sociology,* 9, 1936, pp. 545–555.

Lazarsfeld, S., "Über Eheberatung. Beratungstechnik und Selbsterziehung," *Internationale Zeitschrift für Individualpsychologie,* 8, 1930, pp. 160–165.

Levy, John, and Munroe, Ruth, *The Happy Family,* New York, A. A. Knopf, 1938.

Nimkoff, M. F., "Counseling Students on Premarital Problems; a Function of the Sociologist," *Mental Hygiene,* 19, 1935, pp. 573–585.

Nimkoff, M. F., "A Family Guidance Clinic," *Sociology and Social Research,* 18, 1934, pp. 229–240.

Plant, James F., "Present Problems in Marriage Counseling," *Mental Hygiene,* 23, 1939, pp. 353–362.

Popenoe, Paul, "A Family Consultation Service," *Journal of Social Hygiene,* 17, 1931, pp. 309-322.

Stopes, Marie, *Married Love,* New York, G. P. Putnam's Sons, 1921.

Velde, Th. H. Van de, *Ideal Marriage,* New York, Covici-Friede, 1933.

Weaver, Anne Marie, M. D., "Marriage Advice Stations for Married and Engaged Couples," *Family,* 11, 1930, pp. 85-87.

Wile, Ira S., and Winn, Mary D., *Marriage in the Modern Manner,* New York, D. Appleton-Century Co., 1936.

Wolfe, W. Béran, "Romance versus Marriage," *Forum,* 86, 1931, pp. 166-172.

Wright, Helena, *The Sex Factor in Marriage,* Vanguard Press, 1931.

Yarros, Rachelle S., *Modern Woman and Sex,* New York, Vanguard Press, 1933.

Index

Italicized page numbers indicate those pages on which charts or tables appear.

A

Acquaintance, duration of, and marital adjustment, 164–*165*, *282*, *357*, *406*
Activities, common, of husband and wife, 52–*53*, *60*, *62*, *64*
Adjusted couple, case study of, 178–191, 293–295, *295*–297
Adjustment, marital:
  activities in common and, 52–*53*, *60*, *62*, *64*
  adjustment score as fair index of, 310–311
  affection, demonstration of, and, *53*–54, *60*, *64*
  affectional relations in childhood and, 343–346
  case studies of:
    changing adjustment, 295–299
    doubtful adjustment, 304–310
    fair adjustment, 300–304
    good adjustment, 293–295
    poor adjustment, 290–293
  companionate marriage, 260–261
  comparison of husband's and wife's, 341–343
  confiding, *53*–54, *60*, *65*
  defined, 10–11
  dissatisfaction with marriage, 54–55, *60*, *65*
  divorce contemplated, *73*
  divorced couples, *73*
  fair, 79–80
  good, 79–80
  index of (Chapter V), 58–74
  indications of, 47–48
  interests in common, 52–*53*, *60*, *64*
  measurement of (Chapter IV), 47–57
  personality interaction, 11–15
  poor, 79–80
  prediction research, review of, 350–361
  research:
    future of (Chapter XVIII), 350–374
    institute for, 371–373
    plan for further, 361–370

Adjustment, marital (*Cont.*):
  scoring key for, 63–68, *64–65*
  separated couples, *73*
  separation contemplated, *73*
  social problem of, 1–2
Adjustment score, in relation to:
  acquaintance, premarital, duration of, *165*, *282*, *357*, *406*
  age stopped attending Sunday school, *123*, *278*, *281*, *359*, *392*
  age difference at marriage, *162*, *283*, *357*, *406*
  babies, age first learned origin of, *357*
  brother or brothers, *357*
  by whom married, *358*, *417*
  Chicago, distance from, after marriage, *251*, *410*
  childhood:
    happiness in, *358*
    punishment in, *358*
  children:
    desire for, *260*, *414*
    number of, *259*, *413*
  church attendance:
    after marriage, 88
    before marriage, *124*, *278*, *281*, *357*, *393*
  community, size of, *250*, *410*
  conflict with parents:
    husband's, *93*, *279*, *357*, *378*
    wife's, *97*, *282*, *357*, *380*
  contingency factors, 244–268
  cultural backgrounds:
    general, *78*, *79*, *277*, *281*, *375*
    impress of, 75–89, *324*
  cultural differences, 82–89
  discipline in home, *357*
  economic role, 136–158, *324*
  educational status:
    husband's, *121*, *271*, *276*, *357*, *391*
    wife's, *121*, *271*, *280*, *357*, *391*
  employment after marriage:
    husband's, *263*, *357*, *415*
    wife's, *265*, *419*

Adjustment score, in relation to (*Cont.*):
  employment before marriage:
    husband's, 150–152, *151*, 277, *403*
    wife's, 150–152, *151*, 281, *403*
  engagement, duration of, *168*, *357*, *407*
  factors, five basic, *324*
  family background:
    differences in, 82–85, *84*
    index of, *78*, *79*, 277, 281, *357*, *375*
    index of similarity in, *84*
    size of family, 105, *384*
  father of wife, husband's resemblance to, *358*
  financial index:
    couple's, after marriage, 267, *416*
    husband's, at marriage, *157*, 277, *405*
  friends before marriage:
    husband's, *128*, 278, *358*, *395*
    wife's, *130*, 282, *358*, *396*
  health at marriage, of husband and wife, *118*, *358*, *389*
  height-weight deviation, *120*, *358*, *390*
  home ownership, 254, *412*
  income at marriage:
    husband's, *153*, 277, *358*, *404*
    wife's, *153*, 281, *358*, *404*
  intimate associations with other sex before marriage, *131*, 273, 278, *397*
  keeping company, duration of, *166*, *283*, *357*, *407*
  length of time married, 247, *409*
  meeting, place of first, *358*
  membership in social organizations before marriage:
    husband's, *127*, 272, 278, *358*, *394*
    wife's, *127*, 272, 282, *358*, *394*
  menstruation, age at first, *358*
  mental ability, relative, *358*
  mobility after marriage, 253, *412*
  mother-in-law, wife's resemblance to, *358*
  mother's attractiveness, as rated by husband, *358*
  neighborhood, type of:
    after marriage, 252, *411*
    before marriage, 132–135, 276, 279–280, *359*, *418*
  occupation before marriage:
    husband's, *138*, *140*, 276, *358*, *398*, *399–400*
    wife's, *147*, 280, *358*, *401*
  parents:
    approval of marriage by, *169*, 279, 282, *358*, *408*
    attachment to, *92*, *357*, *377*, *379*
    marital happiness of, as appraised by children, *99*, *101*, 279, *358*, *381*, *382*
    marital status of, *103*, 279, *358*, *383*
  parents-in-law:
    frequency of seeing, 258, *413*

Adjustment score, in relation to (*Cont.*):
  parents-in-law (*Cont.*):
    living with couple, 257, *413*
  petting, *358*
  place in family, *107*, *109*, 275, 279, *358*, *385*, *386*
  position:
    after marriage, average duration, 265, *416*
    before marriage, length of time held, *149*, 277, 280, *402*
  prediction score:
    common to husband and wife, *326*
    husband's *326*, *327*
    premarital, *284*
    wife's *326*, *327*
  psychogenetic characteristics, 90–113, *324*
  punishment in childhood, *358*
  religious home training, *358*
  rent per room per month, *263*, *415*
  residence:
    number of rooms in, 262, *414*
    rural, in childhood and adolescence, *85*, 278, *358*, *376*
    urban, in childhood and adolescence, *85*, 278, *358*, *376*
    with relatives, 257, *413*
  residential neighborhood, type of:
    after marriage, 252, *411*
    before marriage, 132–135, 276, 279–280, *359*, *418*
  response patterns, 159–171, *324*
  savings:
    after marriage, 267, *416*
    before marriage:
      husband's, *155*, 277, *359*, *404*
      wife's, *155*, 281, *384*, *405*
  sex attitudes and behavior, 218–243, *359*
  siblings, attachment to, *111*, *357*, *387*
  size of family, *105*, *384*
  socialized person, 134–135
  social organizations, membership in, before marriage, *127*, 272, 278, 282, *358*, *394*
  social type, 114–135, *324*
  spooning, *358*
  Sunday-school attendance, *123*, 278, 281, *359*, *392*
  unemployment of husband after marriage, *363*, *415*
  weight, *120*, *358*, *390*
  where married, *126*, *358*, *394*
  wife's father, husband's resemblance to, *358*
  wife's intention to work before marriage compared with working after marriage. 266, *419*
  wife's resemblance to mother-in-law, *358*

Adjustment score, in relation to (*Cont.*):
 wife's vocational ambition compared
  with occupation before marriage,
  147–148, *280, 419*
 work record before marriage:
  husband's, *151, 277, 403*
  wife's, *151, 281, 403*
Adjustment scores:
 comparison of, from schedules filled
  out separately by husbands and
  wives, *70*
 of the 526 couples, 68–69
 happiness ratings, *72*
 prediction scores, *284*, 314–316
 reliability and validity of, 70–72
 weighting, comparison of methods of,
  314–315
Affection, demonstration of, and marital
  happiness, *49, 50, 51, 53–54, 60,
  64*
Age:
 at marriage, *20*
 adjustment and, 115–117, *357, 388*
 difference in, and adjustment, 161–
  164, *162, 283, 357, 406*
 at which stopped Sunday school, and
  adjustment, *123, 278, 281, 359,
  392*
Agreements and disagreements, 48–52,
  60, 62, 63, 64
ANDERSON, J. E., 7n
Attachment:
 to parents:
  husband's, *92, 357, 377*
  wife's, *95, 357, 379*
 to siblings, *111, 276, 357, 387*
Aversion, sex, 238–239

B

Baby (*see also* Children):
 at what age learned origin of, *357*
 taking care of, and marital happiness,
  49, 50, 51, 60, 64
BEAM, L., 222, 225n
BENEDICT, R., 76n
BERNARD, J., 352, 356
BERNREUTER, R. G., 173
BINGHAM, W. V. D., 136n
Birth order, *107, 109, 275, 279, 385, 386*
BLUMER, H., 8, 159n
BRIDGMAN, R. P., 7n
BROMLEY, D. D., 9n
Brother or brothers, *357.* See also Sib-
  ling relationships
BROWNE, S., 219
BRYAN, W. J., 8
BURGESS, E. W., 172n, 174n, 245n, 249n,
  356, 363, 368
BUTTENWEISER, P., 172n, 173n
BYFORD, H. T., 225n

C

CARTER, W. P., 107n
Case studies:
 Mr. and Mrs. A., 192–201, 218, 237,
  290–293, 310–311
 Mr. and Mrs. B., 229–230
 Mr. and Mrs. C., 295–300, 310–311
 Mr. and Mrs. D., 300–304, 310–311
 Mr. and Mrs. E., 304–310, 310–311
 Mr. and Mrs. F., 230–231
 Mr. and Mrs. G., 202–216
 Mr. and Mrs. H., 231–232
 Mr. and Mrs. I., 240–242
 Mr. and Mrs. J., 232–234
 Mr. and Mrs. K., 234–235
 Mr. and Mrs. L., 235–237
 Mr. and Mrs. M., 238–239
 Mr. and Mrs. O., 178–191, 293–295,
  310–311
Case studies of marital adjustment (Chap-
  ter XV), 290–312
Case-study outline used in this study
  (Appendix C), 430–435
CHAPIN, F. S., 7n
CHESIRE, L., 39n
Chicago, distance from, *251, 410*
Childhood:
 happiness in, *358*
 in country, *23, 85–86, 278, 358, 376*
 punishment in, *358*
Children (*see also* Baby):
 desire for, *260, 414*
 number of, 27–28, *259, 413*
Church:
 attendance after marriage, 88
 attendance before marriage, *124, 278,
  281, 357, 393*
 wedding in, *126, 358, 394*
Community, size of, *250, 410*
Companionate marriage, 260–261
Companionship, 14–15, 159–171
Confiding and marital happiness, 53–54,
  60, 65
Contingency factors and marital adjustment (Chapter XIII), 244–268
Conventionality and marital happiness,
  49, 50, 51, 60, 64
COOLEY, C. H., 334
COTTRELL, L. S., Jr., 18n, 70n, 172n,
  333n, 356, 367
Courtship, duration of, *166, 283, 357, 407*
CR. See Critical ratio
Critical ratio (CR):
 defined, 80
 use in this study, 80–82
Cultural backgrounds, 11–12, 75–89, *78,
  79, 277, 281*, 317–325, *375*
 differences in, 82–89
 impress of (Chapter VI), 75–89, *324*
 transmitted in family, 75–76

Cultural patterns in marital relations, 216–217

D

DAVIS, K. B., 17n, 36, 351, 356, 357
DICKINSON, R. L., 222, 225n
Desire, sex, 228–242
Disagreements:
  marital happiness and, 48–52, 50, 51, 60, 62–63, 64
  methods of settling, and marital happiness, 49, 50, 60, 64
Discipline in home, 357
Dissatisfactions with marriage and marital happiness, 54–55, 60, 65, 66–67
DOLLARD, J., 336n
DURKHEIM, E., 56n
Divorce:
  contemplated, 73, 288
  increasing rate of, 1–2, 6
Divorced couples:
  adjustment and, 73
  prediction scores of, 288

E

Economic role, 13–14, (Chapter IX) 136–158
  adjustment and, 317–325, 324
  insignificant factor in adjustment, 324–325, 346–347
Economic status and security, 143, 152–157, 261–267
Educational status:
  adjustment and, 121, 271, 276, 280, 357, 391
  before marriage, of husband and wife, 24
  occupation and, 143–145
ELLIS, H., 30
Employment:
  after marriage:
    husband's, 263, 357, 415
    wife's, 265, 419
  before marriage:
    husband's, 150–152, 151, 277, 403
    wife's, 150–152, 151, 281, 403
Engagement, duration of, 167–168, 168, 357, 407
EVERITT, P. F., 39n

F

Family:
  agency for transmitting culture, 75–76
  background, 77–82
    differences in, 82–85, 84
    index of, 78, 79, 277, 281, 357, 375
    index of similarity in, 84
  functions of, 4

Family (Cont.):
  Oriental and Occidental, 2–4, 248–249, 256
  place in, 107, 109, 275, 279, 385, 386
  relationships, 92–95
    Freudian explanation of, 104
  size of, 105, 384
  social trends and, 4–7
FARIS, E., 76n
Father-in-law, husband's resemblance to, 358
Finances and marital happiness, 49, 50, 51, 60, 62, 64
Financial index:
  of couple after marriage, 267, 416
  of husband before marriage, 157, 277, 405
FINCK, H. T., 159n, 160n
FISHER, M. S., 7n
FLUEGEL, J. C., 17n
FRANK, L. K., 7n
FREUD, S., 9, 225, 336
Friends:
  husband's at time of marriage, 128, 278, 358, 395
  marital happiness and, 49, 50, 51, 60, 64
  wife's, at time of marriage, 130, 282, 358, 396
Friendship and adjustment, 128–132
FRYER, D., 136n

G

GOODENOUGH, F. L., 7n

H

HAMILTON, G. V., 17n, 35, 172n, 351, 356, 360
Happiness:
  childhood, and adjustment, 358
  criterion of successful marriage (Chapter III), 30–46
  defined, 31
  objections to, as a criterion, 37–38
Happiness, marital:
  activities in common and, 53, 60, 62, 64
  affection, demonstration of, 50, 51, 53, 60, 64
  appraisal of:
    by husbands and wives, 39, 44
    in husband's parents' marriage, by husband and by wife, 40
    in wife's parents' marriage, by husband and by wife, 41
    in couple's marriage by a member of the couple, and by a judge and by an outsider, 42, 43
  baby, taking care of, 50, 51, 60, 64